ST. JOSEPH CONVENT, MOUNT CARMEL- MOTHERHOUSE, INFIRMARY AND CHAPLAIN'S RESIDENCE

THE PRICE OF OUR HERITAGE

Volume Two
1869–1920

History of the Sisters of Charity
of the Blessed Virgin Mary

SICUT LILIUM INTER SPINAS

B V M

BEATAE + MARIAE + VIRGINIS + SORORES + CARITATIS +

M. JANE COOGAN B.V.M.

MOUNT CARMEL PRESS
Dubuque, Iowa 52001

Only through service to the future can we pay our
debts to the past.

To Mary Frances Clarke, and to those brave women who, each in turn, accepted the burden of leadership and carried it through strenuous and pain-filled years, we dedicate this memorial to their lives and labors.

TABLE OF CONTENTS

Foreword, Sister Joan Keleher Doyle, President
Sisters of Charity, B. V. M.
Author's Note   M. Jane Coogan, B. V. M.

Chapter   Page

PART ONE

MARY FRANCES CLARKE, FOUNDRESS

PART TWO

NEW LEADERS AND NEW STRUGGLES

Sister Jane Coogan, BVM
Dear Jane,

Thank you for the progress report on THE PRICE OF OUR HERITAGE.
The members of the BVM Senate of 1978 want to express gratitude
and appreciation for your loving gift of untold hours of research
and writing.

With the completion of Volume Two, you have provided such a valuable
asset for the understanding of our heritage that it is impossible to
over-estimate the impact of your work on present and future BVM
history.

We thank you, Jane, for your contribution, and we thank God for a
member who has so enriched us.

Your grateful Sisters,

Tenth Annual Senate
Sisters of Charity, BVM

Coletta M. Stanton, BVM

Coletta M. Stanton, Recording Secretary

FOREWORD

Isaac Newton's observation that "If I have seen further . . . it is by standing upon the shoulders of giants" describes the admiration and respect B. V. M. 's today have for those women of faith and vision who brought us to the present era. Three words epitomize their particular kind of courage and leadership: pioneer, practical and faith-filled.

Volume one has told us the story of those brave first years - of Mary Frances Clarke and her early companions starting out as pioneers, leaving the known security of Miss Clarke's Seminary on North Ann Street in Dublin to come to America in 1833. Here they hoped to give their services to ease the burdens of the Irish immigrants in Philadelphia. They pioneered in establishing themselves as an American religious congregation. Successful educators, they developed courses of study for use in the Catholic schools they staffed. After a brief ten years in Philadelphia, B. V. M. 's again joined the ranks of the pioneers when they responded to the invitation of Bishop Mathias Loras to come to the Iowa Territory. Wherever these early members put down roots as women of the Church, they met with steady purpose the varied issues affecting their lives and mission. All their decisions and efforts were born of deep faith in a provident, loving God.

Mary Frances Clarke was sixty-three years old when Father Terence Donaghoe died. She immediately moved into a more active position of responsible leadership in sustaining and directing her embryonic community. Within the year she had completed all the legal formalities for the Sisters of Charity to be incorporated in the state of Iowa. In 1885, two years before her death, she had secured from Rome the final approbation of the Rule for the Sisters of Charity of the Blessed Virgin Mary by which they dedicated themselves to the service of God and neighbor.

For a period of approximately twenty-eight years following Mary Frances Clarke's death, two outstanding women dominated the leadership in the Congregation: Mother Mary Gertrude Regan and Mother Mary Cecilia Dougherty. Tiny Mother Gertrude was sixty-one years old when she was elected Mother General. The spirit of the pioneers was strong within her as she made valiant efforts and took great risks for the financial stabilization of the Congregation while she expanded the facilities of its ever-growing academies and staffed an increasing number of parish schools.

Mother Gertrude, with great foresight, initiated, planned and handled the financial arrangements for the present motherhouse.

She thus proved herself as able expansionist and builder.

Mother Mary Cecilia Dougherty was fifty-six years old when she succeeded Mother Gertrude. One of her initial actions was to limit the further commitment of personnel and finances to new missions and to improve the quality of education in established B. V. M. schools. She encouraged educational conferences, professional excellence in curriculum and methods, meetings of superiors, ongoing formation of the Sisters. She laid the groundwork for following the directives from Rome concerning perpetual vows for B. V. M. 's. She, too, blended vision with the practical.

Brief though her term of office, Mother Ascension Lilly completed the process for perpetual vows. She also sensitized the Congregation to the need for provinces and established four provinces. She created new opportunities for professional training, struggled to meet the grave financial needs of the Congregation, and encouraged the development of the fine arts in the parish school curriculum.

Sister Jane Coogan, the author, has delved into the mystery of these outstanding B. V. M. leaders and has captured many of their elusive qualities in this second volume of the Congregation's history. She gives us a blueprint for builders, a road map for travelers, a model for responding to the needs of the day, based on the lives of our pioneering, practical and faith-filled Sisters who have gone before us.

Joan Keleher Doyle BVM

AUTHOR'S NOTE

The Congregation of the Sisters of Charity of the Blessed Virgin Mary will soon round out a century and a half of its history. The directive of Vatican II which urged upon religious institutes the return to the spirit of their founders has made necessary a study reaching back to the Congregation's earliest beginnings. The purpose of our study has been to search out the spirit of its foundress, Mary Frances Clarke, and to respond to the desire of her Sisters to know all of their Congregation's past that has survived the erosion of time.

Much of what Mother Clarke wrote had been lost sight of, and the details of her life had gone unchronicled. A previous account of the Congregation assigned her only a minor role in its foundations. For many the vision of Mother Clarke and the vocation they shared with her had gradually yielded to the demands of their profession. A growing tendency to equate the religious life with the duties of the classroom, the saying of prayers and the observance of regulations was strongly re-enforced by the promulgation of the Code of Canon Law in 1918. Its revival of old restrictions, out of keeping with the lives and purposes of apostolic congregations of women, and the obligation to incorporate those restrictions into their constitutions, re-enforced the growing dominance of law over spirit and obscured the image each congregation had of itself.

Despite all this, the spirit of Mother Clarke has lived in the hearts of her Sisters through the ninety-one years since her death. It is hoped that the recounting of her lived experiences and the sharing of them with her Sisters will renew for them the inspiration that was hers, and make them ever more conscious of the price paid for the heritage that is theirs today.

A formal history needs still to be written. Happily, this study may serve as a basis for it. My hope is that it may also provide other B. V. M. 's with an impetus to undertake scholarly studies in each of the several areas its contents suggest. May it also furnish research material for students in the fields of Catholic education and the realities of religious life.

My greatest debt in this second volume lies in the contribution made to it by Sister Doris Marie Walsh, B. V. M. , the result of exhaustive research into the lives of Mothers Gertrude and Cecilia. Many years ago Sister was assigned the task of compiling biographical studies of our Mothers-general. However, separating into distinct accounts the lives of women whose labors were so intertwined, and whose concerns and interests were so embedded in the Congregation's history, was a frus-

trating task. So it was that the final writing never came off.
When I undertook the more comprehensive task, Sister turned
over to me the entire result of her efforts. Much valuable
material contained in Sister's notes had been gathered through
personal interviews with persons now deceased. For her service
in research and her generosity in passing on the fruits of her
labors, Sister merits not only my thanks but that of the entire
Congregation.

Thanks, too, to Sister Ann Kathleen McDonnell for the use
of her creation, the B. V. M. symbol on our cover.

M. Jane Coogan, BVM.

July 16, 1978
Feast of Our Lady of Mt. Carmel

PART ONE

MARY FRANCES CLARKE, FOUNDRESS

Her Labors and Her Letters, 1869-1887

Mary Frances Clarke

Chapter One

A NEW HAND AT THE HELM

T he death of the very Reverend Terence James Donaghoe on
January 5, 1869 left much unfinished business for the Community of religious women he had governed for thirty-six years. 1
There were half-established missions, but, more importantly,
there was a half-established institute. Father Donaghoe had left
unheeded the urgent recommendation of the Trappist prior,
Clement Smyth, that he incorporate the Sisters of Charity of the
Blessed Virgin Mary to protect their property rights. Various
community properties remained in his name. His will, made and
reluctantly signed in the last days of his life, conveyed these
properties to Mary Frances Clarke. She, however, promptly
instituted legal proceedings to transfer them to the Community.
    The Constitutions according to which the Sisters had made
their first canonical vows in 1845 had never been presented for
papal approbation, nor could they be presented in the incomplete
form in which they continued from that early date. These first
Constitutions had made no provision for a governing body,
placing instead the Community's entire direction in the hands
of a priest-superior, a role which Father Donaghoe had assumed. His failure to provide a successor to that office allowed Mother Clarke the opportunity to plan the Community's
governmental structure and its incorporation. She assumed
responsibility for the administration of its properties and the
direction of its apostolic activities.
    Mother Clarke, a frail woman in her mid-sixties, had been
long removed from classroom teaching as well as from administrative duties. During an occasional absence or illness
of Father Donaghoe, she was empowered to meet only the most
urgent needs. Now, as a stranger to both tasks, she undertook
the direction of the Community's apostolate and the handling of
its finances and management of its real estate.

There were able women among those to whom Father Donaghoe had entrusted special responsibilities and superiorships. Understandably, these Sisters had looked for years to him for their direction. Only Margaret Mann, capable administrator from Dublin days, had formed an earlier and stronger bond with Mother Clarke, and had suffered the pangs of a divided allegiance. It would be a change indeed for the others to look for direction to the quiet woman in worn black calico and quaint frilled cap, whom they had been accustomed to see engaged in the humbler tasks of the household. The adjustment would not be easy for them nor for her. What seemed so formidable a handicap, however, was quickly overcome, for Mother Clarke structured the new government around those same able women.

Mother chose as her assistant Sister Margaret Mann, then superior of the Immaculate Conception Academy in Davenport, establishing her as superior at the new St. Joseph Academy in Dubuque. Her first major concern was the immediate incorporation of the Community, now consisting of 133 living members. She then transferred to the corporation all Community properties.

The Articles of Incorporation, dated September 30, 1869, constituted

the undersigned Sisters of Charity of the Blessed Virgin Mary of St. Joseph's Dubuque County, Iowa, and such others as may hereafter join them . . . a body corporate for Educational and Religious purposes. . . . The corporation shall commence upon the signing of these articles by nine Sisters, and shall continue perpetually. . . . The officers shall be elected by ballot from professed Sisters, members of the Corporation . . . most distinguished for virtue and prudence, a majority of all the votes cast being necessary for an election.

The minutes of the October 7, 1869, meeting contain, in bold Spencerian script worthy of an engraver, the results of that first election:

President	Mary F. Clarke
Vice President	Margaret Mann
Secretary	Mary J. Clarke
Treasurer	Eliza Regan
Consultors	Bridget McLoskey
	Jane O'Reilly

Articles of Incorporation

— OF THE —

Sisters of Charity, B.V.M.

__St. Joseph Dubuque county, Iowa__

The undersigned Sisters of Charity of the Blessed Virgin of St. Joseph's Dubuque County Iowa and such other may hereafter join them hereby associate themselves into a Body Corporate for Educational and Religious purposes

Article 1

This Corporation shall be known and styled The Sisters of Charity B.V.M. St. Joseph Dubuque County, Iowa and shall commence upon the signing of these Articles by nine Sisters and continue perpetually.

Article 2

Its principal place of business shall be at the City of

Article 12

No money shall be paid out of the Treasury of the Corporation unless upon written order on the Treasurer Signed by the Secretary and Countersigned by the President.

Mary F. Clarke

Mary Margaret Munn

Article 13

These Articles may be amended at any time — by two thirds of the members entitled to vote upon giving two weeks notice previous notice of the Amendment intended to be made.

Rose Foole

Mary Eliza Kelly

Ellen Hogan

Jane O'Reilly

Bridget McCloskeY

Mary Jane Clarke

Mary Eliza Wallas

The seal of the corporation was to have engraved in its center a figure of the Blessed Virgin. The secretary was instructed to prepare and arrange a set of by-laws to be adopted as soon as they had the approval of the Corporation and the Bishop of Dubuque.

Forty-six signatures were appended to an additional article on April 28, 1870, two-thirds of the members entitled to vote having approved it. [2] The article read:

All property now owned by the corporation or <u>any of its members</u> shall belong to said corporation, and upon the death of such members all her /sic/ interest in the property of the corporation shall revert to the corporation, so that no heir of any member shall have any right, title or claim whatsoever to the property of the corporation, it being the intention of the members hereof that this Society shall be perpetuated for educational purposes, and shall apply as well to property heretofore acquired as to property hereafter to be acquired. (Emphasis ours.)[3]

It was later called to Mother Clarke's attention by her faithful friend and attorney, Mr. W. J. Knight, [4] that the above article, and any other addition to the articles of incorporation which had not been registered with the state, lacked validity. Through the years there would be other errors and oversights in such technical matters. To these the lawyer called Mother's attention as they occurred. Fear that she had erred in a serious matter led her to address the following to Sister Mary Gonzaga on May 7, 1872:

The lawyer brought the deed to be signed yesterday. Do you know he troubled me. He doubted the validity of me signing the deeds. He says it is mentioned in the Articles of Incorporation. Dear Sister, you know I have signed to the corporation deeds of all the property in my name, Davenport included. It would be a sad thing if it was not valid. . .

Certainly Mother's signature to deeds for properties willed to her by Father Donaghoe, by which she turned them over to the corporation, would have been valid, the restrictions applying only to properties transferred from the corporation ownership. Subsequent realization of that distinction doubtless gave her great relief.

A study of the names affixed to the article noted above leads to much conjecture. Besides the four living of the original five members, the list includes:

Eliza O'Reilly, Eliza Regan, Julia Donovan, Letitia Burk, Ellen Hurley, Jane O'Reilly, Barbara Isenger, Mary Elizabeth Fullam, Mary Connelly, Catherine Colgan, Mary Ni hill, Anna Quigley, Anne Harron, Bridget McLoskey, Martha Mullen, Anne Seeley, Ellen Cosgrove, Ellen Mulgrew, Catherine Reed, Catherine Butterworth, Margaret Courtney, Margaret Short, Mary Dougherty, Mary Ann Ess, Mary Moloy, Bridget Carr, Catherine King, Mary J. Clarke, Mary Ann Whelan, Catherine Mullany, Anne Ryan, Sarah Ryan, Alice Finley, Bridget Walsh, Mary Ann Corrigan, Mary J. McPoland, Catherine Duffy, Catherine O'Connor, Fannie Linehan, Lizzie Lawlor, Mary Swift and Crissie Sturdevant.

Scarcely a name listed fails to appear sooner or later among those elected to offices in the Community as local superiors or members of the "Board of Managers, " the official title given the body of corporation officers. They were indeed women of "virtue and prudence, " and of varied talents as administrators and teachers.

This apparent delineation of an educated class as distinct from those engaged in the humbler works of the household and farm seems to have stimulated thoughts of a division of the Community into lay and choir members, in the pattern of European foundations. We are told that when Mother Clarke was urged to inaugurate such a change, she called the Sisters together and laid the matter before them. She urged them to discuss it, pray about it, and ponder it well. When they met again, a vote would be taken, its result to be decisive. "If it is decided that we are to have a body of lay Sisters, " Mother added, "I shall be the first to apply. " This announcement seems to have settled the issue, for nothing more was heard of it. 5

Meetings of the Board of Managers took place quarterly, and were ordinarily held in Dubuque, probably at St. Joseph Academy where Sister M. Margaret Mann, and later, Sister M. Josephine Clarke, was superior. Records of those meetings, kept in proper form show a sense of purpose and of organization, as appear in the minutes of January 10, 1871, outlining the "terms for Sisters teaching free schools and schools part-pay and part-free":

Unless the Mission is in a house belonging to the Community, as Davenport or St. Joseph, Dubuque, the priest who obtains the Sisters for his mission shall have a house for school and dwelling furnished, so that the Sisters, if they shall leave, would have nothing to take but their trunks.

If the Sisters have a select school and a free school, as at St. Mary's, Dubuque, the Sisters shall provide fuel for the select school and the priest provide fuel for the free school and pay $20.00 per month for each teacher teaching the free school.

If the schools are part pay and part free, as at St. Anthony's, Davenport, the priest will provide fuel, as he receives the money for tuition and fuel from the children. The salary for each Sister will be $30.00 per month.

Soon after Father Donaghoe's death, Mother Clarke expressed her appreciation to Father Bernard McCaffery, prior at New Melleray, for his services during Father's last difficult days, and enclosed an offering of twenty dollars for a novena of Masses for Father Donaghoe and one for the souls in Purgatory. Since the monks had supplied as chaplains for some weeks before and after his death, Mother hastened to tell Father Bernard that a young diocesan priest had been assigned to them as temporary chaplain. Father returned the offering as a gift to the Sisters, promising to offer the Masses, together with one for Mother Clarke herself, and to remember in his prayers all the Sisters. He added: "We can never repay the hundredth part what has been done by yourself and your house for us. But God will repay you, I'm sure, in due time. "

The young priest, Father A. F. Monaghan, named as their chaplain, served also as pastor at the St. Joseph parish. He immediately set about building a church a short distance from the mother-house, on an acre of ground given by Matthew Powers. On April 4, 1871, the Reverend Alex Hattenberger[6] was assigned as permanent chaplain to the Sisters and pastor of the St. Joseph parish. His appointment to the chaplaincy some-how conveyed to him the idea that he was intended to succeed Father Donaghoe as superior general of the Community. It would not prove easy to disabuse him of the idea.

A souvenir booklet, published in 1893 to honor Bishop Hennessy on the occasion of his silver anniversary as the Bishop of Dubuque, quotes from a letter he sent to the Propagation of

Faith at the time of his accession to the see in 1866. It reads in part:

> . . . in the whole of the present diocese of Dubuque there are only two schools. These were connected with the Cathedral here; one on the north side of it for boys, in which there were eight or ten little boys in charge of one Sister; and a school for girls on the south side of the Cathedral in which there were about fifty or sixty little girls under the charge of five or six Sisters. Both were in a dying condition. (p. 60)

This bit of information would have been a surprise to Mother Clarke if it had come within the range of her vision. Her Sisters were then teaching in four academies and thirteen parochial schools of the diocese. Nevertheless, to correct the supposed deficiency in his school system the Bishop immediately set about the establishment of an elaborate organization - the Free School Association of the City of Dubuque -

> to encourage and promote education, to provide means for the support of teachers and the establishment and recognition of common schools in the City of Dubuque, under the authority and patronage of the Rt. Reverend Bishop of Dubuque for the purpose of educating the Catholic children of such parents as are unable to pay the same.

This beautifully conceived plan died a-borning.

The idea of a college-seminary soon occupied the Bishop's attention. His interest focussed on the elementary school the Sisters were conducting at the site of their earlier hospital, on Fourteenth Street hill. The two Sisters who taught there resided at St. Joseph Academy, nearly two miles away. The difficulty of such a walk in severe weather was a factor in the Community's willingness to release the property. Sisters M. Gonzaga and Agatha were opposed, however, to the Bishop's terms: the use of it for an unlimited time without costs. Nevertheless, his wishes were acceded to, as was also his request for the services of two Sisters for housekeeping duties in his seminary project. Sisters M. Veturia Sullivan and Clotilde Walsh were made available for the work, continuing it until 1872.

The minutes of the Board of Managers' meeting, held on June 9, 1871, indicate the presence of Bishop Hennessy. At this meeting he proposed to the Sisters that they purchase the original Loras residence, then serving as their St. Mary select school, and, together with it, the adjoining land on Emmet Street. The price he named was $20,000, for part payment of which he was willing to take the Butterworth property of forty-one acres, appraised at $5,000, the rest to be paid within ten years at six percent interest. He further proposed that the Sisters build a school at that location. The minutes of the special meeting which followed that same afternoon indicate simply that the Bishop was informed by mail that "unexpected demands and other circumstances" made the purchase impossible. The "other circumstances," according to a memorandum supplied by Sister M. Gonzaga, then superior at St. Mary Academy, included her consultation with a lawyer who declared that the property could not be sold, as the Bishop held it under a deed of trust. "[7] When Sister called this to the Bishop's attention, their friendly relations came to an end.

Another confrontation occurred in 1873, at the time that the Bishop required Mother Clarke to deed to him the property on the Fourteenth Street hill for $3,000. For this he signed three $1,000 notes, payable without interest. The account as given by Sister M. Leo Boyle[8] continues:

> Then he asked Mother to summon Sister M. Gonzaga. He demanded of her that she turn over to him her annuity. Sister M. Gonzaga said to Mother, "Mother, do I have to sign away my annuity?" "You may if you wish, my child," Mother answered. "I don't wish!" said Sister M. Gonzaga, and turned on her heel and was gone.

The Bishop's response was to order Sister M. Gonzaga to leave town before night. This she did, going to Davenport, where Mother Clarke named her superior of the academy. Sister M. Alphonse Mullany came then to St. Joseph Academy, Dubuque, while Sister M. Domitilla King, then its superior, succeeded Sister M. Gonzaga at St. Mary Academy, where she "restored peace."[9]

After opening the Fourteenth Street building as St. Joseph College and Seminary in 1873, the Bishop called again for Sisters for domestic service there. This time Sisters M. Eusebia Grace and Bonaventure Cleary were assigned. They continued there until 1879, when they were succeeded by the Sisters of St. Francis of the Holy Family. A postscript of a letter from Mother Clarke to the bishop, dated January 1878, reads:

Group of postulants in sunbonnets beside the stone Novitiate
Frame Infirmary building and bell tower on left

1. Original parish house. 2. Father Donaghoe's house.
3. Probably the sacristy. 4. Wing of chapel.
5. Body of the chapel.

Father Hattenberger and priest friend in foreground.

I will feel very grateful to you, Bishop, if you will send
what you promised as compensation for the Sisters at the
College. It will be a great benefit at the present time.

Her accounts show that a remittance came in April from the
Reverend P. J. McGrath, president of the college for $200.00.
It is not clear whether the remittance covered the five-year
period of the Sisters' service or only a portion of it.

Shortly before his death in 1865, Bishop Smyth had sought to
arrange for a boys' school at the Cathedral, to be staffed by
the Christian Brothers. It was to this end that Father O'Reilly,
as the Cathedral pastor, had solicited funds throughout the diocese for the construction of a three-story brick building back
of the Cathedral which he named St. Raphael School, in keeping
with the title of the Cathedral. Though the building was completed in 1869, the Christian Brothers did not come to staff the
new school until 1879, remaining only until 1884. Before the
arrival of the Brothers and after their departure, the Sisters
taught in it as in a parish school.

The fact that the Sisters were already expanding beyond the
boundaries of the Dubuque diocese could only mean to Bishop
Hennessy that they must seek the formal approval of a rule[10]
warranting such an expansion. Its approbation would free them
from the direct rule of the local ordinary. It was doubtless as
a counter measure that Bishop Hennessy built, on the Cathedral
property, a two-story brick building to which he invited a colony
of Visitation Sisters from St. Louis. Their rule made each Community an independent foundation; hence the Dubuque foundation
was subject to his jurisdiction. Six Visitation Sisters arrived in
the city on August 26, 1871[11] and occupied the new structure on
the same grounds with the select school of St. Mary's which the
B. V. M. Sisters were conducting in the old Loras residence,
and with Father O'Reilly's St. Raphael School, in which they
were teaching.

Classes were already under way when, on August 31, Father
O'Reilly entered the parish school to inform the Sisters, "Your
services are no longer needed here. The Visitation nuns will
teach the school hereafter. "[12] Word traveled quickly to the
motherhouse, occasioning the following letter from Mother
Clarke:

THE IMMACULATE CONCEPTION ACADEMY, DAVENPORT, ABOUT 1880

St. Joseph's August 31, 1871
All in bed - can't sleep

My Darlings, Sister and Sisters,

None but our dear Lord knows what or how my heart
feels for you. May He support and strengthen you. Have
patience. May His most holy will be done and adored.

I have fixed that there will be adoration from morning
until night tomorrow, first, in thanksgiving to the
Sacred Heart for our cross; 2nd, offering the heart
of each one with all our affairs to His greater honor
and glory, that He may accept of your feelings of body
and mind. 3rd, that He may take each one and all our
concerns - missions, children, houses, property, all
under His holy care, and dispose of all according to
His divine pleasure. My dear Sisters, is it not a consolation to you that you have done your duty? Oh, how
you have labored in every respect to please, and advance the interests of religion in a spiritual and temporal sense, for its advancement. You were the means
of reconciling the people to those they were averse
to. But our dear Lord /knows/ all. I know I ought not
to numerate these things. May God forgive me.

Yet Mother Clarke wished her Sisters to welcome the newcomers, for, as she said, "There is plenty of work for all. "
Sister M. Margaret Mann was then acting as both Mother's
assistant and superior of the boarding and day school, St.
Joseph Academy, at Thirteenth and Main Streets. The opening
of a similar school by the Visitation Sisters in the new brick
building on October 26, with an enrollment of fifty pupils, drew
a number of patrons from the academy. Nevertheless, Sister
Margaret felt keenly the needs of these Sisters, who were suffering the hardships of a new foundation. A letter from Sister
Mary Genevieve King, superior of the Visitation Sisters, dated
December 29, 1871, gives evidence of Sister's response to
their need.

My Honored and Very Dear Sister,

Methinks I should rather style you our own tender loving
Mother, so maternally watchful have you been over us, an-

ticipating our needs lest we should be in want of neces-
saries. Rest assured, Loved Mother, such goodness on
your part is truly appreciated by all and each of our little
band. Yet, Dearest Mother, notwithstanding your past kindness, we dare request an additional favor, emboldened by
your generous and disinterested charity. It is that you will
have the goodness to supply Altar Breads - both large and
small Hosts, for a few months, or until we will be enabled
to purchase Bread irons and Cutters.

It is evident from a letter of Sister Mary Rose of the Visitation Community, written on April 21, 1873, that the favor was
granted, for Sister wrote to thank the "Most esteemed and Dear
Mother" for the altar breads.

What had been so great a disappointment to the B. V. M. Sisters when they were dismissed from the Cathedral School proved
indeed to be an opportunity, for it freed them for a greater
project. In June of the previous year, Father Henry Cosgrove
of St. Margaret Church, Davenport, had written to Mother Clarke
of the desire of the Reverend F. C. Jean, pastor of St. Irenaeus
Church in Lyons, Iowa, to have Sisters for his school. He wrote
that "there are three fine towns together Lyons, Clinton and Fulton,
and eventually these places will be important." Father Jean had
been assigned to Lyons in 1851, following a term as pastor at
Bellevue; from there he had attended Lyons as a mission. The
new pastor immediately built a small brick church, following it
the next year with a brick school where he himself taught its first
twelve pupils. The parish had grown considerably when, in May
1864, Bishop Smyth laid the cornerstone for the present stone
structure, modeled after the cathedral in Father Jean's native
Lyons, France. Pastor and parishioners had worked together,
quarrying sandstone from bluffs north of the city, floating it
down the river on barges, and hauling it to the site in horse-
drawn carts. Returning to his native France for a visit, Father
Jean brought back a replica of the golden crown of France, the
gift of the Bonaparte family to his parish, to serve as a receptacle
for the sanctuary lamp. He next opened a school in the church
basement for the boys of the parish. 13
Despite all his strenuous and successful labors, Father Jean
shortly found himself at odds with Bishop Hennessy. He was
dismissed from the pastorate of St. Irenaeus in 1872. At least
a partial basis for his dismissal was the supposed misuse of
church funds, a charge much like the implication that had dark-

Student sleeping accommodations

Our Lady of Angels Academy, Lyons, Iowa

ened Father Pelamourgues' last days in Davenport. He fought for many years to clear his name and regain his status as a priest, but died without accomplishing either. Probably the full story will never be told as Bishop Hennessy's own records are incomplete, and Father Jean's troubled writings, recovered by Father Griffith of St. Ambrose College, indicate that his mind had become disturbed from much brooding.

There had been dedicated in Lyons on September 15, 1858, an ambitious institution, the Lyons Female College. It had been intended as one of a chain of such institutions subsidiary to a projected university "for the advancement of learning and culture for the gentle sex. "14 The central building of red brick was surmounted by a turret or lookout common to homes of river captains of the day, and this structure was capped by a dome-shaped cupola. Flanked on each side by a smaller brick structure, the building was situated on an elevation overlooking the little town and the river beyond.

The grandiose scheme had failed, and the property, later acquired by the Presbyterian synod of Iowa, was now for sale. The sight of it quickly captured the imagination of the Sisters when they went to Lyons, though not to St. Irenaeus, in 1871. The Reverend L. F. Wieland, pastor of the German parish of St. Boniface, had invited them to a poor little school and log convent a short distance from the site of the vacant buildings. The Sisters were soon able to persuade Mother and her Board of Managers to buy the property so evidently suited to the purposes of a boarding school. Purchased in 1872 for $9,300, the buildings were in a state of neglect and disrepair, calling for much labor on the part of the Sisters, while the smaller building on the south served as a day school for boys and that on the north, for girls. Dedicated on October 2, 1872, the academy was christened Our Lady of Angels. Sister M. Anastasia Mulgrew, as superior, shared the venture with Sisters M. Delphine Conway, Marcelliana McFadden, Regina Cosgrove and Lucy McDonnell.

The academy cared for and educated girls from kindergarten through high school until the days of the boarding school passed. It closed its doors in 1966. Meantime, 112 of its graduates had joined the ranks of the B. V. M. 's.

Under the pastorate of the Reverend P. Leahy, St. Irenaeus parish school provided classes for the boys in the basement of the new church, beginning about 1890. At that time Sisters M. Wenceslaus Shea, Huberta Byrne and Lucille Ivory served as teachers. In 1902, the erection of a school building enabled the parish to provide elementary education to both boys and girls. Our Lady of Angels served the girls and St. Mary's the boys as high schools.

When Mother Clarke took office, two new schools had been promised: a German parish school in Davenport and an Irish counterpart in Cascade, Iowa. As a rule, the German new-comers to the country were in more comfortable circumstances than were the Irish. However, the provision for national parishes with separate schools in the same small town put heavy burdens on both, dividing, for many decades, the limited resources of a struggling population in numerous small midwest towns. The heated rivalry which developed between such schools perpetuated the separation long after ethnic differences had become obscured. We see an instance of this in the little town of Cascade, Iowa.

In 1867, Father Donaghoe had purchased eight lots in Cascade, about eighteen miles from the Prairie motherhouse. The "Irish" parish of St. Martin was then served by the Reverend Michael Lynch, a recruit from Ireland, whom Bishop Loras had enlisted for the diocese. Father Donaghoe had planned and built the two-story convent with earthen cellar; the title of it belonged, therefore, to the Community. A portion of the house was used as a school for the girls, while the boys occupied two small classrooms in a frame building across from the church. In the choice of teachers to serve this new mission there was no problem of nationality. Those assigned were Sisters M. Vincent Donovan, John Cahill, and the newly professed Salome Kinsella.

Smallpox struck the town in January 1873, carrying off at least one member of nearly every family. Ten of the twelve children of one family died in the epidemic, while sixteen boys and as many girls, pupils of St. Martin School, were among its victims. By that time the school had acquired its fourth superior, Sister M. Xavier O'Reilly, Sisters M. Loyola Rutherford and Nicholas Lambert having served briefly after Sister M. Vincent. Sisters M. Xavier and Prudentia Riley attended the victims as long as the epidemic lasted, without themselves incurring the infection.

The story is told that the disease came to Cascade from Chicago in a package containing a long baptismal robe such as was customary at the time. The infant that had worn it had died shortly after baptism, when the family was suffering with small-pox. Thinking that the dress might be useful to Cascade relatives, they had made the mistake of sending it on.

Poverty beset the Sisters and the school, at least partially because of the conservatism of some subsequent pastors. The minimal salary could not always be collected, and even if it had been, it would not have covered the cost of repairs to the deteriorating convent, which in time became a positive health hazard. Cascade was a small town to support two Catholic schools, but in 1906, Father Roche purchased a site from the Sisters and built a coeducational grade school. By 1950, the Irish St. Martin's and the German St. Mary's had added high school courses to their curriculum, the first with an enrollment of 84 pupils and the second, 77: scarcely a satisfactory arrangement from an educational standpoint. A diocesan move to build a central high school in 1962, and the consolidation of the two grade schools under the direction of the Sisters of St. Francis of the Holy Family, led to the withdrawal of the Sisters of Charity after ninety-nine years of service. In the course of those years twenty-three women had entered the B. V. M. Congregation from Cascade.

A second such engagement Mother Clarke was required to fulfill was for teachers for the German parish of St. Kunegunda in West Davenport, or "Germantown, " recently cut off from St. Anthony parish. Its pastor, the Reverend Anton Niermann, had been one of four recruits from Germany introduced to Bishop Loras by Father Emonds of Iowa City on the night before his death. Immediately upon his ordination in 1869, Father Niermann was assigned as pastor to the rock church of the new parish, a position he held until his death in 1914. He lost no time in applying for Sisters. Sister M. Barbara Ess, transferred from Muscatine, Iowa, to take charge, was a native of the Bavarian Alps, where she had learned to yodel and to imitate the sound of the hunter's horn, accomplishments which intrigued both Sisters and pupils. While she would be at home with the German congregation, her companions, Sister M. Benedict McLaughlin, Columba Burke, and Zita Dunn, would require acclimating. 15

Since the Sisters resided at the Immaculate Conception Academy, their walk to and from school was long. When they arrived each morning they had to light the fires and clean the classrooms in preparation for the arrival of the children.

When, in 1883, Father Niermann dedicated a new church for his growing congregation, he changed the name of the parish to "St. Joseph's. " The old rock church then became the school and the frame building which had served as school was converted into a convent. In appreciation for these more convenient living arrangements, the Sisters were expected to work in the sacristy and conduct the church choir, though providing these services required an exemption from their rule.

As the years went by, the rock school building deteriorated, while class sizes increased. At length, local conditions, especially the greatly overcrowded, poorly heated and badly ventilated classrooms, made teaching a near impossibility. When repeated appeals to the pastor proved unavailing, the Sisters were finally withdrawn in 1897, their work being assumed by a German foundation, the School Sisters of St. Francis of Milwaukee.

One matter of concern for Mother Clarke was the management of the more than 1700 acres of land on which Father Donagho was paying taxes at the time of his death. It was certainly not her plan for the Community to make farming a major occupation. The large farm near Prairie du Chien, Wisconsin, which Brother Joseph Kinsella had deeded to Father, had been seriously neglected. This she learned through a letter to Father Donaghoe from I. P. Perret Gentil, land agent there. Apprising him by letter on May 13, 1869, of Father's death, she asked him to put the land up for sale. The acreages nearer home could be used as collateral for building purposes, as demands were made for new schools and academies and for additions to the old. .

For the time, the three Brothers, Anthony, John and Michael, could manage the acres in the motherhouse area fairly well, while other lands were let out to renters. Brothers Anthony Grant and John Ahern did not live long, however, the former dying on August 13, 1873, and the latter on December 23 of the same year. Brother Michael was getting old and as it became apparent that he lacked the tact and the administrative ability needed to supervise so much property, it became necessary for Mother to look elsewhere for assistance. Her own practical acquaintance with agricultural concerns had come largely through the keeping of accounts - the sale of produce and live stock, laborers, and the like. She now sought the advice and assistance of the prominent Dubuque lawyer, W. J. Knight. [16] Lawyer Knight proved an invaluable aid to her, not only in the management of the farm but in the handling of real estate and financial transactions, and of other matters involving legal action.

Even with the many pressures from without, Mother Clarke continued the recording of all cash transactions, leaving to the treasurer the overall records of the Community's finances.

Many of the transactions give hints of the changing times. Professional dental services first appear in a charge of $15.00 for a set of teeth. Extractions had been listed previously as a charge of fifty cents, without identification of the extractor. Charges for surgery include the entry: "To Dr. Bigelow and Son for operating on S. M. Gabriel, Stephana and others, $87.25." Funeral expenses were never great: from seven to twelve dollars for a casket, and a five-dollar offering for Masses covered the cost occasioned by death.

The purchase of a mower and a threshing machine indicated progress in mechanization, while flour bought commercially replaced carrying their own grain to the local mill for grinding. The Sisters were relieved of the heavy task of churning by the purchase of butter. Greater variety in diet became evident with items of canned fruit, catsup, oysters, sardines, figs, currants, and for the sick, beer, lemons and peaches. The purchase of a paschal candle and a supply of coal for the chapel stove, and of wallpaper for the parlor and novitiate were further indications of better times.

Two entries of fifty dollars each covered music lessons for S. M. Gonzaga from a certain Professor Jones, and lessons in voice for Sister M. Cecilia and other Sisters. The purchase of classroom clocks, blackboard crayons, a map of Iowa, a bookkeeping set, and diplomas, and, for the academy in town, pianos and a four-hundred-dollar harp were signs of progress. Then for the graveyard, there was the payment for one hundred metal crosses and a crucifix; for the house and barns, lightning rods; and for the Sisters, merino for habits from Mandel Brothers, and dry goods costing $297.00 from Marshall Field and Company.

The Sisters had been called upon in many parishes to assume a heavy share in conducting the annual fund-raising fairs and bazaars. Mother's belief that the added burden was too much for them led her to forbid the practice, substituting for their labors a financial offering. Such contributions are frequent items in her accounts. But wider demands on charity were met as well. When famine struck Ireland again in 1880, Mother Clarke wrote: "From the Sisters to God and poor Erin, $25.00."

Other charitable items on record were contributions for the poor of Dubuque, and for the colored orphans, with a generous remittance to the sufferers in Charleston, South Carolina where a severe earthquake destroyed churches and homes and resulted in many deaths. A gift of $100.00 went to the Holy Father, Leo XIII, in celebration of his jubilee.

Funds for all these outlays and for the varied building projects were derived from land sales and rentals, the marketing

of farm produce, Sisters' dowry offerings, and, increasingly
as new missions were opened, contributions sent by the missions out of their poverty, for the support of the motherhouse
with its novices and its sick. Occasional entries appear also of
monies Mother supplied to B. V. M. missions in want, or returned to those whose needs she regarded as greater than her
own.

Postulants had been coming largely at their own convenience,
though, until 1879, entrances seem to have clustered around
the greater feast days. In that year, March 19, May 24, August
15 and September 8 were evidently assigned as regular entrance
days. As revealed in the novice record, until 1875 stress was
heavy on the furnishing by the postulants of their own bedding,
and on their bringing what cash dowry they could afford. From
that time the Register of Novices' Clothing was concerned with
the young woman's wardrobe as well. Then, to feather beds,
hair or straw mattresses, quilts, comforters, etc., were
added such items as calico dresses, red flannel chemises, winter and summer night caps and stockings, woolen and quilted
petticoats, muslin and flannel drawers, "breakfast shawls, "
and a variety of other items. To each list the respective postulant affixed her signature, attesting to its correctness. Each
entrant who could was asked to bring fifty dollars to cover the
cost of the merino habit, shawl and other items which would be
provided on her entrance to the novitiate, and a $200.00 dowry
to cover her expenses to profession time. Apparently many
postulants were unable to meet the full costs, or even a part of
them, though some substituted a house or a piece of farmland,
live stock or provisions, while one entrant listed as her dowry
that most sacred of possessions, her "good will. " No one apparently was refused who had the necessary personal qualification

The record of one favored young lady from Davenport who
came under Father Donaghoe's direction in November 1867, includes a dowry of a cabinet organ, a piano, and $1,000, later in-
creased to $5,000, besides the proper wardrobe and supply of
bedding. However, in 1877, Mother Clarke wrote to Bishop
Hennessy regarding the same young lady:

> Although God has bestowed great favors on the Community
> last year, we have met with unforeseen difficulties. One
> of our Sisters who was with us ten years left of her own
> free will without telling her intentions except to a candidate.
> She followed her mother to California who came to visit
> her last summer. We have received letters from her moth-
> er since Sister arrived there. She is distressed, being a

Protestant, lest we should think she influenced her. She requires notes for the money which she brought to the Community, to be paid in installments, which is just. It is over five thousand (5000) dollars. It was given by us in part payment for the purchase of the Immaculate Conception Acad. Davenport. . . .[17]

Mother's account book reveals her heroic efforts to raise the money, borrowing it where she could, to settle the claim as quickly as possible.

A further source of anxiety is revealed in a reference to another former B. V. M. :

The trial of that poor creature who sued us for wages is to come off next Monday the 7th. I hope God will accept all for His own glory.

The "poor creature, " having entered the Community with little more than good will, and only a meager supply of that, had left it several years later, and had then sued for $2, 500 as due her for services performed. In his reply, the Bishop advised that hereafter Mother require from each novice in writing the renunciation of any claim for such services in the event of her leaving. This practice has since prevailed.

Lawyer Knight was successful in defending the Community. When Mother Clarke wrote him to request a bill for his expenses and his services, he complied by sending an itemized statement of expenses incurred, a telegram and carriage hire for two trips to the motherhouse, totaling $10. 70, and added:

I assure you I never had an idea of making a charge for my services in the case, and now have no charge to make for them. If you will accept what little services I have rendered as a slight testimonial of my respect for your order, which, the more I see of its members, it s constitutions and rules, the more I have learned to respect it, I will be more than compensated for what I have done.

Mother Clarke responded:

I am ashamed. I do not know how to express my thanks for your unbounded generosity. But my God, I know, will richly reward you both in this world and in an endless eternity. You must excuse me if I doubt that small bill covers your expenses. However, as I can not do

better, I send you a small relic of better times to settle
it. I have nothing to add but the prayers of a poor old
Irish woman.

> Your humble,
> Mary F. Clarke

What was the "small relic of better times" which accompanied Mother Clarke's remittance? What single precious keep-
sake had her heart clung to from Dublin days, to be surrendered
now in recognition, not only of generous services, but of one
great spirit reaching out to another?

Early October of 1871 brought tragic news from the Sisters
in Chicago. It had been a hot, dry summer, and with large areas
of the city built of wooden houses, sidewalks and fences, there
was much ready tinder for the fire which broke out just beyond
the boundaries of the Holy Family parish. Accompanied by high
and veering wind, it traveled more than two miles in a matter
of six hours. At first there appeared to be little danger to the
church and the parish, but the wind shifting to east drove the
flames directly toward Holy Family. Then, just as the fire
reached the boundary line of the parish the wind turned again,
and the flames spread east and north, away from the area. When
they saw themselves out of danger, priests, Sisters and lay
helpers turned to the task of relieving others. St. Ignatius College quickly became a station for the storage and distribution of
supplies which poured in from all parts of the country. Thousands
of the hungry and destitute gathered at its doors to receive provisions and clothing. Bishop Foley, who had suffered the loss of
both cathedral and residence, took refuge at the college, where
he remained for many months, while the orphans of St. Joseph
home found shelter in its classrooms. The Sisters who cared
for them meanwhile were made welcome in the already crowded
B. V. M. convent.

Father Damen, S. J., who was holding a mission in Brooklyn
at the time of the fire, received word of the tragedy by wire. In
a night of anxious prayer, he promised that if his parish were
spared, its deliverance would be commemorated: he pledged
that as long as the church lasted, lights would be kept burning
before the statue of Our Lady of Perpetual Help. Taking an early
train for Chicago, he arrived to find the main part of the city in
ashes. In a packed church, he offered a Mass of thanksgiving
for the safety of his people, sharing with his congregation the
promise he had made. Then he turned to the task of directing
relief for the sufferers.

Meanwhile, a telegram reached Dubuque from the quickly organized relief committee, requesting bread and cheese for 100,000 persons. But much more than that went, in crates and barrels and boxes, to meet the needs of the destitute.[18] Clearing the refuse and rebuilding would give work to thousands, but not to all, for the weather turned bad. Sister M. Agatha made her own plea to Dubuque parishes and to the Trappist monastery. Later she thanked all in a letter addressed to Mr. Frank McLaughlin, a close relative of some of the Sisters, a member of the committee appointed to solicit aid for the children orphaned by the fire:

Sir: Your draft of $125.00 and 20 brls. of flour have just been received as "Christmas gifts." Never was relief more needed, owing, in part, to the intense cold of this week, which developed cases of individual suffering that would touch your tender heart. A few weeks ago the prospects of the sufferers were comparatively hopeful owing to the demand for laborers and mechanics, but rations, especially tea and coffee, have been shortened and most of the outdoor work suspended - the latter falls heavily on the robust, the former painfully on the hundreds of infirm men and delicate women. The generous hearts of our friends in Dubuque, not seeing the distress, cannot estimate the benefits they confer, nor can language of mine express the gratitude of the recipients. How proud I am of my native state. Dubuque and the monastery parish will ever be fragrant in my memory. . . To the Rev. Father Bernard and his noble parishioners I wish the happiest Christmas they have ever enjoyed, and to you, my dear friend, I say, may your effort to relieve the distressed be a beautiful shamrock in your pathway through a long and prosperous life.

Gratefully,
Sister Mary Agatha

St. Aloysius, Chicago, Dec. 9, 1871

It was not until early November that Bishop Foley found time to thank Mother Clarke for a draft of $100.00 sent for relief. "God has afflicted us severely," he wrote, "but he has also raised us an army of friends to assist and give me countless marks of mercy . . . Where shall we begin, and how can we rebuild our churches and institutions, I do not know. We trust in God."

It was indeed an afflicted church, with so much that had been
built with labor and tears wiped out in a day. Yet help came
from a sympathetic nation and even from abroad, and the re-
placements would no longer be in wood but in brick and stone.

The memoirs of Sister M. Lewine Enderle, B. V. M., recount
for us a timely story:

> A little girl of three or four years, apparently orphaned
> by the fire, was found sitting bewildered in a cemetery
> at the present site of Lincoln Park. Adopted later by a
> Roberts family in Clinton, Iowa, she eventually became
> a pupil in St. Mary School there. When Father McLaughlin,
> who wore a long beard, entered the classroom for the first
> time after her arrival, she jumped up, ran to him and
> threw her arms around him crying, "Daddy, my daddy."
> Eventually she entered our Congregation and was received
> as Sister M. Anysia. Becoming an outstanding primary
> teacher, she spent some years in the elementary schools
> of St. Pius and Blessed Sacrament . . . Sister often ex-
> pressed her longing for her own people, but it was never
> her happiness to know them. She died at the age of forty
> at Blessed Sacrament convent, Chicago.

A more immediate anxiety for the Sisters came two years
later with the serious illness of Sister M. Margaret Mann,
Mother's assistant and superior of the St. Joseph Academy,
Dubuque. In the early fall of 1873, Mother Clarke, learning
of her condition, came to reside at the academy, remaining
there until the death of her confidante and closest friend.
During her stay at St. Joseph's, Mother shared the daily lives
of the Sisters, watching over the patient while they were busy
in the classroom and with the care of the boarders. Sister M.
Margaret, suffering from asthma and a dropsical condition,
found less discomfort in a chair than in her bed. Conscious on
Christmas eve that she was near death, she received the last
sacraments, and asked the Sisters gathered around her to sing
the Christmas hymns. As death delayed its coming, the Sisters
urged Mother Clarke to take some rest. Margaret's eyes followed her from the room, as she spoke a farewell benediction,
"God bless you, Mother Clarke." Death came quietly in the
early hours of Christmas morning to the great-hearted woman.

The funeral Mass at St. Patrick Church on the morning of
December 26 followed the office of the dead. Then the body was
taken to the Prairie where it was met by a procession of Sisters,
novices, neighbors and the children of the St. Joseph parish

school, all led by Father Hattenberger. The coffin was placed on a catafalque near the bell tower, and a service of psalms, hymns and scripture readings followed. The procession then moved to the chapel where a second catafalque, covered with an embroidered white cloth, stood waiting. Here the prayers for the dead were recited. The Sisters kept watch through the night and until eight o'clock in the morning, when Father Hattenberger, with the Sisters' choir, sang a solemn requiem Mass. The procession then conducted the body to the community graveyard north of the convent for interment.

An unidentified clipping carried the following obituary:

. . . It was her nature to bear more than her share of trouble, and to relieve others from bearing any part of it that could be kept from their knowledge. . . . By nature and disposition, she was adapted for the positions she held from time to time in the Community. The position of novice mistress which she held for many years brought the aspirants for a religious life who joined the community in close touch with Sister Mary Margaret's prominent virtues, and there is not of the hundred or more who made their religious profession under her guidance one who did not love her as a mother. . . Among all Sister Mary Margaret's prominent virtues, that of charity - compassion - was predominant - charity, not alone for the members of the Community, compassion that seemed to have no other bounds than that of objects on which to bestow it . . . Hers was a heart that grasped the motherless babe and cared for it with a mother's solicitude. And as it grew and went out into the world beyond her fostering attention, yearned for its welfare as only a heart could which was endowed with more than ordinary resemblance to the heart of Jesus.

Sister Mary Margaret died as she lived, in the full enjoyment to the last of her mental faculties, and in using them as she had for over forty years in meditating on the Saviour and breathing his blessed name in her prayers. Her last words were, "Jesus, have mercy on me. " . . . It was to Sister Mary Margaret's consolation that having experienced the trials, the hardships, the doubts, the uncertainties and the thousand difficulties and obstacles which . . . beset the Community from its birth for over thirty years, that she lived to see it in the flourishing, prosperous and useful condition in which it exists today. . .

Margaret Mann had served as vice president of the corporation's Board of Managers since its inception, and also as Mother's assistant in the general government of the Community during those years. A new election of the Board replaced Margaret with Sister M. Gertrude Regan, who seems, as a matter of course, to have succeeded her in the assistantship.

S. M. Cecilia Dougherty   S. M. Gertrude Regan
Novice Mistress   Mother's Assistant

Notes

1 As a gesture of sympathy and support, at the time of Father Donaghoe's death, the people of Dubuque held a benefit supper for the Sisters, presenting Mother Clarke with its proceeds, $459.60 (Account book 1/24/69).

2 This would suggest that there were sixty-nine members having the right to vote at that time.

3 The article would be found at variance with the provisions of canon law contained in the code of 1918. The code requires that radical ownership of all properties be retained by the Sister during her lifetime, while it guarantees her freedom to grant its "use and usufruct" to whomsoever she wishes, including her Congregation, and her right to dispose of it by will with equal freedom. These safeguards were made clear also by the Sacred Congregation by additions made to the Constitutions and Rules submitted by the Sisters and approved in 1877.

4 The Honorable W. J. Knight, who served the Community for forty-nine years as attorney, friend and benefactor, was born in Ireland in 1838, and died in Dubuque in 1908. Having studied law in the office of the eminent J. W. Griffith, he was admitted to the Iowa bar at the age of nineteen and became a partner in the oldest law firm in Iowa, that of Griffith and Knight. He served on the commission for the codification of Iowa law, acted as attorney for the Illinois Central Railroad, and served three terms as mayor of Dubuque. Only when election to the Iowa legislature took him for considerable periods from Dubuque did he ask to be excused from his many and varied services to the Community, assuring Mother, however, that he would always be happy to give her any legal advice of which she stood in need.

5 As told by Sister M. Albina Craney to Sister M. Lucile Harkin, and by her to the writer. Later a second list of names, including a number of Sisters involved in household and farm tasks, was added to the membership. Many of these had been under vows at the time of the voting spoken of above. It is difficult, in the absence of further data, to explain whatever distinction there seems to have existed, for this second list includes teachers also.

6 Father Hattenberger, an Alsatian, had come to America as

a seminarian, with Father Cretin, on the latter's return from a recruiting tour in Europe in 1848. A hesitant missioner, half regretting his decision to undertake the responsibilities of the priesthood, he was nonetheless ordained by Bishop Loras, serving in Ottumwa and Fort Madison and surrounding missions. As vicar for the German people of the diocese, he fulfilled several assignments for the Bishop, settling problems regarding the German clergy and their congregations. Letters to Loras, pressing for funds for the church in Ottumwa, and for reimbursements to cover travel expenses, including the wear and tear on his horse and buggy occasioned by the fulfillment of his commissions, proved sufficiently annoying to the Bishop that the latter suggested his willingness to give the importunate priest his <u>exeat</u>. (See Hattenberger to Loras, January 2, 1853, Loras file, Dubuque Archdiocesan Archives). However, as the two grew to know each other, Loras learned to value his blunt and energetic vicar. He was still serving in Fort Madison after Loras' death. It was from Milwaukee that he came to accept Bishop Hennessy's assignment to the St. Joseph motherhouse. His service in Milwaukee seems to have been as chaplain to the Sisters of Notre Dame under Mother Caroline. On January 12, 1892, after thirty-nine years of service, Father was stricken with apoplexy, shortly after celebrating the funeral Mass for Sister M. Vincent Donovan. He died two days later, within hours of the death of Sister M. Monica Seery, and their bodies rested together in the convent chapel, awaiting burial. Interment for Father Hattenberger was at New Melleray.

7 Patrick Quigley had donated the land for the first cathedral and rectory, (Lot 603), making out the deed to Bishop Loras and Father Mazzuchelli, as trustees.

8 Sister M. Leo Boyle entered the Congregation in 1872 from Dubuque. As a child she had known Father Donaghoe, and as a religious she knew Mother Clarke for many years. Her account was given to Sister M. St. Magdalen Swift.

9 There has long been a misunderstanding as to whether the Bishop paid the three notes given for the Fourteenth Street property, the impression being that he met them in his own way, by deducting $200.00 each year for a number of years for the services of a chaplain at St. Joseph Academy. Mother's account book indicates, however, the receipt of $1,000 each on January 29, 1876, January 10, 1877, and January 8, 1878. On the second and third of these dates, Mother credited the Bishop with the

full amount, but charged the academy with $200.00, for the salary of the chaplain. The presence in the files of a number of receipts for the salary charge seems to have led to the misunderstanding.

10 For the sake of simplicity, the word "rule" will be used to signify <u>Constitutions and Rules</u>, the more precise title.

11 The Visitation Sisters of St. Louis had been founded from Georgetown. It was their Georgetown convent which had supplied vestments and altar linens to the B. V. M. Sisters when the Prairie motherhouse and boarding school were burned in 1849. Although their enclosure constituted the religious of the Visitation nuns, the title "Sister" is commonly used.

12 Sister M. Valeria Owens, B. V. M. , assigned to the St. Joseph Academy in 1869 and long a resident there, provided the memorandum which tells of the coming of the Visitations, and states that Father O'Reilly's action was in consequence of Bishop Hennessy's directive.

13 St. Irenaeus Parish Centennial Celebration, 1848-1948, Pamphlet, n. a. , n. p. , 1948.

14 Commemoration of the Diamond Jubilee, Our Lady of Angels Academy, Clinton, Iowa, 1891-1946, n. a. , n. p. , 1946.

15 The story is told of the fledgling teacher who found herself on the southbound steamboat at Dubuque where she had been deposited with fare paid, but apparently without instruction as to her destination. Nor had the Burlington superior, on the same boat with her flock of Sisters, been apprised of the destination of the bewildered young Sister. Her doubts were resolved, however, when the boat landed at Davenport. There, running along the pier from end to end of the boat, was a strange man, shouting, "Sister for Dutchtown! Where is the Sister for Dutchtown?" Sister was quickly bundled off the boat and into his care. (Sister M. Lucilla McGrath as told by Sister M. Aquin O'Connor.)

16 Mother Clarke wrote Lawyer Knight in September 1879:
     I have read your clear full statement attentively through.
     The first question is - can you devote a portion of your
     precious time to direct all in the manner you proposed
     - receive the rents, expend what is necessary for the
     convenience of the tenants, and find a man to take care

of the farm, board help, etc., just as you explained?
I am well aware, Mr. Knight, that your time is too
valuable to permit you to visit the farm, but could
not this man bring you the accounts at stated times.
. . . Use the money you receive as you think proper
for the immediate improvements needed. I told
Brother Michael to tell you all that is necessary for
you to know regarding the tenants, and to leave all in
your hands for the future. Brother is not in good health.
It is to this I attribute his lack of firmness and exactness. He means well. Now, Mr. Knight, I wish to
speak to you of another matter. Since you have taken
charge of the building you have sent me an account of
our indebtedness to all parties except yourself. Please
do so at your earliest convenience and oblige me. . . .

17 The following March, Mother received a letter from a
Reverend John B. Reverdy, V. G., requesting detailed information regarding the young lady who then was interested in entering a cloistered Community. Mother wrote simply:
"In reply to all your questions it is sufficient for me to
state, that from our personal knowledge of Miss Mary
C. Sturdevant, we think her entirely unfit for community
life. The young lady means well but lacks health and
stability. "

18 Sister M. Scholastica McLaughlin, in a memorandum,
tells that Mother Clarke gave general permission to the Sisters
to send any items of clothing or otherwise which were in any
way superfluous, for the victims of the fire. When the boxes
arrived at Holy Family Convent, the Sisters recognized Mother's own good woolen shawl among the items. This the Sisters
retained. Moths and relic-seekers among the Sisters have left
the shawl, green with age, quite riddled, though it is still
preserved among the reminders of an earlier day.

Chapter Two

CONSTITUTIONS AND RULES - A CONTEST OF POWER

The Sisters had completed their first year under the Jesuit Fathers at Holy Family when Father Donaghoe wrote to Sister M. Agatha on July 17, 1868, instructing her with reference to the first vows of the three novices who had served for the year in the parish schools:

> Sisters Mary Scholastica, Cleophas and Thomas are to make vows for the diocese of Dubuque, where they received the white veil. Anything else would be wrong, and the vows would be invalid, even if I were there myself. Dubuque diocese is and was the Sacred Fountain for our poor little Community after leaving the diocese of Philadelphia. One of the Jesuit Fathers now at home I hereby empower to receive the vows. The copy of the vows which I send, I suppose you have, as you repeat the same when you renew annual vows.

That formula read:

> I, Mary _____, in the presence of God and the whole court of Heaven renew the promises of my Baptism and take a simple vow of Poverty, Chastity and Obedience for one year, to serve in the Diocese of Dubuque and to engage in all the duties pointed out by our Rule, in the Community of the Sisters of Charity of the Blessed Virgin. To fulfill these engagements, I beg the assistance of our crucified Savior and His Blessed Mother; moreover, it is my intention to renew these engagements annually during the remainder of my life. Amen.

Sister M. Lambertina's Notes contain the following account
of Sister M. Scholastica's renewal of vows at the close of her
summer retreat in 1871, a ceremony in which all the Sisters
at Holy Family Convent, Chicago, participated by their annual
vow renewal:

> Sister Mary Scholastica, after renewing her vows, left the
> copy in her pew while she hastened to get the priest's break-
> fast. Father Koopmans, retreat master, picked it up. After
> breakfast he said to the Sisters: "I see by this paper that
> you are not religious outside of the diocese of Dubuque. "
> Sisters M. Agnes and Angela were furious with Sister for
> leaving it where he could get it. Sister M. Agatha reproached
> her with: "I never knew you when you weren't leaving some-
> thing somewhere after you. " Father Damen next day told S.
> M. Agatha: "I did not know you were not approved or I would
> not have taken you, but now we must go to work and have
> the Rule approved. " Father Koopmans was scheduled to go
> to the Old Motherhouse next to give a retreat there.

It was a strange misconception on the part of Father Donaghoe
that led him to believe that vows for service in the diocese of
Dubuque would satisfy for services they were rendering in
Chicago. The position in which the Sisters were placed by their
obedience was indeed ambiguous, and the subterfuge to which
they evidently resorted - that of omitting from the vow formula
the "to serve in the diocese of Dubuque" - was at least a real-
istic solution to their dilemma. However, the revelation of the
subterfuge gained them the support and assistance of the Jesuit
Fathers in the preparation of a set of rules which would free
them from diocesan control and establish them as a religious
congregation.
The simple rule according to which the Sisters made their
first public vows in 1845, based as it was on government by a
priest-superior, contained no provision for other offices than
those of Mother, Novice Mistress and local Superior. It provided no directives for these offices, nor for the manner in
which they would be filled. Though it specified education as the
Community's single apostolate, it laid down no regulations to
govern the institute as a teaching body. It provided no guidelines
for the admission of candidates or for their training, and it
listed no canonical requirements governing the novitiate or the
profession of vows. All this and more must be supplied before
approbation could be sought.

As Mother Clarke watched age and ill health undermine the faculties of Father Donaghoe, she seems to have quietly planned the missing portions of the rule. By the summer of 1871, her document was complete. The harsher portions of the rule of 1845 were eliminated and the wordier portions condensed. Mother Clarke, completing "in his spirit" the disciplinary regulations the Sisters had observed under him, supplemented these with eighteen brief chapters. These chapters provided the necessary governmental pattern and guidelines for the administration of a religious Congregation, its schools and its local missions. The copy of the finished work submitted to Bishop Hennessy for his approval was written in Mother Clarke's own hand and stitched into a cardboard backing covered with black muslin. [1]

When the Reverend Peter Koopmans, S. J., fresh from the retreat at Holy Family, Chicago, came to the Prairie mother-house to conduct the retreat there, Mother Clarke submitted a copy of the finished rule for his perusal. Convinced of its need for revision, he planned to place it before the rector of St. Ignatius College on his return to Chicago. [2] But that could not be permitted until Mother Clarke was assured of the Bishop's approval of its contents.

During the summer of 1872, the Reverend James C. Van Goch, S. J., retreat master at the Davenport Academy, spoke with deep regret of the fact that the rules had not yet been submitted to Rome for approbation. The following summer, Father Garesché, S. J., conducting the motherhouse retreat, expressed displeasure that the rules were not yet in print. He added that any one of the Fathers would put them in proper form for submission to the Sacred Congregation of the Propaganda, and he proposed the Reverend Aloysius A. Lambert, S. J., for the work. [3]

It is not clear when Bishop Hennessy, having added his own emendations, gave the document his approval, but it was apparently in the hands of the Jesuit Fathers by the end of 1873.

Mother Clarke's next problem was to find a clergyman willing to serve as postulator, to present the rules to the Sacred Congregation in Rome. Her original request was made to the Reverend Philip Laurent, pastor of St. Mathias Church, Muscatine, and a warm friend of the Community. With this in mind she sent him a copy of that first printed rule, containing as it did the emendations supplied by Bishop Hennessy. Her letter brought the following protest from Father Laurent against the Bishop's determination to maintain his hold over the destinies of the Sisters. It was dated July 14, 1875:

I could not in friendship to your order think of soliciting

Rome's approbation on clauses which bind your sisters'
hands and feet and make them slaves in their own houses.
You are forbidden making new foundations without the
consent of the Bishop of Dubuque, and in the diocese of
Dubuque itself you are forbidden to open schools as you
and the respective pastors think proper and necessary.
Does not this mean that you are expected to die out and
the sooner the better? I hope I am mistaken, but I can
see if these clauses are approved and have the force of
law, any court in the land will, at the request of interested parties, pronounce your community dissolved
when this law is disobeyed.

Another clause makes it a duty on all Sister Superiors
to invite the Bishop every year to come and examine
their accounts and see if they have not paid too much for
muslin, calico or cambric. Who is the Sister Superior
who will submit to this or even think of it? By not doing
it every one of them is at fault, liable to reprimand,
troubles. You are again at the mercy of the law. Any
harebrained priest who thinks the Sisters are becoming
too rich can cause them untold tribulations. . . .

On the present action regarding the approval or otherwise of these conditions depends the future of the community. Sister M. Felicitas /superior of the St. Mathias
convent7 will tell you more. She has a clear head and a
good heart. But be sure that God loves the order over
which you preside, otherwise he would not send you all
those trials. This will act as fire on gold, refine it and
make it more precious in his eyes and more useful for
our young and growing churches.

Sister M. Felicitas Carr, superior in Muscatine, wrote to
Mother Clarke on January 8 next, after returning from Dubuque,
where she had apparently discussed with Mother the matter of
postulator. Father Laurent had suggested the possibility of
engaging the Reverend Andrew Trevis for that service, since
Father Trevis was at that time in France where he had gone
for his health. He was suffering from a tubercular condition,
and had been invalided in his Keokuk parish for some months
before setting out for his native France, but now seemed sufficiently well to undertake the commission in the mild Italian
climate. Sister wrote:

I told Father Laurent what you said about paying Father Trevis' way to Rome, and what a favor you would consider it besides, and he seemed pleased. Today he wrote again to him and told him that I was after returning from Dubuque and had told you that he had written to France requesting him to take the Rules to Rome, and that you were pleased and said that Father Trevis would be just the man. He told him that money would be no consideration even though it should cost thousands, and urged him to answer at once and let him know if he would go and that money and Rules would be sent to him. Now, dear Mother, I begged of Father Laurent to urge the matter as fast as he could that I wanted you to have the happiness of having our Rules approved of in Rome before your death. He said indeed he would do his best, and it was his earnest wish that you would live to see that day. . . .

A brief note from Mother Clarke went to Sister M. Felicitas on January 17, 1876:

I'm grateful to Fr. Laurent and have confidence in Fr. Trevis. Will make any sacrifice to get the money required. Will have prayers and Mass for all and the 2 priests. I am resigned if I do not live to see it. The Latin Rules I will have Sr. M. Agatha send to Fr. Laurent. Do not permit him to be at any expense. I will send the amount he has promised Fr. Trevis when you send for it.

Although Mother Clarke had informed Sister M. Agatha that she was arranging with Father Trevis to act as postulator, Sister seems to have become convinced that there was more wisdom in a plan proposed to her by Father Damen, to whom she was also under a certain obligation of obedience. Father Damen had received the promise of Archbishop Wood of Philadelphia that the Reverend Charles O'Connor, then at the American college in Rome, would serve as postulator. It was scarcely a logical arrangement, since Father O'Connor was returning to the States in mid-April. It was to Father O'Connor, however, that Sister M. Agatha addressed the rule, without telling Mother Clarke of her action. That she did not make clear what she had done when she wrote Father Laurent appears from his letter of February 19:

It is only yesterday that Sister M. Agatha wrote to me that the rules had been sent already. I was waiting anxiously to let Father Trevis know and stop further doings about it.

Rev. Philip Laurent

Bishop John Cosgrove

Rev. Andrew Trevis

As it was, I at once sent her somewhat mysterious epistle to Father Trevis, but, I fear, too late to find him at his former address, as I think he may have started already for Rome. Sister M. Agatha says that he may help in the good work, chiefly in case the party from Chicago or elsewhere should not succeed. . . She prudently and mysteriously withholds the name of the interested and interesting personage, so that Father Trevis may use his sagacity and perspicacity in finding him out among the distinguished visitors to Rome from America. I hope he may scent him out at the right time.

It is still my firm conviction, as it always was, that if the Jesuits care about this business, they can have the rules approved without one fifth of the trouble it would cost a secular priest and I hope they have taken it in hand.

Sister M. Felicitas had written Mother Clarke on February 12:

Last night when F. Laurent came from Davenport where he had been attending services for Rev. F. Pelamourgues, 4 there was a cable dispatch written in French from Father Trevis, saying to send the Rule to him at once to the North American college, Rome. Oh, how glad I was. I could not sleep, I was so rejoiced and anxious too to have the Rule there as soon as possible. Father Trevis paid the dispatch which must have been a great deal. Please send him at once the money . . . Father Laurent wants to wait until he asks, but I told him no, because he might think we would go back on our word.

Writing again to Mother Clarke on February 21, Sister M. Felicitas shared with her the pain of mind caused Fathers Trevis and Laurent by Sister M. Agatha's lack of openness regarding her consignment of the rules:

Father Laurent wrote to you on Saturday. He is very much hurt, not at any of your actions or words, only Sister M. Agatha. She dispatched /wired/ here on Tuesday morning and said she would write next day, but no letter until Friday . . . Father Laurent said when his letter did not come in time that she was concocting a letter to make it sound plausible. He was going to send her a telegram telling her

to keep her letter, that she had fooled him long enough.
. . . I never saw him so hurt. He said the idea of rid-
iculing himself and Father Trevis /hurt most/. I really
thought, dear Mother, that Sister M. Agatha knew F.
Laurent better . . . Once he loses confidence in a person it is lost forever. [5] . . . I assure you, dear Mother,
I pitied you last week for I know how uneasy you felt. I
declare I thought she knew how to deal with F. Laurent
better. . . There is nothing too much or noble for him
to do for one who acts simple with him.

Sister wrote again on February 29:

Father Laurent gave me this enclosed letter . . . Father Trevis went to work in good earnest, consulted the
Superior General of the Lazarists and Father Ramière
of the Society of Jesus, who were to give him letters
to the Holy Father, and Cardinal Pitra, Father Laurent's
friend, who would, as his letter states, receive him with
open arms. Father also said for Father Laurent - not a
Sister - to go to the Bishops of Dubuque and Chicago and
secure supplications from them asking to have the Rules
approved. . . . also to have one from Cardinal McCloskey
in New York, who is, Father Trevis has told them, "a
power in Rome superior in this to a dozen other Cardinals. "
Father L. said for me to tell you to send a telegram to
Father Trevis if you thought well of it, and tell him who
the person in Rome was and let both of them work together. He felt worse today after receiving his letter
than I saw him yet, on Father Trevis' account. . . .
Dear Mother, tell me in your next something to say to
Father Laurent, he will expect it. . . I know how pained
you will be when you get this. I could have cried today.

Apparently it was some time before Mother Clarke was able
to secure the following information from Sister M. Agatha in
order to relay it to Father Laurent on March 14:

I am ill. I never was so crushed in my life. Will you for
God's sake telegraph to Rev. Father Trevis. Tell him
it is Very Rev. Charles O'Connor, American College,
Rome, who has the rules.

Father Laurent's response sought to be comforting:

I think you trouble yourself too much about all this. It cannot be helped now and has to be endured. I knew from the beginning that the thing would have difficulties and was not at all surprised at the turn things took. Sister M. Agatha thought she was very cute in doing as she did, and it was the greenest trick she could think of. I know she was afraid to offend both friends, but forgot that a true friend is not offended by what cannot be helped. Now the mistake is repaired. I telegraphed in your name to Father Trevis in Rome and he has delicacy enough not to force his services, if they are not wanted by Father O'Connor. The interest he bears your community and his acquaintance in Rome will not hurt the success of the business. Now, dear Mother, don't trouble yourself any more about this and I am confident all will go for the best.

Meanwhile, Mother Clarke was using more direct means to attain the coveted approbation. A note among her personal effects, dated March 28, 1876, reads:

My dear Lord, I will offer the month of April the devotions the same as the month of March in honor of the passion and Dolors of the BVM, and St. Joseph and Souls in purgatory for the rules and community - all our crosses, in thanksgiving to the holy will of God.

The most crucial aspect of an appeal to Rome for the approbation of a religious congregation of women was the approval of the bishops in whose dioceses the Sisters served, and of these the most important was the clear commendation of the ordinary in whose see the motherhouse was situated. Much, then, depended on the response of Bishop Hennessy to the request for such a statement. However, as we shall see, Dubuque's Bishop was a man of independent mind. Sister M. Felicitas' letter of April 12 to Mother Clarke, having settled the matter of a remittance, gives us an inkling of trouble:

Father L. came in after I had sent your letter with that of Father Trevis enclosed, and requested me to tell you that he sent yesterday 1000 francs or $266.66 to Father Trevis. . . . Father L. says if the Bishop refuses to give his letter of approbation that Cardinal Pitra says never mind, get Bishop Foley's and as many other bishops as you can.

Meanwhile the rules had turned up at the American college and Father O'Connor, on whom Sister M. Agatha had counted to handle the business of the rules, was on his way back to the States, engaged to teach at St. Charles Borromeo Seminary in Philadelphia.

Father Trevis, now possessed of the rules, wrote again, on March 19, and on March 26, giving long and careful instructions as to the steps to be taken and the documents to be furnished in support of the Sisters' petition. There were needed besides letters of recommendation from the Bishops, a statement of the current condition of the Community and its prospects, with specific data as to the number of its members, its houses, resources, etc. ; a formal application; a brief history of the Community, and a biography of Father Donaghoe, regarded as its founder. In face of it all, Mother Clarke's health was failing, as a memorandum in her own hand indicates:

> My troubles and cares are numerous, and my strength going. All that I can do I do this day. I offer my life and my death in union with the death of my Lord and the Sorrows of His Blessed Mother for the Rules, for the missions, the Sisters and the children, and for all my usual intentions. If my Lord will deign to accept, may His holy will be done, although I am unprepared.

In May, Sister M. Agatha went to Muscatine, where she was able to effect a reconciliation with Father Laurent. Of this she spoke briefly in a letter to Mother Clarke: "Father Laurent relented only on Monday, and then he acknowledged that there was no collision intended. We parted good friends. "

All was not going as well in other quarters, for Sister M. Felicitas wrote on May 10 to say:

> Rev. F. L. just received a few lines from Father Trevis. He says that the Secretary of the Propaganda, Father Agnozzi, S. J. , wrote to the Bishop of Dubuque for a letter of approbation in order to proceed to the examination of the rules. Father Trevis says nothing can be done until the letters come, and should none come, nothing could be done except by a miracle.

Apparently Father Laurent had hopes of seeing that miracle accomplished, for he did not delay the writing of an earnest plea to Cardinal Pitra, who had been his teacher in the minor seminary at Autun. In French, and dated May, it reads in part:

At the request of our good Sisters and after having received the advice of their spiritual directors in Chicago,
I presume again to write to you these few lines in order
to interest your Eminence in their favor.

They feel the need of a powerful protector now more than
ever, seeing themselves, so to say, abandoned by the
Bishop of Dubuque who should be their official "protector"
and who refuses to sign their request being sent to Rome.
This refusal is still more singular since he was the first
to approve the new rule.

The letter then speaks of the objections raised by the Bishops
of Chicago and Milwaukee to the restrictions Hennessy had appended to the rules. It continues:

It is not our Sisters' intention nor mine to say anything
about the Bishop of Dubuque that would be opposed to the
respect that we owe to our first pastor, but here in
America everyone has a right to his opinions, provided
that they do not infringe on the liberty of another, and
on the other hand we know that God is present in his saints.
Only it seems, no matter what, that it is the right of our
Sisters to continue without hindrance the admirable work
begun under Bishop Loras and his successor, Bishop
Smyth, the work which has for eight years now been transplanted into the great city of Chicago and which excites the
admiration of both Catholics and Protestants. It is in virtue
of my twenty-five years of priesthood in Iowa, of my being
a disciple of Bishop Loras, and of my admiration for good
Father Donaghoe, their founder, that the young man who
was confided almost forty years ago now to the rhetoric
professor at the minor seminary at Autun comes now,
begging his former mentor, now Cardinal of the Holy Roman
Church, to interest himself in favor of the institution which
has done so much good in our Iowa almost since the establishment of the Church in our distant location . . .

Then on May 13, Sister M. Felicitas wrote that Bishop
Hennessy had received the communication from the Secretary
of the Propaganda, requesting his letter of commendation,
and ventured to ask Mother Clarke:

Would it not be well to call on him again for the letter
or reply, as nothing will be done until that reaches there.

42

Do, dear Mother, although it would be hard after being refused. Still I know you have humility enough to do it.

And she was not mistaken, for on May 17, Mother wrote Father Laurent:

I arrived in Dubuque today, and saw Rt. Rev. Bishop Hennessy. I told him as well as I knew how, what was required from him. He said it was not necessary as his sanction of the rules & his signing was enough; that he received a letter from Rev. Father Trevis, and that he would answer him. I left. In about one hour after, he sent me the inclosed. He thinks it will do. Is it necessary to apply to Cardinal McCloskey? It will be difficult, besides want of time. Excuse this, I have only time to send it.
                    Mary

The enclosure read:

Mother Mary Clarke - Dear Madam
    I hereby declare the approbation over my signature found in the little book containing the constitutions and rules drawn up for the government of your community, the Sisters of Charity of the Blessed Virgin Mary authentic. I remain,
                    Yours truly
                    John Hennessy
                    Bp. of Dubuque
(SEAL)

Father Laurent's response was prompt and characteristic:

I just sent to Rome Bishop Hennessy's letter, for what it is worth, more to show the disposition of his Lordship than for the good the writing will do. He knew full well that it is not what was wanted of him. He had the formula sent to him by Father Trevis, he had the letter of Monsignor Agnozzi, Secretary of the Propaganda, and he knew full well that what he gave you was of no account whatever. Leave him alone, don't go near him any more; the way he deceived you with his small stratagem is unworthy of a gentleman, let alone of a bishop.

I have written to Father Trevis telling him to try and

make them understand in Rome that we cannot get any more
from the man in Dubuque, and that he said it was all that
was necessary. Father Trevis' answer will tell whether
that will suffice or not, and if it doesn't we will try something else. After all, Bishop H's apparent ill disposition
will make it easier to have the iron clauses examined
and changed. Who knows but everything is going for the
best?

Father then suggested the designing of a seal which Sister
M. Josephine could prepare for the engraver and which should
then be used to establish the validity of official papers. Of the
emblems he suggested - the Alpha-Omega, or the crown of
thorns with lilies interwoven, - the latter was chosen.

The file in the Congregation's archives containing many detailed letters in Father Trevis' hand tells of his visit with
Cardinal Pitra and his services as liaison with the Propaganda,
of delays when the Cardinals left Rome during the oppressive
heat of summer, and his own departure for the warmer south
or into his beloved France during the raw, chilly days of the
Roman winter. They tell also of consultors and secret sessions,
of changes and rewritings and retranslations, and of the armies
of Victor Emmanuel on the march, with shadows of impending
war hanging over the city and the country. Yet, faithful to his
engagement, he neglected no means by which the interests of
the Sisters could be advanced.

"Father Trevis, " Sister M. Felicitas told Mother in her letter of June 7, "says Cardinal Franchi will write to the Bishop
in a few days unless his letter soon reaches there. It seems
the Bp. wrote to the Propaganda some three months ago for the
division of his diocese, but they wrote back to him and told him
to first answer the questions they gave him to answer some
five years ago. "

Then there was an address in French to Cardinal Pitra which
Father Laurent had composed for the Sisters. He requested
Mother to have it "copied by your best writer and sign it yourself and the Sisters of the Council. " The handsome new seal,
with its significant crown of thorns surrounding a cluster of
lilies was to make its maiden voyage to Rome, firmly impressed
on the important missive. That there were some mistakes in
the copy was not to be wondered at, but Sister assured Mother
Clarke that "Father Laurent will correct them without it being
noticed. " Father Laurent then wrote on June 10:

I am sending to Rome your letter to Cardinal Pitra duly

stamped with your own seal. I subjoined a few words of
mine, requesting his Eminence to vouchsafe us a little
bit of an answer. It seems so strange to me that holy
Providence has arranged all things so unexpectedly, allowing you to be abandoned by those who should be your
best friends, and placing your cause in the hands of
strangers. But charity knows no nationality and I only pray
that Almighty God may reward your humility. Good Father Trevis will not abandon your cause, precisely because
those who should defend it are found wanting.

On June 12 Mother Clarke's enclosure to Laurent of the Bishop's grudging note had reached Rome and Father Trevis wrote:

. . . I went with the Certificate of authenticity written
by Bishop Hennessy to Mother Clarke on the 17th. This
shabby piece of writing did not altogether appear equiv-
alent to a letter of recommendation, compared with the
warm letter of Foley /Bishop of Chicago/ in behalf of the
Sisters, and coming after so much delay and difficulty.
Bishop Hennessy besides wrote to the Propaganda in answer
to the questions put to him about his diocese, but saying
nothing concerning the Rules of the Sisters. Hence the
Propaganda wants to ascertain directly from the Bishop of
Dubuque whether he has any objection to the approbation of
the Rules by the Holy See, and, if so, for which reasons.
So a letter from the Propaganda will again be addressed to-
morrow to Bishop Hennessy with request to answer it at once.

Father Trevis' letter of June 28 to Father Laurent throws
new light on the motives back of the Bishop's stand:

Bp. Hennessy, who was very anxious to have Iowa divided
at once may perhaps have to wait a little longer. He would
find it but an act of retributive justice to be compelled to
wait when he compels others to wait so long. . . . I did explain personally to Cardinal Franchi and to Msgr. Agnozzi
and to Rev. Pierrantozzi all about the exploits of Bp. Dick
- the question of property, etc. Card. Franchi, hearing
how many children the Sisters were instructing, told me
that Bp. Hennessy should be delighted to have such a help
in his Diocese, and since the property of the Community
was sufficiently secured before the law, he did not see why
Bp. H. should wish to hold the title to it, to which I replied
that the principal reason for him to express such pretensions

should be only his intentions of manipulating the Sisters as he would like. . .

Then he reverted to more personal problems: "Meantime I am eaten up by the fleas! No rest for the wicked. . . . " And to Sister M. Agatha he wrote on July 8:

Good Father Hattenberger /chaplain of the motherhouse7 is importuning me to get for him some documents from the Motherhouse of the Sisters of Charity of St. Vincent de Paul, in which are explained the relations of the Sisters with the Superior, viz. , the priest who is their Superior! and this for his own personal guidance! Well, the whole trouble is simply, as far as I see, that Good Father Hat. supposes himself to be the ecclesiastical Superior of the Community, whereas he should simply consider himself the chaplain, with the obligation of administering to the spiritual wants of the community and giving charitably his advice on matters & things when called for - there is, I think, the misunderstanding! I will advise him to get himself appointed Superior General of the Sisters of St. Vincent de Paul and then he will be better able to apply to his guidance the Rules he wants. We all have a little tendency to become and be great people. Nevertheless, I say & repeat, Rev. Father Hat. is a treasure for the Sisters, & they should try to keep him.

In a letter written July 8 to Sister M. Agatha, Father Trevis returned to the subject of the Bishop:

The fact is the 3rd letter from the Propaganda for Bp. Hennessy is ready and wants only the signature of Cardinal Franchi, and I will go tomorrow back again to get it and send it, if possible by tomorrow's mail. It will go a little hard, I think, on Bp. Hennessy to condescend to reply. Several Bishops in America adopt the stubborn policy of silence toward letters from the Holy See, and with this tactic of silence, Rome can scarcely reach them, but when they are caught, they are apt to pay dear for it. This was the remark made to me yesterday by Mgr. Chatard. . .

You received, I suppose, the scribbling of good Fr. Hatten. My impression is the good man wants a change of position, that is all! or else he would wish to be head and boss, ac-

cording to his own square views & sentiments. Well,
God will continue to provide for you all, especially if,
as is to be hoped, you will all persevere to be faithful
to the original and primitive spirit of your little community. . .

That the problem of Father Hattenberger was a real one,
which would not be solved except by the word of the Holy Father
himself, we see from a second reminder to herself which Mother Clarke wrote on August 28, 1877, a whole year later:

I will commence 1 Pater, Ave and Creed in honor of the
Sacred Heart of Jesus. The Litany in honor of Our Lady
of Perpetual Help. Prayer to S. Joseph & de profundis
for the Souls in Purgatory. 1 Communion - all to continue
to Sept. 8, for Fr. Hat --''s conduct, the missions and
Rome. The same in thanksgiving, whether we obtain it or
not. May the holy will of God be done.

At long last Father Trevis had better news, which he communicated to Sister M. Agatha on August 29, 1876:

Hurrah! all is going now! the Bishop of Dubuque answered
the first letter of the Propaganda. His Lordship's answer,
says Monsignor Agnozzi, Secretary of the Propaganda,
is merely negative, viz., Bp. Hennessy says he has no
objections to the Rules being approved by Rome!! Not a
word of kind recommendation. Nevertheless, as providentially, the Propaganda was made aware of some of
the reasons of this episcopal coldness and stoical indifference from Dubuque. The rules will be handed today to
a Consultor and the regular process of examination will
go on. . .

The good word had not yet reached Father Laurent when, on
Sept. 6, he sent to Mother Clarke the following earnest advice:

It is my opinion that another letter from you to the Bishop
is necessary, and one too that would go to the point. Now
the time has come to rise in the sanctity of your cause and
to speak to him the language of the saints. I do not wish
to dictate to you, as I know that God's spirit guides you,
but I would merely propose to your consideration the sending of a letter somewhat in the following tone:
    Rt. Rev. Sir, We hope you will not look upon this

our new appeal to you as an intrusion. You are our
Bishop, and like most of us you hail from the Island
of the Saints; these are titles which encourage us
to call on you once more. Why should you reject
our prayer when we, in our humble capacity, do
our best and wish to do more to help you in the
teaching and christianizing so many immortal souls
entrusted to your care? We cheerfully carry this
burden for you and incessantly pray for the welfare
of your flock. Our friends both in this diocese and
in Chicago are surprised that you will not say the
only word in our favor needed in Rome, to forward
the approval of our rules, when Bishop Foley kindly
recommended us in the highest terms. We know, Rt.
Rev. Sir, that by this time, three letters have been
sent to you from Rome, and no answer received
from you. Letters often miscarry; but would it be
too much trouble for you to write once more that
simple word that they are expecting in Rome so
long, and the absence of which costs us money which
could be better employed here. Your silence and
your reticence are construed by many as opposition
to us; please tell us and we shall endeavor to become
more perfect. If you want to crush us, tell us openly
and do not hesitate to write it to Rome and motivate
your opposition to us. But above all break this suspicion
and this silence.

Something similar to the above will do, but if anything it
must be more accented and ring with the voice of just in-
dignation.

But the little drama had played itself out, and, while there
would be months more of slow and tedious negotiations, delays,
revisions and retranslations, the way was open to a successful
denouement. In the weary days of waiting when nothing could be
accomplished by enduring Rome's oppressive summer or chill
winter, Father Trevis found refreshment in the following where
his own devotions led him. To Mother Clarke he wrote, in part,
from Castellamare di Stabia on January 26, 1877:

It was last year on the 2nd of February, after one full
week of reflection that I threw myself at the feet of the
Immaculate Mother, offering myself for the work you
were then asking of me for the approbation of your Rules

48

in Rome. Among the spiritual benefits this affair has brought me, besides the precious prayers of your pious community, I must reckon the particular acquaintance with the humble shepherdess of LaSalette . . .

It was probably on this visit that Melanie of LaSalette remarked to Father Trevis: "Father, you are in Rome with rules for a Community in America, seeking their approbation. The rules will not go through due to the objections of a certain cardinal. He will die and the rules will be approved."
In Mother's response to his letter, dated February 18, she wrote:

. . . Rev. Father, I cannot tell you the joy and consolation it gave myself and my dear Sisters in the midst of unavoidable little crosses to hear that you have seen and conversed with the privileged daughter of the Blessed Virgin, Sr. Melanie of LaSalette. What a great favor it was for you to obtain for us a novena in behalf of our rules offered by her and joined by her Rev. Superioress and the Rev. Father. All the houses will be noticed ⁄notified⁄.

The 2nd of February was a beautiful feast for you to offer yourself for the arduous work, the approbation of our rules. We are grateful to hear you say, if God wills it. . . . I know you will be gratified to hear that our Rt. Rev. Bishop is very kind to us. We will offer the devotions of the month of St. Joseph for you, and all your arduous undertakings. I know he will aid you.

I am with respect and gratitude
Your humble
Mary Frances Clarke

Father Trevis had told Sister M. Agatha in his letter of November 19, 1876 that the consultor had done his work and was busy transcribing his notes for printing:

He was pretty much surprised ⁄Father continued⁄ that I had been so favored as to learn his name and to confer with himself on the matter, as generally the Consultors do their work unknown to the parties interested, thereby to secure their impartiality in the report. Of course, what regards the government of your community has been altered so as to leave liberty for new establishments anywhere. At the same time he has it so arranged, he says, that both the Bishop concerned and the Sisters will be equally satisfied, as he bases his report on the canon law of the Church, the Pope being thereby made the Superior, and the Bishops acting only as Apostolic Delegates . . .

It was a clarification of the new relationship the Congregation would enjoy as a pontifical, rather than a diocesan institute.

The report of the consultor, a Capuchin friar, the Reverend Gabriel Guarcino, gave confidence and great encouragement to those most concerned with the affairs of the rules. The introductory remarks of his report call attention to Pope Innocent III's decree given in the Fourth Lateran Council in 1215, that new religious foundations must make use of one of the approved rules - that of Saints Augustine, Basil, Benedict, or Francis - or variations of these. He remarked, however, that "These Sisters operate under no approved rule for their Institute seems to be an entirely new foundation; nor are their Constitutions related to any Rule.

He declared further:

I consider the teaching of these Constitutions and Rules as worthy of full approbation, and certainly of all praise (certain things, however, being excepted) by reason of its precepts of highest evangelical perfection. It seems and certainly is inspired by incomparable wisdom and most ardent love of God. . .

He pronounced the Bishop's clause of "No new foundation in another diocese without the consent and approbation of the Bishop of Dubuque" to be invalid, adding:

After this Sacred Congregation shall have sanctioned these Constitutions with its approbation, all question ceases as to the unrestricted liberty of founding houses in other dioceses without the consent and approbation of the Bishop of Dubuque, because this Sacred Congregation approves this Institute, not for one diocese only, but for all places of missions and for all dioceses.

As for the second troublesome clause, the consultor changed its form to read:

When the Bishop visits the house, it will be the duty of everyone to make known to him any negligence concerning

the observance of the rules, to manifest to him anything
that they may have remarked that is contrary to the spirit
of the Institute, or anything else that in the Lord they judge
should be communicated to him. Moreover, the book of
accounts of moneys received and expended must be submitted to his inspection.

Good news finally came with the month of March, in letters
on the first and third to Father Laurent and on the second to
Mother Clarke:

Now at last, and happy news. The Sacred Congregation
of the Propaganda has just officially examined the Rules,
and the Cardinals in this session have rendered ad
laudem in favor of the Institute of the Sisters. . .

And to Mother Clarke:

I can justly congratulate yourself, Reverend Mother
Clarke, for thus receiving for your dear Sisterhood
such a high pledge of divine blessing, with the incipient
sanction of the Head of the Church, and the blessing
of Pius IX. The rest will come naturally in its proper
time. The good Jesuit Fathers are to go over again a
new original of your Rule which must be sent again for
new examination before receiving the desired approbation
from Rome. From this rule the unfortunate clause which
Bishop Hennessy had seen fit to append was happily eliminated, nor was he given any control over the properties
of the Congregation or its members. In the end he will
give his signature to the approbation, and all will be well.

The celebration of the Holy Father's jubilee in May would
bring many American bishops to Rome, with their problems
to be laid at the door of the Propaganda. There was need, then,
to push hard for final action before that rush of business. Moreover, there were political disorders: Victor Emmanuel's armies
were on the march. Indeed, Father Trevis had written that

The Consultor to whom the documents were submitted had
just leisure enough to enable him to examine and report
favorably when a few days after, he was driven from his
Convent and from Rome by the amiable authorities of
Victor Emmanuel.

Father Trevis urged Sister M. Agatha on April 22 to return with haste fresh copies of the rules with the suggested revisions,[6] - among these, descriptive titles for the several chapters - for

Time here is more than money for you, because the condition of affairs in Europe is such that events may at once upset things here in Rome, and delay the cause of your Rules until after the Dark days!

With the bishops arriving for the jubilee, Father Trevis turned to his own hopes for a second Iowa diocese, with Davenport as its seat, his thoughts reaching forward to "a favorite son" who would some day occupy that see:

No hint that Father Cosgrove is moving toward Rome. . . It is a shame for him not to come to kneel before Pius IX and get his blessing. . . had he come, they might have taken the measure of his head for something.

Meanwhile, Mother Clarke wrote happily to Father Laurent on April 5:

Rev. dear Father,
    It would be impossible for me to express the gratitude of the Community to God and to each and all concerned in the great work of obtaining the sanction of the Church for our Rules and the Community.

I cannot bear to trespass on dear Father Trevis after all the labor and trouble he has had. But if it is possible he could remain to see the end, I think all would be safe. Can I ask you to write for me to him and make this proposition? Tell him not to think of the expense. I will enclose $400 to remit to him and whatever more may be wanting will be ready. Whether he consents to remain or not, send him the money for his traveling expenses. Our prayers shall continue for you and him, and all concerned in this great work.

Father Laurent promptly acknowledged the four one-hundred-dollar bills Mother had enclosed and indicated that he had already carried out her commission, adding that Sister M. Agatha had been there on Easter Sunday, and "we analyzed together the 'remarks' sent from Rome. She is posted on what is to be done now and the less time is lost in doing it the less expenses and delay there will be. "

Then in June Archbishop Wood of Philadelphia renewed his interest in the cause, urging that Father Trevis

> call the attention of the Holy Father himself to the subject, stating that there is urgency on account of the very advanced age and very precarious health of the foundress and superioress . . . She has kept the community for over forty-four years, and if she should die before the Rules are rendered stable and firm by the approbation of the Holy See, there would be serious danger of wreck for that most interesting community.

But Bishop Hennessy had not said his final word. It came in a letter to Cardinal Franchi, and was relayed to Sister M. Agatha by Father Trevis on June 21, 1877:

> The petition of the Sisters was sent without my knowledge and I do not know whether it is better to grant it or defer it. I have written also on more important business which, I trust, will be attended to.

The Cardinals had hoped that, having won the decree of praise, Father Trevis would leave them in peace for other business. He wrote on July 26:

> The Propaganda has been terribly bothered these last two years with American ecclesiastical affairs - Priests against Bishops, Bishops against Priests or Religious Orders, Bishop against Bishop, and especially during the last three months when the North American College has had pretty constantly three or four American Bishops for guests who had some quarrels to settle. Lord have mercy on us!

But Father Trevis himself had little mercy on the beleaguered Cardinals. And on August 29 he wrote to the faithful Laurent that the revision of the rules had been favorably reported to the Propaganda and that the final edition was then in the press. The Decree of Approbation would be submitted to the Holy Father for his sanction the following Sunday, September 2. He remarked:

> It is unusual that even temporary approbation is granted in

Rome so short a time after the Decree of Praise. Meanwhile you may transmit this communication and request that thanks be rendered to Our Lady of LaSalette on the 19th of September next, the anniversary of her apparition. Cardinal Bijarri died two days ago.

On September 15 the Decree of Approbation was issued. Was the death of Cardinal Bijarri in fulfillment of the prophecy confided to Father Trevis by Melanie of LaSalette?

On September 4 there had gone the long-awaited cable to the anxious Father Laurent: 'Rules approved for six years, " and on its heels a letter of rejoicing:

I can announce officially that the Institute and the Rules of the Sisters, BVM, are approved by Pius IX. Glory!!! - for six years. At the end of six years the Rules must be forwarded back to the Propaganda at Rome with the recommendation letters of all the Bishops who will then have houses of the Sisters in their dioceses, each Bishop mentioning whether any change is to be made after their experience of the Rules; thereby it will give an opportunity to our friend, the Rev. Alex. Hattenberger, to mature wisely and squarely his emendation to the Rules. Meanwhile, let him respect them as a good Roman Catholic, and cease to believe he has more wisdom than the whole court of Rome.

Mother Clarke was deeply relieved. Her message went at once to all the Sisters, while a memorandum in her own hand read:

We have obtained the sanction of the Rules. I will offer the Te Deum and Magnificat to the end of September. The first approbation of the Rules by Pius IX. Sister Mary Agatha told me it was beautiful. I did not see it.

She then wrote grateful letters of thanks to all who had brought the work to a successful conclusion, together with monetary gifts to the Jesuit Fathers as expressions of appreciation for their great services.

Father Trevis followed his cablegram with a letter giving details of those last important days and a fatherly reminder to the Sisters:

. . . it is quite unusual in Rome to pass thus a Decree,

even of temporary approbation, so soon after the Decree
of Praise, therefore this result should be for all the Sisters
of the Blessed Virgin Mary a convincing motive for greater
confidence in the Blessed Mother of Mercy, and a new
reason to consider yourselves the children of Providence.

The General Congregation of the Cardinals of the Propaganda with regard to the Rules was held on August 31st.
Each Cardinal brought there his opinion upon the subject
which he had previously studied, a copy of the Rules having
been beforehand submitted to each of their Eminences.
They charged then a committee of two Cardinals, Franzelin
and Martel, the last named a lawyer, the first a Jesuit, to
shape and sum up the corrections of all. This having been
done, the matter was laid before the Pope, who approved as
stated. . . . I pray that the high sanction of the Holy See
in your favor may prove the beginning of a new era in your
community, an era of great fervor and zeal for all that
relates to your own perfection and the instruction of youth,
as well as the edification of all. Rules alone will not do;
the proper spirit must continue to animate their practice.

The visit of three bishops to the motherhouse must have
seemed an appropriate celebration of the great event, for they
too were in a holiday mood. Mother Clarke's letter to Sister
M. Gonzaga gives an account:

Three Bishops dined her last Wednesday - our own, Bishop
Foley and the Bishop of, I believe, Pittsburg. [7] They enjoyed themselves. They were all over the house. It was a
fast day and our Bishop brought pickled fish in his bag
lest we could not be prepared. What do you think of that?
Was it not thoughtful?

There seems to have been some matter which Sister M.
Agatha hoped Mother Clarke had discussed with Bishop Foley
on the occasion of his visit, for Mother gave the explanation
of her failure in a response dated November 21, to a letter
from Sister:

It was impossible for me, dear Sister, to speak to Rt.
Rev. Bishop Foley, the day he was here, Bishops Hennessy
and Shanahan, and Rev. Father Hattenberger being present.
I think my visit was not more than five minutes. You can
apologize to him if you wish, and remark the reason. He

spoke of the Sisters and said you were at his house the day before. It would be hard under the circumstances if he came to the conclusion that I did not approve. I should /have had to/ either speak to him before all present or call him out of the room, which I think would be out of place. Don't you?

Regarding the rule, Mother had written Sister M. Agatha on November 13:

I am relieved and truly thankful to God and to Rev. Fathers Coosemans, Garesché and all who have interested themselves in the most important affair of our Rules. Father Cooseman's advice was in my opinion the most valuable he could have given, that is to ask Father Garesche to translate the entire new copy. It was most charitable of him to consent to do it.

And to Father J. C. Van Goch, she wrote on December 28:

Ever Respected Father
How grateful I feel for your condescension in writing to me. Indeed I often inquired about you, but my only answer was that you were in Milwaukee. You are not forgotten by our poor Community. There is not a day passes but that the Sisters at St. Joseph's say one part of the rosary for you. . . . May you be richly rewarded by God.

I trust in God you will succeed in building your church. If our poor prayers will be useful, you will have them, besides a little Christmas gift of $50. 00 for yourself personally which I enclose. I wish it were more. All I can add are the prayers of an old woman.
                              Your humble
                              Mary Frances Clarke

Together with his directives regarding the application for final approbation after a six-year trial period, the happy Trevis offered in an undated letter the following timely suggestions:

Besides the book of your Rules, would you not do well to record in another book the usages and customs of the community so as to hand them on more faithfully to those who may come after? un contumier, they call it.

On October 10, there came to Mother Clarke a surprise note in Bishop Hennessy's familiar hand: "Dear Madam, This morning I received the authenticated copies of your Rules. They are now approved by the Holy See. I feel pleasure in offering my congratulations on this head. " By the holidays, indeed, he had warmed sufficiently to write: "Wishing you all a very happy Christmas, dear Mother, Yours very sincerely . . "

By November 6 Father Laurent had had time to review the entire proceedings which he summed up in a letter to Mother Clarke:

> The more I think about the affair of the rules, the more
> I am proud of it, seeing how nicely the thing was done,
> without any underhanded doing, and pulling wires, but
> all above board, and even with the express request of
> the Bishop. [8]

Tired and ill as he was, Father Trevis thought to return home to the States. He had missed most regretfully the splendid celebration with which the congregation of St. Mathias and his fellow priests had honored Father Laurent's silver jubilee. He was to face a second disappointment, for, as he was preparing to return he was seized with a hemorrhage and was forced to seek the warmth and comfort of northern France, where he was to remain for four more years. Mother Clarke, always fearful that he would run short of funds, had sent a steady flow of drafts through Father Laurent until both priests had called a halt. Early in the course of the negotiations, she had followed the suggestion of Father Laurent and had urged Father Trevis to make his home with the Sisters on the Prairie, when his work was done. There they could extend to him the loving care his services had merited. But he was wise enough to know that only a hospital would meet his needs when eventually he returned to his diocese. Meantime his unpredictable Bishop sent him faithfully the modest yearly remittance of five hundred francs toward his support. The Sisters of Mercy in Davenport promised him a room, and, if he was able for it, a chaplaincy, on his eventual return.

But Father Trevis had more ahead of him than a room in a hospital. There was important work for him to do, both for the Sisters and for his beloved Davenport, for a new diocese was shortly in the making, and the Sisters would have further business with Rome.

At last the anxieties and long delays had come to an end.
The Community was now a religious Congregation, a papal institute, free to respond to any call where there was need for
their services. Its book of Constitutions was a good one, even
something of a first, and filled with the spirit of God. Rome
had declared it so.

It was in the spirit of Father Donaghoe that Mother Clarke
had added to his written rule the regulations to which the Sisters had been required to conform during his lifetime. However,
when she moved into the area of government, of the Congregation, the schools and within the household, she was in new territory, and was free to speak to the Sisters as her own. But
how greatly changed this portion had become! How much was
lost that she had prayed and pondered over as guidelines for
her Sisters when she was no more!

The Fathers had asked of her a letter which would present
the Constitutions to her Sisters and set her seal upon them.
She had written:

In the presence of Almighty God who sees the intentions
of my soul, and who knows the motives that animate me,
to promote the glory of God, the salvation of souls, and
the good of the Congregation of the Sisters of Charity,
B. V. M. , I give you the Constitutions and Common Rules
of our Congregation.

I have written and compiled them almost verbatim from
the writings of saintly Father Donaghoe, and added,
according to his spirit, that which death prevented him
from finishing. It is my last request and will that these
Constitutions and Rules shall be, in future, your guide
and protection, until high Ecclesiastical authority shall
order otherwise.

May God bless you all, my dear children. I feel confident
that, following these Rules, you will reach the End of
our dear Institute, and having imitated Jesus, Mary and
Joseph, you will enjoy their company in Heaven.

I recommend myself to your good prayers, and remain
                    Your sincere and most unworthy
                        Mother Mary F. Clarke, B. V. M.

It had never been her custom to sign more than her baptismal
and family names to any communication or document. She had

never used the title "Mother" or the identifying "B. V. M. "
These, essential to so official a message, she would never use
again even in later communications with Rome.

But there was little time for rumination or regrets. The
freshly printed rule books, bearing the decree of approbation,
were now in the Sisters' possession. Those at the motherhouse
had received their copies from the hands of Father Koopmans who
had returned for their retreat that August of 1878.

Election for the Mother and her four consultors must take
place at once, for the rule required that it be held during the
summer vacation, and it was now late August. Having notified
the Bishop, Mother Clarke wrote each of the local superiors,
outlining the plan to be followed. The directive required the
Mother, in conference with her Sister-consultors and others
whom she wished to include, to propose the names of three
Sisters whom they judged suitable for the position of Mother,
and six Sisters for that of Consultor. [9] On August 24, Mother's
letter went out, enclosing the required lists. The Sisters who
had been under vows for five years or more were to assemble
in chapter in their separate missions, the letter read to them,
and the lists presented for their consideration. The Superior
was instructed to take

particular pains to make them understand that they may
vote for those nominated, or for any other whom they
please. Then let each one write on a slip of paper with
a lead pencil, the name of one whom she desires for
Mother General, and the names of four others for Consultors.

Then the Superior was to appoint two tellers,

(any two Sisters you please) to collect the votes, after
which one of said tellers will read off the names which
have been written, and only those. Should any other
names be read, the second teller is obliged to correct
aloud and on the spot. According as the names are
read, you will write them on a list, to which you will
sign your own. See that the ballots are burned immediately, then enclose both lists and send them to the
Rt. Rev. Bishop of Dubuque.

After Bishop Hennessy, in the presence of two witnesses,
tallied the votes, he announced on September 2, the results.
In doing so, he confirmed in office Mary Frances Clarke,

unanimously chosen as their Mother General, and Sisters M. Joseph O'Reilly, Eliza Kelly, Josephine Clarke and Domitilla King as her consultors. These, in council session, fulfilled their duty of choosing the other principal officers: as Sister Assistant, Sister M. Gertrude Regan; Sister Visitor, Sister M. Agatha Hurley; and Novice Mistress, Sister M. Michael Nihill.

With these officers properly installed, the new Congregation was launched into its first century of service as an apostolic institute.

Notes

1 That simple document, returned to Mt. Carmel after the
then Archbishop's death in 1900, is the only original writing of
Mother Clarke's which remains to us aside from her letters, a
few brief memoranda on scraps of paper found in her files, and
an essay on educational principles and practices included in the
Congregation's first Custom Book.

2 In 1867, the famous mission team of Father Damen and
Father Cornelius Smarius was engaged for what seems to have
been the first Jesuit retreat given at the motherhouse. The
retreat of 1868 there was conducted by the Reverend Charles
Coppens, S. J. , while the Reverend Bernard McCaffrey, OCSO,
conducted retreats there in August 1869 and July 1870. Following that given by Father Koopmans, S. J. , in 1871, retreats
at the motherhouse and generally elsewhere were conducted by
Jesuits through the succeeding century.

3 The source for the reactions of the three Jesuit Fathers
mentioned here is found in brief memoirs of Sister M. Anicetus
Kearney.

4 Father Pelamourgues, former pastor of St. Anthony's in
Davenport, had died in France shortly before. On his retirement he had returned to his native France.

5 Such did not prove to be the case, however. With the
many letters from Jesuit friends which Sister M. Agatha received on the occasion of her golden jubilee in 1894 there is
one from Father Laurent, indicating the warmth of their early
and enduring friendship:
    . . . Do you remember forty-four years ago at the levee
    in Dubuque when the green French boy was shipped on
    the Steamer Lamartine for Muscatine? I felt lonely in the
    strange country with the strange people and the queer
    language. You comforted me with kind words and a beauti-
    ful farewell. I remembered your brother at the Barrens
    who was a dear friend to me, and his remembrance and
    yours lightened my lonely way to Muscatine. Do you re-
    member twenty-seven years later when you left Muscatine
    for Chicago and I in turn encouraged you in the enterprise
    which then seemed like a rash venture? What a consolation
    to think today that you always tried your best, and never
    impeded God's holy and mysterious designs.

6 It would be a heavy drain on Sister M. Agatha who held herself responsible for the work. She had written on one occasion: "I have nearly finished the copying of the first two chapters ⟨of the translation⟩. It is a real task for me to undertake, but I could not think of asking the school Sisters after teaching all day. " Later Sister wrote: "My shoulder has been paining me so much that I dread seeing pen and ink. "

7 The Most Reverend Jeremiah Shanahan was then Bishop of Harrisburg, not Pittsburgh.

8 There is no other record of the Bishop's "express request. "

9 Doubtless the acting officers of the corporation served temporarily in the role of consultors at this first election.

Chapter Three

IN SEARCH OF A CHARISM

L ike many of their sister-institutes in the process of renewal, the Sisters of Charity, B. V. M. , have taken a backward look to their foundations, and to the circumstances in which the community's Constitutions were formulated. This seems especially important since the members of the B. V. M. Congregation were governed by the rules outlined in those constitutions, with little fundamental change, from the time of its approbation in 1877 to the era of religious renewal following Vatican II.

The deprivation of educational opportunities, together with the status of minors assigned by society to all women of the eighteenth and nineteenth centuries, left religious women totally dependent on male ecclesiastical supervision. Nowhere is this inferior status better illustrated than in the matter of religious constitutions acceptable to Rome, and in the necessity of adapting the feminine religious life style to a rule approved by Rome for an order or a congregation of men.

Apostolic communities of women were relatively new in the Church. Innovative and largely American, they did not - or could not - readily free themselves from the influence of medieval European monastic traditions: distinctive habits, cloister, the chanting in choir of the divine office, and the distinctions of rank between lay and choir members. Rome did not find it easy to give approval to innovation, particularly that of freedom from cloister for religious women. Mary Ward in England, Vincent de Paul in France, and Nano Nagle in Ireland had faced serious handicaps in their efforts to found congregations of women free to meet such exigencies of service as the times called for. Indeed, when applied to canon law, the adage "Law follows life" needs the extension "at a distance. "

The break with monasticism was most decisively made among religious men by St. Ignatius, founder of the Society of Jesus, who devised the plan of simple vows[1] for some of its members, and departed from such ancient practices as the wearing of a distinctive habit and the recitation of the divine office in common, as impediments to the apostolic life. With its professed members pledging their service to the Holy Father for labor in any part of the world where there were souls to be saved, the Society occupied a unique position in the Church. Among the many opportunities for service opened to it was that of guiding young communities in the writing of their rules, or in preparing them for approbation by the Holy See, a task for which their unique position made them singularly fitted.

But the Society had had its day of trial. In 1773, after two hundred years of signal service to the Church, Pope Clement XIV, under the pressure of violent political forces, issued a decree of suppression. A century later the effects of that decree would be reflected in the Constitutions approved by the Holy See for the Sisters of Charity of the Blessed Virgin Mary.

Many factors entered into the formulation of those constitutions as they grew from the early document drawn up by Father Donaghoe under the guidance of the Jesuit, Francis Dyzierozynski, to the finalized form which shaped the lives of the Sisters for nearly one hundred years.

It was as a member of the Society in exile that the Polish Dyzierozynski had been trained, in a milieu vastly different from that in which the Society had had its inception. The forty years of suppression had resulted in an impoverishment from which nearly a century of struggle would be required to restore the Society's leadership in the Universal Church. When the edict of suppression had been finally lifted, the autocratic Catherine of Russia, erstwhile protector of the Fathers, in 1820 drove the surviving members out of her dominion. The Society's restoration called then for an almost total rebuilding of a trained membership, with the necessary adjuncts of novitiates and schools and universities.

Some insight into the problems the nineteenth century American Jesuit experienced in his training is provided in the following reminiscences:

James Van de Velde, S. J., a future Bishop of Chicago, began his study of theology at Georgetown College in 1825, but nine years later at Saint Louis University where he served as minister, prefect of studies, professor of mathematics and Spanish, and for a time as treasurer, his course was still unfinished. . . .

Reminiscing a generation later to Peter Beckx, Roothaan's successor as general, Father Ferdinand Coosemans, by that time provincial of the Missouri Province, threw light on more than one aspect of priestly training in those years when he wrote:

"All the time I have been in the Society I have been occupied with duties without having had a single year free for study. During the second year of my novitiate, I repeated my Rhetoric. While still a novice I was sent to college where, completely immersed in prefecting as also in teaching some four hours a day, I studied philosophy for the space of two years. This study amounted to little more than copying our Father Martin's notes; we had no printed text of philosophy. Fortunately I did not have much to forget when Father Martin's system was prohibited in the Society. I studied for a year and a half without having time to consult other authors; I was at the same time prefect of the students and professors. For one year only did I study Dogma, but I failed in my examination, partly for lack of talent, partly because of the distractions occasioned by my prefecting and teaching. I was ordained priest that same year. Superiors no doubt did not foresee that I should one day find myself in my present position. "[2]

Of the rich heritage Ignatius had left his followers in his comprehensive Constitutions of the Society of Jesus, only the small pocket manual, entitled the Summary /of the Constitutions/ and Common Rules, remained as the vade mecum of the hard-pressed teacher, pastor or missionary. As the Reverend Michael J. Buckley, S. J. , remarked to his confrère, the Reverend George E. Ganss:

In the decades, and even centuries before the Jesuit Congregation /of 1974-1975/ the Jesuit had little contact with the fundamental source of his spirituality; indeed he relied upon the Rule of the Summary, and the Epitome instituti /an abridgment of previous Jesuit legislation still in vigor as each successive edition was compiled/. [3]

Familiarity of the Fathers who prepared the constitutions of the Sisters of Charity with the original Ignatian document would indeed have made a difference in the nature of their efforts. Even the portion of Ignatius' composite document which is strictly identified as "Constitutions, " including their elucidation for the guidance of superiors, numbered 826 articles, some of them more than a printed page in length. It was from these articles that the fifty-three brief excerpts which constitute the Jesuit Summary were taken, a mere remnant indeed of the original legacy Ignatius had intended for his followers, even, in special instances, for his novices. For the Fathers who used the Summary as a guide in their efforts for the Sisters, its brevity seemed a virtue to be exercised even on the simple clarity and economy of words which marked the manuscript rule Mother Clarke presented to them.

As we consider the problems involved in education, and the estrangement from so important a source of his spirituality, we realize that the nineteenth century Jesuit was himself a deprived person, though certainly less so than the average religious woman whom he sought to serve. Had the Fathers lived their years with the full Ignatian document, the richness of their founder's spirit might well have alerted them to the spirit which pervaded Mother Clarke's modest manuscript. As it was, they were scarcely prepared either for that or for a response to insights of hers which we now recognize as akin in many respects to those of Ignatius.

Thus Father Ferdinand Coosemans, former provincial of the Missouri Province, and his companions in the Holy Family community, Frederic P. Garesché, James Van Goch and Aloysius A. Lambert, who generously undertook the preparation of the Sisters' manuscript rule for Rome, suffered under handicaps not of their making. They were preoccupied with the necessity of presenting an instrument of religious government which would find favor in the eyes of the Roman Cardinals who would determine its fate, and who, in view of the Jesuits among them, were favorably predisposed to a document bearing Ignatian earmarks. If the feminine mentality of Mother Clarke's manuscript found little resonance in the masculine minds of the Fathers who were in close association with the Sisters serving Holy Family Parish, how much less would it have struck a sympathetic chord with the distant Cardinals. It was doubtless with something of this in mind that the Fathers set themselves to their task.

The Sisters, in their search today to rediscover the spirit of their foundress, and to analyze the influences that early obscured that spirit, turn first then to an analysis of the transformation effected by the Fathers in significant portions of the manuscript rule which owe their authorship to Mother Clarke.

Mother Clarke's accession to the office of superior general had necessitated a change in the directive on obedience as it had been laid down by Father Donaghoe. His directive had read:

The Sisters of Charity of the Blessed Virgin shall pay
honor and obedience to their Institute, to the Rt. Rev.
Bishop of Dubuque, and their confessor. They shall
also obey the Superior-General of their Society, and
those whom he may direct to visit them, the Mother,
and in her absence, her assistant, and other officers
of the Community in what may relate to their respective
offices.

Since henceforth the office of Mother would be identical with
that of superior-general, and approbation of their rule would
free their institute for service in any diocese, Mother Clarke
wrote:

They shall pay honor and obedience to their Institute
and to the Rt. Rev. Bishop. They shall obey the Mother
and in her absence, her Assistant, the Visitor, and all
other officers of the Community in what may relate to
their respective offices.

This, however, she had prefaced with:

The Sisters of Charity of the Blessed Virgin shall make
it a duty to venerate particularly the authority of the
Holy See. They shall testify in all things a great affection
for and obedience to the Constitutions and decrees of the
Holy Church.

The last article the Fathers deleted as being unnecessary
since, as a papal institute, the Congregation would be obliged
to such allegiance. However, as a clear manifestation of her
position, it is of interest to her Sisters. It is of further interest as it reflects a declaration in the Formula of the Institute
- the fundamental Rule of the Society of Jesus. This states that
not only those who make profession of the four solemn vows,
but the entire Society are "campaigning for God under faithful
obedience to His Holiness, Pope Paul III and his successors
in the Roman Pontificate. "
Mother Clarke made it clear that the Congregation would be
governed by a Sister. She who was elected to that position "shall
be called Mother because the affairs of the whole Community
and the welfare of each Sister are entrusted to her care. " As
to the office itself, she wrote:

The Mother ought to be deeply impressed with a sense of

the great responsibility which her office imposes on her.
Besides her own perfection, she shall labor to make her
Sisters advance in virtue; a mild and humble spirit does
not preclude firmness and constancy, which are necessary. Though humble and affable, we shall therefore
firmly insist on the execution of the orders which she
has given with a view to God's glory.

Among the ten articles on "The Character of the Superior-
General, " Ignatius wrote:

. . . he should know how to mingle rectitude and necessary severity with kindness and gentleness to such an
extent that he neither allows himself to swerve from
what he judges to be more pleasing to God our Lord,
nor ceases to have proper sympathy for his sons.

Mother Clarke continued:

Superiority in a religious house abases rather than
elevates a person; in order to be the servant of Jesus
Christ, the Superioress is the servant of her Sisters.

These two prescriptions were reduced to read:

Let the Mother Superior be mindful that authority
amongst religious consists rather in serving the
servants of Our Lord than in being honored; therefore, let her be persuaded how great and manifold
are the obligations of her office; and, bestowing
her first care on her own perfection, let her strenuously labor that the Sisters make progress in solid
virtue.

While the Ignatian Constitutions assign a chapter of twenty-
three articles to "Aids to the Superior General, " the brief and
simple directives to those who would assist the Mother in the
government of the Congregation were further reduced. Mother Clarke wrote:

The Mother Assistant shall fulfill the duties of her office with fidelity and charity. She is especially charged
with the community of the mother-house. She shall see
that the Sisters be provided with all that is necessary,
and that poverty, cleanliness and decorum be observed.

She shall see that the subordinate officers prepare the meals, etc., at the appointed time and in the place prescribed in the rules; and that modesty and silence be exactly observed. She shall take special care of the sick, that they may have all that is necessary for body as well as the soul.

This read:

The Assistant should be mindful that it belongs to her to help the Mother in all her duties. She shall act as Superior of the Community in the house in which the Mother resides, and shall provide for everything. Should any one be sick, she must with the greatest possible charity, provide everything for soul and body.

Regarding the Sister-Councillors, Mother Clarke requested that

When God shall give them any good thoughts for the welfare of the Community, they shall note them down in order not to forget them, and communicate them to the Mother at the proper time.

To this she added the very perceptive instruction on discernment, a practice distinctively Ignatian:

When called on to deliberate on any affairs, they shall have recourse to prayer, reciting the "Veni Creator," and shall endeavor to have God alone in view, divesting themselves of personal consideration. They should always take the side on which they see the least disadvantage and most good for the advancement of God's glory. If some important affair be proposed to them, and they cannot at once give their opinion, they should ask for time to recommend it to God, and to reflect on it at their leisure.

In the rule prepared for Rome, these directives were reduced to the commonplace

When called upon to consult together, especially concerning matters of importance, let them first pray; for thus they shall be better enabled to advise what seems best in the Lord, and in accordance with the spirit of our vocation.

Of the Secretary, Mother wrote:

The Secretary shall aid the Mother in the government
of the Community. She ought to have a perfect knowledge
of the Constitutions, and of the ordinances of the Mother; and these she should follow with prudence and exactness; she should have a great zeal for the good of the
Community. As her duties are varied and important,
she should preserve a spirit of prayer and recollection.

The letters by the Secretary should be clear, precise
and full of the spirit of piety. In those letters which
she shall write in the name of the Mother, she must assume her spirit and intentions. She shall not write, nor
act, but by her orders, and she shall keep inviolably
secret the things which shall be confided to her.

Mother Clarke's admonition that, in letters written in her
name, the Secretary "must assume her spirit and intentions"
echoes Ignatius' directive that the person "who ordinarily
accompanies" the General "should take on the general's own
person and imagine that he carries on his own shoulders the
general's whole burden. . . . "[4] However, the revision for
Rome read:

The Sister Secretary must know that the office entrusted
to her is of the greatest importance; let her, therefore,
discharge it with the greatest diligence, and at the same
time it behooves her to observe the Constitutions, striving
thus to give good example to others.

Let it be her study that her letters be clear and breathe
the spirit of piety. Besides, she shall not presume to
write or command anything without the approval of the
Mother Superior.

Regarding those to be received into the novitiate, Mother
Clarke wrote:

Their life must have been virtuous and edifying. They
must enjoy good health, and have strength necessary for
the discharge of the duties of the Community. Those
who are of a delicate constitution or have other in-
firmities cannot be received. They must have good
sense and judgment,[5] and be capable of understanding

Rev. A. A. Lambert, S.J.

Rev. Frederic P. Garesche, S.J.

Rev. James C. Van Goch, S.J.

Rev. Ferdinand Coosemans, S.J.

Rev. Andrew O'Neill, S.J.

Brother Thomas O'Neill, S.J.

the spiritual and temporal things necessary for their
salvation and the discharge of their duties. Their natural
disposition must be mild and pliant to good; they shall
not be received who have a violent temper, who are
haughty, stubborn, light, inconstant, proud, idle, or
are cold and insensible to the things regarding God and
their salvation.

Although Ignatius' Constitutions include sixty-six articles on
"Admission to Probation, " the above statement by Mother Clarke
was made to read:

As it is necessary for the religious life to be adorned with
virtue, no one is to be admitted unless she enjoys good
health and strength of mind and body, and is of good disposition, and has a good moral standing, from which we
can prudently judge that the postulant is fit to undergo the
duties of our calling. Therefore, any one who seems to be
much inclined to pride, or the vanities of the world, or
given to inconstancy should not be admitted.

Mother Clarke took particular care in defining the duties of
the Novice Mistress, who, she wrote, "is charged with the
immediate direction of the Novices and Postulants, in order to
lead them more and more to the perfection of their state. "
"It is, " she continued, "her duty to instruct and guide those
under her charge in the knowledge of spiritual things, and in
the practice of the Constitutions and observances of the Institute. " Revision of this by the Jesuit editors must have struck
a responsive chord with Mother, for a prayer which the Sisters
have long spoken of as "Mother Clarke's prayer, "[6] incorporated
the expression "fit instrument in the hands of God. " The revision read:

It is the duty of the Mistress of Novices to form the
Novices according to the proper spirit of our Institute,
and to ground them in solid virtue, that they may be fit
instruments in the hands of God to promote His greater
glory.

Then Mother gave the following penetrating directive to the
Novice Mistress:

She shall attentively study the character of each, in order
to correct her defects, and to cultivate her good qualities,

which serve as instruments of grace. She should also
endeavor to discern the supernatural attraction, and
the way by which God wills to conduct each of the Sisters. She should not wish to make them follow her own
particular attraction or her personal inclinations.

In view of the fact that "Ignatius thought that there was no
worse mistake in spiritual matters than to lead others as oneself, "[7] it is unfortunate that so perceptive an article should
have been reduced to the pragmatic:

Let her carefully endeavor to understand, as well the
natural dispositions as the habits and talents of each
one, that she may be better able to direct them.

Mother Clarke continued:

She shall conduct them gradually to perfection, remembering that they cannot become perfect and practice
great virtues in a short time. She shall be mild and
affable towards all, that she may thus gain their confidence and be enabled to guide them more easily to
perfection.

Ignatius had characterized the person suitable for the guidance of his novices as

a person whom all those who are in probation may love
and to whom they may have recourse in their temptations
and open themselves with confidence, hoping to receive
from him in Our Lord counsel and aid in everything. [8]

However, the revision of Mother Clarke's admonitions read:

Let her most carefully avoid anything like impatience
or excessive warmth, a thing very much opposed to the
direction of souls, but, on the contrary, let her always
show herself affable and kind, for thus she will have the
confidence of the novices, and they will be better formed.

Again Mother Clarke instructed the Novice Mistress in her
role of counselor:

If some one of the Sisters is afflicted or tempted, she
shall treat her with great sweetness, listen charitably

to her affliction, endeavor to console her, and instruct her how to combat her temptation. If her efforts prove unsuccessful, she shall recommend her to God, and obtain prayers for her, and induce her to manifest her pains to her confessor.

Similarly, while Ignatius had written regarding the novices:

They shall be taught how to guard themselves from the illusions of the devil in their devotions and how to defend themselves from all temptations. They should know the means which can be found to overcome them and to apply themselves to the pursuit of the true and solid virtues. 9

Mother Clarke's direction became, when amended, the following colorless observation:

Should any of the novices be tempted, she must proceed with great charity and prudence, by speaking kindly, by encouraging her, and praying for her.

Since the apostolate of education seemed at that time to be the destiny of the Sisters, Mother Clarke planned her brief chapters on the direction of the schools with much care. When we consider the educational limitations of a large portion of the candidates who came to the convent in those early years, and the limited preparation they could be given in the novitiate with the pressures on the Community for teachers, we can appreciate the large part necessarily assigned to in-service training. Hence the stress Mother Clarke's directives put upon supervision and guidance by the directress or the superior. Her most significant instructions with regard to the conduct of the academy read:

The Directress of the Academy is charged with the education of the young ladies who frequent the school. It is her duty to see that whilst making progress in science, they also advance in piety and virtue.

Her conduct should be exemplary. She should show humility and charity toward the Sisters who assist her. She shall distribute the different charges among them. She shall take care that none be overburdened, and that all have time to attend to their spiritual exercises.

She shall exercise a constant vigilance with regard to the Sisters and the pupils. She shall see that the Sister Teachers use the books and follow the method of teaching[10] that has been pointed out to them, and that while acting with sweetness and humility, maintain with firmness good order and discipline in the school. The Directress shall do all in her power to advance the pupils in piety and the love of Christian modesty which is the brightest ornament of young girls; she shall see that they read no book or paper of dangerous tendency. She shall see that they apply with diligence to their studies, and that they are respectful to the Sisters who assist her.

When the Rule was being prepared for Rome, all this was revised to read:

It belongs to this Sister to direct with prudence in our Lord whatever appertains to the schools; to help the Sisters in teaching, and to endeavor strenuously that the children sent to our schools make continual progress both in virtue and learning.

She must be convinced that it belongs especially to her to give good example, as well to the Sisters as to the children.

She must be most careful that no Sister be burdened with too much labor, which would be an obstacle to her spiritual exercises, as well as to her health of body.

She shall see that all the Sisters make use of those books and of that manner of teaching which are approved by our Institute.

Obviously, much of the original unction is lost. The office of a teacher, Mother Clarke wrote:

being a painful one, requiring great application of the mind and exertion of the voice, the Sisters shall take care of their health to be better able to serve God. They should not conceal their indispositions and fatigues lest the proper precautions not being taken, the evil become incurable.

Yet they must not go into their classrooms unprepared:

They shall previously prepare the lessons they are to give in their classes, that, understanding what they teach, they may be able to communicate it to their pupils with clearness and precision. They should devote to their own improvement all the time that is necessary.

Then, lest they grow selfish through the pursuit of their own advancement:

They shall not study any other branches than those prescribed them by the Superioress or Directress, that their progress in science may be accompanied by their progress in humility and obedience.

All this was revised to read:

They must carefully prepare the lessons and recitations to be taught in the schools, for thus they will be able to explain them more clearly and with greater fruit.

They shall not apply themselves to any study without leave of the presiding Sister.

In consideration of each other, Mother Clarke reminded them that

When several Sisters are engaged in the same classroom, they shall take care to moderate their voices so as not to cause confusion; they shall give mutual edification by their meekness and patience.

Then, as a reminder of the communal claim on the riches of the mind as well as of material goods, Mother suggested a sisterly sharing:

They ought to communicate freely to one another whatever learning they may possess for the glory of God.

These injunctions survived only in the form:

Should it happen that two Sisters teach in the same room at the same time they must take care not to speak too loudly, lest they cause confusion to the children.

The next directive of Mother Clarke, however, was lost in the revision. It dealt with the Sisters' contacts with the parents of their pupils. With them,

> their manners shall be full of affability and modesty; they shall not speak of the defects of their children in any way that might wound their feelings, [11] but with prudence and moderation. They shall never speak of those defects to strangers.

Mother reminded the Sister-teachers that they

> should bear in mind while discharging their duties the example of the Saviour calling unto Him little children. All that they will do for them shall be as done unto Himself; this thought should give them particular encouragement.

To those engaged in the boarding schools she added:

> The pupils shall never be left alone either day or night. The Sisters should imitate the charity and vigilance of the Guardian Angels of the children who watch over the souls that are confided to them.

But neither the Lord or the Angels found their way into the revised document. The two directives were instead replaced by the admonition:

> Let it be their principal care to fill the hearts of the young with a very great hatred of every sin as the greatest evil that can befall them in this world.

The superior of the parish school was to assume the duties of directress in the school to which she was assigned. Of her Mother Clarke wrote:

> The Superioress shall cause the method of teaching to be read from time to time, in the conferences of the Sister Teachers, that they may know and follow exactly. It will serve to impress them with noble ideas of their charge, and will furnish them with proper means for succeeding in their labors.

This too was lost in the rewriting.

Regarding those Sisters serving the household in other capacities, Mother Clarke wrote:

> Many other officers are employed in the houses of the Community; such are: the cook, refectorian, laundress, etc. It is not necessary to prescribe for them any particular rules. It will suffice for them to observe the following general directions: They shall observe faithfully the instructions which the Superioress may give them regarding their offices, and endeavor to fulfill them with purity of intention, humility and devotion, seeking alone in all things the greater glory of God and the welfare of the Community.
>
> They shall maintain in their various offices great order and cleanliness. They shall labor without precipitation, but with diligence and with a tranquility that will leave them at liberty to elevate their minds to God, and keep themselves in His presence.
>
> They shall undertake nothing which is beyond their strength. They shall represent to the Superioress what they can perform, taking care not to flatter themselves, and then submit cheerfully to what she shall ordain, in the full confidence that God will assist them to obey.

These directives were omitted in their entirety from the document as prepared for Rome, and with them the stress Mother Clarke laid on "seeking alone in all things the greater glory of God, " so distinctly Ignatian.

The first transcript as submitted to the Congregation of the Propaganda was carefully patterned after the Jesuit handbook, its first chapter bearing the simple heading "Constitutions, " and the second, "Common Rules. " Included under the same cover was a third component of the little handbook, "The Epistle of St. Ignatius on the Virtue of Obedience, " thus completing their similitude.

Thus, though the Fathers had failed to note an affinity in many of the spiritual insights of the two founders, they had shared what they most treasured. In doing so they prepared a document which, with minor alterations, won for the Sisters the security and the recognition of a papal institute.

We venture to compare brief excerpts from the writings of the two founders. Addressing the Novice Mistress, Mother Clarke wrote:

To lead them in the way of perfection she should make them understand that they need the grace of God to conduct them there; that God gives this grace only to the humble and detached souls, and that they should practice humility and detachment from themselves. She should show them that there is nothing sweeter than to overcome oneself courageously for God.

On the "care and progress of the novices, " St. Ignatius wrote:

It will be very specially helpful to perform with all possible devotion the tasks in which humility and charity are practiced more, and, to speak in general, the more one binds himself to God our Lord, and shows himself more generous toward His Divine Majesty, the more will he find God more generous toward himself and more disposed will he be to receive graces and spiritual gifts. [12]

After remarking that "all the Sisters shall entertain great love and esteem for their vocation and consider that God has given them the better part, " Mother Clarke wrote:

They shall have respect, confidence and affection for their Superioresses. They shall honor Jesus Christ in their persons, speak to them with mildness and modesty, love them as their mothers, and address themselves to them in all their spiritual and temporal necessities.

while Ignatius had written:

Likewise, it should be strongly recommended to all that they should have and show great reverence, especially interior reverence, to their superiors, by considering and reverencing Jesus Christ in them; and from their hearts they should warmly love their superiors as fathers in Him. [13]

Thus it was that the spirit of Mary Frances Clarke, so attuned to Ignatian spirituality, yet so completely the spirit of a woman, eager to implant in her Sisters all that was religious and womanly, was, even so early, eclipsed. It is that spirit which her Sisters seek now to know and make their own in these days of their refounding: a spirit so simple that the greatness of her vision escaped the conscious concern of those who would willingly serve her, a humility that sought no least recognition for herself, and a charity incapable of imputing fault to another; yet for all that a foundress, a leader of women, an educator and administrator, but, above all, an heroic servant of God and his Church.

80

Notes

1 In subsequent centuries the simple vows would prove practical for most new congregations.

2 Quoted by John Tracy Ellis in his "Historical Perspective," The Catholic Priest in the United States, Historical Investigations. (Collegeville: St. John's University Press, 1971), p. 7.

3 Michael G. Buckley, S. J., "The Confirmation of a Promise," a letter to George E. Ganss, S. J., Studies in the Spirituality of the Jesuits. (American Assistancy Seminar, St. Louis, Vol. III, No. 5), p. 187.

4 Ganss, Constitutions, Article 800, p. 327.

5 It is of interest that St. Teresa of Avila laid stress on qualities of judgment and good sense in her subjects.

6 Mother Clarke's prayer read: O Lord Jesus, make me a religious, a Sister of Charity of the Blessed Virgin Mary, according to Thine own Divine Heart - meek, humble, patient, chaste, obedient; a soul of meditation and of prayer, insensible to contempt and injuries and sensible only to Thy love and to the things of Thy Holy Spirit. Give me, dear Lord Jesus, the necessary zeal and talent to make me a fit instrument of Thy hands in the salvation of souls.

7 Quoted by George E. Ganss, S. J., in "On How to Become Evangelically Poor," Studies in the Spirituality of the Jesuits, Vol. III, March and May 1976, Nos. 2 and 3, p. 94.

8 Ganss, Constitutions, Article 263, p. 159.

9 Ibid. Article 260, p. 158.

10 A method, simple though it may have been, which won for the Sisters an enviable reputation as teachers.

11 This recalls Mother Clarke's directive noted by Sister M. Regina Cosgrove regarding the all-too-common indulgence of the day, that the Sisters were "to form character and to warn children of the evils of the day, but not to specify drinking lest some child be pained on account of its parents who might drink."

12 Op. cit., Article 282, p. 163.

13 Op. cit., Article 551, p. 250.

Chapter Four

PROGRESS HAS ITS PRICE

There was much besides the rule to concern Mother Clarke during the strenuous seventies. Pastors were pressing for new schools and more Sisters, and, although many applications for admission were coming in, the scourge of tuberculosis was claiming its victims, and striking hardest at the young.

Railroad expansion caused the historic town of Council Bluffs, Iowa, to grow rapidly. Bishop Hennessy met its needs for a pastor by appointing the able and likeable Bernard McMenomy, native of Donegal and fresh from the missions of Missouri. Having built a school, Father applied in 1871 for Sisters. The new mission, more than three hundred miles from Dubuque, called for capable direction. Mother Clarke appointed Sister M. Xavier O'Reilly, who was then in charge of the newly opened boys' school at St. Patrick's in Dubuque, as its first superior. With Sister went Sisters M. Fabian Kane /Cain?/, Adrian McGuire[1] and Berchmans Feller. Sisters M. Assumption Small and Climacus Ryan followed shortly.

A letter from Mother Clarke to the German-speaking Berchmans, written the following spring, responded to one of her own:

My dear Sister,
. . . How grateful I feel to your kind good heart for writing to me, knowing it is such a task for you to write in English. . . I am glad to hear how nicely you manage your German class between you. God will bless your efforts. Indeed you must have suffered from cold all winter with those small stoves. I am delighted you have got such a fine large one now.

Demands grew for upper classes to supplement the small grade school, and, in 1872, the Sisters opened St. Francis boarding

St. Francis as it appeared
in 1902 catalogue

Earliest picture of St. Francis Academy

academy in a newly constructed building. Although the original costs had been met by the parish, Father McMenomy persuaded the Community to purchase building and furnishings from the parish for a total of $9,150, with interest at ten percent.

Meantime, the illness of Sister M. Margaret Mann led to the recall of Sister M. Xavier. In August 1873, with the opening of the academy, there was an almost complete change of faculty. Sister M. Climacus alone remaining of those originally assigned. Mother Clarke appointed Sister M. Nicholas Lambert,[2] then twenty-six years of age, as superior. With her went one professed Sister - Sister M. Dolorosa Iten - and four novices, very young and newly received: Isabella Kane, Bernadette Maher, Vitalis Condon, and Aurelia Keelin. Increased enrollment quickly called for expansion. In 1878, the cost of a new brick building became an added financial burden.

Life on the new mission was one of constant struggle for the growing community, serving as it did both parish and boarding school. On April 7, 1881 flood waters partially submerged the academy, involving the Sisters in much labor and expense. Sister M. Nicholas' letter of May 23, 1881 reads:

. . . We know, dear Mother, that you will not forget us and our wants and needs when it is in your power to do something for us. . . Besides help for the school room, and with the music, one for the work is needed. The Sisters in the kitchen have more than they can attend to. S. M. Ildephonse and Sister M. Boniface are busy all the time, and it is hard for the poor Sisters in the schools to do the extra work before and after they get their school rooms attended to - besides all the washing and cleaning on Saturdays. I would not speak so much about it, dear Mother, but the Sisters are failing on account of being so overtaxed, especially this year, and I feel it is my duty to tell you - and some of them are not strong at any time. Our dear good S. M. Aurelia is suffering very much again from neuralgia - sometimes she does not know what to do to get relief.

Well, dear Mother, I said I would not worry you with repeating these things and here I am at it. . . S. M. Bernadette's cough is better, but her lungs are very painful at times, yet she is keeping up, and with God's help will be better soon.[3]

Then there was question of a new piano. The Chickering which the Sisters eyed with hope would cost four hundred dollars with ten percent interest. [4] It was best, they thought, to get a good one for the pianos were in constant use. Other pressing problems were the cost of milk and the necessity of paying a man $1.25 a day for work about the place. If they could buy a cow, he would milk it, a more economical arrangement than buying milk.

A heating plant but shortly installed was ruined by a second flood in 1884, necessitating a replacement. To prevent a repetition of the damage, it was necessary to raise the academy buildings six feet and the grounds by half that amount. Debts for these repairs rested heavily on Sister M. Nicholas, who was troubled when tradespeople and other creditors were kept waiting for funds long overdue. Finances would have been even more precarious had not Sister M. Nicholas' brother, Captain Lambert, sent her, the preceding year, a gift of $2,000 to improve the living conditions of the Sisters. Sister had forwarded her brother's gift to the motherhouse, as she thought proper, only to have Mother Clarke return it to be used "for the purpose intended."

It may have been Sister M. Nicholas' declining health which led Mother Clarke to appoint Sister M. Damian Kenneally as superior at the Council Bluffs academy in the late fall of 1884. Sister M. Nicholas' last available letter to Mother Clarke, written in January 1885, included a listing of the many outstanding bills and of the problems she had faced in attempting to borrow money. Though Sister was always a frail woman, neither in this letter nor in others, did she make mention of her personal sufferings. She gave no indication of the cancer of the throat which would cause her death two months later, on the fifteenth anniversary of her profession.

One source of the Sisters' financial problems was the reduction of the number of boarding students they were able to accommodate because of the uncompensated space they must give to the classes of day students, members of the parish. In contrast to the pressures on the Sisters, the parish was at the time involved in the building of a handsome and a costly church which fulfilled the dream of their popular pastor. A suitable rectory would be added the following year. [5]

The outlook seemed brighter to the optimistic Sister M. Damian who wrote Mother Clarke on March 20, 1885:

My dearest Mother,
    Your kind letter is just at hand. You did not say anything about the new Sisters' duties. I told Sister M. Brendan to help Sister M. Ildephonsus in the dining

room and the other sister in the baking - I forgot to say the Sisters got home Tuesday morning. We were all glad to see all our own old ones back. I am indeed sorry to hear our dear Sister Mary Philomena and Amata are failing fast.

The house is now about five feet up; they will be all through on Saturday. I mean with the raising, but we now find a difficulty with the other building, that is, the kitchen and all the other rooms connected with it. They are nearly four feet below the main building which will make it very inconvenient for the kitchen and dining room. I spoke to Mr. Brown and he insisted on the men raising it right away. I said I could not think of such a thing without your consent and sanction. Mother, it will have to be done eventually and it will cost less now as the contractor has the machinery on the ground. He figured it out with Mr. Brown. It will cost Four Hundred dollars $400.00, which the latter considers very low (and like a member of the house) he says we will get the money some place. God bless him, he is proving himself a friend this time anyhow. Please, dear Mother, let us know your wish on the subject as soon as possible as the man will move all his machinery next week.

Then, after giving details regarding the securing of a loan, Sister continued:

My dear Mother, I wish you could see us now, we are way up. The air is so pure it seems like a new place altogether. We are thanking God every day for the good weather and the house has not one crack, only where the walls meet and that could not be helped. It was on account of the house being built at different times. Mr. Brown and the contractor are so proud of the work.

There are other things that I would like to speak to you about, but I am so anxious for this to go out tonight so as to hear your decision. Sister M. Regina will be ready to leave by the end of next week. The Holden Sisters will start on next Monday morning. Love from all your children and wishing you love and blessing --

                    I am always
                        Your affectionate child

Mother Clarke was herself burdened with many debts, having recently completed the building of Mt. St. Joseph Academy, and having begun the construction of the new St. Mary, both in Dubuque. Much distressed for money, she wrote to Sister M. Olympia Sullivan, superior at Clinton, Iowa on April 10, 1884:

> . . . I am in great need of $2000, and if you could on your own responsibility borrow in the Clinton bank $1000 for 8 mo. it would relieve me much. I will, with God's help, try to meet it in time. This is confidential between you and me. Don't tell even Father McLaughlin about it.

And to Monsignor R. Ryan, vicar general of the diocese, in February 1885:

> I am very uneasy regarding the money borrowed from you one year ago last November. I had hoped to have been able to pay at least the interest before this. I write to assure you I have not forgotten it, and to ask if I may pay it by installments. I have met with unforeseen troubles in money matters, which has crushed me. All has happened by the permission of God. To Him I trust to be able to meet my just debts. Thanking you, Rev. Father, for your patience with me, and asking your blessing for all,
>
> Your humble
M. F. Clarke

While St. Francis Academy provided a happy homelife for its boarding students, always included among whom were the homeless and orphaned, it never succeeded financially. Facing the need for new and better buildings without the means for their construction, the Sisters decided in 1897 to close the school to boarding students. Alerted by the announcement, the parishioners promised relief, and with their assistance a needed addition and a modern but poorly constructed auditorium were erected.

The academy catalog for 1905 lists 126 pupils, without indicating the number of these who were boarding students. They came from Iowa, Nebraska, South Dakota, Montana and Illinois. They were of all ages, only eight of them to be graduated that year. Courses were offered in music, in commercial and normal training, and in the classical studies. "Post-graduate" courses were made available, leading to the bachelor and master degrees, and in 1897 a bachelor of arts diploma was granted. Two years later a master of arts degree was conferred on the same student, though there is little evidence of an established standard for such recognition. The physical accommodations of the academy included gas and electricity, and "spacious bathrooms with hot and cold water, " whereas the original structure could boast none of these. A course of nine lectures, chiefly by Jesuit professors from Creighton University in Omaha, had been a feature of the school year.

Although the closing of the boarding school was temporarily postponed, by 1908 Sister M. Ignatia Pyne, then superior, initiated a transfer of the boarding students to the more profitable St. Joseph Academy in Des Moines, near the center of the state, a distance of 130 miles. In 1915, Mother Cecilia Dougherty arranged for the sale of the academy property to the parish. The sale price asked was $30,000, but the parish was $50,000 in debt at the time and could not face so large an added indebtedness. Mother Cecilia, rather than lose the opportunity of getting the property off her hands, forgave $10,000 of the $30,000 sale price. Though most of the school facilities were seriously deteriorated, the Council Bluffs academy was reorganized as a parish high school which operated until the opening of the diocesan coeducational high school in 1964. A merging of five grade schools, partially in 1969 and completely in 1972, permitted the withdrawal of the B.V.M. elementary teachers in 1972. The Sisters who continued to serve on the faculty of the high school maintain their residence in the St. Francis Convent, which they share with Sisters of three other congregations. The parish itself was closed in 1975.

During the early years of her administration Mother Clarke was fortunate to have among her Sisters a number of able women on whom she could rely for superiorships, especially for pioneering new missions. Among these was Sister M. Fidelis McLaughlin from County Carlow, Ireland. Having entered at the age of twenty-seven, and being better prepared educationally than most, she was adaptable to various situations. She served for a brief time as superior at St. Margaret's, Davenport before being chosen in 1873 to lead a group of Sisters to Holy Family Parish, Clinton, Iowa. There her nephew, the Reverend P. V. McLaughlin, was pastor. The Sisters made their home at Our Lady of Angels Academy, a considerable distance from the parish school. However, in January Father McLaughlin moved from the rectory, so that it could serve as convent for the Sisters. Returning to the motherhouse for the summer retreat,

Sister M. Nicholas Lambert

Sister M. Josephine Clarke

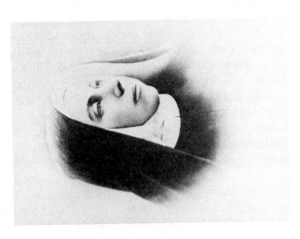

Sister M. Gonzaga McLoskey

the Sisters did not go back to Clinton for four years.

In the fall of 1878, Sister M. Fidelis was assigned as superior
to Garryowen, Iowa. This was one of the earliest Irish settle-
ments in Iowa, and as such one of the Community's early missions. Though a country parish with not so much as a postoffice,
the Garryowen community was a fruitful source of vocations,
providing many able members to the sisterhood. Irish herself,
Sister M. Fidelis was near to the hearts of its people as well as
to Mother Clarke's. Her neighborly letter from Mother Clarke
on October 14 of that year indicates Mother's interest in all
that concerned her Sisters there:

> I received yours of September 11. I was glad to hear you
> all arrived safe home. I hope Sister M. Mildred is better.
> I heard that her family were met on the road after being
> to see her, that she had been very ill. If she was, I won-
> dered that we did not hear of it. Have you heard that some
> of the Sisters returned to Clinton last week? . . . I hope
> you will forgive my long silence. I have had a great deal
> to do this whole year.

Sister M. Mildred did improve, and matters seem to have
gone well at Garryowen, though Sister M. Fidelis suffered the
loss of her nephew, the Clinton pastor, whose untimely death
occurred during the holiday season that year.

Sister M. Fidelis' next assignment was to the Our Lady of
Victory Parish in Waterloo. In 1872, the same year in which
St. Francis Academy was opened, Mother Clarke had responded
to the request of the Reverend Nicholas F. Scallan, cousin of
Sister M. Nicholas Lambert, to provide Sisters for his school.
Although called an academy, it continued under parish auspices,
while providing accommodations for boarding students in the
large frame structure. Week day or "half-boarders" were a
commonly accepted feature of such schools, solving transportation
problems, especially in bad weather. Sisters M. Alexius Butterworth, Crescentia Markey, Hilarion Malony and Bridget and
Louis Byrne constituted its first faculty. By the time of Sister
M. Fidelis' appointment to the mission in 1881 it had already
had four superiors, the latest having been Sister M. Scholastica
McLaughlin. Here, apparently, the Sisters had been subject to
some pressure to provide housekeeping services for the pastor,
as a letter from Mother Clarke to Sister M. Fidelis in November
of that year indicates:

> I hope that woman will continue to keep house for Rev.

Scallan. If not, you will have to tell him to get a housekeeper, that it will bring trouble, as we have refused
others. It would not suit me. I knew, dear Sister, when
I heard what seemed a necessity was granted that it
would give trouble. However, manage and be prudent.

In May, Mother wrote to Sister M. Fidelis that she had permitted Father Scallan's two nieces, postulants, to go with him
to visit their grandmother. In December she wrote again, telling of the grandmother's death. Her brief letter read:

I received yours of the 14th with the sum enclosed safely.
May God bless you for it. I needed it. Rev. Fr. Scallan's
mother is dead. He was here yesterday for Rev. Fr.
Hattenberger to attend the funeral. He seems pleased
with all your family. He said there was peace and quiet-
ness and all doing well. I thank God for it. Give my love
to each of my dear Sisters. I ask God to bless you all
this holy season.

On February 9, 1882, Mother wrote again regarding the serious illness of the Reverend E. McLaughlin who had succeeded
his brother as pastor in Clinton. He was suffering from a severe
case of smallpox through which he was nursed back to health by
Sister M. Olympia Sullivan and her sister, Sister M. Athanasius.

Your Reverend nephew was very ill too. It was a great
mercy that he recovered. He is getting quite well. I
believe we were a month we did not have a word from
Clinton.

From a letter of Mother Clarke's to Sister M. Fidelis on
May 31, 1883, it appears that Sister had been obliged to let an
account run long enough to have troubled Mother, to whom she
had sent a remittance for the support of the motherhouse:

I am sorry Mr. Chuate, being a Protestant, has been
left so long without his money. It looks badly for those
so closely connected with the Catholic Church. If you
think best, try and borrow the money and pay the bill,
but I will return your $100 lest you should be bro't into
any trouble, and you can say you got it from me. Do as
you see and know best.

Responding to a joint letter from the Sisters, Mother wrote

to Sister M. Engratia Jennings on July 31, 1883:

I was much pleased with your beautiful family letter and very glad to hear you had Holy Mass regularly. Your circumstantial account of the general house-keeping was good; as well as the people's thoughtful remembrance of you. I don't wonder you enjoy the good things they send you. God bless all for thinking of my dear Sisters. I see the music keeps you busy. I hope S. M. Lidwine will soon be able to return. I did not hear from her this week; all have returned now but her. I hope dear Sister M. Fidelis and each of my dear Sisters are well. I know you will all be good, obedient children and that you will be a comfort to her. Now, my dear Sisters, you see that your nice family letter has beguiled me into writing you a much longer letter that I intended. With kindest regards to Rev. Fr. Scallan and begging God to bless each of my dear Sisters,

Your affectionate
M. F. Clarke

And a week later to Sister M. Fidelis:

I received Sr. M. Priscilla's letter requesting permission to see her sick Sister. As it is vacation and that good may be done by seeing her father is really my object in letting her go. Do you go with her yourself. Let both of you return after a day or so, as I don't like you to be absent from your charge but as short a time as possible. Write me when you return.

In haste

On the occasion of Sister M. Fidelis' transfer from Waterloo in 1883, Mother wrote, in response to Sister's letter, the nature of which we do not know:

Come home and bring S. M. Lidwine with you. Try to be here by Wednesday next. Fix up the things of the house, accts., etc., and bring your trunk with you. Don't say a word to anyone. I will give you my reason when you come. You can tell Fr. Scallan I have written for you. May God bless you. Poor health is my excuse for delaying so long in replying. Thank God I am better, but very weak.

The Sisters in Waterloo were provided with a new convent in

1897, and in the course of years, extended their services to high school classes. They continued to serve the parish until the opening of the diocesan coeducational high school - Columbus High - in 1968. While the Sisters then withdrew from the elementary school, those who were to teach in the new high school found quarters at St. Francis Hospital, where they continue to the present.

In October 1878, Sister M. Cecilia Dougherty, with a faculty of novices - Sisters M. Valentina Lawley, Florentine Bracken, Lambertina Doran, Simplicia Kennedy and Veneranda Martin - returned to Clinton, where the Sisters purchased a former residence close to the church to serve as convent. The original owner, Colonel Noyes, had lost it through default on a mortgage. However, when he learned the identity of the new owners, he did considerable damage to the interior of the building before they could occupy it. Until it could be put into condition, the pastor vacated his rectory for their convenience, as he had done on the occasion of the Sisters' first coming. However, Father McLaughlin was prevented by ill health and a severe winter from returning to his residence before his death on January 16, 1879. [6]

On December 7, 1880 Sister M. Cecilia was able to inform Mother Clarke that she had paid a note of $1,235.24 toward the purchase of the Noyes residence, most of it having come from their table at a parish bazaar. Sister spoke of her longing to be at the motherhouse for the next day's feast, where she could talk out the many things on her mind. The weather, she added was extremely cold, and "hard coal is so scarce and so very dear ($9.00 a ton), that we can scarcely live. It is amazing all the coal we consume in such cold weather, and yet we are nearly frozen."

Named novice mistress in the late summer of 1881, Sister M. Cecilia returned to the motherhouse, to be succeeded in office at Clinton by Sister M. Olympia Sullivan. Mother Clarke wrote Sister M. Olympia on October 16, 1882:

I received yours of the 3rd, and also a family letter from my dear Sisters on the 4th. I am most thankful to you and to them for their kind and charitable remembrance of me. [7] Tell them, "Don't think I will be tired of your nonsense. It is sweeter to me than good sense from others because you are all my own. Don't you know the crows think their own birds are the prettiest?"

May God bless you, my dear Sisters. Our dear sick Sisters are not well. The weather will try them. Pray for them.

Then, in response to a request from Sister M. Olympia, Mother wrote on November 7:

. . . Yes, dear Sister, you can come to Dubuque. I have written today to Sisters M. Xavier and Anastasia[8] to come up. You can come with them and return with S. M. Anastasia. When you come I will tell you how to arrange the payment of Mrs. Sadlier's bill. Thank God who has aided you to do so well and indeed we need it. May we ever be grateful to God. This is all till I see you. I hope you are getting better and stronger. I was really pleased with the account of the Bishop's /McMullen's/ visit, and pleasure the children gave, but tell my White Birds /novices/ not to be too proud of it. Give them my love, and imploring the blessing of the Holy Family[9] on you and them. I am lovingly your

M. F. Clarke

When later Sister M. Olympia was assigned as superior at St. Mary Academy, Dubuque, she paid a call on Bishop Hennessy. He asked her if she were lonesome for Clinton. She said she was not, but that she was lonesome for the Blessed Sacrament in their new home. The Bishop replied: "But you have no place to reserve the Blessed Sacrament. " To this she responded: "If you permit us to have it, we can provide a place immediately. " A chapel was prepared at once. For the first time in almost forty years, the Sisters in that first of their establishments were permitted to have the Blessed Sacrament in their convent. However, repenting later, the Bishop decided to take the privilege away. It was the Jesuit, the Rev. M. J. Corbett, who intervened, taking the matter to the Coadjutor-Archbishop of St. Louis, the most Reverend Patrick J. Ryan, who, though a lifelong friend of Bishop Hennessy, forbade the removal.

Father Corbett had endeared himself to the Sisters as a kindly pastor and retreat master. Assigned as pastor to a St. Louis parish, he faced the necessity of building a church. Costs were running high, and in a letter to Mother Clarke dated February 16, 1885, he asked if the Sisters could give him some help as the Ladies of the Sacred Heart had done. "I do not ask it of St. Joseph's, as I know it cannot, but if at your suggestion the other houses, which can do a little, it would be a help. " Mother Clarke's accounts tell the rest of the story: "May 18, 1885 Rev. Fr. Corbett's donation. I gave $290. 50, mission Sisters, $209. 50. Total amount $500. 00. "[10]

Ill health plagued Mother Clarke those later years. It was necessary for her to depend on her assistant to make occasional visits to town as well as to undertake for her visits to the more distant missions. Of necessity, she also depended upon others, and especially her assistant, to write faithfully according to her dictation or direction many of her letters. Ordinarily, but not always, Mother signed these. However, there is in a notebook entitled "Copies of Mother Clarke's letters," a copy of a letter dated February 21, 1882, addressed to Sister M. Olympia while she was still superior at the Clinton mission. [11] Since the original is not available, it is impossible to verify the writing or the signature. Quite out of harmony with Mother's spirit, as manifested in all her correspondence, it is certainly at variance with the directive on letter-writing contained in the first Book of Common Observances compiled at Mother Clarke's direction by Sisters M. Xavier and Cecilia. It thus raises a question as to whether those on whom Mother Clarke was obliged to depend were always wholly faithful to their trust. The letter reads:

Sister M. Olympia,
    I feel it is time to put an end to the too frequent letter-writing which you must have felt was out of place and a loss of time as S. M. Cecilia is no longer in charge of that mission. You know, Sister, there can be no restrictions in you or the Sisters writing to me, this is a duty of both, especially of yourself as having charge - but when Sisters write necessary letters to others which you must carefully look over, see that they avoid all flattering, meaningless expressions which common sense and religion forbid. Do not let any letters be written to priests without my permission, and whenever this becomes necessary, they must be very circumspect in their expressions. I would like to hear from you.

Since Sister M. Cecilia was stationed at the motherhouse at the time, surely Mother Clarke would have admonished her directly if she thought there was reason for doing so. Further, the directive on letter-writing contained in the custom book seems to encourage the kind of correspondence a person of Sister M. Cecilia's principles would have carried on. The directive reads:

> In our written correspondence especially with one an-
> other, we ought to bear in mind the advice of St. Francis
> Xavier to the members of the Society who were under his
> charge in India: "The letters you write to one another
> should be exceedingly kind and affectionate. Be particular-
> ly careful not to let a word escape your pen that might
> grieve or discourage them. " We should meet, as it were,
> in our correspondence, for the same reason that we hold
> converse, that is, as members of the same religious
> family, out of pure and affectionate regard for one another,
> to help or seek for help in the discharge of our duties,
> to console in trials, to gladden by the recital of some
> good that God has been pleased to perform through us,
> etc. Such letters will be the links of a golden chain of
> sweet charity, binding together the members, and even
> the missions of the Congregation when distance shall
> have separated us, perhaps for life. St. Francis de
> Sales and St. Alphonsus Liguori were particularly de-
> sirous that their spiritual children should hold this hap-
> py intercourse among themselves.

While this same directive continued to appear in subsequent
issues of the custom book through 1892, the next issue, that
of 1899, twelve years after Mother Clarke's death, contains a
regulation quite in contrast to the above, reflecting rather the
spirit which animated the letter to Sister M. Olympia, written
many years before. The new directive reads:

> Useless correspondence with relatives or others, whether
> members of the Congregation or externs, tends to the neg-
> lect of special duties, and it is at best only a waste of
> precious time. By its means particular friendships are
> multiplied and strengthened, and it keeps alive that ex-
> cessive attachment to family and friends which is so
> great an obstacle to the whole-hearted giving of one's
> self to the service of God and our neighbor which Christian
> perfection demands. Every letter requiring an answer
> should be answered promptly; but it should be a rule
> with every religious to write no letters excepting those
> which business, propriety or affection render practically
> unavoidable.

Superiors should not send out the Sisters' letters with-

96

AFTER AN EARLY SKETCH OF CATHEDRAL SQUARE, DUBUQUE

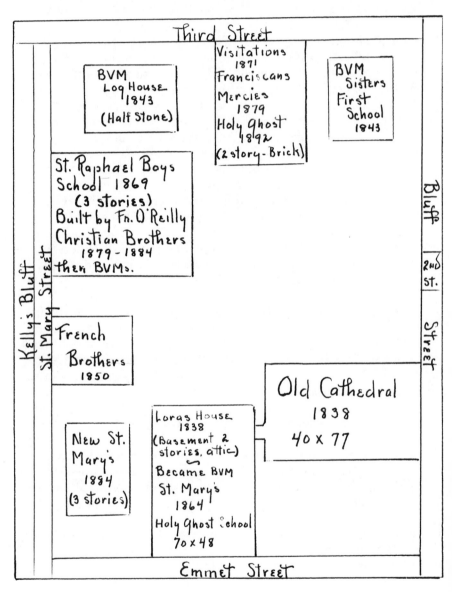

out having read them; neither should they give letters to the Sisters unread. No unnecessary correspondence should be permitted, and Superiors should have the moral courage to refuse to mail sentimental or nonsensical letters written by the Sisters. Should such letters be written to the Sisters, Superiors should feel bound in conscience to withhold them.

All this suggests a divergence of spirits which will show itself again in subsequent events. It raises the question of possible disloyalty close enough to Mother Clarke's person to have been the cause of deep suffering for her.

While Mother Clarke was drawn between the demands for new schools and more teachers, and her anxiety regarding the fate of the rule in Rome, she became pressingly aware of Bishop Hennessy's efforts to introduce into his see city other religious congregations of women. These became subject to his direct jurisdiction as diocesan institutes just at the time when her Sisters were seeking freedom from diocesan control. Already at hand were the Visitation nuns whom he had invited in 1871, and who were then conducting a boarding and day academy on Cathedral Square, alongside St. Mary's select school staffed by the B. V. M. Sisters.

Bishop Hennessy had endeavored to induce the Sisters of St. Francis of Perpetual Adoration of LaCrosse, Wisconsin, to establish their motherhouse in Dubuque. Sisters from that Congregation were then serving the St. Mary - formerly Holy Trinity - parish. But his efforts directed toward the transfer of their motherhouse were of no avail.

On the occasion of his visit to Ireland following the Vatican Council in 1870, Bishop Hennessy called at the Presentation Convent at Mooncoin near Waterford, and invited a colony of teaching Sisters to establish themselves in Dubuque. This they could not do at the time, but four years later, on November 13, 1874, Mother Vincent Hennessey, together with three novices, arrived in Dubuque. To their embarrassment, they discovered that no preparations had been made for their coming. They were forced to depend on sisterly charity, chiefly that of the Visitation nuns until the pastor of Key West sought their services as teachers. [12] He provided them with an unfurnished cottage to serve as house and school, and the people of the parish helped supply their needs. Among the parishioners was a prosperous farmer, John Thornton, who for some years made regular rounds in his farm wagon, gathering from his neighbors meat, eggs, butter and vegetables for the Sisters. [13]

The little convent-school at Key West became the Sisters' first motherhouse. Eventually other schools were made available to them in Dubuque and elsewhere in the diocese. Their permanent motherhouse was later established in Dubuque.

In September 1875, Mother Clarke learned from the Sisters at St. Agatha's, Iowa City, of the arrival there of twenty-nine brown-clad Sisters of St. Francis of the Holy Family, refugees from the hostile treatment of religious by Germany's Iron Chancellor, Otto von Bismarck. [14] Father Emmonds, pastor of St. Mary Parish, had known their community in Germany, where they had cared for an elderly aunt and uncle of his. Hearing of their need, he invited them into his parish. He immediately engaged two of the Sisters to teach German and a third, French, in the private school for advanced students he conducted at the time, entitled St. Joseph Institute. The Sisters were frequent visitors of St. Agatha's, one to study piano, and others to improve their English and learn from the B. V. M. Sisters the ways of their adopted land. A series of misunderstandings with Father Emmonds led to a complete reversal of his feelings toward them. The Sisters were much relieved when Bishop Hennessy invited them in late 1878, to establish themselves in Dubuque.

The pastor of the German St. Mary Church in Dubuque could find no better accommodations for the Sisters and the ten orphans they brought with them than the outgrown Holy Trinity Church which had been abandoned since 1870. The old rock church, scrubbed and partitioned, served the Sisters for nearly a year, a time of extreme privation. Some of the Sisters were then employed as teachers in St. Mary School. This, however, necessitated the dismissal of the Franciscan Sisters of LaCrosse, who had served the parish since 1869.

A legacy permitted the Franciscan Sisters from Germany to purchase property for an orphanage. Their works in the city extended to a home for working girls, established in 1884, in the old Loras residence. It had been recently vacated by the Sisters of Charity who had moved to their newly constructed St. Mary Academy on the same property. The home for working girls soon moved to new quarters. It continues today as St. Mary of the Angels Home. In 1879, the Franciscans replaced the two B. V. M. Sisters whose services Bishop Hennessy had required for domestic work since the opening of his college-seminary in 1873. [15]

Early in that same year, Sisters M. Agatha Murphy and Euphrasia Butler of the Sisters of Mercy, Davenport, responded to the invitation of Bishop Hennessy to establish a hospital in Dubuque. Their arrival occasioned the removal of the Visitation nuns from the two-story brick building on the cathedral property to the former home of Colonel George W. Jones on Alta Vista. Within a year the Mercy Sisters had constructed a hospital on the hill overlooking Cathedral Square. [16] The motherhouse of the Sisters of Mercy was shortly transferred from Davenport to Dubuque.

Establishing their motherhouses there, all four of the new communities became subject to the Bishop's direction as diocesan institutes. All but one of these had made beginnings as close neighbors to the B. V. M. Sisters on Cathedral Square. In the end, the Bishop seems to have found none of the teaching communities completely to his liking, for, in 1892 he established yet another such community, the Sisters of the Holy Ghost, whom he generously endowed. Their temporary school was the ancient Loras residence, vacated in turn by the clergy, the B. V. M. 's and the Franciscan Sisters, while the brick building intended first for the Sisters of the Visitation served as their first motherhouse.

In 1879, five Brothers of the Christian Schools came to staff the three-story boys' school built on Cathedral Square by Father O'Reilly, ten years before. The late Bishop Smyth's dream of a boys' school under the direction of the Brothers was thus fulfilled, at least for a time, for the Brothers remained only five years. Upon their departure, the duty of staffing the school was returned to the Sisters of Charity. This, however, necessitated the dismissal of the older boys, the teaching of whom neither the rule nor Mother Clarke's care for the Sisters would countenance.

When, in 1875, Mother Clarke responded to the request of the Reverend Michael Tierney, pastor of St. James Church in Washington, Iowa, for Sisters, the three assigned there taught and lived in the frame building constructed for them. Out-missions, which took the pastor to a distance, frequently left the Sisters without Sunday Mass. In 1893 it was decided to withdraw them, to the great sorrow of the congregation. The Reverend Bernard Jacobsmeier, who had succeeded to the pastorate, wrote to Bishop Cosgrove of Davenport on November 18, 1899:

. . . Those Sisters /the B. V. M. s/ left here 7 years ago, during Father Moran's time, of their own accord. I made application for those Sisters already 6 years ago and three times since, either personally or in writing, and have done all I could, for I know that these are the only Sisters that can save my school. The people have no con-

fidence in those I have now. . . I was informed a few
weeks ago that the Sisters who have charge of the school
would stay only until June. . .

In 1900, the B. V. M. Sisters returned to Washington, under
the direction of Sister M. Prudentia Reilly. Our Sisters still
staff the school
    In the fall of 1882, Mother Clarke responded to the request
of the Reverend Thomas Gunn of St. Paul Parish, Burlington,
Iowa, for Sisters to staff the Academy of Our Lady of Lourdes,
which he had recently built. Some B. V. M. Sisters were already
teaching in an elementary school in the parish, and others were
commuting to St. Patrick School, which Father Kinsella had
opened in 1870 in the church basement. Sister M. Isabella Kane,
future provincial and superior-general, assigned to the academy
in September of 1877, continued there as a teacher of music
and art for the next eighteen years, serving as superior through
a portion of that time. When the new St. Paul Church was dedicated on January 27, 1925, the name of the academy was changed
to St. Paul High School. The Sisters serve in the new Notre
Dame High School today.

    A recent study made by a former teacher at St. Ignatius High
School, Chicago, in the form of a doctoral dissertation, deals
with the efforts of the Catholic Church to educate its fast-growing immigrant population, especially during the late nineteenth
and early twentieth century. It casts interesting sidelights on
the situations faced by the Sisters, especially in the schools
of that and similar areas.
    Documenting the early marriage of a non-denominational
Protestantism and the public school system, the author holds
that it was this situation which "provided significant impetus
for Catholics to create an alternate system of parochial schools.
He points out that the strong Anglo-Saxon tradition which characterized the public school system made it alien to the growing
immigrant population of which in 1890 the Irish and Germans
constituted over eighty percent. [18] Not only in Chicago but nationally, Catholic children in the early public schools were
"taught to feel ashamed of the creed of their forefathers, which
is often assailed, travestied and ridiculed by anti-Catholic and
prejudiced teachers. "[19] As late as the early 1900's, textbooks
used in the public schools "contained factual errors and offered
insidious or open insult to the most precious knowledge and traditions of the Roman Catholic. "[20]

"In the parochial school, " the author observes, "the immi-grant workingman's children found . . . understanding and tolerance and met with other children on the same plane of equality. "[21] Their teachers, usually immigrants like them-selves, living adjacent to, if not in, the school and working for a pittance, had close ties with their pupils, as did the pastor whose lot was little better.

The Catholic parish was thus the parish of the laboring man who settled his family near the scene of his labors, and thus in areas begrimed with smoke and noisy with the clatter of heavy drays and the screech of switching freight trains. It was in such parishes that the Sisters were early called on to act as buffers against a hostile world, preparing their charges, at a pace they could tolerate, to take their places as loyal and full-fledged Americans.

Thus the 1870's were to witness a rapid growth of Chicago's system of Catholic schools. In this development the B. V. M. Sis-ters had a conspicuous part, especially in those areas of the city where the Irish population was heaviest. They were already well established in the Holy Family Parish, when, in August 1871, they consented to staff a school in Annunciation Parish, on Chicago's near northwest side. It was a site which proved to be just beyond the reach of the great fire in October of that year. The area was being settled largely by Irish who sought work in the roller mills. Their pastor, the Reverend Thomas J. Edwards, had first engaged lay teachers for classes in the church basement. Several of his parishioners who had come from Holy Family Par-ish, where their children had been taught by the B. V. M. Sisters, besought Father Edwards to apply to the Dubuque motherhouse for Sisters. A visit with Father Damen, and through him, with Sister M. Agatha, was followed by Sister's inspection of the premises with Sister M. Seraphina Short, by then an able and experienced educator. Mother Clarke named Sister M. Angela Quigley as superior of the new mission, with Sister M. Seraphina a member of the six-Sister community. During the pastorate of the Reverend Hugh McShane, a combination convent-academy was built adjoining the parish school. Both buildings were pressured for space when the enrollment was at its peak with 850 pupils. Attendance dropped sharply in both school and church when thousands of Polish people moved into the area. Their prefer-ence was for churches and schools of their own, though, as they became Americanized, many came to patronize the An-nunciation School. Further shifts in population led to a general depletion of the parish. The convent closed in 1971, and the school in June 1978, the Sisters withdrawing then.

Reverend Hugh McGuire   Reverend B. S. Hennessy

St. Pius first church

In 1871 St. Pius Parish, on the city's south side, was carved out of Holy Family Parish. St. Veronica School, planned to serve the younger children of the Holy Family Parish taught by the B. V. M. Sisters, became the nucleus of the parish, serving the families of the children who attended. For the first three years of its existence, the Jesuit Fathers were in charge, but in 1874, they resigned the care of the parish to Bishop Foley, who shortly assigned the Reverend Hugh McGuire as its pastor. For a time, the B. V. M. Sisters in charge of St. Pius' School continued to reside at St. Aloysius Convent. They traveled daily in the cumbersome omnibus which served the faculties of Holy Family's several neighborhood schools. Later the Sisters were provided with a small cottage near the church. In 1878 they were given charge of the nearby Holy Angels School, serving it as an out-mission.

Two years later in 1873, a second division of Holy Family Parish resulted in the establishment of the parish of the Sacred Heart, also under the direction of Jesuit pastors. St. Stanislaus School, which had been opened under Sisters M. Veronica and Thomas simultaneously with the larger St. Aloysius in August 1867, was now incorporated into the new parish, Sister M. Veronica continuing in charge.

There were many poor and struggling families in these early parishes. Epidemics of sickness were frequent among them. The Sisters found ample scope for their charity, giving relief to overburdened mothers after school and on Saturdays, and tending them and their families in times of illness. In 1883 the area suffered an outbreak of smallpox. Sister M. Alberic Tench of St. Pius became one of its many victims, having contracted it from the children. Dread of the disease was so great that it was only with much difficulty that any could be pressed into the care and burial of the bodies. On Sister's death, however, the Reverend Hugh McGuire, pastor, who had administered the last sacraments, carefully wrapped the body and placed it in its coffin for burial. Sister M. Hildegarde Whelan, the superior, who had nursed Sister night and day, died shortly after of the same disease.

Mother Clarke's concern for each of her Sisters became especially evident in her response to the needs of Sister M. Maura Hennessy. Professional care became necessary for her shortly after the opening of the Sacred Heart parish school in the fall of 1882, for Sister had suffered a nerve break. Mother had first thought that a return to the familiar surroundings of her own home would restore her, but such had not proven to be the case. It was decided now to commit her to the care of the Sisters of Mercy in their St. Elizabeth sanitarium in Davenport. Mother Clarke wrote to Sister M. Veronica, her superior, to say:

> Yours of the 27th regarding poor Sr. M. Maura is at hand. I enclose sixty dollars - thirty-seven dollars fifty cents ($37. 50) of which is for the first quarter in advance, the remaining twenty-two dollars fifty cents to defray traveling expenses, etc. Sister M. DeSales can send me a receipt. While Sister M. Maura remains there to send me the bill quarterly and word how she is each time, as I will be anxious to hear how the poor child is. I suppose she had better dress the same as while at her father's. You and another Sister had better go with her and let me hear on your return.

Mother Clarke's account indicates that Sister did not improve sufficiently to permit her to return to community life.

Shortly after, Mother began remitting charges through Sister M. Gonzaga for a second Sister for whom she provided in the Davenport sanitarium.

The contract which the Jesuit Fathers entered into with the Congregation for the Sisters' services was generous for the times: $25. 00 a month for those teaching in the grade school, and $35. 00 for instruction in commercial and high school subjects, on the basis of a ten-months' school year. For summer expenses, the Sisters might choose between a payment of $25. 00 for each Sister, or the proceeds from a school entertainment. This arrangement was better than average, for the ordinary compensation contracted with the Sisters did not exceed $200. 00 a year for each teacher. This, if handled with great economy and paid regularly, which was not always the case, met the basic needs of the Sisters themselves. It, however, left little or no surplus for the support of the motherhouse to cover administrative expenses, the training of the young and the care of the sick and the aged. For these expenses the motherhouse was almost entirely dependent on the returns from music classes. As a service to the parish, music teachers were called upon, ordinarily without compensation, for sight singing in the classroom, and for the training of the children's choir and its student accompanist, though not the direction of the choir during the services, that is, the children's Mass on Sunday and requiem and funeral Masses during the week.

Dramatic and musical entertainments in some of these schools, especially that of St. Pius, reached a high level of excellence, especially under the direction of Sister M. Annunciation Hannon, who became something of a master teacher. It was Sister's pride to reach out to such Sisters as were proving inadequate in the classroom and to make of them successful educators.

Both Sacred Heart and St. Pius parishes were able in time to provide good schools and comfortable quarters for the Sisters. The progressive Reverend B. S. Henneberry dedicated a new parish plant at St. Pius' with great fanfare in the course of the Columbian Exposition in 1893. The next year, the school's enrollment reached its peak with 1,335 pupils. Over the years, shifting populations would take their toll. However, the Dominican Fathers, to whom the parish was committed in 1922, have served well the needs of a multinational population, and the B. V. M. Sisters continue their services.

Sacred Heart Parish dedicated a substantial brick church in 1875, the dedicatory address given by Dubuque's Bishop Hennessy. It continued under the Jesuit Fathers until 1931, when it was assigned to the diocesan clergy. The church was totally destroyed by fire on August 18, 1959. The area having deteriorated greatly by that time, the parish was closed and the children enrolled in schools of neighboring parishes.

In August 1876, the Sisters were called upon to teach the girls of the largely Irish St. Bridget Parish, located near the steel mills of Bridgeport, Chicago. Sister M. Sebastian Courtney, a native of Garryowen, Iowa, was given charge of the mission, a position she held until 1880, when Mother Clarke appointed Sister M. Basil Healy as her successor. At the time the Sisters opened the elementary school there, the Brothers of Christian Schools were in charge of the boys' school. When they left the parish the following year, the pastor, the Reverend John H. Grogan, managed the boys' school with the assistance of lay teachers. In 1881 he appealed to Sister M. Basil for Sisters to assume charge of the boys. Mother Clarke wrote in May:

> . . . I am sorry Rev. Fr. Grogan wishes the Sisters to teach the boys. It is impossible for us to supply Sisters to teach and govern boys, except some very small ones, in one of their own rooms, apart from the girls.

The approved rule had limited the Sisters' apostolate to "young girls," a regulation confirming the directive in Father Donaghoe's early rule, which had indicated "young persons of their own sex." However, Father had not demurred when young boys also were committed to the Sisters' care, as had been the case in the Dubuque schools. Mother Clarke was unwilling for the Sisters to be put to the strain of teaching the older boys, rough, and unaccustomed as they were to the restraints of the classroom. [22] The rule given approbation in 1885, was less specific, reading simply "children." It seems apparent that after that date, if not before it, boys and girls were taught, without distinction of age, but ordinarily in separate rooms.

The parish progressed rapidly, and under the pastorate of the Reverend Michael O'Sullivan the parish plant was improved. In 1904 the total enrollment of the school, including its commercial classes, reached 1,100 pupils. By 1920 sixty-eight of its girls had entered the B. V. M. Congregation. Thirteen parishes had been carved out of the original St. Bridget's.

A name especially associated with St. Bridget's was that of Sister M. Landaline Haragan, who, after many years as a successful teacher of the older boys, was made superior in 1919. Sister had organized the Sacred Heart Sodality for young men, admitting only those who had served a year of probation and had been at least one year out of school. Holy Communion in a body each month and on the feast of the Sacred Heart in June was an essential practice. In 1917 when seventy-two of its members entered the service in World War I, they renewed their consecration to the Sacred Heart before leaving. Every month during their absence a Mass of the Sacred Heart was said for their protection. All returned home safe - "not a man was maimed, marre or scarred," though many of them had been in the heat of action. [2]

While the 1870's experienced much stress in the matter of opening Catholic schools, and searching feverishly for religious teachers, the action of the Third Plenary Council of Baltimore made mandatory a situation which previous sessions had foreshadowed. It decreed that a school be erected at once and perpetually maintained in every parish save where the Bishop of the diocese recognized the immediate impossibility of providing one.

The St. Vincent de Paul Parish on Chicago's north side anticipated the mandate by a year, opening a school on August 29, 1883. It consisted of a four-room portion of the original church. Its pastor, the Reverend Edward E. Smith, C. M., a close friend of Reverend Thomas Edwards, pastor of Annunciation Parish, remarked to an acquaintance, "When I have a school, Father Edwards' Sisters will conduct it for me." When it was ready in August of 1883, sometime after Father Edwards' death, Father Smith presented himself to the Sisters as they sat on the porch of the Annunciation Convent one quiet summer afternoon. To them he made the announcement: "I want ye to come over and teach my school. "

Sisters M. Purification and Agatha, who had planned to go to Dubuque on the evening train, promised they would lay the matter before Mother Clarke. The eager pastor did not wait for an answer, but announced to his congregation on the following Sunday that the B. V. M. Sisters would be there the next day to register the children. When the Sisters returned from Dubuque that evening with Mother Clarke's letter of acceptance, Father told them, "Ye are coming. Today I announced to my people ye would be here tomorrow. . . Ye can ride over for a few days until I have your home ready and ye will have your dinner at my house. "[24]

Mother Clarke named Sister M. Ascension Lilly to take charge of the school, and with her, Sisters M. Paschal Campbell, Gregory McGovern and Justa Finnegan from St. Aloysius, with Sister M. Aquilina Jess as housekeeper. The convent was ready in two weeks, furnished with every comfort. As Father took the Sisters on a tour of the convent, he remarked of the empty parlor: "This is not your part. It is the people's. They will furnish it. " During the intervening days, the children came each morning in a body to meet the Sisters, the boys running ahead, climbing trees and jumping fences in their exuberance.

When the Sisters were settled in their new home, Mother Clarke wrote to Sister M. Ascension:

> I was glad to hear from Sister M. Gertrude of your
> school and little home. Sister M. Purification told me
> that the charge of both would devolve on you. I know it
> was hard for her to spare you, but she did so with a
> good will which I am sure God will bless. Sister will
> show you about the keeping of the accounts, and you will
> send them to me quarterly. I will be glad to hear from
> you and the Sisters how all of you are doing. We will
> pray for you all at home. Give my love to my dear Sis-
> ters. I will beg God to bless you and them.
>   Your affectionate
>   M. F. Clarke

While the school opened with 97 pupils, it closed the year with 247. In less than two years more room was needed. In 1889 the Sisters moved to a frame house nearer to the church and school. The new building, constructed for three hundred pupils, opened its doors with three hundred forty-six. To the Sisters' surprise, the children were well grounded in religion, the result of Father Smith's earlier instruction.

In 1917 the DePaul High School became a separate entity under Sister Mary Lambertina Doran. The second building had been constructed in 1902, and now an auditorium and two large classrooms were added, under the pastorate of the Reverend F. X. McCabe, C. M. With the opening of the Immaculata, a central high school for girls on Irving Park at the lake, the high school department of De Paul, as well as those of several other parishes, was closed. The deterioration of the neighborhood and the poverty of the families made the elementary school dependent on archdiocesan subsidies. When in the spring of 1976 it seemed apparent that these would not be forthcoming for the next school year, the Sisters engaged themselves elsewhere, confident that neighboring schools could absorb the diminished student enrollment. When assurance of subsidies came shortly before the end of the term, the parish was faced with the necessity of hiring a lay faculty. The school was closed in June 1978.

Noting the rapid growth of his parish, Father F. S. Henneberry of St. Pius established an out-mission to serve its northern portion, and applied to Mother Clarke for Sisters to staff its school. For some years, Sisters M. Omer Gibbons, Andrew Kinsella and Winifred Gorman walked the mile or so from St. Pius to the new school. They taught in a nondescript building which, since it served also for the celebration of Mass, gained the title "Ryan's Cathedral." In 1885 a rude two-story building, completely without conveniences, was erected nearby, to serve as church, school and convent. The area was then cut off from St. Pius Parish and erected as the parish of St. Charles Borromeo, with the Reverend P. D. Gill to serve as pastor. Assigned here were Sisters M. Florentina Bracken, Ida Harty, Eulogia Dolan and Winifred Gorman. The initial enrollment was 120 pupils. With the rapid influx of immigrants and others, largely Irish, by 1910 twenty-five Sisters were employed in the mission, and in that year ninety-one eighth grade graduates received their diplomas. The physical plant kept pace with the growth of the parish. In 1897 the second pastor, the Reverend Peter J. Muldoon replaced the original structure with a splendid church, and provided a suitable school and convent. [25]

In 1940 Italians outnumbered Irish. They in their turn prospered and moved to the suburbs. A fresh wave of poor and struggling newcomers took their places. As deterioration of the area had set in, the Illinois Medical Center acquired a large tract of land in the neighborhood. Its rapid expansion and the consequent demolition of decaying housing led, in the fifties, to the closing of St. Charles Borromeo Parish. By the time the school closed in 1966, forty of its alumnae had entered the B. V. M. Congregation.

The building of the first Catholic school in Elgin, Illinois, was begun under the Reverend Thomas Fitzgibbons in 1877. Shortage of funds prevented its completion. His successor, the Reverend John Mackin, induced the Sisters to buy the property.26 Here, under the direction of Sister M. Agatha, they opened their St. Mary Academy on February 2, 1880, providing grade and high school training with commercial electives for girls. In 1886 they opened a boys' department.

Apparently Mother Clarke relied on Sister M. Gertrude, her assistant, to give full information as to arrangements made for the new school. Some failure in communication must have occurred. This can be inferred from her letter to Sister M. Agatha on January 6.

. . . You say, dear Sister, "I expected to see you ere this in regard to whom you intended for Elgin. " I thought yourself and Sister M. Veronica knew this before now. Sister M. Alexius is for music, Sister M. Olympia and Ferdinanda are for school, Sr. M. Emerentia for embroidery and small children, S. M. Severina for sewing and general work, and Sr. M. Elizabeth for housekeeping. Sister M Gertrude wrote Sr. M. Veronica when Elgin would open to employ two teachers in place of the two Sisters lent to her. Yourself will take the general superintendence of the Elgin home until the required number of Sisters will be provided. This was already arranged. I must now conclude by wishing yourself and all my dear Sisters a Happy New Year.

Faculty members soon to arrive included Sisters M. Theodore O'Connor, Veneranda Martin, and Elizabeth Horsfield. It was in Elgin that Sister M. Hilary, though a young Sister, began in 1885 a series of superiorships. Among Mother Clarke's letters are two comforting and encouraging her. That of September 8 of that year reads:

My dear Sister,

Too long I have delayed writing but could not help it. I have heard through Sister M. Agatha from time to time how you all were and doing. It is time some one should be placed in charge of the house and I think you, who know all connected with the mission, will for the present be the most suitable. You can write to me regularly and besides take advice from S. M. Agatha in your difficulties.

Have courage, dear Sister, God will help you. Often ask
His assistance. In Him we can do all things. I know the
Sisters will be kind and good. See the Rule kept well, it
will be your protection. Keep your accts in good order.
May God bless you all
In haste,

And to the Sisters of the household, Mother Clarke wrote:

In placing dear S. M. Hilary over the Elgin mission, I
feel that you all who have worked there so long and faithfully with her, will continue to take the same interest.
Do your utmost to gain the dear children. It is one of our
most sacred duties to teach and instruct them. To do this
great work, they must be gained - prayer and patience
will enable you to do this. You are all prayed for at home
and I will ask God to bless each and all. This is our holy
Mother's day. [27] May she watch over you all.
Your affectionate
M. F. Clarke

But evidently the new superior could not muster up the courage Mother had advised, for a second letter to her was on its
way just nine days later:

You see, dear child, I hasten a few words in reply to
relieve all your anxieties. Do not be uneasy. Rely on
God whose aid is never denied to those who ask it. Tell
my dear Sisters I hope to hear that they, as well as yourself, have had your last cry. It consoles me to hear from
S. M. Gertrude that you are all well and doing your best.
Leave the future to God. I have no fears so long as you are
working unitedly but that He will aid as in the past. I am
not uneasy about the finances and am not surprised that
you should be some in debt owing to sickness which told
on your income, but courage, dear Sister, all will be
well. Let me know your troubles and I will help you and
make allowance for mistakes too. Give my love to my
dear Sisters. May God bless you all. Read this to the
Sisters.
Your affectionate
M. F. Clarke

In 1903 Archbishop Quigley purchased the academy from the
Sisters and converted it into a parish school which the Sisters

continued to teach. However, a shortage of Sisters to meet the many demands being made upon the Congregation, a deterioration of the facilities at the grade school, arrears in salary for that school and the problems of dealing with an unpredictable pastor, led the Sisters to withdraw in 1912. They were succeeded by the Sisters of St. Dominic from Adrian, Michigan.

The Congregation opened a mission in Rock Island, Illinois, in 1881. [28] On August 8 of that year the Reverend Thomas Mackin of St. Joseph Church wrote to ask for Sisters. Father's letter reads:

. . . The house now to be used for school and dwelling place for the Sisters will accommodate, with sufficient room for the Sisters, over 60 or 80 pupils. It may be that the zeal of your Sisters will find space for 100. But it is not advisable until, after one year or two, when the school will be built, to fill up with desks rooms needed for the Sisters.

I would rather begin with a small number of Sisters, and increase as we gain influence over the children and parents of the parish. This seems to me the more encouraging way. But in any case, the school must, and will, with God's help, be maintained and made the honor and glory of the parish. The Sisters' requirements for their rooms can be got on the day they come. They can order in the stores what they want and I will pay the bill.

Sister M. Basil Healy was transferred from St. Bridget's, Chicago, to take charge of the new school.

Apparently the pastor, seemingly so openhearted, soon wearied of expenses and decided that the school should be self-supporting. Mother Clarke's letter of November 23, 1881, to Sister M. Basil reads:

. . . Is it possible that it could be thought the whole expense of the schools should be discharged by our labor without other aid? If you took sick and /were/ unable to do your duty, you should come home, and others /must be/ supplied in your place. It would be very hard to expect that "We ought to make the school entirely self-supporting." Besides, after providing your food and clothing /something/ should be sent home to support the novitiate, the sick and the old members. . .

112

A brief history of the parish written on the occasion of St.
Joseph's centennial celebration recalls that:

> In those years girls and boys were taught separately.
> Sisters lived and worked under adverse conditions of
> limited space, inadequate resource materials, sparse-
> ly furnished living quarters, and heating. Most of the
> time they relied upon helpful and generous parishioners
> for food and other necessities.

Of those parishioners, the Geiger and Shields families[29]
were most conspicuous in their generous response to the needs
of the Sisters. The difficulty of teaching in unsuitable quarters
continued until Reverend Patrick Durkin began a thirty-two
year pastorate on January 12, 1919.

The same year that Mother Clarke responded to the call for
Sisters at Rock Island, she honored a similar request from the
Reverend James Touhy, pastor of St. Patrick Parish, Lincoln,
Illinois. Having earlier received Mother Clarke's promise of
Sisters, he wrote in early August 1881, "We will be prepared
to receive the Sisters any day after August 18. " Leaving Dubuque on August 29, four Sisters arrived in Lincoln the following day, hot and grimy from their long train ride. Finding no
one at the station to meet them, they took a hack to the rectory.
There they found that no preparation had been made for their
arrival. A kindly but improvident man, Father Touhy turned
his rectory over to them. Three months later, he was able to
engage for their use a poor little cottage near the church.

Until the arrival of the B. V. M. s, two Ursuline Sisters from
the group conducting St. Mary's German School a block away,
had taught the St. Patrick's children since 1868. The people
of the parish, however, were mostly Irish, many of them immigrants.

The Sisters taught in the sacristy of the frame church, in
two rooms, one above the other. Sister M. Blandina taught the
boys, Sister M. Leandre Swift, a novice, the girls, while Sister
M. Ascella Nagle helped with the girls and taught music. Sister
M. Ambrose Fitzgerald served as housekeeper. All were well
and strong save Sister M. Columba Burke,[30] the superior, who
was shortly replaced by Sister M. Aloysius Curtin. The Sisters'
strength was well taxed, for they, with the pupils, were responsible for cleaning the school rooms and tending the coal
stoves. In addition the Sisters took care of the altar, the sacristy and the altar boys, laundering the altar linens and baking
the altar breads. Although Father Touhy was very appreciative

of their services, he was a poor financier, and was himself sufficiently used to unfavorable conditions not to be impressed with the need for much improvement. [31] However, he succeeded before his death in building a brick school, at which time high school classes were added.

When the scarcity of music pupils led to Sister M. Ascella's transfer to Chicago, the Sisters, receiving as their total salary forty dollars a month, faced a financial crisis. The situation was relieved when Sister M. Lumina came from Clinton, Iowa, to replace Sister M. Ascella. Fortunately, the music class grew rapidly. Somewhat later, Sister M. Gertrude brought Sister M. Lavina Berry to assist with the teaching of the girls. In what free time remained to them, the Sisters visited the poor and the sick.

Father Touhy's death, about the turn of the century, brought the Reverend J. T. Mulgrew, a Bostonian, who did much for the church and the parish. The new pastor soon provided a comfortable convent for the Sisters, and a good brick church for the parish. Today, the schools of St. Mary's and St. Patrick's parishes have merged into Carroll Catholic Elementary School, taught by the B. V. M. Sisters.

In 1884 the Sisters were invited to conduct the St. Mary School in Moline, Illinois. Sister M. Annunciation Hannon's appointment as first superior proved wise, and the nearness to the Rock Island mission insured companionship for the Sisters in both missions. All went well until 1904 when an order came from Mother Gertrude[32] forbidding the Sisters to teach boys beyond the eighth grade or fourteen years of age. The new ruling would inconvenience many school faculties. The pastor of St. Mary's, the Reverend John S. Kelly, turned to Bishop Spalding of Peoria for direction. The Bishop, having besought Mother Gertrude to hold off the enforcement of the directive for a year, met refusal. [33] He then directed Father Kelly to contact a congregation of Sisters who would teach the older boys. The result was the replacement of the B. V. M. Sisters with Sisters of Mercy from Ottawa, Illinois. With regret on the part of both pastor and Sisters, the small band of teachers returned to the Dubuque motherhouse.

Mother Clarke's genuine interest in missions opening in Iowa and Illinois never drew her attention far from the needs of the Prairie motherhouse. Problems of farm and finance, of a somewhat temperamental niece, and of superiors who overstepped the bounds of their authority, compounded her worries. In her letter to her niece, Sister M. Josephine Clarke, we detect the degree of frustration she experienced when relying on Sister. The superior of St. Joseph Academy in Dubuque, Sister M. Josephine, was asked from time to time to transact business which would otherwise necessitate tedious and time-consuming trips into the city for her aged aunt. In May 1879 Mother Clarke wrote to Sister:

> I believe it is a week since I sent to town but it is more than that since I heard from you. I asked how much money you gave Mr. Knight, and did you get a receipt? [34] If convenient, I would like to know, and also if you sent the little accounts of the tenants. Did you approve of what I sent to Father Lambert? I know it is too much for me to expect in your hurry, but if it was only yes or no it would help me.

Then, lest the slight rebuke should leave a sting:

> I sent you a little picture. I think the B. V. M. the most beautiful, and that of her Son - I think I never saw the countenance so infantine and yet mature, and full of sweet holy intelligence. I thought if you liked, you might wish to enlarge it.

An indication of Mother Clarke's problem relative to local superiors and their interpretation of their authority is given in a letter from the Reverend A. A. Lambert, S. J., then on the faculty of St. Ignatius, Chicago. Father Lambert had long been deeply interested in the Sisters' welfare, an interest he had exhibited especially in his translation of their rules into Latin, in the course of their preparation for Rome. Written from St. Ignatius on May 21, 1879, his letter reads:

> Revd. and dear Mother Superior
> It may perhaps be a matter of surprise to you that I should write to inform you about a few things that are going on in your vast and fervent order without perhaps your being aware of them. Let me assure you Revd. Mother that I do it with motives of the greatest sincerity and as I think, for the greater well-being of the whole order. What I am going to say is not mere supposition but are facts, communicated to me by good authority, even by clergymen, whose veracity I cannot doubt.

The first point is: that Superiors take it upon themselves to forbid Sisters to go to Holy Communion -- for some fault or other; Now the Cardinal wrote to me in express terms, that this could not be done, for that the Confessor was the only judge for allowing or forbidding Holy Communion.

2nd. It has often happened that certain Superiors complained about, or reported certain defects or faults of some Sisters, to the Confessor of the house. Now this is one of the greatest evils that could creep in a religious Community. It is enough in my opinion to destroy all the confidence which the religious have in their confessor or Superior, and may be the occasion of even bad confessions. I have taken advice, and asked for the opinion of several eminent Theologians, and they all concur with me in severely condemning that practice. Reports should be made to the Sister Visitor or to you, and never to the Confessor.

3rd. There have been a few cases in which letters from you to the Sisters and from the Sisters to you have not enjoyed perfect freedom, nay have been retained. Now the 25th rule of the 2nd chapter sufficiently explains how sacred such correspondence should be.

Do not think, Revd. Mother that I desire to dictate to you, or that I think that your holy Community does not live up to its rules -- I merely wish to call your attention to these things which I consider of great importance and I do this because I am afraid that they will in course of time do great harm to the order -- Believe me to be

Your humble servant in Christ
A. A. Lambert S. J.

Mother Clarke responded:

Rev. Father,
I received your kind letter. I cannot express my gratitude to you for your great charity in pointing out these matters which are of so much importance. Revd. Father, I am fully confident of the sincerity of your motives for the greater well being of the whole Community. You have proved this by your great labors in

Mt. St. Joseph Academy

Class

of

1882

Mildred Stocking Lila Foote
Caroline Hughes   Susan Donnelly

Mt. St. Joseph Academy, Dubuque, Iowa. The first building opened in 1881. Wing to the right, added 1883

furthering our Rules. My feeble recollection of all you
have done is nothing. I hope the Holy Family will reward
you. This is a favorable time. [35] I will avail myself of it,
and will do all I can to prevent a repetition of these things
which you have taken so much trouble to explain. You
shall have the prayers of a poor old woman.

> Yours humbly
> Mary Frances Clarke

Mother Clarke's most auspicious enterprise was the construction of the Mt. St. Joseph Academy at the site of the
present Clarke College in Dubuque. Plans for the venture began in 1878 when Lawyer Knight was commissioned to make
the purchase of a suitable site. Dated May 19, 1878, Mother
Clarke's letter reads:

Dear Friend,
   Your favor stating particulars regarding the Finley
property was received yesterday, and I am truly grateful
for the special interest you have manifested in our affairs, so important to us and our dear Community.

We have consulted together on the subject, and all are
well satisfied to purchase the property, so I entrust the
whole affair to you with all confidence, feeling certain
that you will act for us in the matter as you would for
yourself. If you succeed in purchasing it for $12,000 (I
know you will if possible) it will be a great help. Again
confidingly entrusting our interest in this matter to you,
next to God without whose assistance nothing can succeed,

> Humbly yours,
> Mary F. Clarke

However, Bishop Hennessy seems to have had his eyes on
the same property, for Mother wrote five days later:

I have considered and changed my mind and concluded
that under existing circumstances I would not be able to
purchase the Finley property.

The copy Mother retained of her letter bears the cryptic
notation: "I wrote the above by direction of the Bishop. "
It was August when Mother wrote again to Mr. Knight:

. . . I have written to Rt. Rev. Bishop saying I have
heard he has declined purchasing Mrs. Finley's property, and asking his permission to purchase it now for
the Community. If his answer is favorable, will you
commence the arrangements for the purchase at once?
. . . I will let you know the result of the Bishop's answer
immediately.

It was decided, however, that the Finley mansion would not
prove satisfactory for their purpose. The property finally purchased was eleven and one half acres at the summit of Seminary
Hill, the site of three lead mines under the ownership of Michael
Carney and Eugene Flynn. The sale was negotiated on May 13,
1879 at $200.00 an acre, plus $300.00 for the mineral rights.
Acting for Mother, the Reverend P. J. McGrath, president of
the boys' college, and Sisters M. Rosalia Ryan and Maurice
Duffy, met Mr. Knight and the Swiss architect-contractor at
the site, making their way through a tangle of weeds and over
heaps of clay from the open mines, to the point where ground
was to be broken. Stone cut from the surrounding bluffs was
used for foundation. The resulting structure, erected at a cost
of $155,000, serves as the college administration building to-
day.

Arrangements were made with the Milwaukee Insurance
Company for a loan of $30,000 at ten percent, with the Butter-
worth property[36] and land in both Table Mound and Prairie
Township as collateral. It was a brave venture with much at
stake.

On January 5, 1881, Sisters M. Josephine Clarke,[37] Rosalia
Ryan, Maurice Duffy, Leocadia Conway, Hilda Fitzgerald,
Daria Lynch, Patrick Brady and Irenea Dolan and their forty-
one boarders arrived at Mt. St. Joseph on Seminary Hill.

The school grew rapidly, and in two years it was necessary
to add a wing to the four-storied structure. Six years later a
music and art conservatory was added. The campus was increased by a purchase of fifty-eight additional acres.

The academy continued to function for forty-seven years,
and was forerunner of Iowa's first all-women's college. Meantime, Mr. Knight, who handled all business affairs in connection
with the building, enrolled his two daughters at the academy. He
showed his further interest by directing the landscaping of the
grounds, and supervising the planting of a thousand evergreens,
his gift to "the Mount."

Immaculate Conception Academy profited greatly by Sister
M. Gonzaga McCloskey's sudden departure from Dubuque in
1873, the object of Bishop Hennessy's displeasure. Permission
for the use of returns from an inheritance enabled her to establish an extensive music department. Income from this made
other improvements possible, including the installation of central heating and indoor plumbing. The academic department
profited by the acquisition of new equipment. Lay teachers were
hired for art and violin, to the advantage of the Sisters as well
as the students. Trips to Chicago for lessons in music at con-
servatories there, and lessons in china painting, etc., were
available to the Sisters. An account book item of $218.19 was
listed in 1893 for "World's Fair expenses for 14 Sisters with
board for same."

While not all the academies conducted by the Sisters were
equally prominent or successful, they all strove for the same
goals, and followed, as nearly as circumstances permitted,
the practices and policies of those in Dubuque and Davenport.
While the academy in Dubuque had a future ahead of it as a
woman's college, that in Davenport closed its doors after ninety-
nine years of service. In 1957 plans for a diocesan secondary
school were fulfilled in Assumption High School. For some
years conducted on the coinstitutional plan, it united the faculties and students of St. Ambrose Academy and Immaculate
Conception Academy. [38] By the time the history of the Sisters'
academy was written in 1940, ninety-four of its former students
had joined their teachers as Sisters of Charity of the B. V. M.

Notes

1 Sister died of tuberculosis on November 25, 1872 at the age of 24. Professed on her deathbed, she was bured in Council Bluffs.

2 Sister M. Nicholas - Annie Lambert - was born in County Wexford, Ireland. She was just five years of age when the family came to Dubuque in May 1851, where, the following year, her father and one sister died of cholera. Annie attended the St. Mary Academy in the original frame building at the corner of Third and Bluff Streets, having as teachers Sister M. Aloysius O'Leary and Philomena Gandolfo, and the superior, Sister M. Catherine Byrne. At the age of twenty-three, Miss Lambert entered religion, making her novitiate under Sister M. Gertrude Regan. Professed on August 5, 1872 Sister was sent two weeks later as superior to Cascade, from where she was transferred the following year to St. Francis Academy. Meanwhile, her sister, Mary E., was received as Sister M. Ildephonse. She spent many years at Council Bluffs, dying there in 1902. In an intimate letter to Sister M. Gertrude, Sister M. Nicholas wrote in September 1884: "I think boarding school is a trial in itself. No matter how we work for or wait on some children, you meet with so much ingratitude, and some parents seem to think that because they pay us a few dollars we ought to be everything for their children. "

3 Sister died in Council Bluffs two years later of tuberculosis.

4 Up to this time Mother Clarke had sent $15, 517. 15 to meet costs at Council Bluffs, besides providing generously for travel expenses of the Sisters going there. She continued to send help as her own resources permitted.

5 "With proceeds and generous donations, he /Father MeMenomy7 built a magnificent edifice, 60x125, on Fifth Avenue and Sixth Street, completed in 1888 for $50, 000, and the next year a $9, 000. 00 rectory. " Reverend John F. Kempker, "The Catholic Church in Council Bluffs, " pamphlet, n. d. , n. p.

6 The Reverend E. McLaughlin succeeded his brother in the pastorate. The bond between Sister M. Fidelis andthis second nephew continued strong, and when Sister suffered paralysis in her old age, Father McLaughlin remained with her until death came on December 1, 1912.

7 October 4 was, and continues to be, observed as Mother Clarke's feast day in honor of her patron, St. Francis of Assisi.

8 Sister M. Anastasia Mulgrew was superior at Our Lady of Angels Academy in Lyons, (North Clinton) from 1871-1887, also 1890-1905. Whether in or out of office, Sister continued to live at the academy. She died there December 3, 1910.

9 The name of the Clinton parish was later changed from "Holy Family" to "St. Mary's. "

10 Mother Clarke was never small in her dealings with the clergy. From the first, her offering for an eight-day retreat was $100. 00. Father Hattenberger's remuneration for his services as chaplain was, besides his keep, $400. 00 a year. Stipends for Community Masses ordinarily ran an additional $60 - $70. As pastor of St. Joseph Parish, he had a second source of income.

11 Sister M. Olympia had succeeded Mother M. Cecilia in that office. The latter was then serving as novice mistress at Mt. Carmel. As an unusually spontaneous and lovable person, Sister wrote with lively affection and interest, a characteristic not always appreciated by her more phlegmatic Sisters.

12 An entry in Mother Clarke's account book dated July 25, 1875 reads: "Sisters of Key West, $30. 00. " Smaller gifts went to the Benedictine Sisters of Nauvoo, Illinois, then in unusual need, and to the Sisters of St. Francis of the Holy Family, recently arrived from Germany and resident for a time in Iowa City. The keeping of the cash account was increasingly difficult as the years went by. At the end of 1874 Mother Clarke wrote: "This ends the accounts of 5 years. I cannot vouch for their correctness. I have done my best under many disadvantages. "

13 Interview with Mrs. Marilyn Coleman, February 28, 1976. The present Sisters M. Margaret and Madelena Thornton, B. V. M. , are grand nieces of Mr. Thornton.

14 Only an unexpected delay in their departure saved the S ters from boarding the Deutschland, the tragic end of which was the subject of Gerard Manley Hopkins' "Wreck of the Deutschland. "

15 The labors of the Franciscan Sisters contributed much to

the success of the college, but demands for personnel made by their rapidly expanding apostolate compelled their withdrawal from the college in 1957. The year 1925 had seen them established as a papal institute. (Details from They Have Taken Root, the Sisters of the Third Order of St. Francis of the Holy Family, by Sister Mary Eunice Mousel, OSF, PhD, New York: Bookman Associates, 1954.) There is evidence that the Sisters of St. Francis later occupied the two-story brick building vacated by the Sisters of Mercy, visiting and caring for the sick in the neighborhood, and providing a home there for a few orphans they came upon in the course of their ministrations. Their duties included the care of Bishop Hennessy in his declining years, and of the elderly Ellen Hennessy, his sister. The care of Miss Hennessy was undertaken by Sister M. Dolorosa Iten, B. V. M., after the Franciscan Sisters withdrew from the site.

16 The Sisters of Mercy of Dubuque are now members of the Union established in 1929. As such they belong to the Detroit province. They now staff an extensive Mercy Medical Center in Dubuque, and maintain schools and hospitals throughout the Dubuque diocese.

17 James W. Sanders, The Education of an Urban Minority: Catholics in Chicago, 1833-1965. (New York: Oxford Press, 1977), p. 19.

18 Ibid, p. 57.

19 Ibid, p. 21.

20 Ibid, p. 25.

21 Ibid, p. 87.

22 In the neighborhood schools of Holy Family Parish, the Sisters were teaching the younger children, both boys and girls, while the older girls in the upper grades and high school classes were taught at St. Aloysius. The boys were under the care of Brother O'Neil, S. J., at Holy Family or at St. Ignatius College.

23 Quoted from accounts contained in the Congregation's mission files.

24 Ibid.

25 Always a warm friend of the Sisters, Father Muldoon was consecrated auxiliary Bishop of Chicago in 1901, and in

1908 was named the first Bishop of Rockford, Illinois.

26 The Council voted to purchase house and lot in Elgin, with a cash payment of $1,000.00, and a mortgage of $5,000 at 6% interest. Date April 26, 1879.

27 September 8 is observed as the birthday of the Blessed Virgin.

28 In 1869, for a brief time, the children of the parish had been taught by Sisters M. Basil Healy and Stella Reid who crossed the Mississippi each morning on the ferry from Davenport. But permission for that small venture seems to have been withdrawn by the Bishop.

As a young girl, Sister M. Basil had attended Mass in the old St. Joseph Church when her family were migrating west. Returning as a teacher, though briefly, she and her companion so impressed their pupils that six girls from among them followed the Sisters into the Community.

Sister was born in 1847 in Granville County, Wisconsin, and attended the Brown Deer School near her home. The family moved to Iowa in 1862, and settled near Iowa City where Sister attended the St. Agatha Academy as its first pupil. There were five sons and six daughters in the Healy family, three of whom entered the B.V.M.s. Sister M. Basil was the first of these, entering in 1867. She was followed by two sisters, the future Sisters M. Flora and Claver. While Sister M. Claver died in 1889, Sister M. Basil survived six superiorships and several terms as consultor at the motherhouse. Sister M. Flora died in 1930.

29 Each of these families provided the Congregation with a member: Sister M. Joseph Therese Geiger and Sister M. Jean Ellen Shields. Monsignor John T. Shields, for many years pastor to St. Mary Church, Pontiac, Illinois, was always a kindly friend to the Sisters.

30 Sister M. Columba Burke was a native of Garryowen and a cousin of Sister M. - later Mother - Cecilia. Sister returned to the motherhouse from Lincoln, and died there two years later.

31 The area was not a very desirable one at the time. Across from the Sisters' cottage was the "gas house," a public utility distilling domestic gas from soft coal. A second factory beside it made caskets, and beside that stood a "dead shoe" factory,

manufacturing shoes for wear in the coffin, an item long since dispensed with. A monument works on the triangular lot on which the first church stood, added to the lugubrious nature of the neighborhood.

32 Word came from Rome some years later (1909) forbidding the teaching of older boys by religious women, a ruling which was later withdrawn, apparently as the result of pressure from American bishops. The directive also forbade the teaching of boys of any age in the same classroom with girls.

33 However, Mother Gertrude exempted the St. Mary Academy, Elgin, Illinois from this regulation, the older boys might be retained in the commercial and other higher classes. The only restriction there was against teaching men in evening classes, doubtless in religion courses.

34 Lawyer Knight had undertaken the management of the farm at that time. Mother Clarke, doing her business in cash rather than by check, was careful to keep receipts as a matter of record.

35 Many superiors would be coming home for retreats. New appointments were made during the vacation, and those appointed could be properly instructed.

36 This corrects an error on page 405 of Volume I which indicates that the Butterworth property alone was adequate for the insurance company loan.

37 An item in Mother Clarke's account book shows that Sister M. Josephine received $1,000.00 in gold in 1881, while a second item of $1,000.00 came to Sister two years later. This second amount was indicated as "her own." It is possible that these amounts came to Sister from her brother, or the settlement of his estate in Australia, or though less likely, from her widowed mother in Dublin. As "her own" Sister may have been permitted to use the funds for the equipping of the new school, as Sister M. Gonzaga had used the income from her brother's legacy for the Davenport academy.

38 The buildings of the girls' academy were sold at a sacrifice to the neighboring Palmer School of Chiropractic, and today houses a junior college.

Chapter Five

A WOMAN FOR OTHERS

D espite Mother Clarke's high regard for the clerical state, she was not long free of problems in her dealings with members of the clergy.

In 1865 the Reverend John M. Brazill, V. G. , obtained from Father Donaghoe a corps of teachers to staff his St. Ambrose School in DesMoines. The tone of his request had been more demanding than petitioning, and it was with foreboding that the request was granted. Knowing that Father's death had left the Community in the hands of a frail and elderly woman, Father Brazill presumed to pressure her for unwonted services on the part of her Sisters. Her response to his letter, dated October 24, 1870 reads:

> Very Reverend Father,
> I received your letter of the 9th inst. I will simply state the following: Our Rev. Father Donaghoe did not wish that his Sisters should ever be a burden to any priest. His motto was that the laborer was worthy of his hire. And to pay and to be paid. He did not wish the Sisters to have anything to do with the choir, altar or church. Neither make, mend, wash, or scrub for it.
> The priest has a right to direct what he wants with regard to his schools.
> The Sisters should have a house for their dwelling, and schools, furnished, so that if they leave they have nothing to take but their trunks. They should be paid by the people according to the advancement of the classes and their means. If there are children who can not pay any it cannot be expected that the poor Sisters should substitute the teaching of the public schools at the expense of their own labor. A provision should be made to

pay one or two Sisters a given sum, monthly or quarterly for teaching them.

After the support and clothing of the Sisters, whatever they have to spare should be sent home to St. Joseph's for the support of the noviceship and those returning from the missions, the sick and the old.

Very Rev. Father, you wish to examine the Sisters' account. It is the first time that any Gentleman - not even our Right Rev. Bishop - required that. Therefore you will excuse me for positively and finally declining.

There are altar societies now at the Cathedral and older churches. It would be well that there was one in DesMoines. Then fewer Sisters would be required.

I am with respect
Your humble
Mary F. Clarke

So ended the correspondence on this subject. In time a new problem presented itself.

In 1881 Mother Clarke received from Sister M. Baptist Seeley, superior of the St. Ambrose School, DesMoines, information concerning a two-room school named St. Michael's, being built by Father Brazill to serve children on the east side of the DesMoines River. He considered that the two Sister-teachers could reside at St. Ambrose Convent and commute daily. How they are to get back and forth is not clear. Sister wrote:

The house on the east side is nearly finished, notwithstanding all my doubts. Our Very Rev. Pastor, Father Brazill, is gone today. I think he will call on you for the two Sisters you promised. He will lend them his little summer oilstove so they can cook their dinner and have a cup of hot coffee or tea every day. They can send nearly all the children home for dinner; the few who live too far can take their dinner in one room and the Sisters have the other. I think they can manage to be pretty comfortable, but whether they will have to work for nothing as most of us do, time will tell. Our Very Rev. Father is so fond of having the Sisters keep their vow of poverty, that he'll not concern himself much about the teachers if the scholars are provided for. He does not know how to get money for his people, even for himself. I have the bedding to prepare for the two Sisters you will send for the new school, so if Father Brazill proposes to bring them along,

let them come and they can help us while waiting for the
plaster to dry. He will not let them go to the school until
the first Monday of November. The Sisters are all well
and attending diligently to their duties. We have in school
192 girls and 115 boys, making a total of 307. So you see
we have plenty of work.

However, Father Brazill had much besides the new school on
his mind, for it was in that year that the long-pending division of
the Dubuque diocese was finally effected. Even from the time of
Bishop Smyth's death in 1865, Father Pelamourgues of St. Anthony
Church, Davenport, and administrator of the diocese, had urged
the division, with Davenport as the most suitable see city. The
firmest argument he had given in its favor was the fact that income from properties on St. Anthony Church square would help
substantially toward the support of the bishop and diocesan institutions. Difficulties subsequently arose between Pelamourgues
and his new Bishop in the matter of finances, concerning which
Pelamourgues invited the Bishop

> to come to Davenport to survey all things and receive
> his accounts. What passed between them is not known,
> only that Bishop Hennessey would give no account to any
> man about what he considered his rights, but continued
> to administer all the affairs of St. Anthony Block to the
> time Davenport was made into a new diocese. [1]

While Bishop Hennessy persistently urged on Rome the division of the diocese, and while Father Trevis, nearer at hand,
pressed the matter, no one looked more eagerly toward the
mitre than the pastor of St. Ambrose Parish, DesMoines.
Further, he envisioned DesMoines as the episcopal city of the
new diocese. It was painful, then, for him to learn[2] that Pope
Leo XIII had given a decision in favor of Davenport and had
named John McMullen, vicar general of the Archdiocese of
Chicago, its first bishop.
    Bishop McMullen, an able and completely dedicated prelate,
acted characteristically when he gave as first payment for the
property on which St. Ambrose College would be erected, the
$5,000.00 gift of Chicago friends. His episcopate was a short
one, death from cancer claiming him after two years. [3]
    The several months' illness of the Bishop gave time to think
about a successor. None was more eager in the promotion of
his own cause for that office than the former vicar general of
the Dubuque diocese, Father Brazill. But, while he was extreme

ly popular with the politicians and other prominent men who frequented the state capital, [4] he had aroused the animosity of many of the diocesan clergy by an arbitrary exercise of his authority as vicar general. And none had a more active dislike for him than the gentle Father Laurent, who berated him without mercy for his overweening ambition. [5]

Yet the name of the Irish Father Brazill went to Rome on the terna[6] sent by the Archdiocesan synod of St. Louis. The possibility of his appointment was a matter of grave concern to the priests of the diocese. Father Niermann of St. Joseph Parish, Davenport, considering possible alternatives, made the remark to Father Trevis: "Henry Cosgrove is an Irishman, but he's all right." Whereupon Trevis organized a fevered campaign to secure the signatures of as many of the clergy as possible for the appointment of Father Cosgrove, who was then serving as administrator of the diocese. Fearing that the petition would not reach Rome in time for the decision there, he cabled a request for delay. It was to him, then, that the announcement of the appointment came, naming Cosgrove as the second Bishop of Davenport. [7] His consecration on September 14, 1884, was an auspicious occasion, with Archbishop Feehan of Chicago the principal consecrator, Bishop Hennessy first assistant, Bishop John O'Connor of Omaha second assistant and Father Trevis notary. Archbishop Ireland of St. Paul preached the sermon. Father Brazill continued as pastor of DesMoines.

Sioux City, in the northwest corner of the state of Iowa, was still frontier when, at the request of the Reverend B. V. Lenehan, the Sisters arrived there in 1881. The proximity of the Winnebago reservation occasioned the frequent sight on the downtown streets of blanketed Red men and their squaws, and in the classroom, the presence of French-Indian children among the white, who were chiefly French, Irish and German. Sioux City was still within the Dubuque diocese when the well-loved pastor of St. Mary Church, Father Lenehan, petitioned Mother Clarke for Sisters. Those assigned to the mission were Sisters M. Sebastian Courtney, Isidore Motie, Mary of the Angels O'Connor, Bertha and Cyrilla Curran and Germanus Hiberger.

Arriving by the Illinois Central railway, the Sisters received a hearty welcome, and were taken by omnibus to a residence prepared for them. [8] An old church housed the Sisters' first school for ten years.

During their first winter in Sioux City, Sister M. Sebastian suffered an illness which occasioned a letter from Mother Clarke to Sister M. Germanus, the housekeeper, in February 1882:

My dearest S. M. Germanus,
I have given you reason to think I have forgotten you. How pained I was to hear of dear Sister M. Sebastian's illness. It makes me easy that you are with her. I enclose in this a little money lest you may want it for her use. Don't let her want for anything, and if you want more, write and I will send it to you.

Apparently Father Lenehan had observed a need of boarding accommodations for Catholic girls living in the rural areas of the parish. He consulted with Sister M. Agatha at the time of her visitation in 1885, and submitted to Mother Clarke a letter requesting the establishment of a boarding academy. To this Mother Clarke responded:

Dear Rev. Father,
Last evening I received from S. M. Agatha yours of the 19th inst. to her. I hasten to answer, as it regards the purchase of property in Sioux City, to assure you that it is impossible for me to think of incurring any additional expense on the Community, which I am resolved not to do. We have boarding schools enough, and I desire to inculcate in my Sisters a love for the parish schools, where so much more good can be done. I thank you, Rev. Father, for the kind interest you have taken in the matter, also for your kind care of the Sisters under your charge. I hope the Sisters will have patience with me awhile longer for the Sister who will replace S. M. Sebastian. [9]

In 1891 the Reverend Timothy Tracy, as pastor of St. Mary's, built a three-story brick structure on the corner of Tenth and Pearl - later, Grandview - to serve as school and convent for the Sisters. Increased enrollment in later years sent the Sisters across Pearl Street to crowded quarters in the Villa Marie, a building which served principally as a home for working girls. Here they remained until the building of the present convent, about 1900.

In 1932 the diocese of Sioux City was established, and the Right Reverend Philip J. Garrigan, D.D., vice-rector of Catholic University, was consecrated bishop. The St. Mary Church was then renamed Epiphany Cathedral.

The St. Joseph elementary school in Sioux City was not established until 1891. In that year Sister M. Ascension Lilly and five companions took up their residence in a large frame building which served as church as well as convent. The parish was then, and continued to be, relatively poor and struggling. Yet within a year of the Sisters' arrival, the Reverend E. W. J. Fowler, pastor, had erected the present church and rectory. The present pastor, the Right Reverend Monsignor Edward Lilly, provided a new convent for the Sisters in 1961. They continue to serve the parish.

The Sisters were invited in 1902 to establish a grade school in the Immaculate Conception Parish in Morningside, a suburb of Sioux City. The Reverend J. L. Kerby, formerly stationed at the Cathedral, served as pastor. Beginning with sixty pupils in the church-school combination, Sisters M. Mauricia Shay and Emma Healy taught there for seven years, commuting from the Cathedral Convent. The extreme inconvenience led to their withdrawal in 1912. They were succeeded by the Servants of Mary from Cherokee, Iowa.

By 1965, when Heelan High School, named after Sioux City's second Bishop, supplanted the girls' high school at Cathedral, sixty girls from the St. Mary (Cathedral) Parish had entered the ranks of the Sisters of Charity, B. V. M.

On May 1881 death claimed the third of Mother Clarke's Dublin companions, Sister M. Eliza Kelly, then seventy-three years of age. Sister had been a patient sufferer for many years from a form of rheumatoid arthritis. Though death had come as a merciful relief, there was sorrow for Mother in the parting. A letter from Sister M. Baptist in DesMoines, dated May 11, and addressed to Mother Clarke speaks of her passing; word of which had come in time for them "to offer our Sunday Communion and Mass also for her. Since that Fr. Brazill said Mass for her. One by one your dear companions are leaving you, but our beloved Father must be delighted to see them coming home. "

It was at this time that Father Lenehan was arranging for Sisters to serve as faculty for St. Mary School in Sioux City. Knowing that Sister M. Agatha, as visitor, was expected to arrive shortly in Council Bluffs, he wrote to Sister M. Nicholas, superior there, asking that Sister should come directly to Sioux City from Council Bluffs. However, as Sister M. Baptist continues:

She could not go from there as so much of the track was under the high water, so she went from here /DesMoines/ this morning and expects to be able to return tomorrow night.

Sister M. Baptist was grateful for the respite those two days provided her before Sister's visitation, as it would give her

that much more time to square up my accounts which are as usual behind-hand. I'm glad Sister Mary Agatha can see for herself how good for nothing I am in time to let you consider giving me a release from a position I was never capable of filling in a suitable manner. Don't fear that I would fret or grieve at being removed. I'm surprised that you could leave me here so long.

Then Sister M. Baptist requested from Mother a memorandum of amounts and dates she had forwarded to the motherhouse during the previous two years, as an aid to her in clearing up her accounts. She continued in a new vein:

The Sisters are all pretty well and working away at their duties as hard as they can - but they will find it very hard to get up at 4:30 in the morning as the heat here in this sand-pit prevents any sleep until 11 & sometimes 12 and they get up in the morning feeling like rags rung out. Sister Mary of the Cross has enrolled 70 little girls and Sister Mary Maxima has 80 . . .
                              Your unworthy child,

Mother's response went promptly:

You make me sad. I think you are depressed. You have been a comfort to me. How often your letters came as if you knew I needed them. The Holy Family will bless you. You are only severe to yourself. I send the memorandum from my books as follows:

Mother then listed the date for each of five remittances of $100.00, adding "as you are badly situated, sleep to 5 o'clock for the present. Don't be discouraged. "
    The DesMoines parish of St. Ambrose was divided in 1883, and that portion east of the river, or East DesMoines, was placed under the patronage of the Blessed Virgin and is known as Visitation Parish. The pastor, the Reverend J. F. Nugent, changed the name of the school from St. Michael's to that of the parish. The Visitation School grew rapidly and several more Sisters were soon teaching there.
    The Sisters at St. Ambrose were giving consideration to the establishment of a select school adjacent to the parish plant,

while the question of a boarding academy was also presenting itself. The first consideration called for fresh dealing with Father Brazill. The concern of Mother Clarke for the needs of the Sisters, her views on boarding schools in general, her trust in Sister Mary Baptist who had pioneered at St. Ambrose, and the precision with which Mother discussed business arrangements became apparent in the following correspondence:

March 31, 1884

My dear Sr. M. Baptist,

I have received yours of the 25th ult. and have read it carefully. I see its advantages and disadvantages. If you build where you now are you would be near the school and church, which is something not to be overlooked, especially for those who teach to get a warm comfortable dinner, but of course the house would be on church property. From what S. M. Gertrude tells me the size of the ground you now occupy for school and dwelling would, I think, be sufficient as there will be no boarding school there. We have five of them now which is more than enough. Select and parish schools will be much better and less laborious and won't require so much help.

The pastor, however, had his own plans, losing no time in arranging for a site. He apparently remembered his previous encounter with Mother Clarke sufficiently to transact his business through another. Mother's letter to Sister M. Baptist continued:

Dear Sister, I don't understand what Rev. Fr. Brazill means by saying the first payment $3000 won't be due until Dec. or Jan. next, as I have not made the purchase yet, and would not make the purchase before having it well secured from all future claims by any one, if you are all satisfied that the lots are all you wish and that Father Brazill gives them as I understand for $17,000. Do you think that young Catholic lawyer there has experience enough to transact the business for us? When all is satisfactorily arranged and the property is ours, I would like to make a payment of $3000 with our united aid, and the remaining $14000 in seven notes of $2000 a year with .06 interest from the time the notes are drawn. Dear Sister, if I have not made myself understood tell me. I will expect to hear from you soon about all.

You don't expect to build until the ground is paid for,
on account of the interest. We could not meet all. In
the meantime the lots could remain rented which would
help.

Dear Sister, we too need more room here at home and
aid to do it, but God is all sufficient. In Him we will
trust. I will ask God to bless you all.

> Your affectionate
> Mary F. Clarke

Apparently Mother Clarke had decided on the purchase of one
lot, and had sent payment, when Father Brazill changed his
plans. Meantime, Sister M. Baptist had learned of another site
at some distance from the school one which could serve the
double purpose, if necessary, of both select and boarding school
Mother wrote her on June 3:

Yours of the 27th is received. As I went to a great deal
of expense and trouble in procuring what I sent on to you
for that corner lot and that Rev. Father Brazill thought
proper not to give it to us, I won't take it now. Where
does he intend you to go or what to do for your support
if he puts the Christian Brothers where you are now? I
like what you say of the five acres, but could you have
a school there if you were not living there, and how
could you be accommodated for Mass and the Sacraments,
as the Street Car does not run that far? I would like to
know all this and your views of it. May Almighty God
direct all for the best.

And on June 14:

I received your letter yesterday. I will send a Sister
out next week who will aid you in selecting one among
all the places you named - although I felt Fr. Brazill
going back on his agreement; yet, if when you both
examine all and that you see it to be the most desirable
of all the others you can take it, if it is still to be had,
but wait for all this till Sister is with you. May God
direct all as He sees best.

Then in response to Sister's apology for some supposed
fault, Mother wrote:

Dear Sister, I have nothing to forgive, for you, as well as I, only tried to do for the best. It is I should ask forgiveness of God and you. While Sister is with you speak together of all matters, and if all conclude it is best to have boarders I won't object, although I must say I prefer the parish and select schools. . .

On September 26, 1884 Sister M. Baptist wrote of the proposed purchase of an estate which included a large residence that would serve for a time, as a boarding school.

. . . I would not decide on the purchase till the Sisters tried a walk out there and I let them go out one morning that we had no Mass. There is a good sidewalk all the way and I think it is not farther than the East side school. At all events, they said we could easily walk it if we had to do it. There are apple trees on it, bearing now, and you would smile to hear Sister Mary Venantius talk about getting the apples for winter.

Then on October 30 Mother wrote:

Yours of the 26th giving the very satisfactory statement of the purchase was received yesterday. It is well you have it rented as we cannot possibly give a Sister for there until the 19th of March. I wish for your sakes I could send them now. There are four of them in a dying condition, two came two days ago. One of them is S. M. Clemence. She was anointed yesterday and is going fast to her last long home. We will include your kind friend Major Cavanaugh in the daily prayers we say for our benefactors. I thank God that you and the children were able to attend the mission so well.

On October 22, 1884 the W. R. Welch estate on Grand Avenue was purchased for $20,000. The Sisters quickly christened it the Villa Marie. Only a few alterations were needed to prepare the building for the admission of boarders and "select day pupils." Complete furnishings would, of course, depend on the Sisters. Mother Clarke wrote in February:

We have a trunk ready with a few sheets, pillow cases and spreads that will be a help to you. The beds, etc., for those who go there will be boxed; you can arrange them as you think proper. God grant you can have the

house blessed and Holy Mass in it - you must all pray
for this. Won't you see there will be no sleeping apartment over the Chapel and make yourself sure by inquiring if anything should be over it. Get the Altar, Confessional and all that will be necessary. I will try to
have a few purificators, corporals, etc., made here. If
there is anything else we can make out for you we will
do so. I did not hear if S. M. Maxima came or not - if
she has & calls, we will send the trunk with her. We
heard her dear Mother died and are praying for her.

Then regarding matters, personnel and otherwise:

Sister M. Landaline has a decided objection to going to
DesMoines, having left it so recently - there is no fault
with her; it is much easier to go to Chicago, and cheaper
too, than to DesMoines. It is very kind of that lady to
leave her piano with you. I beg of God to bless all who
do a kindness to my dear Sisters. You will have time to
let me know the best routes & time for the Sisters to
leave. If the weather permits it would be better for yourself to take a child and come on for them. Should there
be anything else necessary write and tell me. I will ask
God to bless you all.

Apparently Sister M. Baptist had been the victim of a fast-
talking salesman and had become painfully aware of her mistake.
Mother wrote her on April 14, 1885:

Yours of the 11th reached me safe, also your two letters
regarding the linen purchase. I admit it startled me,
but your repentance relieved me and will prevent in yourself the recurrence, as well as enable you to guard others
against such persons. You did well to repack them lest
anything should happen by delay in keeping them. I would
willingly be at the expense of returning the box if you
know where he resides - if you judge it safe to do so.
Don't you think, dear Sister, you have done sufficient
penance for it now?

Then her letter turned to other affairs:

I wish you would send S. M. Antoinette to the Bluffs,
they are distressed for help. I will give you as good
in August. How many boarders have you now? And are

your terms the same as our other boarding schools? It would not be just for you to do otherwise. Now about the 6 acres. I think the $11,000 is reasonable, but before deciding if it can be taken just now, I must know from you when the next payment on the 10 acres becomes due and amount of it - as I would not undertake any more extra debt till I know what may be expected from your resources.

Sister M. Baptist's response reads:

. . . Many thanks for the trunk and boxes with their contents. I hope you will be able to send us good Sisters and good teachers made of good women to meet the needs of our new school.

Mr. Welch says we will surely realize a dollar here for every 50cts. in DuB - and he has secured two boarders for us. They will also leave their horse, a fine strong, gentle fellow, for our use while they are in Dubuque. The sisters here think it would be cheating Saint Joseph not to give him the name of the new place and begged me to write again and say they vote for it to be St. Joseph's.

. . . The Bishop may be out in a few days & he will see if we can get Mass on Sundays and Fridays - we are having all the children pray that we may get the Blessed Sacrament on St. Joseph's day. [10] We would be so happy to have our Blessed Lord with us. I do not know whether I can leave or not to go for the Sisters. Sister Mary Michael & I will have to go out today if Mrs. Welch gets away; for if the house were burned we would not get a cent insurance if there were no one in it to take care of it. All pretty well. Pray for

Your dutiful child,

The new St. Joseph Academy was blessed and formally opened on March 19, 1885, under the direction of Sister M. Baptist. Mass was celebrated there for the first time that day. In June Mother wrote reminding Sister that

It is a long time since you wrote, perhaps not to you who must be very busy between both houses. S. M. Maxilinda is in delicate health and her Sister, Mrs. McCormick, has written requesting to have her go to DesMoines for a

Welch mansion purchased for an academy and
select school and first named Villa Marie

St. Joseph Academy, Des Moines

St. Joseph Academy, Dubuque

while. Would it be advisable, and could she stay with you while there? Let me know immediately as I want to answer the lady. . . When will you have to make a payment and will you be able to meet it? Tell me whether or not immediately, as I will try to collect all I can to help. Give my love to all. I will ask God to bless you.

The previous summer Mother had written Sister in response to a request made by Sister M. Seraphia, a widow, whose daughter,

Mrs. Smith asked if she sent a free pass to and from where she lives, if Sister would be permitted in vacation to see her as it would be too hard for her to travel with her two babies. Let me know your views before I write to Sister M. Seraphia.

While no responses remain, it is altogether probable that Sister replied in the spirit in which Mother had written, and the two requests were granted.

Meanwhile Mother had gathered the contents of two additional boxes of supplies for the new boarding school.

We have crammed everything we could into them. . . We have made out a chalice, and I have dear Father's little censer which I know you will be careful of. We won't venture to send them this time but will as soon as possible. The things go by the Milwaukee Road.

The two-story frame residence on the west side of the city stood in a wilderness of trees. A large stable provided protection for the horses and carriage that brought a priest three times a week for Mass. The car lines did not extend so far, though at long intervals one might hope for a "bus." The first year brought thirty students, including one small boy, but no boarders. Soon, however, boarding students stretched the house to its elastic limits. While the girls took their meals in the dining room, the Sisters ate in the kitchen. The older girls slept in the attic, while the younger occupied the "upstairs," the Sisters separated from their charges by calico curtains. A metal tub graced the single bathroom.

The school's first graduation - 1892 - was held in the parlor, the two graduates wearing long, hand-sewn gowns of white wool with "street trains." A medal bearing the name and the date of graduation supplied for a diploma - a custom commonly followed in academies of the day.

Meantime, Mother Clarke had not been unmindful of needs. She wrote on April 8, 1886:

> I sent you a draft for $650.00 to meet your next payment. I cannot promise to be able to help you any more this year. God is good and if He, who knows all things, gives me the means, I shall share it in helping you, but you must not be disappointed if I can not. The expenses this year with us are enormous between sickness, death, etc., but God permits all. I hope we will be satisfied with His holy will.

The year was indeed a hard one. Death had claimed thirteen Sisters in 1885, three of them after just two years of religious life. The next year would bring nine more deaths, most of them of Sisters only a brief time in the Congregation. The usual cause of death was tuberculosis.

In August 1887, not long before her death, Mother wrote Sister M. Michael Nihill confirming Sister's appointment to the superiorship of the academy.

> . . . I will send word through S. M. Baptist when you are to take charge of the academy.

Then, as though Sister had proposed some difficulty, Mother continued:

> You seem to think there is self-will in what you propose. I think you are right, but have courage and confidence in God who is always ready to help our weakness. I know you will take my advice and brave temptation and I will say a few of my poor prayers for you. Have courage. The enemy wants to prevent the good you can do. May God bless you.
>   Your affectionate

Almost immediately the Villa Marie was supplemented by a substantial brick structure, and as the school prospered, new buildings were added. The academy absorbed the boarding students from St. Francis, Council Bluffs in 1908, and continued to prosper for another sixty years. By 1951 the demand for boarding schools had so declined that their maintenance seemed no longer justified, and the academy was closed to boarders. In 1972, the erection of a diocesan central high school and center for adult education in West DesMoines, named Dowling High School-St. Joseph Educational Center, marked the closing of the academy. The entire plant was then sold to the College of Osteopathic Medicine. The academy meanwhile had contributed more than a hundred members to the B. V. M. Congregation.

Not every young woman who entered the Community was equally in earnest about living up to its requirements. There were those among them whose unwillingness taxed even Mother Clarke's long-suffering patience, as we see from the following letters. The first of these was addressed in March 1884, to Sister M. Purification McDonnell, superior at Annunciation Convent, Chicago. It concerned the former Elizabeth Bolger who had entered the sisterhood from Lake Forest in April 1881, at the age of "24 6/12" and received the name Sister Mary Humiliana.

I have tried to answer S. M. Humiliana's letter. She seemed very much depressed. She seems to have lost all confidence in teaching. I feel sorry. She can only restore it by humility.

A year later, Mother wrote to Mr. J. J. Bolger, Sister's father:

I deem it a duty to write you regarding Sr. M. Humiliana. We cannot employ her as she wishes which makes her very unhappy. It will be necessary for you to come on as we fear her health, physically and mentally, will give way if things continue as they are. [11]

The following January, Mother responded to a letter from a second Miss Bolger, a former B. V. M., who had entered from Chicago, but who suffered from a similar problem.

My dear Miss Bolger:[12]
    Yours of December 28th was duly received and your request to return duly considered. You have made a trial, dear child, of over three years, both in the Novitiate and in two of our mission houses. As the same cause for dissatisfaction would still exist for you I can not in justice to yourself or the Community admit you again among us. This must not discourage you, dear child, as this decision must be the will of God. I am sure you will serve Him well and

be a good Christian in the world. May God bless you. I
hope you got your package and letter safe.

> Your affectionate M. F. Clarke

Mother Clarke had erased the name from the copy she kept
of the following letter dated November 14, 1884:

My dear Sister,
    I got your last letter yesterday. Since you leave the
result of your going or staying with me, I have concluded that as you can not teach in our schools and are
not able for work, having offered you the lightest duty
we have - sewing - which you decline, I see nothing
more that I can do but refund your money and let you go
in peace. I am satisfied you will never do anything un-
becoming a good Christian. Let me hear from you at
once, and then I will send you a good trunk and your
money. I will pray for you and ask God to bless you.

Of another Sister, Mother wrote, Bishop Hennessy on September 29, 1885:

Painful as it is to me to again trouble you, I feel it is
no longer a matter of choice but of duty I owe to the
Community. It regards Sr. M. Casilda who, as you may
remember, was dismissed about three years ago, and
whom we again took back for further trial. Now we are
more than fully satisfied of the utter impossibility for us
to retain her longer. Were she confined to a bed of sickness and that the most loathsome kind, [13] most willingly
would she be attended to with us; but it is not so. She is
in usual good health and well qualified to maintain herself by teaching, having given herself entirely to study
here. She has not been under vows for four years. We
are all far below her idea of what religious should be so
it will not surprise any of us to hear of unkind and unworthy reflections. Poor child! if she finds the world
as forbearing as we have been, it is more than I look
for. May God give her grace to look into herself and
protect her.

> Your humble
> M. F. C.

Then we have the account of a gifted and very attractive
young Sister whom Mother had assigned as superior to an elem-

tary school then opening in DesMoines, for it was Mother's custom to choose the more attractive for beginnings so that first impressions would be good. It was not long, however, before the young Sister had formed a somewhat too obvious friendship with the assistant pastor, a fact which had begun to create talk such that older Sisters in the convent thought Mother should be made aware of the situation. Sending for the Sister, Mother told her of the reason for calling her home and suggested that it might be best if she did not return to DesMoines. The response was a vehement protest and the insistence that by returning she could show proof that the rumors were unfounded. Mother listened carefully, then proposed a plan. The Sister was to remain at the motherhouse for a week of prayer; meanwhile Mother would pray earnestly to know God's will. Sister must then be prepared to accept whatever decision Mother had determined upon. At the week's end Mother's own words were:

Now, child, knowing how easily we can be tempted, human nature being what it is, I have decided that it will be best for you not to return. There is an opening in Chicago where your talents will be appreciated, and I'm sure you will be happy.

After much unsuccessful pleading, the young Sister exclaimed defiantly,

I won't go. I'll go home first.

To which Mother responded,

Perhaps that will be best, Sister.

With that Sister hastened to Sister M. Gertrude for her support. The latter came quickly to remonstrate,

Mother, you can't let her go. She is so beautiful, so gifted, so able. She will be a great loss.

Mother answered quietly,

I grant you, she is all that, but she is not obedient, and we cannot keep her. [14]

The story is told that on one occasion when Mother Clarke was obliged to dismiss a Sister, the Sister remarked to another:

I will go, but will return when Mother Clarke dies.

Mother, hearing this, said,

Poor child, she will be dead long before I am.

And such proved to be the case. [15] Writing to Sister M. Agatha in her capacity as visitor, Mother outlined the regulations which she wished to have followed on the missions. The date of her communication to Sister was February 7, 1885. In keeping with her directives, the Sisters were not to entertain priests in the convent after eight o'clock in the evening, were never to provide cigars or serve alcoholic beverages of any kind to them, or to invite them to their own table.

Regarding poverty, Sisters receiving gifts of fine cashmere for habits, etc., were required to have them returned, to be exchanged for habit serge or for merino to be used in a shawl. Presents of money were to be acknowledged by the Sisters who received them and immediately incorporated into community funds. Sizeable gifts of money were to be sent to the motherhouse. Signs of worldliness, such as buttoned or side-laced shoes were not to be tolerated, nor were ready-made quilted winter or summer underwear.

Other restrictions involved "sleigh-riding or carriage riding merely for pleasure." While the Sisters might accompany the pupils on such occasions to care for them, they were never to go otherwise. Nor were they permitted to take refreshments of any kind outside the convent, except as provided for in the Custom Book.

More an exemption than a restriction was the directive regarding music teachers, "who must not be required or allowed to take more than twenty-five music pupils," and no lessons of any kind were to be given to outsiders after dark.

Infractions of any of these regulations were to be reported promptly. As early as April 1872, Mother had written to the Sisters regarding poverty:

For the future at Christmas or at any other time do not send to me, or to any Sister, presents of clothing, framed pictures, books or other articles, except for the general use of the Community. Send nothing to any individual except pictures for prayer-books.

Sometimes corrections and admonitions had to be given. On these occasions, Mother was firm but never harsh nor carping.

One letter, addressed to a Chicago superior with reference to a problem in her household read:

> . . . I am very sorry there is any misunderstanding among my dear Sisters when I know they are all trying to work for God's little ones. But this must not discourage you. God permits the cross to test our fidelity. May our sweet Immaculate Mother obtain for my dear Sisters peace and unity in order to please God. Knowing your faults, I'm sure you will pray to correct them. May God bless you.

Then to another who seemed to be taking herself too seriously:

> I would give my poor advice if it is worth anything. It is that you conquer your too sensitive feelings and try to forget the greater part of your varied knowledge. It is an injury to you. A more simple course would be best, and cause you less trouble and make your Sisters more happy. If you walked into the school rooms every day, your presence would be better than teaching, unless you thought proper to teach an odd class. It will save the appearance of watching the Sisters and speaking to them before others. It sours their temper and does no good. You must bear with young people for God's sake, and you can speak to them another time with more profit to themselves and peace to yourself. Don't encourage them to be tale bearers, but in conscience let them tell whatever they see or hear which may give disedification. Be moderately cheerful with them and they will be cheerful and happy.

And regarding an especially unpleasant matter, Mother wrote the following:

> Something must be done about those who stay in bed in the morning - from the time the bell rings for prayers until the bell for Mass they are dressing and going through the rooms. Sisters who are able to dress immediately after all leave the bed room should try to rise with the bell and be at prayers and meditation with the Community. Borders and collars have been taken and parts of other sewing torn off. I request Sisters who have charge of things of the house to come and tell me when anything is

taken. I am ashamed and grieved at this dishonorable mode of acting in any of my Sisters. I am always willing each should have what is necessary but to ask for it.

Then there were problems regarding the regular hours of recreation. Lest some of the Sisters take refuge in a book instead of participating, Mother added:

Let no reading be in the noon and evening recreation without my permission. Sister M. Terentia will see that all reading matter is put away during these hours. Avoid speaking of the faults of each other and curiously inquiring into the affairs of missions and Sisters. By doing so and keeping together at all times you will avoid many faults and save yourselves many regrets. During the hours of silence be careful in keeping it - it will preserve you from a thousand faults.

Then, in keeping with the regulation of long standing which had been retained in the new Custom Book:

Sisters should go to confession according to number or tell me when they cannot do so.

Endeavoring to maintain faithful adherence to the officially approved rules and to long established customs, Mother was faced with psychological problems with which she was scarcely prepared to grapple. The seeming necessity for confining within such narrow limits the natural interests of the Sisters must have sometimes haunted Mother. This would be especially a problem for Sisters engaged in household tasks, who had little intellectual refreshment available to them. What subjects of conversation had they to fill those hours as they sewed, mended or quilled?[16] What would have been more normal than for them to turn their minds to the missions and the Sisters on them, even perhaps to their vagaries, and to bits of family news? Rubbing elbows as closely as the Sisters did with others of their own household, they must often have been painfully conscious of each others' faults and foibles. Well kept silence would indeed help many grow in tolerance, but it could also permit estrangements to grow and flourish. Doubtless Mother realized all this, but there was little she could do to provide diversion or broaden the outlook, especially of those resident in the rural setting of the motherhouse. Few among them shared her gifts of contemplation or her lifelong quest for knowledge.[17]

"Theatre" was a bad word in ecclesiastical circles in the
nineteenth century. Attendance at theatrical performances was
strictly forbidden the clergy in many dioceses, and third order
members had long been indoctrinated with the evils of the stage.
Mother Clarke's reaction, then to the request of Sister M.
Alphonsus of the Davenport Academy on June 8, 1870, for permission to accept the offer of the Burtis Theatre to host an
academy performance should not come as a surprise. The offer had come at the request of Father Brazill of DesMoines
when one of the Sisters mentioned to him that the projected
audience would be much too large for their cramped quarters.
This would be especially the case since Father Brazill, as
vicar general - Bishop Hennessy was at that time on his ad
limina[18] visit to Rome - was to hold a council in Davenport on
the day following the performance, and almost every priest in
the diocese would be present. To her request, Sister added:
"Dear Mother. . . if you decide in favor of it, which I hope you
will, I think it advisable to preserve Father Brazill's letter
authorizing our doing so. " A second letter to Mother, written
on June 19, gives the denouement:

Dear Mother,
    Believe me I am truly sorry for having caused you to
feel so sad. I thought I would never do that; please forgive me and forget the fault, and I trust in God I shall
not be again guilty of the like. . . Though I did insert
the clause saying I hoped you would consent, indeed I am
glad you refused. The stage is now up in our schoolroom
as usual.

    Then, as if she had submitted the program for Mother's ap-
proval, and Mother thought a portion of it a bit too frivolous,
Sister added: "There is now no comic piece whatever. . . "

    Mother Clarke had followed through on the suggestion made
by Father Trevis that she have a book of customs or common
observances compiled, and had charged Sisters M. Xavier
O'Reilly and Cecilia Dougherty with the task. It was a severe
little book, compiled as it was of the practices that had prevailed from the earlier days of the Community. Many of its
provisions continued with little revision to the middle of the
twentieth century, despite new theological and psychological insights into the meaning of Christian perfection. One directive,
unique to that first printing, regarded travel. It read:

We are required, when travelling, not to stay or lodge over night with Religious of another Order, lest we disturb the regulations of their rules. When there is no house of our own Community near, we must go to a hotel, taking care to secure a private apartment for ourselves, and keep as retired as possible. We should not go to the public table, but take our meals in our rooms.

The regulations included reminders of the prayer to be said when the clock strikes, and of the aspiration to be given and responded to when two Sisters met each other, or on entering a room where there were others present; the custom of adoration "introduced by our Reverend Founder as a reparation for some horrible sacrileges committed in this country, " the necessity of going to confession "according to number, " that is, in the order of profession, the nine rosaries for a deceased Sister to be construed as nine fifteen-decade rosaries or "chaplets, " and strict regulations regarding the "modesty of the eyes, " and silence. Then there was the classic view of the superior which read:

We must never forget that our Superior holds, in our regard, the place of God, and that, having devoted ourselves entirely to the Divine service, we should look upon every Superior as an angel sent by God to direct us in the fulfillment of His holy will, and resign ourselves to her guidance, as little children in the hands of their parents.

The letter which went to the superiors of all the houses at the time the copies of the new book were circulated was written by Sister M. Xavier O'Reilly and signed by her with Mother Clarke's signature added. Dated October 23, 1882 it said simply: "We depend on you to see that these 'Customs' be strictly observed. "

A second item which went in the same mail was a copy of the "Course of Study, " with the request that the superiors would

Please introduce it into your schools immediately, as we are most desirous to give it a two years' trial. Be particular to notice how it works, and report to Mother after each semiannual examination, what you find in it commendable or otherwise. We can have this copy framed, but we think it advisable not to have it copied till it proves its worth.

As an aid in conducting graded schools, we recommend you

to procure for your teachers a copy of "How to Teach, " by Henry Kiddle, A. M. , published by J. W. Schermerhorn & Co. , New York. Also a copy of Guibe's "Method of Teaching Arithmetic, " published by S. R. Winchell & Co. , Chicago. This little book fully explains the method of teaching "Combinations of Numbers, " as mentioned in our primary Grades.

The letter then adds as a postscript: "Please have Formula of Examen copied from the Custom Book, and kept in the chapel for daily use. " The Formula followed the five points prescribed by the Jesuit retreat masters.

Mother submitted a copy of the book of customs to Father A. A. Lambert, S. J. , for his comments. These came in a letter giving her the assurance that he had "read your book of customs or regulations. They are admirable, and contain the spirit of the approved rules. " It is not surprising that he found "three or four expressions which are not clear, " for religious have a way of creating a vocabulary of their own. However, "dear Sister Gonzaga in Davenport told me how they are understood by the Sisters. "

A second edition of the custom book published in 1884 closes with a fifteen-page study entitled "Regarding School. " It is a remarkable study, manifesting an insight into the essential and enduring principles of education which have persevered through a century and are proclaimed by the best educators today.

Since the Rule allowed but a single three-year term for the offices of Mother and her councillors, the Sisters, anticipating the end of that first term, applied to Rome through Father Trevis, who was still in Europe, for the privilege of reelecting Mother Clarke for a second term, 1881-1884.

On December 1880 Father Trevis wrote from Nice, France to Father Laurent, acknowledging the Sisters' petition:

I thought first on opening the long list of Sisters' names that there was some general insurrection, but no, it was simply a petition to continue in her office the Venerable Mother Clarke. To me, the question does not seem of vital importance, though it is very near the heart of all the Sisters, and, though it seems fit that the Foundress should be the object of their devotion and respect. However, I concluded to start for Rome and have the question settled while Bishop Hennessy is there. . . The Sisters must now see that the rosaries and litanies they so charitably offered for me when I was a prisoner in my room in

Keokuk has turned partly to their benefit since the new
lease on life they obtained for me has been partly employed in their cause. [19]

While waiting for the office of the Propaganda to open after
the Christmas holiday, Father Trevis saw Bishop Hennessy,
"who is well disposed to help our cause. Nevertheless he seems
preoccupied with his own affairs."

On February 4, 1881 Father Trevis wrote again to Laurent:

Herein you will find the answer to the petition of the
Sisters for the re-election of Mother Clarke. It is a
faithful copy of the original document which I will confide
for transmission to the kindness of Bishop Hennessy.

He added facetiously:

It only remains that Mother Clarke be alive for re-election,
that two-thirds of the votes given secretly be for her, and
that in the counting of the ballots there be no cheating:
therefore, on that occasion, let the ballot box be carefully
watched that the ayes may have it.

Unaware of the Sisters' petition, Mother Clarke wrote to
Bishop Hennessy who had just returned from Rome:

As the time of election is approaching, I feel anxious. I
am ignorant of all that may be required of me. I abandon
myself without reserve to your judgment to be directed as
you think proper. I send the Sisters, commissioned to receive whatever advice you think well to give.

It was a happy surprise to her to learn of the Sisters' early
action.

Shortly after his return to the States, on June 21, 1882,
Father Trevis wrote Mother Clarke from Mercy Hospital, Daven
port, where he was chaplain, reminding her that the period of
temporary approbation for the rule would soon expire. He then
gave her careful instructions for the application to be made
for its final approbation. A second thoughtful reminder came
from Father Lambert, S. J., the following April. On July 18,
1883 Mother wrote to Father Trevis:

This is the last day of our retreat and as no one knows
better than you, our dear, trusted valued friend, I beg

you will pray for us that we may do God's work, and in
the manner He wills it, and for the final sanction of our
Rules. How happy, dear Father, it would make me if,
as of old, you were in Rome to attend to them for us -
but I must submit to God's good pleasure and await His
in this matter as in other things. Begging your blessing
for myself and all my dear Sisters,
Your humble,
M. F. Clarke

At the same time, Mother sent to Abbot McDonald at the
monastery an offering of fifty dollars for Masses to be said for
their varied needs. This the kindly Abbot returned, but with
the assurance that her reque st would be attended to promptly.

Since the election of 1884 came while the matter of the rule
was still under consideration, the Sisters made a formal request that Mother be permitted to remain in office for life.
Meanwhile they were solicited by Mother for any changes in the
rule which they wished to propose. Their proposals were to be
sent to the Bishops of the dioceses in which the Sisters were
involved. After giving them consideration, the Bishops were
expected to add any suggestions of their own. Bishop Hennessy
directed the Jesuit Fathers to send all resulting documents to
Rome. Suggestions for change must have been few indeed, for
the rule finally approved on March 15, 1885, contained only
the most superficial changes.

At Father Trevis' suggestion, a long and gracious letter,
written, one might suspect, by Sister M. Xavier but signed by
Mother, went to Right Reverend L. Hostlot, rector of the North
American College, petitioning him to undertake their cause. Although Father Trevis had left at the College full data regarding
the Rule and recommendations of the Sisters and their work,
Mother requested Monsignor Hostlot that Father Trevis' name
not appear on the petition for approbation, this apparently at his
own request. We will remember that at this time the appointment of Davenport's second bishop was pending, and Father
doubtless preferred not to be involved in two separate causes
at the same time. Having graciously accepted Mother's charge,
the Monsignor assured her that he would respect her confidence
in this matter.

A source of anxiety arose for Mother Clarke from the delay
necessarily involved in submitting the required documents to
the propaganda. Since the temporary approbation of the Rule,
granted for six years only, would expire in September 1883,
she was troubled lest the approval granted the Congregation it-

self would lapse on that date. Monsignor Hostlot hastened to assure her, however, that there was "no necessity for a renewed approbation /of the Congregation itself/ since the approbation holds good until either the rules have been approved or the approbation is formally withdrawn. "

On September 20, 1883 the documents reached Rome, including letters from Archbishop Feehan of Chicago and the recently deceased Bishop McMullen of Davenport. Strangely enough, a third letter, from the erudite Bishop of Peoria, John L. Spalding, came in English, instead of the traditional Latin, and without the proper episcopal seal. Together with these, three copies of the Constitutions in Latin and one bound copy in English were enclosed.

In July Monsignor Hostlot had written: "Nothing can be done until the papers arrive from the Rt. Rev. Bishop /of Dubuque/. His letter of acknowledgment in September added: "I have not yet received the letter you mentioned in your last from the Rt. Rev. Bishop of Dubuque. " He wrote again a week later: "The letter from Rt. Rev. Dr. Hennessy has not come as yet. " He had, however, assured Mother that

> I will not sleep over the matter, nor will allow the others to do so, as I feel that the approbation of your Rule would be a great encouragement for your Community to work with greater ardor in the noble work undertaken.

The next communication came from the Very Reverend A. J. Schulte, vice-rector of the American College, on January 13, 1884, informing Mother that Monsignor Hostlot was ill with pneumonia, a condition which soon resulted in his death. Monsignor Schulte, however, carried the work forward. He advised that there was need for twenty more copies of the Constitutions, each marked with the desired changes, and with these should come a more formal application than the one originally provided. [20]

A gracious letter came from the Bishop to Mother Clarke on Christmas eve, 1884:

> . . . I did not anticipate this delay in the confirmation of your Rule. They are somewhat slow in Rome; they will take their time, but all will be right in the end. . . I was sorry to hear on my return from Baltimore that your health was somewhat delicate. I sincerely hope that it is improved now. I hope also that the health of your Community is good. Wishing you a very happy

Christmas and many returns, I am, Dear Mother,
Yours sincerely in Christ,

The action confirming Mother Clarke in office for life was delayed beyond the election date for 1884, and Monsignor Schulte twice obtained permission for a delay of the election. Meantime he was happy to confirm by letter dated March 27, 1885, his cablegram of a few days before:

At last your long cherished desires have been fulfilled. Your Institute has received final approbation. I sent you a cablegram to that effect last Monday. Out of the seventeen religious orders of women who have applications to the same effect at the Propaganda, yours is one of the first to receive attention, though some of the others had sent their applications long before yours was received. 21

On March 15, 1885, the day the cable arrived, the Bishop wrote Mother again:

I sincerely congratulate you on the good news from Rome, and I hope that the petition for your appointment for life will be granted. Indeed I think it almost likely that it will, as it would be no more than the complement of what is already granted. Hoping you are well after the long and severe winter, I am, dear Madam,
Yours truly

Within a month Monsignor Schulte wrote again to Mother that "As for retaining you as Mother Superior for life, that was left to the decision of Bishop Hennessy. " Quite naturally, this message left the Sisters in a state of uncertainty until the following July 26, when Sister M. Cecilia, writing in haste to Sister M. Agatha, gave her the good news. Her letter cast the Bishop of Dubuque in an unfamiliar role:

Joyful news! glad tidings! Are you all ready to hear? Well, - our Rt. Rev. Bishop made his appearance in our midst yesterday, and with all the delight and gladness and happiness of a devoted son of Mother's, proclaimed to us all assembled that he had just received orders from the Eternal City to confirm our dearest Mother in her office of Mother General for life; and right heartily and joyfully did he make the proclamation, I assure you. He received the letter from Rome while at his dinner, and as soon as he had dined, took his buggy and drove right out here. He saw Mother first, then left her in the parlor until he stole in on the whole of us just as we were, (guess that part) and began to frisk about and joke just like a big boy - gave us, without being asked, three days of "unbounded jolification, " and "moderate recreation" until retreat opens, and lots of other jolly good orders - then told us why he gave us all that. He called for a violin and actually I believe the man would have made us all dance, and dance with us himself if we had one. Then he marched all the Sisters down to the parlor to congratulate Mother - took his chair and sat down beside her, while we all came in single file and each came and kissed Mother, then stood up and shook hands with her himself, and congratulated her with all the warm-heartedness of a dutiful son. Then, after some chit-chat here and there through the crowd, he blessed us all and started for home. . . Now didn't I tell you good news? Come home and help us rejoice.

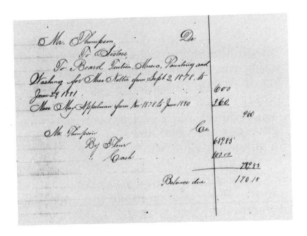

Notes

1 Recollections of Teresa Laurent, niece of Muscatine's pastor, Griffith files, Davenport.

2 The news came in a cablegram on May 9, 1881 to Father Trevis, who had now returned to Davenport.

3 Patrick W. Riordan, named Bishop of San Francisco in 1883, visited his dying friend before going west. Realizing that he had no other gift for the newly consecrated Riordan, the sick man reached out to him his own pectoral cross, with the words, "Take this, I shall not need it any more. " (Miscellaneous notes, Griffith files.)

4 On Brazill's death, the Iowa State Register carried the longest and most fulsome obituary it had published up to that time.

5 See Laurent to Brazill, January 31, 1882, Griffith files. As early as 1876, while Father Trevis was still in Rome, Sister M. Felicitas had written to Mother Clarke, though her message had been premature:

They are dividing the Diocese of Dubuque in Rome now. F. L. got 4 pages of foolscap on the subject from F. Trevis. They even know at the Propaganda about the piece of poetry composed for Father Brazill the time they called him suspender. F. Laurent, I guess, got it up, but he wonders how it got to Rome.

Father Brazill had so exasperated Father Laurent by the abuse of his authority as vicar general in suspensions and threats of suspension of the clergy that the latter took the occasion of reminding him of certain irregularities in his own past. A number of the priests had presented him, as a reminder of his arbitrary actions, with a Christmas gift of a pair of suspenders. It was this which provided the inspiration for the poetic attempt which brought much mirth to the sedate Cardinals.

6 The word terna signifies the list of three suggested candidates to fill a new or a vacant see, sent by a synod of Bishops to the Holy Father as an aid to his selection of a suitable and acceptable candidate for the office.

7 The Reverend D. J. Flannery, pastor of St. Anthony's from 1882 to 1916, contested the diocesan claim to the property

which included the St. Anthony square. In a dispute in 1898, he asserted that the revenues were due to the parish, and not the diocese. Bishop Cosgrove, as the legal successor of Bishop Loras, to whom, with Father Mazzuchelli, the property had been ceded by Antoine LeClaire, claimed that Father Pelamourgues, as pastor, had acted with the power of attorney in leasing the land, the return of which he had sent to the Bishop. The most Reverend Sebastian Marintelli, Apostolic Delegate, decided the case in favor of the diocese. (John F. Smith, St. Anthony's, 1837-1953.)

8 The Tom Malone family living across the street, be-friended the Sisters in many ways. Their little daughter Alice was soon quite a favorite with the Sisters. As Sister M. Josephin Sister was destined to be a provincial and later, a college president.

9 Sister M. Isidore Motie was later assigned to succeed the ailing S. M. Sebastian.

10 March 19 is celebrated in honor of St. Joseph. It was for many years celebrated as a holy day of obligation in the Congregation.

11 Mother Clarke recorded the following: "April 16, 1885. Returned to S. M. Humiliana Bolger $100.00. Travelling expense and clothing $45.00."

12 The Community register indicates that Anna Bolger, dismissed in December 1885, had the religious name of Peragrina, while the Sister dismissed on April 22, 1885, was Elizabeth Bolger. The former Sister M. Peragrina had entered from Chicago, March 19, at the age of 27. It is likely, though not certain, that they were blood sisters.

13 Mother seems to have referred in her own mind to a situation recounted on page 10 of the Doran Journal. The account the setting of which appears to have been Philadelphia, tells of two children who had been confined in a garret in near-starvation for some years, by an uncle who was intent on getting money which would rightfully have come to them. When they were discovered they were in a shocking condition. The boy died soon after, but the girl, feeble-minded or deranged from her experience, lived for some years in the care of the Sisters who came to speak of her as Sister Mary. The account says graphical

ly enough: "She was diseased, and taking care of her was a loathsome task. After her death the house was filled with a most delightful odor. "

14 Account given by Mother Isabella Kane to Sister M. Ernestine Henthorne when the latter was doing a portrait of Mother Clarke.

15 Sister M. Leo Boyle attested to the truth of the above, giving the account to Sister M. St. Magdalen Swift.

16 The stiff, finely fluted "border" worn about the face was prepared for wearing by working a pair of flat wooden "quilling needles" through a hem of soft white material, then starching and drying. To remove the border from the needles the "quills" were broken apart and the needles deftly slipped out. But the hazards were many - scorching in the drying process and splitting or tearing the material while removing it from the "needles. " The border was then sewed to a white starched cap. Then there was the precision needed in making a set of borders. Indeed, at that period there was the necessity of making every item of one's clothing, much of it by hand, and the expense involved in the purchase of material good enough for long wear and color fastness. The labor of laundering the several pieces of headgear, especially the ironing of the twice-starched hood, was a time-consuming process of remarkable proportions. This was especially the case when the summer heat literally melted the many starched pieces into a limp and sticky mass humiliating and uncomfortable to wear. While the Sisters today may sympathize with nostalgia over the bonneted and swathed religious of earlier years, recollections of those trying days leaves them cold.

17 We recall Mother's acquaintance with the botanical names of flowers, and her interest in astronomy to which Father Donaghoe once made reference. Her attraction for science did not seem to end there, for in the margin of a page in her boarding school accounts, we find an unusual list of words which she apparently had come upon and the meaning of which she intended to investigate. They were: Ozoic, protoz/oa7, bilocation, anodes, cathodes, bituation, otiose, megatherium, and nil - Did the last introduce a Latin phrase? Possibly "Nil nisi bonum de mortuis" or "Nil disputandus de gustibus. "

18 Literally, "to the threshold. " The expression refers to

158

the ten-year report a bishop is expected to give to the Holy Father in person on matters concerning his diocese.

19 The improvement in Father Trevis' health, which he attributed to the Sisters' prayers, had enabled him to be of much service to them.

20 The Reverend Walter Hill, S. J. , who gave the motherhouse retreat in the summer of 1884, seems to have prepared the rule for final approbation. In his notes, in the Congregation's archives, there is a gracious commendation of the Sisters' work and their history, to which, however, he added as his personal reaction to the rule a remarkably violent denunciation of it. His remarks can scarcely have been justified, especially since the rule which received final approbation differed only superficially from the one which had been temporarily approved. A letter from Father Hill addressed to Sister M. Agatha from St. Louis many years later speaks with much warmth of his contacts with Mother Clarke on the occasion of retreats given at the motherhouse, and of his years as director of the Sisters at Sacred Heart School in Chicago. His letter reads:
> Word from you and the Sisters gives me much pleasure. It brings back to me sweet memories which often come to my thoughts: of the retreats I gave at your sweet old historic home where Mother Clarke died in her humble room which she told me she would never leave except for her grave. I gave many retreats to the Sisters at other houses, and for twelve years had spiritual charge of the Community of the Sacred Heart church, Chicago. I thus learned to value highly and to love the B. V. M. Sisters. . . My desire was always greater than my power to do good for the Sisterhood.

21 The appointment of Bishop O'Conner of Richmond as the new rector of the North American College resulted, much to Monsignor Schulte's dismay, in his own transfer from Rome to a professorship at the Philadelphia Archdiocesan Seminary of St. Charles Borromeo at Overbrook. Feeling himself more than compensated financially for his services, he sent to Mother from the seminary a box of religious articles blessed by His Holiness, Leo XIII, "as a small token of gratitude for all your past favors, assuring you again and again that I am ever at your service. "

Chapter Six

THE END CROWNS THE WORK

T he last four years of Mother Clarke's life were full. During
them she concluded arrangements for the opening of thirteen
new missions, extending the services of the Sisters to three
parish schools in Kansas City, one each in Milwaukee and San
Francisco, and two boarding academies, in Holden, Missouri
and Wichita, Kansas. [1] Meanwhile tuberculosis claimed the
lives of many members of the struggling community. [2]

Mother had largely given up the effort to keep the daily accounts, and at times, depended on others to transcribe her pen-
cilled letters. Her assistant, Sister M. Gertrude, and the official visitor, Sister M. Agatha, [3] were in personal touch with
the various missions. Sister M. Gonzaga, superior at the
Davenport academy, was occasionally called upon for similar
services. As Mother Clarke's correspondence reveals, she
kept in close touch with each new situation, while writing many
personal letters to individual Sisters and to the established missions. It was she who maintained communication with pastors
and bishops.

As prelude to those last years, there was the celebration of
the fiftieth anniversary of the Congregation's founding, given
officially as November 1, 1833, and the golden jubilee of its
two founding members, Mother Clarke and the patient Rose
O'Toole. Few details remain of that celebration; a couple of
letters, a memorial card, a brief account in the Sunday School
Messenger published by the Jesuit Fathers of Holy Family parish, Chicago. But in the local paper, there was nothing, though
there were then four hundred living members, and the Congregation had served the diocese and city of Dubuque for forty years.
Besides a gracious letter of congratulations from Father Trevis,
there must have been messages from Father Laurent, Father
Damen, S. J. , and many others, and doubtless numerous gifts.

But of all these no evidence remains.

Gatherings were planned at St. Ambrose, DesMoines, at St. Aloysius, Chicago, and at the academies, as well as at the motherhouse. On October 21, 1883, Mother's assistant, Sister M. Gertrude, wrote to Sister M. Agatha, and probably sent similar messages to other central houses:

> The approaching feast of All Saints is our loved Mother's "Golden Jubilee" and the Fiftieth Anniversary of the organization of our Community - in other words, our "Double Jubilee." With Mother's permission, I send you these few lines, that we may, united in spirit, becomingly celebrate these, to us, all-important events.
>
> It is proposed that the three days previous be spent in greater recollection, and that on the Feast, the Holy Sacrifice of the Mass, Holy Communion, and Benediction of the Blessed Sacrament be offered in thanksgiving to God for past favors and to implore a continuance of the same in the future.
>
> Mother wishes all our Sisters in Chicago to spend the day with you; they will be notified to that effect. It is also proposed that each Superior send Mother such a donation as her means will allow, to aid in erecting a monument in memory of our revered and sainted Father.

Sister M. Baptist wrote to Mother Clarke from DesMoines on October 28:

> . . . I told our good old Fr. B. yesterday that we were going to have a grand celebration; that you were our Mother for 50 years, & he exclaimed, "50 years! Well, I think she might celebrate." It is also the 18th anniversary of our arrival in DesMoines, so we have three celebrations to make. Your little circle of 50-year children is narrowing. I believe Sister Mary Rose is the last, unless Sister Mary Clare comes within the 50 years. What a crown these fifty years must have won!

The occasion brought the Dubuque Sisters and those from nearby missions to the motherhouse where the celebration centered about Mother Clarke. The account in the Sunday School Messenger spoke of "about 600 B. V. M's, " listing their various academies and estimating an enrollment of 10, 000 children

161

under the care of the Sisters. As for Chicago, the Messenger account continues:

> In this city there are nine schools and 100 Sisters, having under their care 5,000 pupils. Three of these are in the Holy Family parish, one each in Sacred Heart, Annunciation and St. Bridget's, and two in St. Pius; and a school in the parish of the Vincentian Fathers on the North Side which was opened this year. St. Aloysius', one of the largest, if not the largest female school in the United States, having over 1000 children.

The account tells of the papal blessing cabled from Pope Leo XIII, and adds:

> The good accomplished by the foundress of the Sisters of the Blessed Virgin is incalculable, and is only exceeded by her great humility which shrinks from all honor or praise of which she is so worthy.

However, it was business as usual during that auspicious year. The establishment of two small schools in Iowa and one in Illinois preceded many major foundations. In 1883 the Reverend Michael A. McCarthy from Boston, who was destined to spend his entire priestly life in Assumption Parish, Cresco, Iowa, opened a school there in a large residence. As was generally the case in rural situations, the building was without central heating or indoor plumbing. Four B.V.M. Sisters came to staff it: Sisters M. DeChantal O'Regan and of the Cross Fitzgerald for the classrooms, Lidwina Carney as music instructor, and Januarius McGowan, housekeeper. The school opened with eighty pupils. Sister M. Tertulla Reynolds was shortly added to their number, making it possible in 1884 to add high school courses. The presence of Bishop Hennessy honored the first graduating class in 1889. Favorite teachers were Sister M. Engratia Jennings, music, and the diminutive Euphrosina Hennessy, the "baby-teacher." Among the boys, Sister M. Claver Barry was held in high regard.

The Reverend Thomas Murtagh, succeeding to the pastorate, built a new convent-school in 1910, classes having been suspended for a year during the construction. Fire destroyed the church in 1929, but it was replaced by a much larger one, dedicated the following year.

The diocesan reorganization of its school system in 1951 resulted in the assignment of Cresco's two schools to the Sisters of Notre Dame, Indiana, and the withdrawal of the B. V. M. Sisters, to the regret of the parishioners. By that time their graduates included fourteen B. V. M. Sisters and seven priests, two of whom became bishops: Edward A. Fitzgerald of Winona, Minnesota, and Edward D. Howard of Portland, Oregon. The Reverend Lloyd Glass was for many years a Maryknoll missionary in China, and Monsignor Leslie V. Barnes of the Lincoln diocese served for a time as army chaplain.

Meanwhile, in Dubuque in 1883 the old Loras residence, in use as St. Mary School "in which the Sisters reside and teach" was declared unsafe for school purposes, and the Sisters' council in its meeting on August 20 authorized Mother Clarke to lay the matter of its replacement before Bishop Hennessy. This she did at once, and "the board reassembled at two o'clock that afternoon to hear the report of the president." Mother Clarke reported that "the Right Reverend Bishop was most willing that a suitable building be erected on the corner of Emmet and St. Mary's Street, he offered to donate the property; he also gave permission to hold a fair or two if necessary, in the Cathedral parish to defray the expense of erection." The minutes added: "Report received and thankfully accepted." However, the land was the inalienable possession of the diocese, and could not be "donated" to the Sisters.

The new building was erected at once. The generosity of the Sisters' families and friends made possible its furnishing. Classes in the new building extended through high school.

By 1903 the three-story structure Father O'Reilly had built as a boys' school, now being conducted by the B. V. M. Sisters as a parish school, was in serious need of replacement. The rector of the cathedral, the Reverend John J. Toomey, was planning with the parish council for a total reorganization of the parish facilities. St. Mary Academy was proving a financial liability to the Sisters. The tuition was low and many of its pupils were taken free. The cost of heat and maintenance in the three-story, high-ceilinged structure was prohibitive. Father Toomey recognized all this and offered to take the building off the Sisters' hands and build them a suitable convent, since it was serving as residence for the Sisters teaching in the parish school. As he wrote Mother Gertrude on June 23, 1903: ". . . I am anxious to ameliorate the conditions if possible of our hard-working Sisters. . . Our Sisters deserve every reasonable encouragement." Pressing Mother for a prompt response because of imperative deadlines, he received the following decision, arrived at by Mother and her council: ". . . We propose that our entire building of St. Mary's be left

CATHEDRAL SQUARE, DUBUQUE, IOWA, AFTER 1890

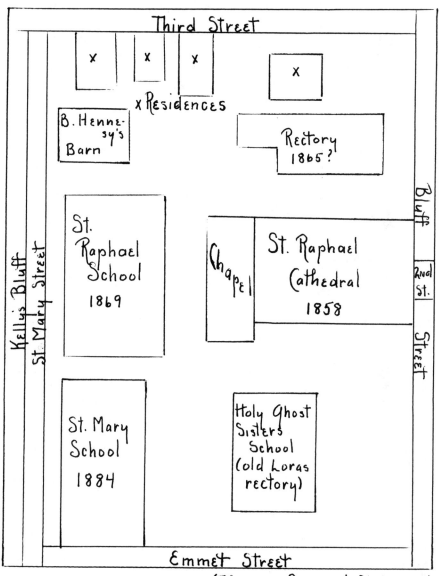

(After an Original Sketch 1902)

for the accommodation of our Sisters. . . " Mother's answer
was an evident disappointment to Father Toomey. He responded:

> . . . if the Sisters at St. Mary's will be happy and con-
> tent in their home, I don't know that I should interfere.
> But when I spoke of such an arrangement sometime past
> to our Sisters /Sister M. Gervase Tuffy was superior at
> the time/ they said the building was unsuited for that pur-
> pose /the housing of the grade school faculty, as the aca-
> demy was closing/. Moreover it was too large and very
> expensive /to maintain/.

On July 15, 1903 the Sisters' council offered to make a gift
of the building to the archdiocese. This the parish council rejected for the people thought it best to build a new school and
leave the convent to the Sisters.

However, the matter was dropped. The Loras residence,
which had been serving the Sisters of the Holy Ghost as school,
was demolished, and with it, the building that Father O'Reilly
had erected. In their place Father Toomey had the present St.
Raphael School erected, opening its doors in 1904.

Grade school girls who had been attending the academy were
enrolled in the parish school, and those of the high school who
wished it were received at the St. Joseph Academy on Thirteenth
and Main Streets.

Not until 1923, when Sister M. Alcantara Vogt was superior
at St. Raphael's, did the cathedral pastor again interest himself. Then the Reverend Edward Daugherty assumed responsibility for repairs, light, heat and water for the oversized convent, and agreed to pay the Sisters $35.00 a month as salary.
The Sisters continued paying the insurance, however, as they
had through the years. Finally, in 1966, under the principalship of Sister William James McGonegle, title to the academy
building was signed over to the parish. In 1965 the pastor,
Monsignor Norbert Barrett, had considered plans for the erection
of a suitable convent. However, the area was in a process of
change, and the plans were deferred. By 1976 enrollment had
dropped to such a level as to make the maintenance of a school
no longer feasible. After a service of 143 years on cathedral
square, in June of 1976 the B. V. M. Sisters withdrew from the
scene of their initial labors in the diocese to which the pioneer
Bishop Loras had invited them.

The Reverend Peter O'Dowd, pastor of St. Mary Church,
Ackley, Iowa, built in 1876 at a cost of $13,000 a large brick
structure to serve as Sacred Heart Academy. On his transfer

in 1879, he was succeeded by the Reverend D. H. Murphy, brother of the famous Chicago surgeon, Dr. J. B. Murphy. Ill health led to his resignation after three years. During the years 1876-1879 the Sisters of the Presentation from Dubuque staffed the academy. They were succeeded by the Sisters of the Holy Cross from Notre Dame, Indiana, and they, in turn, in 1883 by the Sisters of Charity from Dubuque. Meantime, the Reverend Lawrence Burns had been assigned as pastor.

Matters did not go well for the Sisters, as the following correspondence indicates. The first is a distressing letter from Sister M. Leandre Swift, superior, to Mother Clarke in November 1886:

Dear Mother,

There are only seventeen cents in the house, and several wants and calls for money. I do not know what to do. There is not a dealer in the place wishes to have anything to do with us except one Catholic gentleman to whom we owe over a hundred dollars. Said person is himself heavily in debt, but too gentlemanly to demand settlement. Rev. Fr. Murphy spoke of him when he was here and said he (Mr. Higgins) was tired waiting. He owes seven thousand dollars bearing ten per cent interest, and it is not right that we keep his money from him. I know it must be circulated through town that we are either dishonest or unable to pay. I have not been speaking with Fr. Burns since the receipt of Sr. Mary Gertrude's letter, but I am sure things would not have altered had I. It is evident he wants to keep away from us, anyway he has been ill for over a week. I think it useless to harp at him any more; he will just talk and that is all. There is no money to come in for some time yet, the music pupils all settled before vacation, and they have never been in the habit of paying in advance. The wood is all consumed, and when it was ordered this morning the man said he did not have it. I think he did not want to trust us; we have been similarly treated by others. What do you want us to do? Will await your decision.

Mother immediately referred the matter to Bishop Hennessy.

Rt. Rev. Bishop,

The enclosed I have received from the Sisters in Ackley - it speaks for itself. I cannot answer until I hear from you.

It was agreed before they went there to give the two teachers each $25 per month; had this been given, they would have struggled, with economy, to keep out of debt. Each vacation I was obliged to pay their fare back, and supply other necessities. Besides the debts specified in the inclosed letter, they borrowed money in the Bank to pay for some articles that were left there by the Sisters who preceded them; on this they are still paying interest. I shall be most grateful for a few words of advice when you are returning the enclosed. Hoping you are well and asking your blessing for all,

Your humble
M. F. Clarke

Five days later the Bishop responded:

Dear Madam,

I do not know what advice to give you in the circumstances. I would write to Father Burns on the subject were it not that I intend to make a change very soon in the pastoral care of Ackley. It may be better for you to await the change before deciding to withdraw the Sisters which would seem your only remedy if the contract made with them be not kept. This information is intended for yourself only.

I am, dear Madam,
Your obd. serv.
John Hennessy, Bp. of
Dubuque

This was apparently not the first difficulty that had arisen in Ackley, for on July 16, 1885 Bishop Hennessy had written to Mother Clarke requesting that she not withdraw the Sisters from the mission there, but that she "let them continue according to your instructions."

A few days later Mother Clarke received a visit from Father Burns who presented her with the following letter from Bishop Hennessy:

Dear Madam:

The bearer, Rev. Father Burns of Ackley, tells me that the school in Ackley cannot be supported as a day school, there being only a few children in that city and a few families to whom he could look for the support of a school. He says it could be well supported with the aid of

the country people which cannot be secured unless their
children are received as boarders, as otherwise they
would have no interest in it. As he stated the case, if
the Sisters do not take some boarders there can be no
school.

I should be very sorry to see Ackley without a Catholic
school, or see the Sisters leave it, and would therefore
be very glad if you would permit the Sisters to keep some
boarders (as the existence of the school depends thereon)
till such time as it could be supported without them.

But the care of such boarders as the Sisters took seemed
only to add to their indebtedness. [4]

Father Burns was not replaced until 1889, when the Reverend Michael Meagher was appointed to St. Mary's. The Bishop
apparently placed great hopes in the new pastor, for he established the parish as an irremovable rectorship, little reckon-
ing on the good man's longevity. The huge granite Celtic cross
which marks his grave bears the dates of his priestly career,
1887-1926. Matters must have shown some improvement during
his early years, but the Sisters' salary, meager though it was,
became increasingly difficult to collect, until they finally became dependent on the generosity of the parishioners for their
very sustenance. In 1917 they finally withdrew, departing quietly to avoid any altercation with the aging pastor. By withdrawing the irremovable status from the pastorate, Archbishop
James J. Keane saw to it that the difficulties resulting from so
secure a position would not be repeated.

In 1884 the Reverend Joseph Ascheri of Holden, Missouri,
a town about fifty miles southeast of Kansas City, applied for
Sisters to conduct a school. When she accepted, Mother Clarke
did not understand that the plan involved the keeping of boarders
but, having made all arrangements and having settled the Sisters there, she did not withdraw them.

Having appointed Sister M. Purification from Annunciation
Convent in Chicago, to be the superior of the new mission,
Mother wrote her on September 1, 1884:

Do come home, bring S. M. Balbina with you. I will send
S. M. Urban to S. M. Basil for the time, as it is possible
that the Holden school will not be ready till near Christmas. Bring S. M. Eusebia with you. I will lend her to St.
Mary's, Dubuque for the time. Don't fear, you will get
them back the moment they are wanted. Sister M. Ven-

St. Cecilia Academy, Holden, Missouri

Science Laboratory, Immaculate Conception Academy, 1890

eranda will come with you. Bring her and S. M. Balbina
direct out home when you come. Don't worry. God will
bring all things right.

When word came from Father Ascheri in early October that
he had rented a house for the Sisters until the building then
under construction was ready, Mother wrote to Sister M. Purification:

Sisters Mary Seraphina, Eusebia and Balbina[5] will be
with Sr. M. Gonzaga at latest by Wednesday or Thursday
next. You and Sr. M. Urban can meet them there and
leave from there for Holden. The Rev. Father will rent
a house for the time being, otherwise I would not be willing to let the Sisters go there till the building was finished.
Write to me when you leave Davenport and after you get
to Holden. May God give a blessing to your journey and
efforts there. I will pray for all.

The Sisters were settled in their permanent quarters in the
new St. Cecilia Academy when on January 8, 1885 Sister M.
Purification wrote the following long and troubled letter:

We opened the school in the new house on Monday. It
rained all day. Sr. M. Eusebia had only ten boys and
Sr. M. Seraphina twenty-seven girls. Of course, they
all pay well. There are others to come next week, but
I do not know how many. There are some to come from
the college, but their term will not be up until the first
of Feb.

I said everything I could to Fr. Ascheri against keeping
boarders, but he would not be satisfied. Two came this
week, and we kept them, because I knew their father
would go to him if we refused them. I made no agreement with them nor took any money from them, so that
we can dismiss them at any time, but it will be very hard
to be here if we have to be working against him or dis-
puting with him; however, I will do whatever you tell me.
I know you said you would rather we would not keep
boarders this year, but under the present circumstances
what shall we do? Please write and let me know. He has
put advertisements in the two papers for boarders and
day scholars; this was in the paper before we came here,
and he has renewed it this week again. I think we will not

have much of a school here this year on account of having
begun so late in the season. I am very sorry this mission
was ever begun. It may be good yet, but it is very troublesome now.

Since we moved into the new house he comes oftener than
ever, but perhaps it is because it is a novelty to him yet.
I know he has done a great deal, and has left himself
poor and uncomfortable on account of this house. He has
taken the stoves out of his own rooms to dry this house,
and has had to suffer many other inconveniences also. He
supplies all the coal, bought the beds, chairs, stoves and
desks. All the other things he has left for ourselves to get.
There is not one bit of carpet in the house, but he got
excellent stoves, $60 apiece.

There is a man here that offered to work for his board,
and I thought it would be well to have him while we are
beginning in this house as he saves the Sisters from a
great deal of hard work, such as carrying coal and cleaning the rooms after the workmen finish, etc. After a few
weeks we shall be able to do without him. He sleeps in
Fr. Ascheri's barn. There is a great deal of work to be
done in a new house, besides the water is very inconvenient, but we are to have a well beside the kitchen in
a few days. I know Fr. Ascheri is doing all he can to
help us, he has worked here like a laboring man day
after day, but it is hard to have him visiting so often,
and I have to treat him very coldly on this account in
order not to encourage the visits. Sometimes I pretend
not to see him when passing through the house, and do
not even salute him. I know this is not very polite, but
if I did not act this way he would come oftener.

You see, Mother, I have to tell you all my troubles. I
think it is better to tell them to you than to anyone else,
for you will help me by your prayers and advice, as you
have always done.

The next extant letter of Mother Clarke's was dated November 29, 1885, when sickness had added to Sister M. Purification's problems:

I got your letter with note enclosed. I am sorry but
these things can't be helped. Dear Sister, if Sr. M.

Bertina is no better it may be well for you to let her come home with Sr. M. DeChantal. But if Sister is better and able to help, I have no objection to her remaining with you, but how will we manage, as Sr. M. DeChantal can't come home alone? In March, I will give you a Sister but not before it. How is Sr. M. Seraphina? Give my love to her and all my dear Sisters. May God bless you all.

But Sister M. Bertina Noonan was not destined to get better. She, Sister M. Wenceslaus Riordan and Sister M. Urban Prosser - "an exceptionally beautiful and talented nun" - and her niece, Katie Lawless, were all victims of tuberculosis in those first years at Holden.

Despite all the early discouragements, St. Cecilia's Academy prospered. In 1890 at the suggestion of Father Ascheri the Sisters purchased a former Presbyterian college with its ten-acre campus, and transferred their boarding school there, where they received day students as well. For a time, the boys of the parish remained in the earlier situation, but the arrangements were so inconvenient that a place was made for them at the new site in rooms apart from the girls.

Boarding students came from a distance, especially from Oklahoma and Colorado. In 1900 the school received five Indian girls from Oklahoma. Recollections of the school and teachers came in later years from their alumnae. These indicate that the school regularly served approximately one hundred girls, chiefly in the high school department, where about one third were boarding students. The eighteen members of the graduating class in 1891 passed examinations which secured proper accrediting for their school. Sister M. Urban was "loved by all," wrote one alumna. Sister M. Bertilla was "one of the most brilliant women I have ever known, and an excellent teacher. However, at the time we thought her a veritable ogre. She was very stern and very strict and demanded our best." Sister M. Flavia Littig was a "great pianist." One alumna spoke of a man and wife who attended classes to complete their high school education. The school itself provided "an atmosphere of beauty and holiness," and offered "an excellent course of study."[6]

The academy provided facilities for summer retreats which were attended for years by the Sisters from Kansas City. However, in 1908, the school was closed as a result of an order from the Apostolic Delegate requiring that all novices be retained at the motherhouse for their full canonical year. Since there were thirty-two such novices on the missions at the time the order came, arrangements were made to recall sixteen of them that year, and the remaining number the next year. This necessitated the closing of the boarding schools at Council Bluffs and Iowa City, and the entire school at Holden, as the most expendable of the Congregation's missions. The building at Holden stood idle for some years. In 1914 the property was exchanged for 560 acres of land near Pensacola, Florida which was sold in 1925 for $14,000.

Schools in Kansas City, Missouri would claim the services of many B. V. M. Sisters in the course of the years. Of these, Mother Clarke was responsible for the opening of the first three: Annunciation, St. Joseph and St. Aloysius. At the request of the Reverend William Dalton, Mother assigned six Sisters to open the Annunciation School. They arrived in the city on August 26, 1884. Sister M. Gonzaga, superior of the Davenport academy, and Sister M. Lambertina had gone ahead to make sure that all was in readiness. On their way they visited the Sisters at St. Cecilia Academy in Holden, and had just arrived at the Annunciation rectory when the six pioneers reached there also. They had assembled in Davenport and left there a day or two earlier than expected. The new arrivals included Sisters M. Philippa Sheridan, Leocadia Conway, Eva Whalen, Edna Murphy, Lourdes Brophy, and Chrysostom Dougherty. They were accompanied by Sister M. Editha Flanagan who returned to Davenport as Sister M. Gonzaga's companion.

Father Dalton received all with great graciousness. Although the convent had been painted and its walls whitewashed, its furnishings were incomplete. However, when the parishioners heard that the Sisters had come, they brought many items needed to make the home livable.

Reporting on their first day in Kansas City, Sister M. Gonzaga wrote to "My dearest Mother, "

We thought it would be a beautiful thing to have our Lord come to the house the very first evening of our stay, and, nicer still, to open our new labor of love for God by His blessing and Benediction. When we went to supper, we asked our good Father if he would allow us that great privilege, and he most cordially assented. The day was extremely warm, but we went over, washed and cleaned the altar and prepared the best way we could for our Lord.

They spread new sheets for altar-cloth and antependium, and a blue "counterpane" as a rug on the floor before the altar, borrowed candlesticks and candles from the church, and a small organ from the rectory. With Sister M. Editha at the organ, and Sisters M. Lambertina and Edna forming the choir with her, they had their first Benediction.

Father Dalton was most considerate of the Sisters, and their first years went pleasantly. However, by 1896 the parish had undergone many changes and could no longer support both school and convent. Both were closed in August. However, in 1917 the school was reopened, as an outmission from St. Vincent's, with Sisters M. Celesta Murphy and Melanie Russell in charge. Final closing came in 1966 when schools in the area were merged.

On May 3, 1887 Mother Clarke responded to a letter from the Right Reverend J. Hogan, D. D. , the first Bishop of Kansas City, regarding the opening of a school in the new St. Joseph Parish.

. . . Am I to understand from yours of today that you wish us to have the school building erected? If so, I am sorry to say we have not the means; it would be impossible for us to attempt either to purchase or build. I would do all in my power to provide Sisters, though, as stated in my letter of yesterday.

The Bishop's reply reads:

. . . The ground and house near St. Joseph's church in this city intended for the use of the Sisters are parochial property. The pastor and parents will be required to pay for the property as soon as the bishop may judge them able to do so. Also, of course, the parish will be required and is expected to build the school without delay. It is my wish and you have my invitation to occupy these premises and begin the work of the parochial school without delay. I hope you will be able to do so.

A small mission, opened in Tomah, Wisconsin, in 1880 had just closed with the indebtedness to the Sisters of $500. 00. A notation in Mother Clarke's account book indicates that the Bishop of LaCrosse asked that the pastor's check for $200. 00 be accepted in full payment for the debt. The closing of the mission freed Sisters M. Scholastica McLaughlin, Etienne Fleming and Bonita Breen, who were assigned to St. Joseph School, Kansas City, where Sister M. Albina Craney joined them. Little remains of the history of the school except that it became an out-school from St. Vincent's in 1912. It closed finally in 1914, and the building was converted into a hospital for Negroes.

A third mission opened in Kansas City in the Jesuit parish of St. Aloysius in August 1887, the Reverend James A. Dowling, S. J. , having petitioned Mother Clarke for Sisters. He was not in a position to furnish them with a convent at the time, but they would be accommodated at Annunciation Convent. Their travel would cost nothing as the Sisters were not required to pay fare on the street cars. "From my personal knowledge of the success of your Sisters at our schools in Chicago, I prefer having them, " he wrote. His letter continued with specifications for the Sisters to be sent:

> I would like two Sisters, (1) who have had some experience in schools, & one, at least, in managing - (2) who will be apt to make a favorable impression on our people who most of them of the better class, and (3) who have enough energy and self-denial not to be discouraged by the little difficulties apt to occur in a new school and parish. As far as the spiritual advancement is concerned of the Sisters you may assign, I shall see to that.

Father Dowling's long letter closes with the following assurance of his independent position:

> I shall be candid enough to tell you now, though some would not do it, that your Sisters are my first choice; but I do not bind myself to wait for them in case you refuse them for September coming; especially as some of our Fathers who have other Sisters teaching in our parishes, naturally speak an encouraging word of their favorite teachers, & would only be too glad to aid me in getting them.

Since Sister M. Agatha was willing to spare two Sisters for the place, the school was opened on September 17 as an out-mission from St. Joseph's, however, instead of Annunciation. Sisters M. Esther Warren and Ermine Elliott were in charge of the new school. Father Dowling had fitted a small cottage, 15x15 in dimensions, as classrooms, accommodating thirty-six boys and four girls. Work was started at once on a new school. The new building with its three classrooms was ready for opening the following September. In it, Sisters M. Ermine and Esther, and Sister M. Rosamunda O'Neill taught, the last attempting the impossible in the third room, wall to wall with small boys and girls. After three months her health broke, and Sister M. Tertulla Reynolds came to take her place. Sister M. Melitta Fleming was assigned as music teacher.

It is scarcely surprising that contagion would spread quickly in such crowded quarters. Several of the children died of diphtheria in the winter of 1889-1890, while Sister M. Angelica Small, who had come later, contracted measles, Sister M. Laetitia, whooping cough, and Sister M. Ignatia Pyne, typhoid-malaria. In that year also, Sister M. Remi Wallace was brought home to die of tuberculosis. Yet, after all its early difficulties, the school saw brighter days. A high school for girls was added, many of its graduates joining the Congregation. The changing conditions of the neighborhood may have occasioned the departure of the Jesuit Fathers in 1948. The closing of the high school followed in 1953, and the elementary school in 1966.

A short-lived mission, opened in 1885 at Waverly, Iowa, had Sister M. Lutigarde Ryan as its superior until her death on June 2, 1888. The mission was closed four years later, with no reason recorded for its closing. However, nine young women from Waverly have entered the Congregation in the course of the years, two of them artists, Sisters M. Blanche Fosselman and Blanche Marie Gallagher.

The Holy Rosary School in Milwaukee was opened on October 12, 1885, with Sister M. Crescentia Markey in charge. The school had been built on 2031 Oakland Avenue, Sister M. Agatha superintending the construction. Since the church was still in the planning stage, the Sisters walked each day to the cathedral for Mass.

Planned as a girls' school and financed by the Sisters, it accommodated the small boys also, continuing thus until 1893, when it became fully coeducational. Its early teachers included Sisters M. Rosina Harrigan, Pulcheria McGuire and Evangelista Ryan. After the first year, Sister M. Huberta Byrne came to free Sister M. Evangelista for music. Sister M. Eusebia Mulally served the parish for twenty-six years, ending her days there, where her death was deeply mourned. Another favorite who gave the parish long years of service was Sister M. Rosina Harrigan, who lived out her later years at the Holy Angels Academy, Milwaukee.

Mother Clarke's letter assigning Sister M. Crescentia as superior was typical:

My dear S. M. Crescentia,

I am going to give you charge of a mission. It will not be a heavy one. I beg you not to show any difficulty you may feel about going. God will assist you and I will pray Him to bless you. Show the Sister who replaces you what

you think necessary for the school. I am greatly hurried
- you will hear from me again. May God bless you.
Your affectionate
M. F. Clarke

The contract made with the parish seems strangely one-
sided. The Sisters were to build and finance the convent-
school, their "successors and assigns" to maintain "on the land
hereby conveyed, a Catholic parish school of sufficient capacity
to meet the requirements of the parish in which it shall be
located. " The salary paid the Sisters for their services, even
in a new contract dated 1903, was placed at $200. 00 a year for
each Sister, and "never to exceed $1600. 00 a year for eight fully
capable teachers. " It provided that two or three rooms in the
B. V. M. -owned convent be provided for school purposes, rent
free; that these be supplied with heating apparatus in full repair,
and the necessary toilet facilities. The parish on its part would
pay $50. 00 a year to cover the cost of heating each such room.
As for the teachers, they must be fully competent with "knowledge
of the branches taught and of the latest improved methods, and
have the ability to maintain order. " They were further "to encourage love for vocal music, especially of a sacred nature,
for the purpose of preparing pupils for future service in the
choir. " They must also follow the teaching manual of the
Archdiocese.

High school classes were soon opened under Sister M. Gregory
McGovern, who included in her room the eighth grade girls.
Three seniors and two eighth-graders were graduated at the end
of the 1897-1898 school year.

The price the Sisters paid for serving the parish met its reward, for some eighty young women from it have joined the
ranks of the Sisters in the course of the years. The Sisters continue to staff the school.

In the early 1880's Mother Clarke had discontinued the practice of sending novices on the missions, but she had run into
another problem - the effects of holding them out on the Prairie for two full years beyond their postulancy. Educational
resources there were quite limited, and cultural opportunities
lacking. Their days were taken up largely with the rough labors
of their rural situation. Life on the missions offered them at
least a degree of preparation for the classroom, and a chance
to test their fitness for a life of teaching before the taking of
vows. It was a problem Mother thought proper to discuss with
her Bishop.

St. Joseph's Prairie, Dubuque, Ia.
Feb. 4, 1886

Rt. Rev. Bishop,

It seems unkind in me to write you at this time to bring my little troubles before you while /you are/ suffering on a bed of pain. [7] Yet I rely on your indulgence to bear with me. It regards the two years' novitiate.

The deaths of many of our young and promising members make me feel if the time were divided into one year at home and one year of mission life, it would be less of a strain on them, and afford them a better opportunity of testing their vocation and making them more useful members.

It was never either our Rev. Father's or my intention to keep them two years at home and I feel God had not blest the doing. So I am satisfied that when divided /into one year at home and one year of mission life/ as they return when school closes in June to the Novitiate, they will have until August 15th to prepare for their vows.

We have had so many deaths and such a drain for help that it has been a painful source of trouble to me. I submit the matter as I feel it to you for advice, before bringing it before the Consultors.

When you are able I shall be most grateful for a line. Trusting your limb is improving, and assuring you of the prayers of all,

Your humble
Mary F. Clarke

The plan Mother suggested seems to have been followed for some years thereafter, until again pressures grew in the early 1900's. Then a visit from the Apostolic Delegate led to the recall of thirty-two novices to the motherhouse for their full canonical year. No question was then raised of a second year novitiate to be spent at the motherhouse.

The new parish of St. Brigid's, San Francisco, had been established by Archbishop Alemany on September 10, 1863, and placed in the care of the Dominican Fathers. In 1875 the parish was transferred to the diocesan clergy, and the Rever-

end Peter Bermingham was assigned as its pastor. Several
years later, in the hope of engaging religious to serve a school,
he built a frame schoolhouse, with rooms on the upper floor as
residence for the Sisters. In 1887 Archbishop Patrick W. Riordan,
who had been in contact with the B. V. M. Sisters in Chicago, appealed to Mother Clarke for teachers. Mother sought the advice
of her Bishop as to the wisdom of sending the Sisters to so great
a distance.

> The enclosed letter from the Archbishop of San Francisco
> is the second application which I have received from him
> in regard to sending Sisters. The first was an appeal for
> an academy which he wished our Sisters to open, but
> which I was obliged to refuse owing to our not having the
> members at the time. The second, as you see, is for
> Sisters to conduct a parish school which I do not like to
> refuse, and I think by the time he requires them, we
> would be able to supply them. Do you approve of my send-
> ing them to him if matters can be arranged satisfactorily?
> I will await your answer before giving him a definite
> reply. Please have the kindness to return me the en-
> closed letter. Hoping you are well and asking your bles-
> sing for myself and Sisters,
>   Your humble
>   M. F. Clarke

The Bishop's reply was immediate:

> Dear Madam,
>   The only objection I see to sending Sisters to San
> Francisco as you can spare them is the great distance
> and the difficulty of directing or governing Sisters so
> far from the motherhouse. But considering the growth
> of your Community, manifestly the day is not distant
> when your Rule will have to be revised and other Centers
> of authority created, as it will be found impossible to
> govern a Community so widely dispersed as yours is
> likely soon to be from any one point.
>
> I do not wish to give any advice on this matter, but if
> you conclude to send your Sisters to San Francisco you
> may count on my approval of your action. In that event
> you should send Sisters in whom you have the fullest
> confidence that they would take care of themselves.

Hoping you continue well, I am, dear Madam,
                Yours truly
                John Hennessy, Bishop of
                Dubuque

    Mother Clarke selected Sisters M. Maurice Duffy, Arcadia
Haugh, Magdalen McCristal, and Seratina Mulick for the mission. However, it was not until a week after Mother's death that
the Sisters set out on their long train ride to the coast, their
total fare $197. 52. Departing on December 11, they were ac-
companied by Sister M. Gertrude as far as Sabula, Illinois,
where they met the westbound train from Chicago. The journey
involved four full days of travel. They did not reach their
destination until December 15. All was not yet in order for them,
and the four Sisters were given hospitality until Christmas day
by the Daughters of Charity of St. Vincent de Paul.
    School opened on January 9, 1888, with 140 pupils, but the
attendance grew so rapidly that four more Sisters were soon
added to their number. Arriving on February 4, they were Sisters M. Philip Powers, Prudentia Reilly, Delphine Conway,
and Ascella Nagle. When Mother Gertrude arrived for visitation
on a spring day in 1890, she found Sister M. Ascella in a dying
condition. A second death that spring was that of Sister M.
Magdalen. The Reverend Peter Bermingham, pastor, died too
before the year was out. He was succeeded by the Reverend
John E. Cottle, who still lives in the memory of the Sisters for
his kindness. Within a year of the Sisters' coming, they received as visitors Sister M. Josephine Clarke and Rosalia
Ryan of Mt. St. Joseph Academy in Dubuque.
    For more than sixty years the school's average enrollment
was 500 pupils. St. Bridget[8] Academy served the girls through
their high school years. New buildings were constructed in 1928
and 1936, the centennial year of the parish. The present spacious
convent was constructed in the pastorate of Monsignor John Cant-
well in 1930. Recollections of the 1906 earthquake and other early
missions await the final volume of our series.
    It is unfortunate that after eighty-five fruitful years at St.
Bridget's, its most reverend pastor panicked at the adaptations
to modern needs made by the Sisters after their chapter of renewal in 1967-68. He required their replacement in 1973, preferring the more conservative Sisters of Mercy from Dublin. His
decision was greatly regretted by many loyal parishioners.

    In 1887 Wichita was a rapidly growing town in the Kansas

wheat belt, six hundred miles southwest of Dubuque, with favorable railroad connections. While the general population was open to any of the latest religious fads, most citizens were generally in agreement in their opposition to the Catholic faith. However, with the arrival of increasing numbers of Catholics and the establishment of the diocese of Wichita in 1887, there was promise of greater acceptance. The Reverend Michael J. Casey, as administrator of the diocese pending the appointment of the Most Reverend John J. Hennessy, [9] sought the establishment of a grade school at the pro-cathedral, and a boarding academy for girls. As a close friend of Father Dalton of Kansas City, Father Casey had learned of the B. V. M. Sisters then teaching at the Annunciation School, and was determined to have them for the new diocese. Following his request, Mother Clarke sent Sisters M. Gonzaga and Agatha to investigate the situation. Father Casey's application for Sisters enclosed a statement of conditions to be met in their coming. Mother Clarke's response, dated May 5, 1887, read:

> Your favor of the 18th ult. was duly received, and the enclosed "Statement" is most satisfactory to us, if the terms on which our holy Rule permit us to accept your conditions are satisfactory to you. According to your "Statement, " All Hallows Academy is to be a "quasi Motherhouse. "

> Now, according to our Rule, we are permitted to have but one Mother House proper, and that must be in the County and diocese of Dubuque. We have three principal or "Central Houses, " as we call them - one in Chicago, one in Davenport and one in DesMoines. All Hallows Academy could be a fourth "Central House" of the order, [10] but not a Motherhouse, since we can have but one Novitiate, and that must be here. Now perhaps this may not satisfy you, and I am anxious that you should know it in time. There will be no difficulty about the "three-thousand-dollar" condition, and the salary for two Sisters is satisfactory. If I am not mistaken, our Sisters who visited Wichita told me the house would be furnished for the Sisters; is that so? I could not procure the three thousand dollars in the given time were I obliged to furnish the house besides defraying travelling expenses for the Sisters. I shall be most anxious, Rev. Father, until I hear from you.

Father Casey's reply of May 12 assured Mother that he had

not intended a condition in conflict with the rule. For the academy to be a "Central House" would suffice. He promised to do all he could for the Sisters when they came.

The Sisters for the new mission made an early retreat with a Trappist director, and set out on their long journey, Sister M. Veronica Dumphy,[11] superior of the band of five. The ill-equipped cars chugged along on badly constructed track, spewing smoke and cinders into the windows. It was a weary and dishevelled group that Father Casey met at the station on the twenty-sixth of July, the feast of St. Anne, in 1887. Until the building was completed in mid-August, the Sisters were provided for in the home of Mr. and Mrs. Tangney in the city. When Father Casey drove them out to the site in a hired carriage they must have viewed in dismay the four-story brick building which was to be their boarding school, as it stood stark against the windswept plain stretching to the horizon. Remembering the lush green of her native Iowa, Sister M. Veronica would soon set out rows of seedlings which she watered and tended, only to see them uprooted and blown out of the sandy soil by the persistent Kansas wind. Only by patient replanting of saplings of a sturdier growth, and by much watering, was Sister able to make the beginnings of the beautiful campus that eventually surrounded Mt. Carmel, as the academy came to be called in 1902.

Two of the Sisters were driven each day by the academy's handyman to the downtown school, near the pro-cathedral, while the rest began their labors at All Hallows with twenty boarders and ten day students, all in grade school classes. However, by the end of the year, their number had increased to forty-four. Completing their elementary courses, the students begged to stay on for high school work. Among the first academic graduates in 1892 was Grace Guyton, whose younger sister, the future Sister M. Carlino, was also a boarder in the school.

Meanwhile, however, there had been four years of crop failures, resulting in a severe depression and a drop in the enrollment to just twelve boarders, a time of near destitution for the Sisters. While times improved thereafter, inconveniences continued for many years. The water supply, pumped into the building by a windmill, was as fitful as the wind itself. Stove heat and the light from kerosene lamps required much tending. Two epidemics, of diphtheria and of scarlet fever, brought classes to a halt, and resulted in one death. However, by 1919 the enrollment had grown to two hundred students, and, with the aid of generous benefactors, building had kept pace, adding a wing to each side of the original structure. The discovery of oil, some of it on Indian lands, resulted in prosperity to the area, and the bringing of many bronze-skinned girls to the academy.

The Zingra Club at the first All Hallows Academy

Pupils at All Hallows Academy, September 1887

By 1897 the Sisters for St. Aloysius pro-cathedral school had been provided with a convent, but in that year Bishop Hennessy dismissed them without ceremony when Mother Cecilia refused to permit them to care for the altar and sacristy and to attend evening devotions. Such activities, prohibited by the Constitutions, were to be a bone of contention with many pastors in the next few years.

Mt. Carmel Academy had a long and successful career. Besides the sound intellectual training it provided, the school prepared its graduates for gracious and productive lives. However, as local schools and transportation facilities improved boarding academies became obsolete.

In 1962 when the Christian Brothers purchased the academy property for a boys' school, the Sisters of Charity built a handsome new high school in the city, one of four such schools, two for girls and two for boys. However, by 1973 it had become necessary to merge schools, and the Jesuit-conducted Kapaun joined with Mt. Carmel as the coeducational Kapaun-Mt. Carmel, using the facilities of Mt. Carmel.

In time Father Casey had been disappointed to find himself transferred to the poor little town of Weir, Kansas. Mother could not refuse him when he requested Sisters there, Sister M. Veronica agreeing to be among them. But the people were too poor to support a school, and the Sisters were withdrawn at the end of the year.

While calls for parochial schools were coming increasingly from urban situations, in 1887 the small town of Boone, in the center of the Iowa corn belt, applied for Sisters to staff its Sacred Heart elementary school. Sister M. Borromeo Condon was assigned as superior to the little band of four that constituted its first faculty. The people, predominantly non-Catholic, drew their living from farming or from railroad occupations as the Northwestern Railway early situated its yards there. The early history of parish and school is obscured by the lack of correspondence. The school was never large, each room providing for two grades, but the allegiance of its people to their school was marked. A new Ryan High School, completed in 1969, continued in service but a single year, a shortage of teachers forcing its closing. The elementary classes then moved into the new building where the Sisters continue to serve. Despite the strong Protestant influence in the town, by 1952 twenty-four of its young women had joined their former teachers as B. V. M. 's.

Mother Clarke's health, never robust, had been failing for

some years, yet she continued to carry out the duties of her office. Her last letters, as we have seen, were as clear and decisive as those of her earlier years. Father Damen, S. J. , had given the motherhouse retreat August 6-15, 1887, and, while he asked for Sisters to visit the sick in his parish, it had become quite clear to him that the pressure for teachers had left none free for that work. Mother had seen the Sisters off to Milwaukee, Boone and Wichita, and had made the final arrangements for those who were to leave for San Francisco. A Community of 130 living members at the time of her accession to office had increased to 499 in the eighteen years of her administration, despite the scourge of tuberculosis which had carried off more than one hundred. When she took office, the Community staffed fifteen parish schools and three boarding academies, in addition to their own St. Mary Academy and the Prairie motherhouse. The number had increased to forty parish schools and nine community-owned academies.

The governmental pattern Mother Clarke designed had proven sound, and the administration of the many schools was in the hands of able women, loyal to the directive she had laid down. Her crosses had been many, but in her eyes, all had come from the hands of a loving God. When illness, in the form of severe bronchitis, struck in late November, it came as one more token of that love.

Only a few days before Mother Clarke's final illness, a strange thing happened. Preparations were under way for a reception ceremony on December 8. The white veils and other items of headdress for the clothing of the new novices were to be laundered in ample time. For many years Sister M. Martha Quinn had directed the work of the laundry and cared also for the altar and sacristy. On Saturday afternoon she had prepared for Monday's washing, laying the fire in the wood-burning laundry stove, and placing on the stove the copper boiler filled with fine wash. She planned to draw the water to soak it late Sunday. Then, hurrying to the chapel, Sister began to prepare the altar and vestments for the next morning's Mass. Sister M. Martha, then quite deaf, had been in the sacristy for sometime when she distinctly heard the words, "Go to the laundry. " Thinking she imagined it, she continued with her work, but again the voice came. Again she ignored it, until, as she was leaving the chapel, the warning came a third time. It was quite dark by then, so Sister beckoned Sister M. Mathias, who had been praying in the back of the chapel, to accompany her. Together they hurried across the yard to the laundry. Opening the door, they found the room full of smoke, and flames leaping from the boiler. A spark hidden in the ashes had caught the kindling of Sister's carefully laid fire. The Sisters removed the boiler from the stove, only to find all its contents in ashes - all, with the exception of Mother Clarke's two frilled caps which were not so much as scorched. Sister's spontaneous reaction was: "Mother will never go to purgatory. The fire would not touch even her caps. "

The Sisters often pondered the incident during the ten days while Mother lay ill. The doctor's diagnosis "pneumonia" sounded like a death knell, and they could only pray. All day Thursday, December first, Mother lay in perfect quiet, scarcely breathing. On Friday, Father David Sullivan came from the monastery to administer the last rites, and to watch at her bedside. At three o'clock that afternoon a cablegram arrived from Pope Leo, addressed to her. Though she seemed unconscious, Father bent over her, saying, "Mother, our Holy Father, the Pope, has sent you a blessing and grants you a plenary indulgence at the hour of death. " As she opened her eyes, a look of surprise and delight passed over her face, and she responded: "Thanks be to God. I need it. " Those were her last words. Breathing almost imperceptibly, she lingered until a few minutes past midnight on Sunday morning, when, with the Sisters kneeling about her, the end came. When word reached Father David of her death, he exclaimed, "A saint has died in our midst. "

Of those last hours, the Sisters wrote:

Lightly did the relentless finger of time touch dear Mother Clarke. Her kind face bore few traces of the keen suffering, the many trials and privations attendant on her life work. Her beautiful eyes, in which we had so often read the mildness and sweetness of her disposition, needed no artificial aid even in examining the voluminous correspondence that was so important a part of her daily task. Her gentle hands trembled not when embracing her children, who knelt, one by one, to receive her cherished blessing for the last time. Her vigorous intellect was not weakened even when the chill of death manifested itself; she was fully conscious that her last hour had come, and she approached the judgment seat of God in the same holy dispositions with which, as a truly humble servant, she had ever been blessed.

The Dubuque Daily Herald for December 7 bore on its front page the following simple account:

Yesterday morning all that was mortal of Mother Mary
Frances Clarke was laid in its last resting place. The
funeral was very simple and very impressive. Hundreds
of priests and Sisters of Charity were in attendance,
coming from Chicago and many nearer places where the
order has established houses. High requiem Mass was
celebrated and a touching sermon delivered by the Rt.
Rev. Bishop Hennessy. The feeling of sorrow was universal, and it was made apparent how strong a hold
Mother Clarke had upon the love of all with whom she
ever came in contact. Requiescat in pace.

Meantime, in preparation for her burial, Sisters M. Cecilia
and Lambertina dressed Mother Clarke's body in the habit she
had never worn in life, and a local photographer took the inevitable picture she had so dreaded. Enlarged and framed, it
would hang on the wall of every community room until, after a
careful study of its features and with the guidance of many who
had known and loved Mother, her youthful likeness was caught
in the portrait which has become a favorite with the Sisters
today.
     All the Sisters who could be spared from the missions were
present for the services. Taking turns, they kept vigil beside
the simple casket in the chapel, and day and night continued the
recitation of the rosary. On Thursday morning the clergy of
Dubuque and a large number of priests from the many missions
the Sisters served assembled in the little adobe chapel. There
they chanted the office of the dead. After it, Bishop Cosgrove
of Davenport sang the solemn requiem Mass, assisted by Fathers M. Flavin of DesMoines, L. Roche of Cascade, Roger Ryan,
vicar general of the Dubuque diocese, Hugh McGuire of St. Pius,
Chicago, and P. J. Smith of Iowa City. The final absolution was
given by Bishop Cosgrove, assisted by Father McGuire. Preceded
by a cross-bearer, the body was borne to the grave by six priests
followed by a long procession of clergy and Sisters, the silence
broken only by the rhythm of Gregorian chant. After the casket
had been lowered into the grave, the clergy advanced, one by
one, and dropped loose earth upon it. "Slowly the crowd dispersed, but the Very Reverend Father Alberic, superior of the
Trappist monastery, and Trappist Fathers David and Gregory
remained and quietly, even tenderly, filled up the open grave. "1
     The account of Mother Clarke's death as recorded in the
Sunday School Messenger published by Holy Family Parish,
Chicago, carried the following tribute, a reprint from the Milwaukee Sentinel. Its author would seem to have been Father

Van Goch, S. J., pastor of the Gesu Church there:

> Mother Mary Frances Clarke was one of the most re-
> markable and saintly women in the history of the Catholic
> Church in America. Selected by Divine Providence for a
> sublime mission, the establishment of a congregation
> devoted exclusively to education of youth, she passed
> through many trials and difficulties, but ere called to
> her eternal reward she had the consolation of seeing
> her work crowned with success, and bearing the seal of
> the Church's approbation in the approval of the Supreme
> Pontiffs, Pius IX and Leo XIII. From the little band of
> five who formed the nucleus of the Order, she beheld
> arise a numerous and prosperous Community, thorough-
> ly organized, well equipped for their work, with thou-
> sands of children under their direction and a wide field
> of usefulness open before them.
>
> The life of Mother Clarke when written will form some
> of the brightest pages in the Catholic history of our
> country, and be another proof that Almighty God watches
> over His Church at all times and in all places, and
> raises up those who are to supply its special needs in
> every age and clime. Mother Mary Frances Clarke was
> undoubtedly such a chosen instrument. By her life-work
> and her virtue, she has written her name among the just
> who are held in everlasting remembrance. May she rest
> in peace.

On December 11, Father David sent to the Reverend Editor
of the Ave Maria, a monthly published at South Bend, Indiana,
a deeply appreciative account of Mother Clarke which appeared
in the next issue of that publication. His account ended with the
lines:

> Her simplicity, sincerity and kindly disposition, like a
> secret magnet, attracted all who came within the range
> of her acquaintance. Their affections were drawn by her
> good qualities, and their veneration by her great ones.
> The most convincing proof of this was the many bitter
> tears shed around her bier when God called her home.

Twelve years after Mother's death, the Reverend Michael
Nichols of Nevada, Iowa, wrote to a postulant:

. . . The good example of Mother Clarke, the most pious,
most holy and humblest creature I ever laid eyes on, is
enough to encourage you in your holy calling. I have seen
millions of people, young and old, on both sides of the
Atlantic, both secular and religious, but no person has
ever laid the impression on my mind of true humility put
in practice as Mother Clarke. I have no doubt but that she
will be numbered among the canonized saints of the Church
of God.

But the most complete tribute paid to Mother Clarke was contained in the eulogy pronounced over her by her Bishop at the
burial Mass:

. . . My acquaintance with her was comparatively slight.
I saw her not more, perhaps, than twice a year on an
average, since I came to Dubuque, and then only for a
few minutes. But few and short as were the interviews,
they left impressions that were highly favorable to her.
Those impressions, like those of heat and cold on the
body, were spontaneous. They were made without a
thought of making them on the one side, or of receiving
them on the other. The visits were on business and
were as short as the business in hand allowed.

The appearance, the dress, the bearing and the surroundings of Mother Clarke spoke to you of humility, meekness,
the spirit of poverty in the midst of abundance, self-
denial, mortification and similar virtues. To a stranger,
she would look like a poor, desolate old lady, whom the
Sisters in their charity had taken in to provide for in her
old age. No one would think of her as the foundress of
a large and prosperous community. . . To her, prosperity
and adversity were welcome alike. She regarded them as
coming from the hand of God for his own honor and glory.
Like all good Christians, she was in the world but not
of it.

Beneath that very humble exterior of this feeble little
woman, there was a remarkably clear mind and sound
judgment, and a wealth of information at all times on the
matter under consideration. Her letters on business connected with her office were models. They were clear,
concise, and to the point, and ever characterized by humility and charity. I was so struck by the simplicity and

precision of these letters that I asked more than once
whether they were or not written by herself. That humble exterior hid away a mind of no ordinary ability, an
ability which became manifest at the call of duty only,
and then in the utmost simplicity and apparent unconsciousness.

I never perceived in Mother Clarke the least sign of
selfishness or worldliness, or ambition, or of any in-
ordinate desire regarding the growth of the community or
its temporal prosperity. Her only desire seemed to be to
do the will of God in all things, regardless of consequences.
She seemed to keep that holy will ever before her and to
bow to its dispensations. On all important occasions she
sought its expression from the lips of the Bishop. I do
not think she ever made a foundation in this or in any
other diocese without having obtained, directly or indirectly, my sanction, or without believing that it had been obtained. The submission of these undertakings to me was
not only an act of submission to her Bishop, but seemed the
promptings of faith to ascertain the will of God. Had I at
any time refused sanction, or had I discouraged any project, how dear soever to the community or to some of its
members, I believe that from that moment all her influence
would have been directed to its abandonment.

Mother Clarke led the life of a recluse. She loved solitude.
I saw her plain apartment only once, I think, a few months
ago, and it appeared to me admirably suited to the tenant.
To love solitude is not an impulse of nature. . . She loved
it because it was to her a place of mental activity, a place
of prayer, of meditation, of conversation with God and her
guardian angel, and of profitable thought as to how she
could best correspond with God's designs and promote His
glory. . . It is in that solitude she nourished and strengthened that life and those habits of thought and speech and
action which belonged decidedly and definitely to the supernatural order, though they seemed as easy and as natural
and as simple as the movements of a child. She was a child
of grace and an instrument in the hands of Divine Providence
for the performance of a great work. It is such as she
God loves to choose, according to the saying of St. Paul:
"The weak things of the world hath God chosen that He
may confound the strong."

And to the Sisters the Bishop said:

A new era is now opening before you. Heretofore, as a
community, you have rested on a solid granite base of
humility, poverty, mercy, justice, truth and sanctity.
Mother Clarke was this foundation. She is no more. Let
it be your fervent prayer that her spirit may descend to
you and to her successors. Keep the memory of her virtues forever in your hearts.

In the face of all this, it becomes trivial to repeat the following. Yet that the record be complete it seems necessary to include the testimony of one who knew Mother well, having cared
for her room and her wardrobe for many months. Sister M.
Henrietta Motie attested that she and others had seen Mother
Clarke at times raised in the air after Holy Communion. Father Donaghoe had, for that reason, required that she receive in
the sacristy or in her own room.

Sister also testified to a phenomenon of which others have
also spoken - too many to be lightly dismissed - of encounters
with evil spirits which left marks and bruises on Mother's person. Sister added that she and many others had seen the marks,
but Mother had strictly forbidden them to speak of the matter.

It was one of the Sister's duties to bring Mother her mail.
She often saw Mother, after reading a letter, kneel beside her
chair wholly absorbed in prayer and quite unconscious of Sister's presence.

Mother Clarke's poverty was extreme. Sister M. Henrietta,
having laundered her simple calico dress, found it badly worn
and asked Mother if she could make her a new one. She was
met with a quiet refusal and the dress was in use long after.
The one small stove in her room she fed sparingly, and she
would not waste the least scrap of paper or length of thread. 13
Copies of her letters written on the backs of old envelopes remain in the files today.

Accounts are many of tearful novices sent to Mother Clarke to
report a broken cup, a torn apron or a habit snagged in the
tomboyish climbing of a tree or the scaling of a fence. Tears
were quickly dried when, after appraising the damage, Mother
would suggest that Sister M. Rose, or another practiced in
mending, would make it quite as good as new. As for the cup
or the dish, perhaps it had been cracked before - at any rate,
it wasn't broken purposely, so no great harm had been done.
A sip of wine and a sweet cracker, or a bit of candy was a

soothing antidote, and the smile and blessing with which such a session ended provided a memory cherished through a lifetime.

While no signed and witnessed testimonial remains of these details, they confirm stories that have long been a part of the Congregation's oral tradition.

St. Mary academy, Emmet Street, Dubuque,
built in 1884

192

Notes

1 The account of some of these establishments has been recorded in earlier chapters.

2 By the time of Mother Clarke's death in December 1887, 119 Sisters had died of the disease, the first of these, Frances O'Reilly in 1845, and one of the original five, Catherine Byrne, in 1866. Of the 696 who had entered since the Congregation's beginning, 190 had died or departed.

3 Sister M. Agnes Burke had served a brief term as visitor - 1881-1884.

4 A number of small remittances to the Sisters at Ackley appear in the account book during this period, indicating that Mother Clarke met immediate needs without relieving the pastor of his responsibility.

5 Sisters M. Seraphina Short, Eusebia Mullaly, Balbina Durbin, and Urban Prosser.

6 Sister M. Claude Coffey, aged ninety-six and presently a resident of Marian Hall, the Sisters' infirmary in Dubuque, went to Holden in 1898, as a second-year novice. The people of Holden, she says, were largely Protestant and many of the boys who attended the day school were non-Catholic but most respectful. Sister taught science, performing simple electrical and other experiments. Sister speaks of a non-Catholic astronomer who, on going to Europe for a year of study, left his telescope available to the Sisters. They found much interest in studying the constellations on clear nights.

7 The Bishop was suffering from a broken leg at the time.

8 The spelling of the parish name seems gradually to have anglicized to the present St. Bridget.

9 The most Reverend James O'Reilly had died as the first Bishop-elect of Wichita.

10 In 1915 when the system of provinces was established, the central house promise was fully realized, the academy then being established as the official residence for the provincial of Holy Family Province. A sophomore at the academy, Helen

Wright, the future Mother Consolatrice, recalls the arrival of the first provincial, Sister M. Adora Caverly, when she came on visitation and to establish her residence at the academy.

11 Sister, whose family name is sometimes written "Dunphy, " had entered the Community from Burlington, Iowa in 1861. She was the only novice to make her novitiate at the Davenport academy where her novice mistress, Sister M. Margaret Mann, was superior at the time.

12 Details from unidentified notes in the B. V. M. archives.

13 The above details were communicated to Sister M. Corita Slattery, B. V. M. , by Sister M. Henrietta Motie, who entered the Community from Davenport in 1867, and who was Sister's superior at St. Mary Convent, Pontiac, Illinois from 1912-1918. It was during those years that Sister M. Henrietta shared many early memories. The writer lived in the same mission with Sister M. Henrietta from 1922-1924, and knew her as a woman of sound mind and lovable disposition even in her advanced years.

SELECTED LETTERS
OF
MOTHER MARY FRANCES CLARKE

T he basis for our selection of Mother Clarke's letters is our desire to reveal, insofar as they permit, her personality, her spirit, and her relations with her Sisters and with others with whom her correspondence has been preserved. Care has been taken to avoid duplication of subject matter and the inclusion of matter that has no particular significance. They have been edited for easier reading, especially as to punctuation and the supplying of connectives omitted in hurried writing. Only occasionally has it been necessary to correct spelling. Since all letters were addressed from the St. Joseph motherhouse, that heading has been eliminated.

To Father Donaghoe at the academy at Davenport:

Feb. 23, 1865

Very Rev. and Dear Father
I wish you every happiness both spiritual, and temporal on this your seventieth birthday. Father Kinsella arrived last evening, heard the confessions said mass this morning and gave Holy Communion. He was writing to his sister and I thought it a good chance to send this to the post. All here are just as you left. I trust in God you are well. I hope you will take care of yourself. I hope Sister Mary Margaret's eyes are better. Give my love to her, Josephine, Alexis, and all my Dear Sisters. Mrs. Golden* is well and was out this morning. Father is waiting. May God send you safe home.

Mary - -

* Father Donaghoe's widowed sister, Jane Golden, spent her last years with the Sisters at St. Joseph's.

The following is the only extant letter of Mother Clarke's to Sister Margaret Mann, then superior at the Immaculate Conception Academy, Davenport. It is dated June 21, 1867.

Our dear Father received your letter last evening. He told me to write a few lines to you, and tell you not to be cast down or discouraged, but listen to all without reply, no matter how unjust or injurious to us it may be. He thinks that when all that can be said and done is exhausted, his good Mother will come to our aid, as she has always done, and bring us through. Put the Sisters on their guard to be prudent, and silent, and if even our schools are injured for a time don't be uneasy. Go on steady and quiet, and offer all you suffer through the sacred heart of our dear Mother to the holy heart of her dear Son. They will help us, and all will come right again. You know that in Chicago and other places there are several communities*, and as our dear Father says, if God is served it is no matter by whom. He is midling well, thank God, but not strong as he is living on gruel. I don't think it would be prudent for him to go down in the great heat, and he thinks it will not be well for you to come up.

Father Scallan was here yesterday; he did not comply with the conditions of building, so he will not get Sisters. The sick Sisters are about the same; they were at Mass, and received Holy Communion yesterday. They seem quite happy. I fear you are suffering from the heat, as well as your anxieties. Don't lose courage. After thirty-five or six years of bitter crosses and labours, you will gain the crown at the end. Keep up the Sisters, give my love to them. Father will soon write to you himself. We commenced a novena to St. Aloysius today for all our schools.

Your ever affectionate

Mary

* It seems that other communities were coming in to Davenport, but none is listed in the Catholic Directory until the establishment of Mercy Hospital there in 1869.

The following letter is addressed to her lawyer and agent, the Honorable W. J. Knight, who gave Mother Clarke signal service in many aspects of her administration.

April 24, 1879

Respected Sir,

I send you all the detached receipts I have to my knowledge. I also send you Mr. McNulty's book. It may aid you. I send plats of surveys. You will see in one the names of persons who bought land from Rev. Fr. Donaghoe be-

fore his death; none has been sold since, although we
have some land that is useless to us which we have
wished to dispose of, but I do not know why we have
been disappointed always. I send you papers belonging
to mineral lots in Dubuque. It is thought they are near
the late purchase and contain about 8 acres. I have
tried to keep all the deeds and papers belonging to the
community safe. If you think necessary at some leisure
time to see them I shall send them to you. But if you
do not charge the full amount for your labor and trouble
to repay you for your valuable time I would not have
satisfaction in proposing these affairs to you.
    I pray God to bless yourself and family.
    Yours humbly,
Mary F. Clarke

    The following three letters are unaddressed. The first is to
a young Sister undergoing her first classroom experience:

My Child,
    I hope you are well and that you are quite grown up and
serious by this time as becomes your important duty. I
need not tell you to be kind and affectionate, and to have
patience with the dear little boys. Teach them to know
God and His Blessed Mother. Teach them their prayers
and catechism, and teach them obedience and respect
for their parents. All this they will never forget, and
it may be the means of saving their precious souls at the
end of perhaps sinful lives, for there is no one safe in
this dangerous world. Do not lose sight of the children
for a moment while they are under your care. You will
have a great reward.

Dec. 30, '82
My dear Sister,
    I received yours with the enclosed sum safely. May
God bless you for it. My crosses are numerous, but
thank God they are more against myself than any one
else. I will try and bear them as well as I can and offer the merits if any for my dear Community. Excuse
this poor scribble. Give my love, asking God to bless
you all.
    Your affectionate
Mary F. Clarke
It is so dark today I cannot see.

Nov. 26th, 1886

My dear Sister

Your remittance came safe. I needed it. I hope you
and my dear Sisters are well. Did I tell you we lost our
hogs which was a great loss to us. They died of some
sickness. I would ask you if you could lend me a little
money if you had it to spare before Christmas. I never
asked such a favor from the Sisters before but I can not
help it now. If you can not spare it, don't send it. May
God bless you all.

Your affectionate

M. F. Clarke

This letter addressed to a prospective postulant was the introduction of Sister M. Eusebia Mullaly to the Community. Sister entered in 1881 from Dubuque receiving the Community
number 500.

Dear Child,

Sister Mary Sebastian did speak of you to me, but as
it is a whole year since that time, I waited to hear from
yourself, as I could then be certain you were still earnest
in your desire to consecrate yourself to God. Now that I
am assured of this, and being urged thereunto by the Sisters who know you, I will not hesitate to admit you August
15th or Sept. 8th. Sister Mary Michael also recommended
you, having known you favorably in school. Pray fervent-
ly that God may direct you in your choice. The list of clothing you will find enclosed.

November 10, '83

Rev. E. Gray
Dixon, Illinois

Dear Rev. Father,

Your favor of the 7th inst. is at hand. You state the
Archbishop has already conveyed the Dixon property to
our Community. This astonishes me. I was not aware that
any such agreement had been made. Sisters Gonzaga and
Agnes returned to me immediately after seeing you in
Dixon and informed me that they came to no decision as
to the purchase of that property; that they told you we
could do nothing before March next, in the way of pur-

chasing or sending Sisters; and that, in the meantime,
you could dispose of it to other parties, should a favorable opportunity present itself.

Now, Rev. Father, owing to the pressure of the times,
I find it impossible to purchase the property on any conditions; but will, according to promise, send you Sisters
in March or September next, should you so desire, providing that the necessary arrangements can be made.
I am, Rev. Father,
        Most respectfully yours,

                            Mary Frances Clarke

The Sisters of St. Dominic, Sinsinawa, Wisconsin, served this
parish under the Rev. Thomas P. Hodnett from August 1874
until Father Hodnett's transfer to a Chicago parish in 1883. His
successor, The Reverend Eugene Gray, "a very old. . . typical
Irishman. . . kind-hearted . . . of an impetuous disposition, "
succeeded him, and closed the school in 1883. It was not reopened until 1897. (Sister M. Paschala O'Connor, O. P., Five
Decades, 1849-1899. Sinsinawa Press, 1954, p. 181.)

                                    Jan. 28, '84
Rev. Fr. Damen,
        Your two letters of Nov. 6th and Jan. 19th were duly
recd. Poor health is my apology for delaying so long in
replying. Thank God, I am now better but very weak. I
am grateful that our Sisters under your kind care and
that of Rev. Fr. Corbett are so comfortably fixed. Regarding the retreat, I will be satisfied with any arrangement that may be made as I have always done. I regret
not being able to comply with your request for two Sisters to visit the sick. There are no Sisters but novices,
the sick and old.

Like many of the copies of letters Mother Clarke retained, this
was unsigned.

        The following three letters were addressed to Sister M.
Baptist Seeley, DesMoines.

                                    May 17, 1884
My dear Sister,
        Your letter containing the draft came safe. How strange

about those two places. God in his wise designs must
direct it so. I trust He will direct in the future what
will be for our good. I don't know what would be advisable about that place in the suburbs. It is a matter
you should well consider and take advice regarding it
and let me know, as I only wish what will be for the
glory of God, the welfare of my Sisters and the good
of the children. How near to the church and school
are the two colleges you mentioned?

S. M. Seraphia* sent me word by S. M. Gertrude
that her daughter, Mrs. Smith, asked if she sent a free
pass to & from where she lives, if Sister would be permitted in vacation to see her, as it would be too hard
for her to travel with her two babies. Let me know
your views before I write to S. M. Seraphia. I hope
yourself, S. M. Michael and all my dear Sisters are
well. I will ask God to bless you all.

Your affectionate

M. F. Clarke

* Sister Mary Seraphia, Mary M. Mix, widow, entered from
Dubuque on December 8, 1879, at the age of 47. She died
from a heart condition at St. Joseph Academy, DesMoines,
September 2, 1887.

Undated

My dear S. M. Baptist,

It is a long time since you wrote, perhaps not to you
who must be very busy between both houses. S. M. Maxilinda is in delicate health & her Sister, Mrs. McCormick,
has written requesting to have her go to DesMoines for a
while. Would it be advisable, and could she stay with
you while there? Let me know immediately, as I want
to answer the lady. How is S. M. Michael, and all my
dear Sisters in both houses? When will you have to make
a payment and will you be able to meet it? Tell me whether
or not immediately, as I will try to collect all I can to
help. Give my love to all. I will ask God to bless you.

In haste,

M. F. Clarke

April 8th, 1886

My dear S. M. Baptist,

I send you a draft for $650.00 to meet your next pay-

ment. I can not promise to be able to help you any more
this year. God is good, and if He, who knows all things,
gives me the means, I shall share it in helping you, but
you must not be disappointed if I can not.

The expenses this year with us are enormous between
sickness, death, etc., etc., but God permits all. I hope,
dear Sister, you are well. How is dear Sister M. Venantia?
Is she better? Give my love to my dear Sisters.

Your affectionate

M. F. Clarke

Anne Seeley, Sister M. Baptist, entered March 1, 1853, from
Elk Grove, Wisconsin, at the age of 24. Superior at St. Ambrose,
DesMoines, 1877-1885, then at St. Joseph Academy, 1885-1886.
She spent her later years at the motherhouse where she held official positions until her death, June 19, 1897. She was a convert to the faith during her years as a student at the Prairie
academy.

To a Sister in need who had written with too much diffidence
to make her situation clear, Mother wrote:

I received yours of the 28th ult. in which you did not
explain your circumstance as clear as you have done in
your last of the 17th, or at least I did not understand
you so well. If I did I would have sent you $100.00 which
I enclose now. It troubles me to think you have suffered.
You know our dear Lord, who is our banker never lets
us want.

Your affectionate

M. F. Clarke

Addressed to Sister M. Emerita Fahey

Aug. 8th, 1885

My dear Sister,

I have just read your letter, and have only time to say
if your dear mother is dangerously ill, you can go see
her immediately after retreat. May God bless you.

Your affectionate

M. F. Clarke

Julia Fahey entered April 16, 1879 from Muscatine, at the age
of 15, and served as superior of Our Lady of Angels Academy,
Lyons, Iowa, from 1924 until her death in 1929.

Nov. 10th, 1885

My dear Mrs. Brown,

I have just learned through a letter received from
Sister Mary Josephine of Mr. Brown's noble gift to the
Sisters of Mt. St. Joseph's. This act, with those he did
personally for them while living shall ever be held in
grateful remembrance by myself and Community.

We have been praying for him as a benefactor, but
this adds to our obligation of ever doing so for him, yourself and your devoted children, for whom I ask God's
choicest blessings. Assuring you, dear Mrs. Brown, of
my deep, heartfelt thanks and prayers for you and yours,

I am very sincerely,

Mary Frances Clarke

This letter of condolence went to the father of Sister Teresa
McDonald on January 8, 1886:

My dear Friend,

Our little angel Sister Teresa passed away from earth
about fifteen minutes ago, at a quarter of 10 A. M. Not
a struggle or even a sigh. We tried to send you a telegram but could not get it to you in Holbrook. Please
notify her brother James. Katie did not come.

May our dear Lord comfort you, my dear Friend, in
this your sorrow, and remember, our sorrow is her joy
at this moment. She is a happy, happy child - no more
care, no more sorrow, no more of life's bitter trials
for her. She is safe in the arms of our Father in Heaven.
Again may God comfort you, you have all our sympathy.

Your sincere friend,

Mary Frances Clarke

And to Sister M. Laurinda on the death of her sister:

I was truly sorry that you were not in time to see
your dear sister before she died, but God permits all
that happens, and will accept the sacrifice. Her loss to
your loved parents and family is her gain. And her happy death must be their great consolation now. Sister
M. Agatha is here and tells me what a loss your dear
sister is to your aged parents. Now, dear child, as
you have given satisfaction, I will let you remain for

the present with S. M. Agatha in order to give them
consolation in seeing you, and that your advice may be
a solace and comfort. I feel that you will be as faithful in the future as you were in the past. Be a good
obedient child and give my regards and sympathy to
your good parents. We are praying for the soul of your
dear departed sister. May she rest in peace. May God
bless you.

The following three letters have been selected from ten written to Sister M. Benvenuta, O. P. , at Sinsinawa, Wisconsin,
regarding her sister's condition. Written under Mother Clarke's
direction, they all bear her signature. Sister M. Flocella,
B. V. M. , died September 10, 1886. The originals of the letters
are in the Dominican archives at Sinsinawa.

J. M. J.

Feb. 5, 1886

Dear Si ster Benvenuta,
    It pains me to have to tell you that our dear child Sr.
Flocella begins to sink rapidly. Indeed if she continues
as she has been during the past three days, she can
scarcely last till the middle of March.
    Since I wrote you last she has had various changes
from better to worse. Yet, we did not give her up. We
made several novenas for her, and she and we had every
hope until now, when there seems no hope left. Evidently our dear Lord wants her, and will take her, and surely she can not go in a better time. She is well prepared
and quite resigned, although she did not give up hope of
recovering until 2nd inst. We have written to her home.
I know her poor father and mother will feel her death
very, very much. Indeed, so will each member of the
family. That is the only thing troubling her - "how they
will feel at home. " May our dearest Lord console them
each and every one, as only He can do.
    Begging the prayers of your Community for our dear
young Sister, and assuring you of our sympathy for you
and the entire family, believe me,
        Yours very sincerely,

Mary Frances Clarke

Undated

Dear Sister M. Benvenuta,

Your kind letters were received this morning. Our dear Sr. M. Flocella is writing you a few lines herself; and I will only say this time that she is giving you a correct account of her condition at present. She has been getting better ever since I wrote you last. How permanent this improvement may be, God alone knows. You and your good Sisters will, I am sure, continue to unite your prayers with ours for her, and who knows what God may be pleased to do. Surely so many prayers, Masses, Communions, etc., offered in such good faith must have great weight with God. Her brothers in the city, as well as all at home are very kind and attentive, doing everything in their power to help us to keep her alive & well. We are indeed truly grateful to them all. They do not worry her at all, but keep up very bravely before her. Her poor father finds it impossible to keep in her presence, so he comes but seldom to see her. Of course, the boys keep him posted. You will hear from us often.

Most truly yours,

Mary Frances Clarke

J. M. J.

Aug. 27, '86

Dear Sister Benvenuta,

Our dear child Sr. M. Flocella still lingers - is just alive, and not much more. No telling how long she may be with us. Some of the Sisters think she may last through next month, others think she cannot possibly hold out so long. These warm days are terrible on her. She was so pleased to hear from you, and is glad you are remaining at home this year. She is patient and good and resigned as usual - is very much weaker and thinner than when you were here.

She sends you her warmest love, and says please continue to pray for patience for her, and thank all your good Sisters for their prayers, and beg them to continue. When she goes to Heaven, she will pray for you all in return.

Very truly yours,

Mary Frances Clarke

Sister suffers much from the cough, and from the same pain she had when you were here. . .

Sister M. Flocella died September 10, 1886.

June 11th, 1886

My dear Sister Mary Aimee*

I was glad to get your letter. It pleased me much to know you are nearly as well as ever. I am sure you will be a nice little housekeeper in time, and a good little manager and will try to improve by your mistakes. I know by experience. I could give you examples by my own mistakes. It has given me compassion for others. I did not lose courage and by that I conquered. I am told you have a great plantation the care of which will surely make you well. May God bless you all.

Your affectionate

M. F. Clarke

*As a novice, Sister M. Aimee Watson had the care of Mother Clarke's room. She entered September 8, 1882, from Chicago at the age of 17. Childlike in her ways, she often forgot herself and sang as she went about her work, to Mother's quiet delight.

Addressed to Reverend John Kemper, historian for the Church in Iowa

Mar. 25, '86

Dear Rev. Father,

You are no doubt looking for the promised "items" for your book, but I hope I do not disappoint you too much when I tell you that upon reflection, I have yielded to a certain natural repugnance of mine to have anything of the kind in print during my lifetime. I refused good Father Laurent the same request once before.

Had I been able to see you when you were here, I could have better explained my objections than by writing, but I feel you will understand me, even as it is.

Your kindness to our Sisters merits that I should gratify your every desire, but this one your extended kindness will release me from. Believe me, dear Rev. Father,

Yours gratefully & sincerely,

Mary Frances Clarke

Addressed to the Reverend William Dalton, Annunciation
Parish, Kansas City. Father Dalton merits the appreciation
of the Congregation as the first priest to manifest this consideration for the Sisters. However, it was a privilege Mother
Clarke was not prepared to grant, especially as it could not
be shared by all.

Dear Rev. Father,
    Your favor of the 3rd inst. was received yesterday. I
remember hearing of "Excelsior Springs" last vacation.
It is exceedingly kind of you to make provision for our
Sisters there, and I assure you, Rev. Father, I am more
grateful than I can ever express. But, I am sorry to say
I cannot grant permission for the Sisters to go there lest
it should give rise to difficulties which you can understand - rather, anticipate - only by being in my position.
Trusting that you will understand me, as I understand
you and your great kindness in this instance, I remain
in J. M. J. ,
    Your humble serv't,
                                        Mary F. Clarke

Addressed to Sister Mary Leobina Moore

                                        July 3, 1887
My dear Sister,
    You tell me next year your term for vows of three
years will be up. So, dear child, you can just renew
them again, and I trust in God that at the end of the
next year it will be a pleasure for me to admit you
again for another term. I am sure if you keep Rule well
it will ensure for you the blessing of God and fidelity
to all the Vows require of us. Unless we keep Rule we
will neither be good nor happy religious. I know too that
you thank God who has aided you all so much. Love Him
much, dear child, in return for all. May He bless you.
    Your affectionate
                                        Mary F. Clarke

Katie Moore entered March 19, 1883 from Davenport at the age
of 19.

May 12, 1887

My dear Sister M. Ignatia,
Your dear letter so long received I kept before me
till now, so that I could send you even a few lines. It
is a great pleasure for me to hear from my loved and
devoted Sisters, but I fear many of them have me down
in the black book as a bad correspondent. I know I
deserve it richly, yet my heart is with each and all, no
matter how distant from me, and daily do I recommend
you all to God's loving care and that of the Holy Family.
May they bless each of my children at dear Immaculate
Conception.
Your affectionate

M. F. Clarke

Libbie Pyne entered July 7, 1877 from Chicago at the age of
20. Sister had a long life of superiorships: at St. Pius, Chicago,
1890-1894; St. Mary's, Dubuque, 1897-1900; St. Mary's, Elgin,
1900-1903; Council Bluffs, 1906-1908; St. Joseph Academy,
DesMoines, 1908-1912; I. C. A. , Davenport, 1915-1921; and St.
Aloysius, Kansas City, 1925-1931.

July 13, 1887

My dear Sister Mary Anacleta
I did not see your dear little letter with the others
and I am pleased you sent me word so promptly as I
would be very sorry to overlook you, dear child. I do
grant you the desired permission with all my heart to
make your holy vows, also to renew them at the proper
time. May our sweet Mother and St. Joseph obtain grace
for you to observe them well. Thank God often, love
Him much in return for all His gifts. Pray for sinners
& for the holy Souls in Purgatory.
Your affectionate

Mary F. Clarke

Lucy Grady entered August 15, 1884 from Chicago at the age
of 22.

August 25, 1887

My dear Sister M. Xavier,
Just a few lines to say I have written to dear S. M.
Gonzaga who will give you this note - that you are now
to take charge of the Academy. I know you will be con-

siderate for Sister and she will aid you. And God, I
trust, will bless you all. We will pray for you at home.
In haste, your affectionate

M. F. Clarke

Addressed to Sister M. Antoinette Murphy.

Aug. 26, 1887
My dear child,
Yours of the 24th is just received and I hasten to
relieve you. Yes, child, I will let you come up to
S. M. Thecla and will write to S. M. Veronica to go
with you as far as Kansas City and S. M. Andrew will
come to Dubuque with you. I only sent you there thinking
it was for the best. May our sweet Mother and St. Joseph
assist you, my dear child, under this very heavy trial,
which will be in future years a trial for others in similar
circumstances. May God bless you and aid you to bear
this generously for His love.
Your affectionate

M. F. Clarke

Lizzie Murphy entered September 8, 1883 from Chicago at the
age of 18.

Addressed to S. M. Veronica Dumphy, superior at All Hallows, Wichita.

Oct. 26, 1887
My dear Sister,
The first few lines I write shall be to you. I was not
able before. The letter containing the money and all your
other dear letters was received by me. It pained me to
hear you were so overpowered and yet to be unable to
send you help from here. I am most anxious to hear from
S. M. Agatha, but not a line since she went there.
Write and let me know how you and all are. God bless
you and all my dear Sisters. I would write to them were
I able. I thank you and all for your many acts of kindness.
Your affectionate

M. F. Clarke

Margaret Dumphy (Dunphy) entered March 1862 from Burlington

at the age of 19. She was the first superior at Sacred Heart,
Chicago, 1873-1884; at All Hallows, Wichita, 1887-1893;
Council Bluffs, 1896-1897; Mt. Carmel, Dubuque, 1897-1900.
Sister then volunteered for the short-lived mission at Weir,
Kansas.

Addressed to Sister M. Marcelliana McFadden at Our Lady
of Angels Academy, Clinton. Sister had just replaced Sister M.
Anastasia Mulgrew as superior of the academy, where the latter had served from 1871 to 1887. It would seem that Sister M.
Anastasia was not too happy at having been relieved of office.
She would serve again, 1890-1896 and 1899-1905, remaining in
residence there from its opening in 1871 until her death in 1910.

My dear Sister,
    Do you think, dear child, I have forgotten you, or
that your letter and those of the other dear Sisters from
Our Lady of Angels were not appreciated? I assure you
and them, the more so as it gratified me to hear they
acted as Religious should when the change was made. I
missed my dear S. M. Anastasia's letter among them.
I can never forget what she has been to me during her
charge of the house. God blessed her efforts there, I
am sure, and I pray that He may continue His blessing
on all. Give to all my love, and thanks for their nice
letters. I read every one of them but this must serve
as an answer to all, so read it for them. I hope you are
all well and the school doing well. I am anxious. Let
me hear from you soon. May God bless you and each
of my dear Sisters. I would name them were I able.
    Your ever affectionate
                                    M. F. Clarke

REGARDING SCHOOLS

The following educational principles and directives were
included by Mother Clarke in Chapter IX, "Regarding
Schools, " of the Custom Book of 1884. They were repeated in succeeding issues until that of 1908. In that
year only specific directives contained in the chapter
were retained, the principles enunciated all being sacrificed, perhaps as taken for granted.

It is from the motives that animate us, that all our actions
are pleasing or displeasing to God. As Religious, and especially as Religious Teachers, how much more does this apply to us
than those trying to sanctify themselves in the world.

The end of our Institute being the salvation of our souls,
worked out in the salvation of our neighbor through education
of youth, how deeply penetrated we should be with the importance
of fitting ourselves thoroughly for this sublime vocation. Of one
thing, then, let us be convinced from the beginning, that we can
never attach our pupils to us and cause them to take pleasure in
acquiring a knowledge of our Holy Religion, unless we can justly merit their confidence and that of their parents, in our ability
as efficient teachers; if both one and the other find not in our
schools what they could find in others. Let us then, acquire
and impart secular knowledge with a view to this, and with a
holy and intelligent zeal, keep our schools progressive with the
times in which we live; by inventiveness and forethought, utilize
our knowledge and our time to advance our pupils judiciously,
and thus secure for our schools a good name, which will be the
bait to draw young and innocent souls from the schools of in-
fidelity and immorality.

The profession of teaching is so fraught with interests that
are to tell both for time and eternity, that to assume such a
duty without study or preparation, is a responsibility that the
reflective mind must instinctively shrink from with fear. And
this dread responsibility cannot be avoided once we enter the
profession, for by our example -- by our very presence alone,
we teach for good or for evil, whether we will it or not. As
Religious, we have not assumed this great charge; Obedience
has directed us; but individually we must labor strenuously,
according to the spirit of our vocation, by prayer and study, to
discharge this duty in a manner worthy of teachers through
Obedience.

We are, to a certain degree, responsible for the bodily growth and the health of our children, either of which, and perhaps both, may be impaired by our culpable ignorance of the laws of health, and from overtaxing the mind. Parents may be as often to blame in this respect as teachers, but on account of our profession, we ought to be better informed. Gymnastic or Calesthenic exercises, properly taught, will improve both the health and appearance of our pupils, and also aid in the discipline of the school.

For the moral training of our pupils we are no less responsible than for their physical. Home culture and other influences may often retard -- maybe counteract, all our efforts to ennoble a child's nature; but let us not be discouraged by the obstacles that may arise, bearing in mind that as their bodily and intellectual faculties are strengthened by exercise, so, by our constant inculcation of truth and honesty of purpose as the groundwork of a great moral character, and this not only by word, but by example -- for children are quick to learn from this, we may hope to see, if not immediately, at least in time -- a corresponding development of their moral faculties.

And if we are to hold ourselves responsible, and gravely so, for our pupils' physical, intellectual and moral training, what are we to feel concerning the crowning motives of all our endeavors, of all our labors -- the Religious training of the thousands and thousands of precious souls committed to our charge? That we may not lose sight of the end for which we have undertaken all, but more especially this most responsible of our duties, we must daily invoke the assistance of our Blessed Mother and St. Joseph to help us in its fulfilment, and to obtain for us purity of intention, that we may see in each of our pupils the Holy Child Jesus, and so act toward each that we may merit the blessing of this Divine Child, both for our pupils and for ourselves.

As to their Religious training then, we must scrupulously instruct the children according to their age, in all the practices and duties of Religion, such as to make the Sign of the Cross correctly, to recite the Lord's Prayer, the Hail Mary, the Apostles' Creed, the Confiteor and the Acts of Contrition, Faith, Hope and Charity perfectly and devoutly. We must also teach them how to examine their conscience, and how to prepare for and make their Confession. They must be taught how to assist at Mass -- uniting their intentions with those of the Priest, in offering the Holy Sacrifice for the intentions of the Church, that they may participate in Her merits.

They must also be taught the practice of making mental prayer, using subjects suited to their capacity. All who have made their First Holy Communion should be taught this practice daily. Teach them that to meditate means to think; that to meditate on a religious subject is simply to think on it as we would about the preparation of a lesson, or about some game we have planned and are going to tell our playmates -- show them how, in religious thinking, or meditation as it is generally called, we first read, or listen to the fact or truth placed before us -- then think how we stand before God in the light this truth has thrown upon our mind. What virtue does it show us that we stand in need of, or what vice or sin do we discover in ourselves? Then as naturally as we think comes the thought, "What must we do?" and so follows the resolution, either to strive to acquire the virtue, if wanting, by performing such, or such acts, or to root out the evil, avoiding or refraining from what we know has been the cause of our yielding to temptation. By some such explanation as this, clearly, simply and earnestly given, children will understand and be impressed with the importance of meditation, and so be led to think, and above all to think rightly, for if the young mind learns to reflect upon religious truths it will soon conform its motives and actions to this mode of thinking, and so cannot fail to think and act rightly -- having a correct basis of thought. This is the great want of our day, and with the Prophet we may say "With desolation is the land made desolate, because there is none that considereth in the heart." Teach the children to meditate, and for them, at least, much of this desolation will be obviated.

Not less important for them to be taught is how to make the daily particular and general examen, making them understand how easy a means this is to overcome their faults and to advance in virtue. Impress deeply on their minds the end for which they were created, and the absolute necessity each one is under of working out his own salvation, and therefore the constant need of prayer and the wonderful strength acquired by it against temptation; teach them, then, ejaculatory prayers, and a great devotion to their Guardian Angel, for these prayers and this devotion will help to keep them in the Presence and Grace of God.

Teach and explain to them the mysteries of our Holy Religion and how to meditate on them when reciting the Rosary, also how to perform the devotion of The Way of the Cross. They should be taught hymns, and required to sing them frequently, for by this means they learn many religious maxims and principles that cannot readily be effaced from the mind.

The Sisters engaged in teaching must scrupulously employ the hour allotted for study, and also any time left after the performance of their several household duties, in the preparation of the lessons to be taught in school and in their own improvement; to accomplish this latter requirement, they must adopt some order in their method of study. Though, perhaps much cannot be done at a time, still let them not be discouraged; a little study every day will show surprising results; if any one fails, having the proper means, it will be from want of utilizing the time at her disposal.

The Sisters teaching in the Primary and Intermediate Departments must be very particular in this point, as their grades require almost constant oral teaching; the Sisters must qualify themselves to impart general elementary knowledge with ease, grammatical accuracy, and in language intelligible to the young.

In teaching we must avoid two extremes, viz: giving too much aid, or too little. When children come to us for an explanation -- or even in teaching our class, we should endeavor to make them think -- speak to them about the general principle which the matter under consideration involves, or upon some elucidation previously given upon something similar. This should be done kindly, not in a cold or formal manner, but with a kind interest, and in a way that will set them thinking, and invite them to express their thoughts, and, crude though they be, we will often be surprised at the correctness of their reasoning. This way of teaching them, without seeming to teach, as it were, will open their minds, put them in the way of working for themselves, which is simply the only way of educating rightly, for we should remember that what is done for children, without due study on their part, makes but a feeble impression, and is soon forgotten.

We must wake up their minds by constantly calling into action their powers of observation and reasoning, and incite them to ascertain for themselves. If we do not do this, or if we do it poorly, they will grow up blind, so to speak, to the manifold beauty of God's creation; they will study none of the plans of nature that are constantly working so wonderfully above, around and beneath. But to so direct the minds of our children we ourselves must be alive to our surroundings in this beautiful world of the visible creation of God. We must acquire a general knowledge, not studying for our own gratification or pleasure simply, but as Religious, to increase our influence and usefulness as a means to accomplish the end of our holy vocation.

We must carefully study the characters of the children we teach, that we may deal with them in the way best suited to each; and if it be allowable to manifest a special interest in any one pupil, let it be in the child of inferior abilities.

We must be particular to keep our rooms neat and orderly, and require the same of the children -- to keep their desks in good order -- occasionally instructing them in personal neatness and polite deportment, and requiring them to put these lessons in practice while under our supervision.

We must watch over their conduct well during the time allotted for play; in fact, we will find that if we wish to acquit ourselves well of our responsible charge that from the moment the children present themselves in the morning until dismissal in the evening, we will have to give them our undivided attention. During the time of Intermission, and, of course, never in school, are we permitted to engage in any kind of needlework, nor in reading any book or paper, but must give our whole attention to the welfare and progress of the children while in school, and to their conduct and the care of the school furniture, etc., during the time of recreation.

In giving correction we will find it best to give reproof to the individual pupil in private. We will thus win the child's confidence. Every expedient must be tried before resorting to corporal punishment; still, it is a necessary form of correction; for even to know that it will be inflicted, if their conduct merit such, will often of itself preserve discipline in the school. Our Superiors deem it advisable that when obliged to administer correction in this manner we do it privately or during intermissions. We should always be calm and self-possessed in the presence of the children, but especially so when obliged to inflict corporal punishment. Make the child feel and acknowledge the gravity of his fault, and that you are pained to be forced to deal so severely with him. Girls should never be punished in this manner.

Animated by the spirit of our vocation, in our conduct toward each other, we should ever evince the deepest regard and affection, especially before externs. Can they say of us as was said of the first Christians: "Behold how they love one another!" Are we mindful of this in the presence of the children, who are daily witnesses of our reciprocal relation? What scandal if they perceive that there is not a good feeling among us; if they should see the least mark of disagreement! Do not let us be deceived; children are more clearsighted than many of us seem to suppose; a look, an impatient word, a smile even, may do more to scandalize them than years of after teaching will be able to remove. To avoid such sad results let us love one another sincerely, "As Christ loved us. " By this we shall prove ourselves His disciples, and so merit His benedictions for ourselves and for our pupils.

Holidays are to be granted rarely. Indeed, the national holidays of the year might be considered sufficient. Still, it will help very much to attract and endear to children their own school if they are permitted to celebrate certain days of special interest to the school alone. Such, for instance, as Patron Saints' day, the anniversary of some important event in the history of the school, etc. A little ingenuity on the part of the teacher, judiciously carried out, will make these occasions beneficially happy ones.

As incentives to study, it is proved by experience that Monthly Reviews, followed by Reports of the same to the parents or guardians of the pupils, and semi-annual Examinations, followed by class or individual promotions, are productive of better results in the school, of better feeling among all concerned, more especially the children and their parents, than by the distribution of premiums, therefore our Sisters will adopt this method as a proper means of exciting emulation. The Reviews should be held in the presence of the Rev. Pastor, Sister Superior, some of the other Sisters, if possible, and, if expedient, a few invited friends of the pupils.

The Scholastic year shall be divided into two terms of five months each. At the end of each term there must be a Public Examination, to which the children's parents and the patrons and friends of the school must be invited. These Examinations must be just, thorough and complete.

All our words and dealing with the children tend to the formation of their character; therefore we must be particularly care-

ful to put before them noble ends for all their actions. Teach
them first to refer all their thoughts, words and actions to God;
to work for His greater honor and glory; that they owe a debt
of gratitude to their parents and teachers, which they can best
pay off by acquitting themselves well of their duty as pupils;
their own advancement is also a commendable motive to urge
them to work for, when it is not selfish in its object. Teach
them to wish and to labor to be useful members of society, and
that they cannot hope to be such without a good Catholic education. We should frequently examine ourselves on this. See if
the principles we inculcate are of a nature to form the children
to virtue, to union among themselves, to respect for their
superiors, to love for their parents. True, some will not correspond to our wishes, but our labor will not be lost on all.
It will not be without some result favorable to their salvation,
that the children of our schools shall have listened to so many
religious instructions, shall have passed so many days in
innocence and in the fear of God. Such thoughts as these must
encourage us in our duty, for our Lord Himself assures us,
"He that shall do and teach, he shall be called great in the
Kingdom of Heaven. "

WHAT ARE THE MARKS OF A RELIGIOUS FOUNDRESS?
WHAT CONSTITUTES HER CHARISM?
THE CHARISM OF HER COMMUNITY?

The following study is an adaptation of a definitive treatise
entitled "Founder and Community: Inspiration and Charism, "
by the Reverend Juan Manuel Lozano, CFM, and published in
the Review for Religious, Volume 37, Number 2, March 1978.
It has been shared with and approved by Father Lozano[1] as
conforming accurately with his own documented sources.

We have traced the life of Mary Frances Clarke through fifty-
six strenuous years, witnessing her trials and her response to
them. We have shared her hopes and her anxieties, her understanding and her love for those who constitute her religious
family. We now observe her against the background of the qualities and characteristics according to which the Church defines
a foundress:

> The history of a religious community begins with a per-
> sonal calling which later develops into the vocation of a
> group. Everything that community has done has been initiated
> by the call of the foundress. A certain light in the intellect
> of a foundress focuses on a specific need of the Church, while
> a corresponding impulse in her will moves her to offer her-
> self as an instrument of God. God prepares and educates her
> by gradually imprinting in her heart the idea of a future con-
> gregation, helping her to discover in her own life what she
> will propose later to others.
> The inspiration received by a foundress is intimately re-
> lated both to the gospel and to her historical situation. A way
> of life, a spirituality, structures, formation develop gradual-
> ly around this axis. The full dedication of a foundress to the
> service of God, her love, her humility, her prayer-life make
> those in close contact with her aware of her sanctity. She be-
> comes a woman "according to the heart of God, full of grace
> and doctrine. " Specifically:

1. A FOUNDRESS HAS AN AWARENESS OF BEING CALLED
BY GOD TO CREATE A NEW RELIGIOUS COMMUNITY.

When God wants to help his Church, he first raises up a
person and gives her a special grace and impulse under
which she may serve in a particular manner.

Three religious congregations were established in Dublin during Mother Clarke's youth and young womanhood. Instead of choosing one of these she braved the hazards of ocean travel and the uncertainties involved in a New World situation. In Philadelphia she could have laid down the burden of leadership and solved several immediate problems by joining the Sisters of Charity of Emmetsburg. She later showed no interest in Bishop Smyth's efforts to "aggregate" the Sisters to the Sisters of Mercy.

2. A RELIGIOUS COMMUNITY BEGINS AS A GROUP OF DISCIPLES OR COMPANIONS GATHERED AROUND AN OUT-STANDING PERSONALITY.

Mary Frances Clarke was from the beginning the acknowledged leader of the first five. Their first joint project was given her name - Miss Clarke's Seminary.

3. A FOUNDRESS IS MARKED BY SANCTITY.

While the written account of her mystical experiences was deliberately destroyed, Mary Frances Clarke was widely regarded as a holy woman. Two bishops and the Trappist Fathers as well as other priests, and eminently those nearest to her, her Sisters, gave recognition of her sanctity and revered her for it.

4. A FOUNDRESS IS THE SOURCE OF TRADITION. SHE PRESENTS THE RULE TO THE HIERARCHY, DEFINES THE AIMS OF THE COMMUNITY, IS THE SOURCE OF INSPIRATION THROUGHOUT THE COURSE OF ITS HISTORY.

The congregation's traditions center in Mother Clarke. She not only presented the Rule to Rome, she was author of all of it not ascribed to the Jesuits through Father Donaghoe directly or indirectly. Though much of what she wrote was lost in its preparation for Rome, its spirit and its directives had already been embodied in the lives of her Sisters. The name of Mother Clarke has been associated with all that was best in the congregation from its earliest days. Her letters and other writings are the source of inspiration to her Sisters today and are fundamental to the spirit of their new Constitutions.

5. A FOUNDRESS ORDINARILY GOVERNS HER COMMUNITY.

For nearly nineteen years Mother Clarke was the freely chosen head of her community, and it was at the earnest petition of her Sisters that she was confirmed by Rome in her office for life.

6. THE VITALITY OF A GIVEN RELIGIOUS FAMILY DEPENDS ON THE SPIRITUAL FULLNESS OF THE PERSON TO WHOM IT OWES ITS EXISTENCE IN THE CHURCH, i. e. , ITS FOUNDRESS.

Despite a published account which was too long accepted as the congregation's history and which gave first place to Father Donaghoe, the memory of Mother Clarke in her life and her works is the vital force in the community's efforts at renewal though she has been dead for ninety-one years.

7. SUFFERINGS MARK THE PATH OF A FOUNDRESS, COMING TO HER EVEN WITHIN THE RANKS OF HER OWN COMMUNITY.

Who can measure the pain Mother Clarke suffered in seeing her community governed for thirty-six years by a spirit foreign to her own? in being set aside in conspicuous ways during what should have been the most productive years of her life and the most crucial for the formation of her sisterhood? Allegiance of a portion of her Sisters to Father Donaghoe meant their alignment with a spirit irreconcilable with her own.

8. THE OFFICE OF A FOUNDRESS IS THE OFFICE OF SPIRITUAL MOTHERHOOD, HENCE THE TITLE "MOTHER. "

From very early years the title "Mother" was assigned to Mary Frances Clarke, and her title to it has never been disputed.

9. A RETURN TO THE SPIRIT OF THE FOUNDRESS CONSTITUTES THE COMMUNITY'S RENEWAL.

The spirit, the labors, the letters and other writings of Mother Clarke have been central to the congregation's efforts at renewal.

CHARISM

A foundress' calling is a particular grace given her directly by the Holy Spirit for the good of the Church. It is she who formulates it and proposes it to others. Her aims, her spirit and her charism are reflected in her community. She still intercedes for the community she has created.

The personal vocation of one called to share in the vocation of the foundress implies certain graces thanks to which a religious may be faithful to her calling. Her vocation among the people of God constitutes her charism.

Those elements which pass from a foundress to her community, that is, the share the community has in her vocation, constitute the charism of her community.

It should be a source of great consolation and assurance to her Sisters to recognize how completely Mary Frances Clarke meets the standards of the Church for the exalted position of a religious founder. They may well rejoice in the blessing that is theirs in the claims they have on her as their spiritual Mother.

---

1 To his approval, Father Lozano has added the following comment: ". . . if you keep studying your Foundress, you will be able to see more clearly in which particular way she actualized her charism of Foundress. There are often very interesting differences in the way Founders become aware of their calling. "

ADDENDA

WE LEARN OF A MEETING BETWEEN TWO FOUNDRESSES

Sister M. Johnetta Monahan recounts for us the following significant incident. Ten years ago when Sister paid a visit to the Presentation Convent, George's Hill, Dublin, an elderly religious took her to a second floor room in the convent where she said Mother Clarke had visited with Mother Catherine McAuley. Mother McAuley was at that time, 1829-1831, making her novitiate with the Presentation Sisters in preparation for the final establishment of the Sisters of Mercy. Certainly the two foundresses had much in common, and might well have spent many hours in prayerful discussion of their hopes and plans.

Knowledge of this meeting would lead us to conjecture on the likelihood of another meeting, that between Mother Clarke and Mary Aikenhead, foundress of the Irish Sisters of Charity established also in Dublin in 1817.

Such exchanges certainly clarified for Mother Clarke the image of the Congregation she envisioned, and determined the path she was to follow as far as later circumstances permitted.

AND OF AN UNSCHEDULED DEPARTURE

There is an interesting episode, heretofore unnoted, related to Father Donaghoe's departure for Philadelphia in 1844. It is told, though with inaccuracies both as to date and destination, by the French Jesuit, the Reverend Augustus Thébaud, in his account of Forty Years in the United States, 1839-79. (New York: United States Catholic Historical Society, 1904.)

As Father Thébaud and a compatriot, Father DeLuynes, were enroute to Dubuque, where they were to spend a week with Bishop Loras, their boat made a brief stop at a village just south of Dubuque. An Irishman, recognizing them as priests by the cut of their coats, came racing down to the boat in great excitement, evidently wishing to convey a message to them. As soon as he could speak,

he begged us when we reached the Bishop's house, to let him know that Mr. Donaghoe had left the place for Europe the day before, and that there would be no Mass the following Sunday unless the Bishop sent another priest.

This was puzzling indeed, but we did not fail to report
it to the good Bishop, who smiled - though he appeared
a little vexed - and explained that Mr. Donaghoe was
an excellent man and a most zealous priest; but that he
was at the head of a community of Sisters and had probably gone either to Ireland or Rome for some purpose
of his own. "He would have done well, " he added, "had
he written me a note, and not been content to convey
the news to me by one of his countrymen. "

A CHANGE OF ADDRESS

A single line notation belatedly found in the archives states
that Mother Clarke lived in a comfortable house on Bride Street,
Dublin. We know that her brother Edward's family lived at a
Bride Street address, and that, at least in her later years,
Martha Clarke had an address near his on the same street.

Bride Street is south of the Liffey. Residence there would
have put the family in the St. Nicholas Myra Parish, where
Martha carried on her charitable labors for many years. It was
in this parish that the Kenrick family resided, and that Bishop
Kenrick's uncle, the Reverend Richard Kenrick, served as
pastor. However, Franciscan influence was strong in the area,
so that the tradition of Mary Frances' baptism by a Franciscan
priest becomes much more acceptable than if the family lived
in the St. Mary Parish, then the pro-cathedral - as indicated
in The Early Days. A search of the St. Nicholas Parish records
failed to reveal evidence of the Clarke family baptism there.
The Bride Street area is now given over to industry. As for the
North Ann Street site of "Miss Clarke's Seminary, " that area is
presently listed for urban renewal.

PART TWO

NEW LEADERS AND NEW STRUGGLES

1887-1920

Mother M. Gertrude
1888-1894
1900-1906

Mother M. Cecilia
1894-1900
1906-1912
1915-1919

Mother M. Ascension
1912-1915

Mother M. Isabella
1919-1931

Chapter Seven

A NEW HAND AND THE HOUSE SHE BUILT

T he name of Sister M. Gertrude Regan, the fifteenth member
to join the sisterhood, was one of three placed in nomination by
the consultors to succeed Mother Clarke in the office of superior-
general. Sister had been repeatedly reelected as treasurer of
the Congregation from the time of its incorporation in 1869, and
on the death of Sister M. Margaret Mann in 1874 was named assistant to Mother Clarke and vice president of the corporation,
a joint office she retained until Mother Clarke's death in 1887.
Familiar as she was with community affairs and remembered
kindly by the novices whom she had trained throughout her fifteen years as their mistress, it was perhaps no surprise that
Sister M. Gertrude was given the unanimous vote of nearly five
hundred electors. The consultors chosen to assist the new Mother were: Sisters M. Loyola Rutherford, Agatha Hurley, Gonzaga
McCloskey, and Cecilia Dougherty. The choice as assistant to
Mother Gertrude was Sister M. Baptist Seeley, while Sisters
M. Agatha and Cecilia were confirmed in their offices of visitor
and novice mistress, respectively.

The newly elected Mother General was scarcely a prepossess-
ing figure. Sixty-one years of age and less than five feet tall,
she was gnomelike in face and form, her mouth slightly twisted,
and her features without distinction. She spoke with a decided
lisp and her voice was low and hoarse. With little concern for
externals, neither her headdress nor her habit ever seemed
quite settled into place. But her powers of endurance and her
dedication to the interests of the community knew no limits,
and the daring she manifested in building ventures to meet growing needs was equaled only by her deftness in financial matters.

While Mother Gertrude kept as her headquarters the small,
poor room from which Mother Clarke had governed the Congregation, trusting much to local superiors and sisters-visitor,

the new Mother was to exercise a more immediate control. She relied on the support of her four consultors in major decisions, but she also sought first-hand knowledge of each local situation, a plan which called for almost constant travel. Through snow and sleet or floods and summer storms, early and late, in drafty trains and those open to grime and smoke, Mother seemed impervious to inconvenience. Hurrying from convent to convent or to business appointments in horse-drawn cabs, she kept a killing pace which left little time for the amenities even of religious life. Yet no matter how taxing the trip had been, how early she had risen or how late she reached home, Mother's practice was to rise with the community for morning meditation and Mass.

The problems facing the new superior were manifold, the first of which was the need for a new motherhouse, providing facilities for a growing novitiate and for the care of the sick and the elderly. Then rapidly expanding boarding academies in Dubuque, Davenport, Clinton, DesMoines and Council Bluffs, Iowa, Elgin, Illinois, Holden, Missouri, and Wichita, Kansas[1] were calling for additions and new buildings, while bishops and pastors were pressing for more and larger teaching staffs.

During her first double term of office, that is, from 1888-1894, Mother Gertrude pursued a program of expansion which included the present motherhouse and a boarding academy in Boulder, Colorado. She purchased a house in Milwaukee to serve as an academy, bought six acres of land in Chicago for a future high school, and when she learned that the vacated Presbyterian college in Holden, Missouri was to be sold at a sacrifice, she purchased it for the St. Cecilia Academy. Besides in those six years Mother Gertrude opened parochial schools in Emmetsburg,[2] Sioux City, Cedar Rapids, Cedar Falls, LeMars and Marcus, Iowa, in Lincoln, Nebraska, Kansas City, Missouri[3] and Petaluma, California.

The motherhouse on the Prairie, architecturally unsound, inadequate for the increasing numbers, and nine miles of unpaved roads from the nearest railroad station, must of necessity be replaced. Conference with Bishop Hennessy confirmed her judgment that a new motherhouse must be situated in or near the city. While Mother Clarke had long seen the need, other pressures had been too great for her to meet it. By the time of Mother's death, the change had become imperative.

Following Bishop Hennessy's advice, in the summer of 1888, Sisters M. Gonzaga and Loyola visited recently constructed motherhouses at Maryville and St. Vincent's in St. Louis, St. Joseph's and Loretto in Toronto, and Hotel Dieu and Villa Maria in Montreal. At a special meeting of the consultors on September

10, over which the Bishop presided, the two Sisters presented their findings. As a result, the consultors resolved on the early purchase of a site.

Second thoughts as to the financial burden involved in the venture, however, led the Sisters to hesitate. St. Francis Academy in Council Bluffs, and Holy Rosary School in Milwaukee were in debt. The Wichita academy was mortgaged, St. Joseph's in Des Moines was in need of expansion, as was the Davenport academy, and plans for a conservatory at Mt. St. Joseph in Dubuque were pending. Perhaps an added building on the Prairie would meet their immediate needs, and there was hope that a railroad was to pass nearby. It was a hard moment for Mother Gertrude, who saw the larger picture. However, on September 24, Mother, accompanied by Sisters M. Cecilia and Baptist, the only members of the council immediately available, drove into Dubuque to present to the Bishop their plan to expand the facilities at the old motherhouse. He returned with them to the farm, and in a dour mood pointed out the impracticality of their scheme, advising them to purchase suitable property immediately.

It was a brilliant future which Bishop Hennessy envisioned for the Congregation. [4] The Christian education of youth, in which they were now completely engaged, was the need of the day, and "if met at all that need would be met by religious women, not religious men. " Providence had placed the Sisters "in the heart of the republic, the Mississippi Valley. . . at the juncture of three of the finest states in the Union. . . . Already in San Francisco, they had been invited to New York and to Boston, to Europe, to Ireland, the richest mine of religious vocations in the world . . . to Australia also. " The proposed motherhouse was to be "what the heart is to the human body, the central source of life and health and vigor. " It should then be "all that a good architect can make it . . . as impressive as circumstances will allow. " As for the grounds, "they are the frame of the picture. " His sanguine hopes called for a stone structure, or cluster of structures, large enough to house 1, 500 religious. Realities would reduce that dream to a single stone-trimmed brick building with a capacity of nearly five hundred.

A site of twenty-seven acres was first purchased for $15, 000 "at the head of Locust Street, " across from their Mt. St. Joseph Academy, but on more careful examination, it was found to be too small and otherwise ill-suited to their needs. [5] The property finally purchased was an area of 110 acres situated on a bluff overlooking the Mississippi, and giving a panorama view of Illinois and Wisconsin at their juncture. The owner of ninety-one of those acres, Henry L. Stout, a wealthy lumberman and fancier of fine horses, used the property for grazing purposes. [6] The purchase from him was effected in September 1889, also for $15,000. An additional nineteen acres purchased from the Vincentian Fathers of St. Louis for $5,000 brought the limits of the property to the end of Grandview Avenue. Work was to begin in the early spring of 1890.

Meanwhile, however, the "foremost architect of the age," J. J. Egan of Chicago, had drawn up a set of plans for the Locust Street site. With these Mother and her consultors were highly pleased. However, when the plans were submitted to Bishop Hennessy he indicated to the architect that neither he nor "the Sisters" were happy with them, disturbing word indeed to Mr. Egan when their production had cost him $550.00, in addition to his long hours of labor. Assured, however, that any of the Sisters "who had seen the plans," were happy with them, he felt the better of it and asked to be recompensed only for his cash outlay. He was quite as pleased as the Sisters with the new site, variously called Grandview Park and Summit Hill. All were agreed that it was "God himself who had directed us to it for our future home." A new set of plans more suited to the situation was soon in the making. At the suggestion of the architect, the laying of a siding on the Milwaukee Road at the foot of the bluff permitted building materials to be delivered there and hauled up the 226-foot elevation to the building site, while water pumped from the river served the masons in their work. It was to be a stately structure, with a frontage of 250 feet, a wing 220 feet long on the south for chapel and novice quarters, and one on the north, four stories high, referred to as "the professed wing," to extend 245 feet. Limestone, quarried on the grounds and faced with Bedford stone, gave a solid foundation, seven feet thick at its base. Local pressed brick would face the superstructure. Interior partitions fifteen inches thick and of solid brick were to be finished with plaster. All flooring, even that on the ground level, to be of hard maple, and with all other woodwork in solid oak, it was built to last.

Work, under the direction of a local builder, John Keenan, was well under way when the great accord which had for the time existed between the Bishop and the Sisters was put to a test. Bishop Hennessy was suddenly fired by the dream of a school system of his own, in the hands of a congregation ideally to be trained in a normal school which he proposed to establish. The Sisters would be at his disposal for service in the many small towns of his diocese which other religious could not afford to serve.

It was while Mother Gertrude was waiting at the Cathedral
rectory for her assistant, Sister M. Baptist, to return from an
errand regarding contracts for the new motherhouse that the
Bishop approached her with his proposal. As the nucleus of his
young order he wished to have a group of four B. V. M. Sisters,
then teaching at St. Raphael School - Sisters M. Beata Griffin,
Redempta Coleman, Maude Tallman, and Columban Heffernan -
to be freed for that purpose. In a letter written that night of
April 22, 1890, Mother anguished: "My first thought on hearing
the Bishop's views was to wish myself in the middle of the
Mississippi sooner than bring any trouble now or in the future
on the community. " She was subsequently to spend anxious mo-
ments outside his office door as he interviewed each of the
chosen four. Great was her relief when she learned that each had
held fast to her commitment, while Sister M. Redempta, whom
he had hoped to have head of the new community, requested to
be sent "as far from Dubuque as possible. "[7]
   Mother's anxieties were far from over, for his gaze then
turned to the able group of Sisters at Mt. St. Joseph Academy.
Sister M. Angela Fitzgerald, on the staff there, told of Mother's
driving in from the Prairie in an open wagon, arriving hot, dusty
and very troubled. Hastily assembling the Sisters, she told them
of the Bishop's desire for recruits. The decision must rest with
each Sister. To Mother's deep relief, the Sisters came, one by
one, and kneeling before her, each renewed her allegiance as a
Sister of Charity. The Bishop would have to look elsewhere for
candidates for his proposed diocesan congregation. [8] Eventually
they were named the Sisters of the Holy Ghost.
   At this time an event of major importance to his personal
career distracted the Bishop from his interest in the motherhouse and his recruitment of Sisters. That event was the celebration on September 30, 1891 of the silver anniversary of his
consecration as Bishop of Dubuque. The occasion called for a
pontifical Mass, which drew large numbers of clerical visitors.
Archbishop Patrick Ryan of Philadelphia preached the sermon.
The banquet following the ceremony was the most elaborate so
far served in the state, its seven courses making use of a silver
service purchased especially for the occasion. A torchlight procession of 10, 000 people held that evening ended with a display
of fireworks and the firing of twenty-five volleys from many guns
   The diversion permitted Mother to carry out plans more in
keeping with her means. Indeed the limitations on those means
had led to a cessation in the building process, and work was not
resumed until the following spring. When it was, however, the

convenience of an elevator was sacrificed, a decision which the architect regarded as a serious mistake in so large a building. Financing the costly project put great pressure on the community. Yet Mother Gertrude, though faced with her building plans, had purchased through Father Muldoon of St. Charles, Chicago, in 1890 six acres of land in Chicago as the site for a high school, "a place for the Sisters to have retreats and hold teachers' institutions."[9] Debts on Holy Rosary School pressed and the Ackley Sisters, dependent on tuition they couldn't collect, were destitute. Meantime, Mother was called upon for Sisters to staff the St. Theresa Cathedral grade school in Lincoln, Nebraska, whose first Bishop, Thomas Bonacum, had been named just three years before. Other pastors and bishops were pressing for Sisters.

St. Teresa's, the one small church in Lincoln, served Bishop Bonacum as his first cathedral. At his request four B. V. M. Sisters[10] came in 1890, with Sister M. Constantia O'Leary as superior. Of these, Sister M. Columban Heffernan was to spend the next twenty years in Lincoln. Coming somewhat later, Sister M. Sophia O'Connor gave twenty-five years of her life to the mission. Sister M. Letitia Murphy, on the other hand, being recalled in 1891 because of failing health, died just as she left the train at Savanna, Illinois, where Mother Gertrude had gone to meet her.

Sister M. Ascension Lilly twice served as superior to the Lincoln elementary and high school, a three-story building which Bishop Bonacum had provided near the center of town. Here she won esteem as an educator and the respectful affection of parents and students alike.

The struggle with poverty was constant for the church in Lincoln, and the Sisters lived in a succession of abodes. A modern high school building was finally under construction in the late twenties under Bishop Francis J. Beckman. Lack of funds as a result of bad investments led to its abandonment even before it was roofed in. Later sold to the public school system, its loss was partially compensated for after thirty years by the erection of the Pius X High School, replacing the old Cathedral high. The B. V. M. Sisters continued to serve for some time both in the elementary and the high school. Bishop James V. Casey, appointed to the diocese in 1957, replaced the old St. Mary Cathedral with the beautiful Christ the King, a departure from the traditional type of church architecture. The B. V. M. Sisters serve both Sacred Heart and St. John parish elementary schools today.

Deaths from tuberculosis were on the increase. So many

were returning from the missions with "lung trouble" that Mother realized provision must be made for their care. A sanitarium in Saranac, New York was reporting improvement from situating patients in dry or mountainous areas.

In the summer of 1890 Mother sent Sisters M. Loyola Rutherford and Faustina Kirk to Santa Fe, New Mexico to investigate the offer of Bishop Salpointe for a mission there. On their return to Dubuque they made a stopover in Denver, where Sister M. Theodore O'Connor was attempting to recover from a "dry cough" under the care of her brother, Dr. Walter O'Connor, surgeon-general for the Denver and Rio Grande Railroad. The doctor took the three Sisters to Boulder, urging that they open a house in which tubercular patients could be accommodated. Then he arranged a visit for them with Bishop Matz of Denver.

In a letter dated October 21, 1890 to Mother Gertrude, the Bishop assured her that a day school in Boulder would face no competition from other orders, and that the Benedictine Fathers would gladly serve them. However, since the Sisters of Loretto were just then opening a boarding academy in Denver, he could permit no other order to accept boarding students until the Loretto Sisters had gained a foothold. Sister M. Loyola, sent to consider the situation, returned delighted with the possibilities of a day school.

A plot of ground given the Sisters at the foot of the precipitous slopes of the Flatirons, a sandstone range of the Rockies, was remote from the church. Though there were but thirty Catholic families in the area, and those were of modest means, plans went forward for building what they decided to call Mt. St. Gertrude Academy in honor of Mother Gertrude. Sister M. Theodore was named the academy's first superior. Meanwhile, the Sisters[11] lived and conducted a small grade school in a house near the station secured for them by Mrs. K. O'Brien, wife of Sister M. Rose O'Toole's nephew.[12] Shortly, however, they moved into a small brick house much nearer the church, conducting the first Sacred Heart parish school in rooms available in the rectory of the Benedictine Fathers. Sister M. Lumina Farrell, who came to teach music, was soon supplied with more students than she could handle.

Sister M. Theodore was near death before the academy building was completed, but in her eagerness to see it opened, she requested that the Sisters move into the remote, half-finished structure in late September 1892, although the doors were still unhung. It was an eerie experience, the dying woman in the bare, three-story structure, open to the winds which whistled through it, rattling windows and banging loose boards. A pack of coyotes which darkness brought down from the canyon added their dismal wail. Death came as a release to Sister on October 8.

The opening of school later that fall brought thirty pupils, girls and small boys. Sister M. Blandina Lyons, who succeeded Sister in office, lived only until the following June, when hemorrhage struck as she was preparing for a trip to Dubuque.

Poverty and heavy labor marked those early years, especially trying to the Sisters sent there in the hope of recovering their already impaired health. Building costs had tripled their estimate. To improve their situation they resorted to taking in a number of "lady boarders, " women who had come west for their health or for prolonged vacations. These had presented unique problems. Only after much pleading on the part of the Sisters and their friends was permission granted in 1917 for them to accept boarding students. [13] The academy thereafter knew relative financial success.

One of the most significant figures in the development of the academy was Sister M. Oswald Armstrong. As Janet Armstrong, Sister was born in Fifeshire, near Edinburg, Scotland on September 11, 1855. Her parents were Helen Lennox and John Armstrong, an officer in the English army. Her school life was begun in Edinburg under the direction of the Sisters of Notre Dame de Namur, and it was doubtless this contact that first interested Janet in the Catholic faith. While she was still young, Mr. Armstrong brought his family to Chicago. Becoming acquainted with the Sisters of Charity, Janet entered the Congregation on May 6, 1879 at the age of twenty-three. Sister served in its schools for forty-five years, teaching in Burlington, Lyons and DesMoines in Iowa, and in Chicago. As superior at Mt. St. Gertrude from 1914 to 1920, Sister directed the building of a large addition, containing chapel, classrooms and living rooms. But she is especially known for the warmth of her personality, the tender regard for the "motherless bairn, " and her way of comforting a lonely child with her characteristic "You're ma ain dear lassie noo. " Death claimed Sister in a Denver hospital on December 7, 1926. She is among those buried in the Sacred Heart of Mary Cemetery in Boulder.

Mt. St. Gertrude Academy won the confidence of the professors at Colorado University for the level of scholarship it maintained, and served both day and boarding students for many years. It graduated in the course of those years twelve hundred young women, many of them daughters of mountain ranchers for whom schooling would otherwise have presented great difficulty. In the course of those years, the academy contributed much to the faith and culture of a fast-growing area. The acad-

emy was, however, to suffer the fate of many small schools as
state requirements called for laboratory courses in science
requiring specialized teachers and an outlay which small classes
could not warrant. The last of the B. V. M. boarding schools to
open, it was the last to close, continuing as it did until June of
1969. The parish school of Sacred Heart continues to prosper,
having celebrated in 1975 its seventieth year as a separate mission. [14] Prior to 1905, the Sister-faculty had resided at the
academy.

One of the warmest associations with the academy through the
years was that with the Reinert family, three of whose sons became Jesuit priests: Father Carl of Creighton University and
Fathers Paul and James of St. Louis University. The bond of
friendship with the Sisters remains unbroken.

In September 1892 three small parish schools in Iowa - St.
Patrick's, Cedar Falls, St. Patrick's, Cedar Rapids; and Lorett:
(later Holy Name) in Marcus - were due to open. Mother and
companion had made a hasty trip to each site to make certain
that all was ready for the Sisters. While the first two situations
were satisfactory, that at Marcus called for major changes in
arrangement. Twelve Sisters were needed for these three
schools.

It was a hot day in late August when Mother brought in from
the Prairie twelve B. V. M. 's, all properly cloaked and bonneted,
and gathered them about her, together with their motley array
of luggage, on the Illinois Central platform in Dubuque. Having
purchased twelve tickets, she parcelled them out, four tickets
for each of the three destinations, in this way indicating to each
Sister her year's assignment. She had provided a meditation
book and small volume entitled "Visits to the Blessed Sacrament, " for each of the three budding communities. The recipient
of these was the designated superior of the group. Each four
Sisters included two classroom teachers, one music teacher
and a housekeeper. At least one member of each group was a
novice.

School-convent arrangements were in order when the respective groups reached Cedar Rapids and Cedar Falls. However, it
was not to be so simple a matter for the Sisters who left the trai
in the little country town of Marcus at six o'clock the next evening. The pastor, startled by their unheralded arrival, could
only offer them the hospitality of the rectory, since the school-
convent was still undergoing the alterations Mother Gertrude
had required. Their total cash assets - the single dime that
Mother had entrusted to the prospective superior - would tide
them over until they received their first monthly check from

the pastor, provided they opened a charge account with the local grocer.

After a week in the crowded quarters of the rectory, they determined to move into the unfinished school. Rural living was primitive in those days, innocent of indoor plumbing and water supply. Carrying their wood from the shed and water from the well and the cistern provided more than sufficient outdoor exercise. "Half-boarders" added to their indoor labors and gave occupants to the gaunt, high-ceilinged top floor. Early discovery that the novice-housekeeper had little disposition for work was disconcerting indeed.

In early November the pastor gave orders to Sister M. Alexander Powers, superior, [15] to accept boys as boarders, or "pack up for Dubuque. " Taking the next eastbound train, she laid the matter before Mother Gertrude, whose blunt response was that Sisters were too scarce to waste where they were not wanted. If the pastor insisted, they were to return to Dubuque without further ado. He, however, thought better of his order and they stayed on.

Cold and hardships deprived the school of its music teacher, a victim of tuberculosis. The following March she returned to Mt. Carmel. There was no one to replace her, yet, with it all, the mission survived. The people were kind and made every provision they could for the Sisters. The school was destined to grow and in time to add high school classes in cooperation with the local public high school. Only when state requirements and a shortage of Sisters forced the closing of the high school in 1964 and of the grade school in 1972 did its history end.

The four Sisters[16] assigned to Cedar Rapids settled into the old frame St. Patrick's Church structure which had been converted into a two-story school-convent. The Sisters' sleeping quarters shared the second floor with the kindergarten, while the lower floor accommodated grade and high school classes and living facilities for the Sisters. Two students constituted the first graduating class in 1896. Father Finnegan, S. J. , present for a mission, conferred the diplomas. [17] The parish has prospered and the B. V. M. Sisters continue their services in a modern school and a pleasant convent, conducting a second grade school, that of St. Jude, as an "out-mission. " The high school department has been transferred to LaSalle High, with a B. V. M. faculty.

All started well in the small grade-high school situation in Cedar Falls, [18] but Mother Gertrude was called on by the end of the year to settle differences, which she did by changing both the superior and the music teacher. It was soon realized that

so small a high school was not feasible. However, the elementary grades were continued until the reorganization of diocesan
schools took place in 1969 when the B. V. M. Sisters withdrew.

Besides the three Iowa houses opened in 1892, Mother Gertrude
responded to the call of the Reverend James Cleary, pastor of
St. Vincent Parish, Petaluma, California. The parish had been
in operation for thirty-five years, the Daughters of Charity conducting its first school from 1867 to 1888. They were succeeded
by the "white-robed Sisters of Notre Dame de Namur" who were
established in the "beautiful and majestic building which had
been christened St. Vincent academy. "[19] These Sisters were
withdrawn in 1892.

Sister M. Leocadia Conway, B. V. M. , [20] the first superior,
was succeeded by Sister M. Redempta Coleman in 1898. Under
the superiorship of Sister M. Rose Rourke, the Sisters moved
into a new convent, leaving added room for students in the academy building. In 1937 the upper story of the academy was removed, and the building given over to the high school classes,
while the grades were moved into a new school building. Sister
M. Casia O'Connor, an especially loved woman, served as
superior from 1919 to 1924. St. Vincent's is a thriving parish
today with thirteen Sisters in residence.

But beyond all these concerns, Mother's principal preoc-
cupation was financial. Her assistant, Sister M. Baptist Seeley,
provided her in 1891 with a memorandum needed as a basis for
negotiating loans on her building projects. Showing tax payments
of $493. 56 in 1890, it listed properties which Sister evaluated
at $693, 000. Its larger items included the following:

Our Farms	45, 000. 00
Mt. St. Joseph	150, 000. 00
New Motherhouse property	60, 000. 00
Locust St. Place	25, 000. 00
13th & Main St.	25, 000. 00
St. Mary Academy	10, 000. 00
Immaculate Con. Acad.	100, 000. 00
O. L. A. Acad. , Lyons	30, 000. 00
St. Agatha Academy	40, 000. 00
Cascade house and lots	8, 000. 00
St. Francis, C. B.	50, 000. 00
St. Joseph Academy, DM	40, 000. 00
Chicago land	10, 000. 00
Holy Rosary, Milwaukee	10, 000. 00

All Hallows, Wichita	20, 000. 00
St. Cecilia, Holden	20, 000. 00
Boulder land	3, 000. 00
Sisters' lots, etc.	22, 000. 00

We note that the estimates of value were considerably beyond the price paid for the property purchased for the new mother-house and that on Locust Street. Doubtless it was wishful thinking or an eye to the future that caused the Sister to draw up an inflated listing as a basis for future borrowing. Certainly much of the above property was placed under mortgage to meet the need for funds, but even to keep up with interest payments presented difficulties. In face of this, it became Mother's practice as pressures grew to make hurried visits, especially to the Chicago houses, inquiring of the superior whether she had money in the bank. Often she required that the whole amount be surrendered to her. The strain under which this placed the local mission was such that some superiors resorted to concealing their household funds.

The pressure for personnel with the opening of so many new missions also made existing missions vulnerable. Alerted by grapevine communication that Mother was in the area, superiors found sudden errands for their young Sisters lest they prove reminders to Mother of needs in other missions. Stories abound of Mother's sudden forays. We hear of her unscheduled arrival during a house cleaning bee at the Wichita academy. A messenger dispatched to a young Sister found her on her knees scrubbing a classroom. Flushed, and drying her hands on her work apron, she appeared before Mother to be told, "Sissy dear, get on your cloak. " Her skirts damp with scrub water, Sister obeyed, only to find herself on the way to the railroad station. Not until the two got off the train in Davenport and Mother gave directions to the hack driver did Sister know that her destination was the Immaculate Conception Academy, where, incidentally, she spent the next several years. [21]

On one occasion, holding a cab at the motherhouse door, Mother sent a courier in haste to find a Sister whom she had come to take to St. Mary's, Chicago. She then sent a second Sister scurrying to pack a suitcase for the traveler. Others coming to the rescue, proffered from their meager wardrobes, a fresh border, a clean cape - any item that could speed her on her way. [22]

And again, returning from DesMoines with a sick Sister, Mother instructed a novice to be ready in twenty minutes to

depart in her place. When the young traveler arrived breath-
less at the door, taking the cloak from the shoulders of the sick
Sister, Mother deposited it on those of the now black veiled
novice, and they were off to catch the return train to DesMoines.[23]

But it was not always to meet a sudden need that novices were
taken from their studies. Mother seems to have wished to expose
them to classroom situations as early as possible. Mother
Gertrude had just been put in charge of the novices at the close
of her term of office as superior general when, in the late spring
of 1894, she took Sister Robertine Welch, a young Sister, to
one mission after another in Chicago in an effort to place her.
Father Curran, S. J., at Holy Family was the tenth and last of
the pastors to refuse her, none wishing to introduce a raw recruit into a classroom at that time of the year.

Shortly after that humiliating experience, Sister was sent to
St. Brigid's in San Francisco. There Father Cottle, who had
succeeded Father Bermingham as pastor, had arranged for a
summer place in the mountains for the Sisters, even damming
a small stream to provide a swimming pool for them. Since
her assignment for the fall was to seventh grade girls, Sister
M. Robertine was instructed to bring the necessary texts with
her on their vacation, with the assurance of Sisters M. Simplicia Kennedy and Rose O'Rourke that they would go through
the year's work with her. Then, during the school year, Sister
M. Rose, as principal, frequently visited her classroom, observing, or demonstrating methods by teaching a lesson for her.

Mother Gertrude leaned heavily on the Holy Spirit in her assignment of music teachers. To one young Sister, Mother said:
"I'm going to have you teach violin. " To her protest, "But, Mother, I don't know violin, " she was given the assurance that she
could take lessons every Saturday, her teaching and learning
thus progressing together. In the course of the years, Sister
M. Rosalita McLaughlin developed into a superior teacher of
music. [24]

The spring of 1892 found Mother Gertrude so ill that there
was imminent danger of death. No indication is given of the
nature of her illness, but the severe epidemic of grippe or influenza prevalent that year caused many deaths. She was herself again when in July Sister M. Rosina Harrigan, superior
of Holy Rosary School, Milwaukee, wrote her regarding the
desire of their graduates for secondary education. The desire
was seconded for the girls of his parish by the pastor of the
nearby Gesu Church, the Reverend J. J. Foley, S. J. Sister

relayed the word also that the Daughters of Charity were giving up the Gesu grade school and that the Jesuit Fathers were eager to have the Sisters take it over. This Mother promised, and Sister M. Seraphina Short was appointed first superior of the Gesu elementary school.

Father Foley, in turn for that favor, interested prominent Catholics, Mr. and Mrs. Robert Johnston, [25] in search for suitable quarters for an academy. They suggested the purchase of the former residence of Dr. Nicholas Senn at the corner of Twelfth and Cedar Streets, which the Sisters purchased at a cost of $30,000.00. Mr. Johnston assisted in arranging for the necessary loans. Eight Sisters[26] were sent to take charge of the new Holy Angels Academy, which opened that fall with Sister M. Lamberta Fitzgerald as its superior. Twenty students, among them several small boys, constituted their first enrollment, their tuition $3.00 a month. By 1897 the enrollment exceeded the capacity of the house, and ground was broken for a second building on an adjacent lot. By 1899 the Reverend W. B. Rogers, S.J., then pastor of Gesu, had become disturbed that many of the smaller children who rightfully belonged in the parish grade school were actually in attendance at the academy. He assured the Sisters that if that matter were adjusted, the Fathers would compensate by helping to enlist students for the high school classes. To this arrangement, Mother Cecilia yielded readily, sending additional Sisters to teach in the parish school. [27]

Accredited to the Catholic University of America in 1912 and to Wisconsin University in 1915, the academy was "deemed worthy of special commendation" by the State Normal School. Its superiors in the course of its early years were among the best known members of the Congregation: Sisters M. Bertrand Foley, Regina Lynch, Angela Fitzgerald, Seraphina Short, and Michael Flynn. It enjoyed the services of the Jesuit Fathers as teachers of religion and was commemorated by the Reverend Francis Finn, S.J., in three of his popular books for boys. The Johnstons continued to be among its benefactors, though the largest single financial gift, $90,000, came from Mr. Charles Knoernschild,[28] father of Sister M. Virginita. It was theirs and other gifts which enabled Mother Isabella to engage the well-known architect, Barry Byrne, to construct in 1928 the handsome academy building which in 1929 hosted the ninth biennial convention of the National Federation of B.V.M. Alumnae. Succeeding years added to the impressive record of attainments both in the field of fine arts and of scholarship.

As the neighborhood deteriorated, however, parents feared to send their daughters into it, and the enrollment dropped in

Graduates of 1896

Graduates of

HOLY ANGELS ACADEMY, MILWAUKEE

Senn Home and New School

Final Structure

1970 from nearly six hundred students to 339. Both it and the Divine Savior High School for girls, which drew from much the same clientele, were operating at a deficit. It was, then, with much regret that the student body of Holy Angels was transferred to the more happily situated school, to be known as Divine Savior-Holy Angels High School under the combined faculties of the two schools. By the time of its close, Holy Angels counted 6,081 graduates, 101 of whom entered the ranks of the sisterhood.

The year 1893 was significant for two reasons. Though it began in a mood of prosperity, panic had struck by fall when the great international fair, the Columbian Exposition was officially opened in Chicago's Jackson Park. The interests of the schools centered in the more than 1,000 exhibits of class work submitted from every state in the union, and from France, England, Spain, Ireland, and Africa. In charge of the exhibits was Brother Maurelian, F. S. C. Among the addresses of the day were those of Bishop Hennessy of Dubuque and of his close friend, Archbishop Patrick Ryan of Philadelphia. Professor Peabody, chief of the Liberal Arts Department of the World's Fair, declared that the "Catholic Education Exhibit of Chicago was the gem of his department." Cardinal Gibbons brought the encomiums closer home by declaring the Holy Family schools, then in their zenith, "the banner schools of the nation," a comfort indeed to the sorely pressed Sisters, as well as to the Jesuit Fathers.

1893 was a banner year also for Bishop Hennessy and his diocese. On May 19 Dubuque was raised to the rank of an archdiocese, with Davenport, Omaha, Lincoln and Cheyenne suffragan sees. Cardinal Gibbons came from Baltimore to confer on the new archbishop the pallium, symbol of his office. Archbishops Ryan and Feehan, as well as three hundred priests of the new metropolitan see were present for the occasion. As was usual on such occasions, the gathering brought many clerical visitors to Mt. Carmel.

Construction on the new motherhouse was going well in the summer of 1893. The workmen had finished the great shell of the building and were starting the work of plastering, plumbing, heating and lighting. Mother Gertrude was anxious to move into the new building by November 1, or, at latest, December 8, as the year 1893 marked the fiftieth anniversary of the Sisters' coming to Dubuque. Indeed Mother Gertrude's historic sense had been stirred, for in April of that year she had written to Sister M. Loyola requesting her to begin the writing of a community history, for, she said: "We have been dilatory in that matter, " but Sister had as much as she could do to fulfill her other assignments. [29]

On November 11, 1893 the anxiously awaited move was made.[30] The sixteen lively postulants, three of them fresh from the land of the Gael, were lined up and ready to go, each with a clock, a lamp or a picture in hand for safekeeping. For them there was a horse-drawn bus, the "black Maria, " as they dubbed it, lined with long benches. Dishpans filled with dishes lined the aisle. A funeral hearse had also been lent for the occasion. The farm wagon bedded with straw, and spring wagons lent by neighboring farmers provided for those professed[31] who were then to leave the old home and such novices as had not been sent to the missions, as well as for various household items. All were well bundled up against the chill November weather.

The sight of the new home was a delight to all eyes; its size, its grandeur and the interest of its location high above the river; and indoors, its spaciousness, its broad stairs and corridors and great stretch of dining room, community room and novitiate. The snowy lavatories, the gas fixtures for lighting and cooking, the facilities for steam heat with fireplaces to supplement - all were added wonders. Only the lower floors were completed, and for a time a dormitory would serve for chapel. There was little furniture at hand, but that was being remedied for Sister M. Loyola was purchasing a supply of tables, chairs and other items from the recently closed World's Fair.

There was moderation in those early enthusiasms when turning the tap brought no water, when no light came from the gas fixtures, and the great iron radiators stayed cold. It would all take time, for neither water nor gas mains had been extended so far by the city. There was a well, and ways could be devised for collecting the rain run-off. Meanwhile a dipperful served for nightly ablutions, the fireplaces somewhat moderated the deadly cold of winter, candles and grease lamps served, as they had at the old home, and the novices counted it a lark to drive out to the Prairie with the family laundry. A succession of novenas to St. Anthony encouraged the men who were boring for water. The following June they at last struck the sandstone layer, 280 feet down, and water from this well served basic needs until the city main brought a plentiful supply some years later.

It soon became apparent that the two lavatories in the novice wing, or even the four in the wing for professed Sisters, would be inadequate. The architect's masterly drawings show the plan for the "annex" to be constructed, providing a large lavatory off each landing of the broad stairs in the center of the house, a supply tank above them providing the necessary pressure. This was later supplemented by a standpipe in the rear of the building. City water would not be available for ten more years.

There was much work to be done, and the ten new postulants which December brought were doubly welcome. Little time could be given to lessons except for Sister M. Crescentia's classes in Christian Doctrine.

With spring came wagonloads of trees and shrubs, and Sister M. Loyola was busy laying out the orchard of apples, pears, plums and cherries. Then the lines of evergreens were set along the "pine walk" which led to the proposed new graveyard. The shade of the oaks already standing was supplemented with that of maples, elms, ash and conifers: spruce, pine and arbor vitae. Lilacs and other flowering shrubs, and many of those first trees, today provide a living memorial to the capable Loyola.

Mother Gertrude had been returned to office by an easy majority in the election of December 1891, with Sister M. Baptist Seeley again her assistant. The consultors at that time included Sisters M. Josephine Clarke, Loyola Rutherford, Sebastian Courtney, and Faber Montague. Sister M. Cecilia was named general secretary and novice mistress; Sister M. Loyola, treasurer, and Sister M. Agatha returned to the office of visitor. However, by the time the election of December 1893 approached, the Sisters' mood had changed.

As Mother Gertrude's second term of office was coming to a close, Sisters M. Agatha and Gonzaga favored her reelection, an action which would have called for confirmation by Rome. For this purpose they called as many of the superiors as were in reasonable distance for a meeting at the Prairie motherhouse. They were directed to Mother Clarke's room, and when they had assembled in that familiar setting, Sister M. Gonzaga announced: "Sister M. Baptist will tell you the object of this meeting. "

But Sister M. Baptist returned emphatically, "You tell them yourself. " Sister M. Gonzaga then explained that in view of the new building and for other reasons especially those concerned with finances, it seemed best to have Mother Gertrude's time extended. She asked for the opinion of the other Sisters. They, with a single voice, responded "No! " and opening the door, abruptly left the room. [32]

The election resulted in the choice of Sister M. Cecilia Dougherty for the office of mother-general, with Sister M. Rutherford her assistant. The consultors named were Sisters M. Basil Healy, Sebastian Courtney, Maurice Duffy, and Rosalia Ryan. [33] Sister M. Crescentia Markey was named secretary, Sister M. Loyola continuing as treasurer, and Sister M. Basil as visitor. The office of novice mistress was assigned to the retired Mother Gertrude.

Notes

1 In 1889 the Sisters teaching at St. Aloysius pro-cathedral were given their own convent. To that time they had been residing at the academy. Members of the new household were: Sisters M. Philippa Sheridan, Roberta Reynolds, Adelbert McGuire, Adrian Miller, Lavina Berry, and Protase Peters.

2 The Emmetsburg mission will be treated with later missions there.

3 St. Joseph, Kansas City, had been an out mission until 1887. The faculty that first year consisted of Sisters M. Scholastic McLaughlin, Bonita Breene, Melitta Fleming, Firmina Smyth, Anysia Roberts and Catherine McGovern. St. Aloysius, Kansas City, was made a separate community in 1888, with Sisters M. Ignatia Pyne, Esther Warren, Irmina Elliott and Simeon Dillon as its members.

4 Quotations that follow are from notes in the Bishop's hand and contained in the Congregation's archives. No record remains of requests from Ireland or Australia, but the Bishop thought big.

5 Later a portion of this land was sold to the city for the erection of the Julien Dubuque Senior High School, and the rest added to the Mount campus.

6 The story is told that it was disappointment over the loss of his favorite horse, killed by a fall over the cliff, that induced Mr. Stout to sell the property.

7 Sister was assigned to the new Petaluma mission in California a short time later.

8 Although the Archbishop on his death had left it well endowed, the Congregation of the Holy Ghost Sisters never flourished. It was suppressed after twenty-two years by Archbishop James J. Keane. Some of its members then entered other congregations, though some clung to their situation at St. Anthony's convent-school until, in 1917, the Archbishop gave orders that the B.V.M. Sisters would supplant them in the classrooms. They continued, however, to care for the altar boys and the teaching of music. The last remaining member, Sister Agatha Kerns, died January 29, 1974, at the age of ninety-three. Sister had spent her last years at Holy Family Hall, a residence

for the elderly maintained by the Sisters of St. Francis, Dubuque. (Sister Rita Clare Becker, archivist).

To supply the school, Mother Cecilia placed Sister M. Wilfreda Linot in charge. Then choosing two novices, Sisters M. St. Thecla Mahoney and Clara Louise Reuter who had taught before entering, she obtained the Archbishop's permission for their early profession. The three Sisters made their residence for many years at nearby Mt. St. Joseph.

9 This was not, however, the site used for St. Mary's in 1899.

10 The other Sisters who opened St. Teresa's, Lincoln, were: Laetitia Murphy, Columban Heffernen and Avellina Boyle.

11 These early Sisters included: Sisters M. Theola Harrington, Theodore O'Connor and Faustina Kirk.

12 Rose was one of the five founding members of the Sisters of Charity.

13 See letter of Bishop Matz to Mother Cecilia, dated March 6, 1917, written in response to the plea of Father Garrett J. Burke, a close friend of the Bishop's.

14 The Sisters who formed the first Sacred Heart Community were: Sisters M. Marcelliana McFadden, Anthony Dacey, Andrea Heffernen, Cephas Healy and Laeta McNamara.

15 The other three Sisters for Marcus were Valerian Cullen, Engratia Jennings and Lewine Enderle.

16 The only Sisters whose names appear in the register for Cedar Rapids were M. Adrian Miller, Adaline Walsh and Polycarp Keas.

17 Of the two sons of Nellis Christopher McCabe, among the early graduates, one became associate editor of the Washington Star (D. C.) and the other a Jesuit teacher at Creighton University, Omaha.

18 The four Sisters who formed the first community in Cedar Falls were M. Bertille English, Leandre Swift, Anthony Dacey and Gratia Barker.

19 Historical Sketch of St. Vincent de Paul, 1857-1962, Petaluma, California. Souvenir Booklet Prepared for Dedication of New High School, March 17, 1962.

20 The other Sisters who pioneered in Petaluma were: M. Philip Powers, Omer Gibbons, Bertina Palmer and Nepomucene Gutchenritter.

21 Sister M. Immaculata McCann as recounted to Sister M. Philippa Coogan.

22 As told at recreation by Sister M. Rosanna Darragh.

23 Account given by Sister M. Lewine Enderle.

24 Sister and her companion, Sister M. Virginus Austin, also a teacher of music, were killed instantly on November 1, 1921 when they were struck by a hit-and-run driver on Grand Avenue, DesMoines, directly in front of the academy.

25 Mr. Johnston was a successful business man, and both he and Mrs. Johnston proved themselves especially generous benefactors to Marquette College, soon to assume the status of a university.

26 The first four Sisters to arrive for the Holy Angels Academy were: Lamberta Fitzgerald, Stanislaus Keas, Gerina Curran and Veneranda Ryan.

27 Gesu School grew rapidly, its eventual enrollment reaching 1,300 pupils. Sister M. Pancratia Coyle remained as seventh and eighth grade teacher for thirty years. Among the seven hundred boys who passed through her hands during those years, there were many who later became priests, a number of them Jesuits. A large number of her graduates honored her in a reunion in 1928 coming from various parts of the country for the occasion. During these early years the Sisters resided at the academy. Only in 1911 did they have a convent of their own. The Sisters who formed that first separate community were: Sisters M. Ildephonse Kennedy, Devota Ennis, Pancratia Coyle, Urbanita Stapleton, Genese Hayes, Harold Kinsella, Bernardus O'Brien and Donata Purcell.

28 Mr. Knoernschild, a millionaire and a philanthropist, was killed in an auto-train collision not long afterward.

29 Sister M. Michael Nihill was also encouraged to take on the task of historian. While she conducted countless interviews with the Sisters at Mt. Carmel and made pages of notes, ill health had robbed her of the drive necessary for the task. Sister M. Pulcheria McGuire used some of her material when ten years later she set herself the task of composing The Annals.

30 Many of the following details have been gleaned from tape recordings made by Sister M. Angelita Kramer in 1953 during a succession of interviews with elderly Sisters in Mt. Carmel's infirmary.

31 The first professed Sisters to occupy the new home were: Mother M. Gertrude, S. M. Baptist Seeley, Loyola Rutherford, Cecilia Dougherty, DeChantal O'Regan, Antonia Flanigan and Martha Quinn.

32 Sister M. Lambertina Doran's notes attribute the account to Sister M. Ignatia Pyne who was doubtless present on the occasion.

33 On the death of Sister M. Rosalia in August 1895, Mother Gertrude was chosen to replace her as consultor.

NEW MOTHERHOUSE UNDER CONSTRUCTION
Students from Mt. St. Joseph with Sister M. Benedicta

Chapter Eight

A GRACIOUS LADY, EDUCATOR AND MOTHER

M ary Dougherty, the future Mother Cecilia, was born in Boston
on February 2, 1838, the daughter of Irish-born Thomas Dougherty
and his wife, Cecilia Burke. The family later came west, settling
with their many compatriots in Garryowen, Iowa. From there,
on February 2, 1856, her eighteenth birthday, Mary's father
drove her in a sleigh over the frozen roads to the motherhouse on
the Prairie, where her aunt, Sister Mary Agnes Burke, had been
the first postulant to enter the sisterhood after their arrival in
the west. As her father bade goodbye and turned his team for the
lonely ride back home, Mary's novice mistress, the large-hearted
Margaret Mann, urged her to warm herself at the grate fire.
"You must be cold; why, even your braids are frozen;" and they
were, for they had served to wipe away the furtive tears that
kept gathering as she sat snuggled close to her father on the
long, cold drive.

"You're number 86, " observed an interested novice. And "86"
would be more than Mary's laundry number and the indication of
her relative position in the community, for the simple number
often identified her to close friends to whom she wrote in later
years.

Received into the novitiate on July 2, Mary was given the
religious name Cecilia, a daily reminder of her home and mother. Professed on December 8, 1858, Sister's first assignment
was to Davenport, where, with her novice mistress and eleven
of her Sister companions, she played her part as directress
and music teacher in the establishment of the Immaculate Conception Academy. There she remained from July 1859 to September 1877, when she entered into a year of service as novice
mistress at St. Joseph Prairie. Then three years as superior
of Holy Family Convent in Clinton, Iowa, were followed by
thirteen more years as novice mistress at the Prairie mother-

house. In the course of that time she served in the position of consultor to Mother Clarke for six years and to Mother Gertrude for three. Now, on February 2, 1894, with a long and varied background of experience, Sister M. Cecilia assumed the responsibilities of superior-general. It was the thirty-eighth anniversary of her entrance and her fifty-sixth birthday.

The contrast Mother Cecilia presented to her predecessor could scarcely have been more striking. Tall and slender, she possessed a gracious dignity and a charm of manner which won her many friends. Always trim and well groomed, she encouraged others, as she had her novices, to preserve an appearance in keeping with their dignity as religious women. Her ready affection and personal warmth, even her firmness, kindly as it was, had endeared her to her academy students and her many novices, and would serve her well with many who were now her subjects.

While Mother Gertrude had proven herself an able and dauntless builder and financier, her record as educator had left much to be desired. Mother Cecilia, on the other hand, was fearful of incurring debt and had little aptitude for finance. She proved however, an able and far-sighted educator.

There had been little time or thought in Mother Gertrude's crowded days for academic concern. Indeed, Mother Cecilia as novice mistress had been sorely tried in carrying out her program of academic and spiritual training of her novices for raids on the novitiate were often and unexpected. Now with a reversal of positions, the new Mother could modify that pattern.

It was her first intention to relieve pressure on the Sisters by refusing to open more schools than they could reasonably supply. Those undertaken during the years 1894-1900 included only a short-lived mission at the small settlement of Eagle (Postoffice, Streator), Illinois, Blessed Sacrament and St. Agatha parish schools in Chicago, a staff of grade and high school Sisters to replace the Franciscan Sisters withdrawing from St. Mary's, Iowa City, [1] and a central high school for girls in Chicago.

Mother Cecilia called Sister M. Maurice Duffy back from California to assist Mother Gertrude in her duties as novice mistress, for she felt the need of her predecessor's guidance and assistance in many of the matters of administration. While the instruction of the novices on the vows and the spiritual life were regularly left to Mother Gertrude, Sister M. Maurice met their day to day needs, taught them geology and took them for field trips and occasional hikes over the hills as Mother Cecilia had done. [2] Happy recollections of her years in California fired many of the young with the desire for an assignment to the West.

Sister M. Michael Nihill, who had returned from DesMoines to recuperate from surgery, was assigned the task of training the novices in composition and rhetoric, while Sister M. St. James Kinsella gave them lessons in perspective and other aspects of drawing. Sister M. Teresita Butler, a former university student from Iowa City, taught Latin, while Sister M. Crescentia Markey, continued her lessons in Christian Doctrine, and Sister M. Baptist Seeley introduced them to the spiritual principles of the Catechism of Perseverance. However, classes were not held as regularly as Mother Cecilia might have wished on account of occasional funerals, Monday's laundry, and at times the pressure of other household duties. Moreover, demands on the teachers, several of whom were involved in administration, sometimes kept them from the classroom.

Mother Cecilia was equally concerned about the upgrading of the quality of education in the schools. As a means toward this she sought ways in which beginning teachers might share in the methods and ideas of the more competent and experienced. For this purpose she called together at the motherhouse in July 1894, all the superiors, first for a retreat and the renewal of the spirit of religious observance, and then for a six-day conference. It was to be the first General Council of the Congregation, and for it the agenda had been sent to them in May. Since the conference was to be on school matters, each superior was asked to bring with her her best teacher. Fifty-two superiors were in attendance from Iowa, Illinois, Missouri, Kansas, Nebraska and Colorado. Only the superiors of St. Brigid's, San Francisco, and St. Vincent's, Petaluma, California, were deemed too far away to come.

Prominent among the Sisters present were Sister M. Agnes Burke, superior of St. Agatha's in Iowa City, who was in touch with the direction educational courses were taking, and Sisters M. Michael Nihill, Crescentia Markey, Annunciation Hannon, Philippa Sheridan, Ascension Lilly, Lambertina Doran, Isabella Kane, Octavia Burke and her sister Edmunda, Ignatia Pyne, Hilary Regan and Benedicta Prendergast, each of whom had shown a special aptitude as master teacher or administrator. Sister M. Benedicta was then superior at Mt. St. Joseph Academy, and encouraging her Sisters to make such preparation as they could for the teaching of college subjects, while Sister M. Lambertina, superior at All Hallows, Wichita, was planning the publication of a text entitled Lessons in Literature, intended for seventh and eighth grade classes.

The school session, which was to serve for a pattern for other such meetings, opened with a lecture by the Reverend Joseph Rigge, S. J. , nationally known scientist from Creighton University. The Sisters had been assigned to specific committees, each with its chairman. Twice each day panelists presented background for problems to be discussed, suggesting possible solutions. Discussion from the floor followed. The topics assigned for that first conference were: the uniformity desirable in student papers, order in the classroom, methods of classroom organization, grading, religious instruction, and the advisability of teaching boys and girls in separate classrooms.

The final work of the conference was a three-year plan for regularly-graded course of study to cover the eight grades and the four academic years. While the Sisters recognized that some schools would not be able to put the full program into effect, they urged weekly lessons in classroom singing and drawing, and recommended instruction in science and languages wherever possible. Little was attempted by way of individualized laborator experiments, work in the area of science being fairly confined to a study of Steele's <u>Fifteen Weeks</u> in each of the several branches of scientific study.

During the subsequent years of Mother Cecilia's administration, on three Saturdays of each month, sessions were held in Chicago for the exchange of ideas and methods in teaching various class subjects. This program was especially effective in the city, where teachers of the various grade levels met in conveniently located centers and were directed by master teachers. While it seemed best not to put the pressure of summer institute on the Sisters the next three summers, they were resumed in 1898, with extensions to serve the Sisters outside of Chicago. These were located in the various boarding schools. Superiors were urged meantime to provide special help for Sisters needing it.

Even at that first meeting, Sisters M. Agnes and Crescentia had spoken together of the need for Catholic summer courses at the college level. Obstacles were many, however. The summer vacation did not begin until the last week of June, and the Sisters were expected to be at their missions by the middle of August since their schools ordinarily opened a week before the public schools. The novices were required to spend the summer at Mt. Carmel, and, for all the Sisters as well as for them, there was always an eight-day retreat. There was, further, the problem of a general cleaning to be given for both convent and school, usually including a certain amount of scraping and varnishing of desks, the slating of blackboards, etc. , tasks which otherwise would not be done and which the Sisters regarded as essential to a well-kept classroom. Every item of the Sisters' wardrobe was "homemade" and hand-mended, while the costly habit serge and veiling underwent many transitions before they were finally discarded. Furthermore, the summer was especially a time for visiting the sick and the parents of the pupils, and doing necessary planning for school. All this left little time for summer courses.

But these were not the only obstacles to regular classwork. There was not a single Catholic college or university open to women. Priests were either forbidden or at least discouraged from teaching women, and Sisters were forbidden to take classes from laymen. [3] As for attendance at secular colleges or universities, this was not to be countenanced. In time all that would be altered, but meanwhile much would be lost.

At the time that Mother Cecilia came into office the new motherhouse was still without a name. The consultors had pondered the title "Nazareth Heights, " but it suggested no link with the past, while its alternate, "Mt. Carmel, " had been used to designate the hill on which the Prairie motherhouse stood. The decision was finally made by a vote taken at the consultors' meeting on March 22, 1894, and the bluff that overlooked the Mississippi and the busy town on its banks was to be known thereafter as Mt. Carmel. As for the house itself, that would, like the old home, be St. Joseph Convent.

The huge debt of $120, 907. 00 which remained on the new home, as well as the indebtedness for additions on the several boarding academies seemed quite overwhelming to Mother Cecilia. Faced with a heavy payment of interest due on April 1, she beseeched the entire congregation to make a fervent novena in honor of St. Joseph, closing on his feast day, March 19. It is an interesting fact that on that date a bequest of $12, 000 came to Sister M. Alphonse Boyle from a family estate.

In early 1894 the consultors, at the urgent request of the pastor of Assumption Church, Cresco, Iowa, decided to permit the Sisters to attend evening Benediction in the parish church, a permission withdrawn later when the same request was being repeated elsewhere. The article of the rule which forbade the Sisters to take care of the altar and sacristy of the public church had likewise been set aside in several instances. However, when Mother Cecilia reviewed points of discipline with superiors at their summer conference of 1894, questions regarding these exemptions had arisen. Then in 1895 she called the superiors home for a Holy Week retreat, and to impress upon them their

responsibilities as guardians of the rule. In a circular letter
that followed the retreat, Mother directed the Sisters to live
according to the original intent of each rule.

When the ladies in early Dubuque complained to Bishop Loras
that the Sisters were leaving an excess of oil on the pews in the
course of their Saturday cleaning of the cathedral, he solved the
problem by turning the cleaning chores over to the ladies themselves. Then there had been more Sisters available than there
were classes to teach. Those times were no more. Classes were
large, requiring much preparation and correcting of papers.
Cleaning of classrooms and convent duties taxed even the most
rugged in the absence of modern conveniences, without adding
to these the care of altar and sacristy. Since the rule of silence restricted all but the most essential communication, the
one hour of evening recreation was almost the only release from
the tensions of the day. For pastors to add parish devotions to
the heavy regime of the Sisters' spiritual exercises and thus to
deprive them of that one brief hour for the sake of edifying his
parishioners was to draw from the urbane and gracious Mother
Cecilia more fire than they were quite prepared for. She was
quite prepared for them when they began to press her with their
complaints. Rough drafts of some of her letters remain in her
files. One of these is addressed to Bishop Bonacum of Lincoln,
Nebraska, where Sister M. Ascension Lilly was superior at
the cathedral school of St. Theresa's. It reads:

> Sr. M. Ascension tells me you requested her to write to
> me again, before the Sisters discontinue the care of the
> altars in the church in Lincoln. In regard to this matter,
> I think I can add nothing to what I have written to Rev. Fr.
> Nugent. The care of sacristies in public churches is em-
> phatically against our rule, as you may see by reference
> to our Constitutions, Chap. 11, Art. 38; we have for
> weighty reasons found it necessary to withdraw dispensa-
> tions which allowed work prohibited by this rule to be
> done in certain places. The withdrawal of dispensations
> to be effective must be general - no exceptions can be made.

> Sr. M. Ascension says that in case our Sisters discontinue
> the care of the altars, you will be obliged to get Sisters to
> come from the other side of the city to take care of them.
> This will be an inconvenience, I know. Would it simplify
> matters for you, Rt. Rev. Bishop, were I to withdraw our
> Sisters from Lincoln, and thus leave you free to give your
> school in charge to any other Community who can better

SISTERS FROM ST. BRIGID'S, SAN FRANCISCO

At San Rafael, 1899

S.M.Casia O'Connor	Mrs. Parrott	Mrs. Rowan	S.M.Arcadia Haugh	Climacus Ryan
S.M.Rose Rourke	Delphine Conway	Redempta Coleman	Consolata Connell	Luciola Mariga
S.M.Leonella Conway	Letitia Lee	Gaudentia Hallinan	Prudentia Reilly	Simplicia Kennedy

On Mt. Helena with Father Cottle

serve the interests of your parish in accordance with
their rule? Do not for a moment hesitate on our account. We are doing what is judged best for our Community and its special work; and, of course, you are
justified in doing whatever you think will best serve the
interests of your diocese.

The Bishop seems to have caught the message, for the Sisters continue to serve the Lincoln diocese to this day.

There remains also the reply to the Reverend E. W. Fowler,
pastor of St. Joseph Church, Sioux City. To the Bishop's complaint regarding evening Benediction, he added also that regarding the care of the altar and sacristy, Mother wrote:

> In regard to those things which you find so distasteful
> and which you are pleased to call "new regulations," I
> have only to remark that there is nothing new about them.
> They are only our expressed rule or the things implied by
> its spirit and necessary to its observance. Our Constitu-
> tions have received the approval of the Church - a suf-
> ficient guarantee that we may safely follow them without
> fear of spiritual loss. I did not force the rule on the
> Sisters. At her profession, each religious of her own
> free will promises God solemnly that she will observe
> the rule; and I cannot, without sufficient cause, dispense
> her from her obligation. As to forcing "regulations" on
> you, I never dreamt of such a thing. Before you engaged
> the Sisters to teach your school, you knew, I suppose that
> we are exclusively an educational order; that we do not
> profess to be sacristans, sextons, nor directors of choirs
> in public churches. These things are forbidden us, as you
> may see by reference to our rule, a copy of which is, no
> doubt, in your possession.

> Yes, I heard that you applied not only to one but to three
> different communities for Sisters to take your school, and
> I regret very much that some of them could not accom-
> modate you.

> Now, as to the choir: the Sisters may train the children
> in the school or the convent, but no Sister may sing in the
> choir, nor may she direct the choir, during such services.
> Whether composed of children, or of grown up people, the
> choir, on those occasions, is the choir of the public church,
> and we are not permitted to sing in it, or to direct it. I have

no objection to the Sisters sitting in the gallery and looking over the conduct of the children.

The Sisters may see that the altar boys are vested for Mass,
or for any other service, held in daylight; and they may keep
the boys in order while waiting for the service to begin.

The fact that laughter from the Community room could be
heard in the church would seem to indicate that the Sisters
are living in very unsuitable quarters. [4] The Sisters work
hard all day; they have their spiritual exercises at appointed hours; and the rule allows them a certain amount of
recreation in the evening. I can not deprive them of this
recreation. Of course, I admit that under present circumstances, the Sisters ought to be careful and the talking and
laughing should be moderate.

Now, dear Rev. Father, whatever you may think about it,
our experience is that we render the greatest service to
both priests and people in those places in which we most
faithfully observe our rule and devote ourselves to our work
as efficient teachers, leaving the church, the choir, and the
conduct of public worship to those to whom such things rightfully belong.

Trusting that all misunderstanding may be now amicably
settled, I am, dear Rev. Father,
                              Very sincerely yours,

A third protest came from the Reverend J. Henry Tihen, later
Bishop of Lincoln and then of Denver, but at this time pastor at
the pro-cathedral in Wichita. Father's protest regards attendance
at evening services in the church. We quote just the essence of
that letter:

I am not in the least apprehensive that the Sisters in Wichita,
or anywhere else will suffer spiritual loss through exact
observance of our rule. . . As to giving scandal, is it not a
fact, borne out by all history, that the congregations of religious men and women who have scandalized the faithful are
precisely those who have departed from their rule? Not
long ago a gentleman, eminent for his virtue and learning,
speaking about the attendance of religious at night services
in public churches, said: "No right thinking man believes
that the streets of great cities, or of country towns and vil-

The earliest available picture of the Wichita Academy.
The original All Hallows Academy building is seen at
the right.

Immaculate Conception Academy, Davenport in about 1890.
The original Hill house is seen at the right.

lages are, at night, proper places for unattended women. Religious edify seculars most by keeping their rule; and at night services in public churches, the empty benches of religious women give greatest edification. In saying this, I believe I voice the sentiments of all enlightened Catholics. " I have only to add that if those who possess jurisdiction in the matter think that by observing their rule, the Sisters will become a scandal and an obstacle to the best interests of Catholicity in Wichita, we shall take this as an evident sign that Wichita is a field in which God does not intend us to labor.

Father Tihen returned with the suggestion that it would save any possible scandal if the Sisters were to reside at the academy instead of in the parish convent. To this Mother replied:

In answer to your letter, received yesterday, I would say that past experience has taught us that it is not practical for our Sisters in Wichita to attend the parochial school from the Academy. The long ride back and forth in the winter, the cold dinner that must be taken, and other inconveniences connected with such an arrangement are hardships which we have no right to inflict upon the Sisters. If it is agreeable to you, we will vacate the house by recalling the Sisters to Dubuque. Is it your wish that we do so at once? Or, if we remain until you can secure another Community will we be allowed to observe our rule as we understand it?

The Sisters remained at the pro-cathedral until sometime later, as we shall see.

Mother's position was strongly reinforced by Father Friedan, S. J. , director of the superiors' retreat in April 1896, when he reminded all of the obligation placed upon them by their rule.

In a letter addressed to Sister M. Aloysius Curtin on July 19, 1897, Mother Cecilia wrote:

I cannot permit the Sisters in LeMars to take care of the Church. You write that in the event of your not being allowed to comply with Father Barron's wishes in the matter, he wants me to remove you all. I now do so. Pay all your debts. Leave the house in good order, and come to Dubuque as soon as you have settled everything.

The Sisters[5] arrived in Dubuque, July 21, 1897.

It is difficult to reconcile the firmness and independence of
mind which Mother Cecilia manifested in these letters with the
immaturity which she seemed to foster in two young women
whom she had directed as novices, as seen in the following letter addressed to Sisters M. Blanche and Benezetta Fosselman,
and dated June 13, 1897. The former had been in the Congregation
eight years and the latter six. The occasion of a family gathering, in all likelihood the last, the poor health of the parents, and
the sacrifice they were making of a third child to the religious
life - all, would seem to call for a response in direct opposition
to that Mother outlines. The letter reflects instead the dichotomy
then existing in the minds of the pious between the "holy" and
the secular, "the life of perfection" and "the world,"" the supernatural and the natural. It reflects, too, the misconception that
an attitude of dependence is a necessary adjunct to a life of
obedience. Mother's habit of underlining persists through all
her personal correspondence.

I have consented to let you visit your home in Waverly for
two days and two nights only - and you are to reach there
on 24th inst. Rev. Fr. Burke wrote for your parents' sake
and begged the favor - Frank is to be there too; and you
are allowed to go because your parents are not well - and
because Frank is going to take the Franciscan Habit in a
short time - and you may never be together again. Now -
my dear Novice Children, I want to be very proud of you -
so be on your best cheerful religious behavior. Remember,
you are not girls or ladies of the world now. Do honor to
your Habit and to your holy profession, by your religious
deportment. If strangers - not members of the family -
are at the table, don't take your meals with them: Mama
will give you your meals by yourselves. If there are no
strangers at table, you can take meals with the family.
And do not remain up longer than 9 o'clock at night. Slip
off for noon examen - into your bed room - ten minutes -
and manage to make your meditation - say your rosary -
and night prayers - also a wee visit to your bed room after
dinner & supper - to speak to our Lord. Being religious,
this will be expected of you. Read a chap. of the "Imitation"
at night. Now be good - lovely - happy - and may God bless
you both! My love to all at home. Thank Fr. Burke for
asking this favor for you. Be gravely nice to Fr. Burke.
Your loving
Sr. M. Cecilia

The letter suggests something of the watertight nature of the Sisters' daily schedule. In general, regulations imposed on the personal lives of religious women, and not of B. V. M. 's more than of others, were especially stringent in view of the fact that they were applied to adult, freely committed women. These included the following in one form or another:

1. The obligation of superiors to read incoming and outgoing mail, the restriction of letters to those merely "necessary, " and the withholding of such letters as they deemed "sentimental, " or "nonsensical. "

2. The necessity for a companion in the parlor and for even the briefest foray outside the convent.

3. The restriction on the borrowing of books or other reading matter except with the express permission of the superior to whose scrutiny each item was to be subjected.

4. The prohibition against leaving the convent for any purpose on Sunday without the permission of the mother-general.

5. The obligation of attendance at the high Mass on Sunday of at least a portion of the local community for the sake of giving edification, though this ordinarily meant the hearing of a third Mass.

6. The observance of silence on the street and in street cars, or at least the refraining from unnecessary conversation.

7. The limiting of communication with externs to the unavoidable.

8. A report to be made by both the superior and the Sisters involved when a delay keeps Sisters out after darkness has fallen.

9. Silence at all meals except with the special permission of the mother-general. [6]

To these general regulations each superior-general added those peculiarly their own. Mother Cecilia's included the admonitions:

"Never be guilty of the improprieties of chewing gum or

playing croquet, " and "games playing with playing cards are not to be permitted. "

Her regulations regarding school entertainments were enforced by her early successors also:

There is still much that is censurable in the entertainments prepared by the Sisters. I have called your attention to this many times and still there was dancing as an important part of many closing exercises this year. In one place the priest stopped it at the last moment, and I commend him for it. Not only has there been dancing, but boys and girls dancing together on the stage; and a Sister teaching such things, picking up her skirts and dancing before the children to teach them. I am ashamed of this work, and I beg you to put a stop to it. Present in your public exercises only those things that a good religious should be proud of teaching. Hereafter let there be positively no dancing of any kind whatsoever in entertainments given by the pupils of our schools. Our Custom Book distinctly states that the Sisters must not permit the pupils to use powder, rouge, or things of the kind even when they are preparing for entertainments.

While loyal support was generally given to such directives, it was sometimes at a heavy price. The Record of Events kept by the secretaries-general lists what seems to have been an undue number of nervous breaks and unscheduled departures.

Yet Mother Cecilia was a kindly and very lovable woman, often herself subject to some of the same corrections she made. She was not a good traveler, and it helped her to chew gum, which she once quite unconsciously continued to do throughout a train conversation with the Archbishop of Dubuque. She often renewed the request that the Sisters avoid the use of shortened or nicknames for each other, yet she repeatedly fell into the same practice. She excused Sisters readily for small faults and inadvertences, as an incident recounted by Sister M. Conrad Curley intimates.

Sister was a new postulant at the time. In the course of dusting the convent parlor she climbed on a chair to wipe the heavy frame of a large print of Father Donaghoe. The picture wire broke and the picture crashed to the floor, the glass shattering over the room. Mother was not at home at the time. Sister M. Esther Warren, then in charge of the postulants, assumed her sternest manner, telling the postulant that she would have to report the matter to Mother. It was a long and troubled time of

waiting. When at last Mother came, the tearful postulant told
her the story amid sobs. "Did you hurt yourself?" was Mother's
anxious question. "No, Mother, but the picture -. " "Never mind
the picture, " Mother answered. "That can be fixed, or we can
get another, but we couldn't get another one of you. "

To queries made of elderly Sisters regarding Mother Cecilia,
the reaction is uniformly warm and clearly affectionate. One
who knew her well responded: "If you didn't know Mother Cecilia
you missed half your life. " Others recalled that on Mother's return from a business trip or the visitation of houses, the novices
would run to meet her and throw their arms about her, a greeting to which she would respond with lively stories of her experiences. It was Mother Gertrude herself who commented on the
contrast of their greeting of her, who was then their mistress.
On one occasion when Mother Gertrude returned from a trip,
her novices, as was usually the case, stood about stiffly. One
who was quite young and exuberant, ran up to her, put her arms
about her and kissed her. To this Mother remarked, "If I were
Mother Cecilia you would all be up here. "

The name "Holy Family School" referred to the "Brothers'
School for Boys" of the Holy Family Parish, conducted by Brother
Thomas O'Neill, S. J. , with a faculty of laymen and women,
Brother serving as prefect of discipline. His was no small task
when the enrollment ran between 1, 500 and 2, 000 boys, "containing all the life and energy for which Irish immigrants were
noted. " After eighth grade the boys who were inclined, or in a
position, to continue their schooling, attended St. Ignatius, a
six-year preparatory-college combination just east of Holy
Family Church. Neighborhood schools of the parish, taught by
the B. V. M. Sisters, continued to provide for the younger boys
and girls.

St. Aloysius School at 210 Maxwell Street, also taught by the
B. V. M. Sisters, or "Black Bonnets" as they were familiarly
called, provided schooling for the girls of the upper grades.
There the academic course, supplemented with commercial
subjects as electives, was taught by three Sisters. Priests
from St. Ignatius College conducted classes in logic, ethics
and mathematics. Steele's popular books on science, including
chemistry, physics, geology, physiology, astronomy and botany
were studied. The classes were small and the subjects were
well taught. A number of its graduates entered Chicago Normal
College to train for teaching in the public schools.

The Sisters had by 1891 established a formal system of classi-

fying their pupils according to grade level. [8] Sister M. Agatha
Hurley had served as superior of all the B. V. M. Sisters teach-
ing in the various Holy Family schools, and as principal of St.
Aloysius from 1867 to 1887. For a brief time Sister M. Agnes
Burke was her successor, followed by Sister M. Seraphina
Short during a three-year term in which Sister M. Agatha
served as visitor to the Congregation at large.

At this time Holy Family was a rapidly changing parish. The
Irish and German families that had prospered were moving
farther west and north, their departure hastened by the arrival
of large numbers of Russian Jews fleeing from pogroms in their
own land. By 1892 the area about the west end of the Twelfth
Street bridge was known as "Poor Jews' Quarter. "[9] It was an
area of sweat shops, junk dealers, street hawkers and kosher
markets. Italians too were coming in numbers, and settling in
"Little Italy" in the area of Halsted and Taylor Streets. Whole
families crowded into single rooms in the gaunt, grimy houses.
Unskilled as they were, these newcomers became "street
sweepers, boot blacks, fruit peddlers, rag pickers and organ
grinders," while the little boys sold newspapers and shined shoes.

It was no longer the "single great Irish workingman's parish
whose 5,000 children accounted for one-sixth of all Chicago's
Catholic school children. "[10] But, like the Irish and Germans,
these people too would prosper and move on. Meanwhile it was
through a fast changing neighborhood that the Sisters were conveyed by their horse-drawn carry-all or long bobsled to the
neighborhood schools. As they came and went the Jewish children
shouted epithets at them. Breaking windows, throwing stones at
the convent and pelting the girls with anything they could pick up,
they made their most concentrated attack on the convent on
Christmas night of 1895. Conflicts between Irish and Jewish
children, and later between Irish and Italian, were frequent. As
a consequence of the many changes in the area, the schools' enrollment was dropping rapidly.

On September 10, 1895 Brother O'Neill died. His brother,
Father Andrew O'Neill, S. J., supervisor of the several parish
schools, was approaching his seventieth year. The Jesuit Fathers decided it was time for a reorganization.

Letters of the Reverend James Hoeffer, S. J., addressed to
Sister M. Hilary, then superior, in the late summer of 1896,
outlined the new arrangement. "Holy Family School" was to
constitute the central school for boys and girls beyond the
fourth grade. None but the Sisters were to teach. The St.
Aloysius School on Maxwell Street was soon to be sold. Father
Hoeffer's estimate of an anticipated enrollment of 1,600 chil-

dren indicated a need of from thirty-two to thirty-four Sisters. The course of study was to be outlined by the reverend prefect of studies for all the schools. It was his duty to draw up quarterly examinations for all grades, to judge of the efficiency of the teachers, and to "decide upon any question with regard to the school which may arise. "

The girls in the high school classes which had been conducted at St. Aloysius were left with but little choice. Those who continued enrolled in the public schools. Bands and the drum and bugle corps for the boys, with their splendid uniforms, were no more. By way of compensation, however, they were included in the choruses, declamations, cadet drills, tableaux, calisthenics, and dramatic performances which took up the final week of the school year. [11] Though all the parish schools were to be coeducational, boys and girls were taught in separate rooms and assigned to separate playgrounds.

The St. Aloysius school building was sold in the early summer of 1896 to the public school system, thereafter to serve as the Oliver Goldsmith School for small boys. Until the completion of a convent at 1010 S. May Street, the Sisters lived first in the former boys' school, then in a rented store building opposite the church.

It was a comfort to the Sisters after all the changes to receive the praise of the prominent Chicago layman, the Honorable W. J. Onahan:

The introduction of the Sisters of Charity of the B. V. M. , was one of the happiest events for Catholic education in this parish and city. This wonderful Community seemed to possess, from the beginning, a special fitness and aptitude for the task of parochial schoolwork, into which they entered with the greatest ardor and for which the Sisters have demonstrated the highest capability. [12]

The B. V. M. Sisters continued with the parish schools amid the vicissitudes of a decaying neighborhood. [13] They serve today, not in the school, but in the ministry of the Jesuit Fathers to a rapidly growing congregation of Blacks and Chicanos. They also conduct a house of prayer to provide the wearied and the disheartened of the area an occasional refuge and source of refreshment. In 1922 when a vocational summary of the parish was made, it was found that 187 girls from its schools had entered the Congregation of the Sisters of Charity. [14]

Fifth Grade, St. Pius School, Chicago, 1895

All Hallows Academy, Wichita, ca. 1890
Rev. Henry Tihen, later Bishop of Denver

The same year that the Sisters took over the reorganized Holy Family School, 1896, Mother Cecilia was called on to supply Sisters for a school in the new Blessed Sacrament Parish in the village of Lawndale. Laid out after the fire of 1871, the village was surrounded by a broad stretch of virgin prairie on the far outskirts of Chicago. Blessed Sacrament was to be the first of a succession of new parishes which would form a crescent about Chicago, from St. Jerome's in Rogers Park on the north side, Our Lady of Lourdes, Ravenswood, St. Gertrude's, Edgewater, St. Agatha's, Douglas Park, Our Lady Help of Christians, Austin, Our Lady of Angels and Presentation, Garfield Park, Queen of Heaven, Cicero, Holy Cross, Englewood, and St. Dorothy's, Grand Crossing, as well as St. Thomas of Canterbury in Uptown Chicago. To each of these, B. V. M. Sisters responded.

Previous to the establishment of the new Lawndale parish of Blessed Sacrament, Father Henneberry from St. Pius and Father Muldoon from St. Charles alternated in attending the Catholics in that area.[15] Accompanied by two B. V. M. Sisters and two altar boys, on Sundays the priests drove out to hear confessions and say Mass in a public hall, while the Sisters taught catechism to the children. These the priests had recruited by traveling about on horseback, distributing from their saddlebags copies of catechisms to likely subjects.

The brick school erected by the Reverend John M. Dunn, its first pastor, proved a magnet for Catholic families and the town grew rapidly. The coming of the Western Electric[16] and International Harvester plants and the Lawndale Avenue carhouse added significantly to its population. Prepared for two hundred students when the Sisters came in 1896, the school had enrolled 484 by the end of the year. In its jubilee class of 1947, 108 children received diplomas. However, the neighborhood was then beginning to change from Irish and Bohemian to Black. It is almost entirely Black today, save for the B. V. M. Sisters[17] who continue to serve it. Long-time pastor, the Reverend John Morrissey, like many others of the time, is especially remembered for his care of the poor during the great depression of the thirties. Father Raymond O'Brien's well-known boys' book, Brass Knuckles, was dramatized by the graduating class of 1947 under the direction of the Sisters. Thirty-five B. V. M. 's and twenty-nine priests have been among the school's graduates.

The St. Agatha Parish, bordering on Douglas Park, was founded in 1893 for the Irish of the Lawndale area, and named after Sister M. Agatha Hurley who taught catechism at the Douglas Park bandstand before the parish got under way. The

B. V. M. Sisters[18] came when the first school building was ready in 1895, enrolling ninety-eight pupils. By 1910, its peak year, 750 children were in attendance. The parish was never large, its residential area being limited by the extensive Douglas Park. As the neighborhood changed, both priests and Sisters sought to meet the needs of its new Black population, despite the deterioration of the plant and the general impoverishment of the area. Though their number is much reduced, the Sisters continue to serve the parish.

In 1893 the academy at Wichita was seeking permission for a building project at an estimated cost of $10,000. The fact that the academy was already in debt led the consultors to reject the request. At nearly the same time Mother Cecilia was faced with the necessity of refusing a request for Sisters at Newton, Kansas. This double disappointment in matters of importance to his diocese put Bishop Hennessy in an unhappy mood. As a result, he asked Mother to withdraw the Sisters from the school at the pro-cathedral, in favor of a diocesan community of Sisters of St. Joseph. To his people's protest, the Bishop's response was that he knew he was injuring himself by his action, but that it was "necessary that my authority be maintained."

A cemetery was opened in the spring of 1895 at the new motherhouse, a decision made when the funeral procession of Sister M. Francis Mulligan bogged down in deep mud on its way to the Prairie burial grounds. The following September the Reverend John Daly, motherhouse chaplain, blessed the large plot and the recently erected crucifix. There was no attempt at that time to transfer the bodies from the country graveyard. In 1898 Father Donaghoe's remains were removed from its place under the altar in the little adobe chapel to the nearby graveyard, and a granite monument erected. A marble shaft was then placed to mark the grave of Mother Clarke.

In 1895 also, the Sisters at the motherhouse adopted the monastic habit of going in two's to chapel and dining room, reciting the Miserere or other psalms or hymns alternately as they walked. The steam laundry was set in operation and a telephone was installed in the motherhouse that year. The year 1903 saw also the death of Father Trevis in Davenport.

Financial pressure led to the decision to offer the St. Joseph Academy at Thirteenth and Main Streets for sale. Fortunately for its future, the offer brought no buyer. An earthquake jarred Dubuque on November 3 of that year. Tragedy struck twice in early 1896. On April 6 the twenty-five-year-old Sister M.

Class Picture, St. Vincent's, Petaluma, 1898
Sisters M. Redempta Coleman and Damian Kenneally

Probably a group of sodalists, Sioux City, 1898
(1) Mayme (2) Nell Malone, Sisters of S. M. Josephine
Malone and aunt and mother of Sister M. Benedict Phelan

Patricia Faherty died at the Council Bluffs academy of burns received when a mixture of beeswax and turpentine she was preparing for floor wax caught fire. In late April Sister M. Damian Kennealy, teacher of art for the novices, was thrown from a street car in Chicago and seriously hurt. Death from her injuries occurred in October after months of suffering.

On July 22, 1896 death took General George W. Jones, former Indian trader, soldier, Wisconsin pioneer, friend of Mazzuchelli and of Jefferson Davis, territorial representative, senator, ambassador to Bogota, convert to the faith and generous patron of Mt. St. Joseph Academy.

A home for the chaplain had been made ready by the construction of a two-story brick house, its first floor to serve temporarily for the workmen employed at the motherhouse. A gift of $300.00 from Bishop Cosgrove was used to install fire hose in the new home, and the large tubular bells used for calling the Sisters' to their exercises were erected, the gift of the Reverend John Hanley and Mrs. Kinsella Duggan. From candles and grease lamps the Sisters turned to kerosene lamps for lighting in time for Christmas 1896, city gas not yet being available to them.

The motherhouse remained unfinished. In 1897 the Sisters' council decided to complete the cell wing assigned to the professed Sisters, and because it was believed that germs traveled upward, they located its infirmary section on the upper two floors. The little chapel prepared there they described as "the prettiest room in the whole convent."

In March 1897 the Congregation instituted a suit against the company that had contracted for the roofing of the new motherhouse, charging the use of inferior materials. An award of $8,400.00 was eventually granted by the court. That fall Mother Cecilia and companion made the visitation of the California houses, leaving Dubuque on October 30. Their total expenses for "travel, sleeper and pocket money," was $85.00. Meantime many and varied changes had taken place.

Many requests for Sisters had come from various parts of the country, as well as an urgent call from the Jesuit mission in British Honduras with the appended note that the mission called for women prepared for great self-sacrifice. They were not enough Sisters to meet this need or those of many others, including Father Jennings' that they build a high school in his parish of the Presentation, Chicago, on land which the Congregation owned there. This they could not do for that called for a more central situation. In 1900 they did, however, provide Sisters for his parish school.

While the problems of finance pressed heavily on Mother
Cecilia, Mother Gertrude was able to relieve her of excessive
interest charges by refinancing the Congregation's debts at the
low interest rate of four percent.

Concern was growing for the secondary education of Catholic
girls on Chicago's southwest side, a concern which Sister M.
Hilary, superior at Holy Family, communicated to Mother
Cecilia and her council. On November 21, 1897 Mother wrote
the pastors of that area:

> For some years we have been considering the project
> of a Catholic high school for girls in the City of Chicago.
> We are inclined to think that the time is now ripe for such
> a work, but before entering on this important business,
> we feel that we ought to consult with those interested in
> our schools and competent to afford us wise counsel.
>
> May we infringe upon your charity and good will by re-
> questing you to meet us on Monday, 28th inst., at 3 P. M.,
> at St. Charles school, 12th and Cypress streets, to discuss
> the advisability of such a step and the proper location for
> such a school? Please favor us by considering this subject
> and by being present at the meeting. The above project
> has the approval of the most Reverend Archbishop.
>
> Yours humbly in Our Lord,
> Sister M. Cecilia, CBVM

Sisters in other parish schools of Chicago's west and south
sides were offering secondary subjects to the few girls who had
not exchanged the classroom for a factory assembly line, for
cleaning or for domestic service. The most successful of these
schools was the St. James parish high school under the direction
of the Reverend Hugh McGuire, a capable and farsighted educator.
In 1897 his already thriving school occupied a new building, adequate in every department, and regarded as the model parochial
high school of the archdiocese. Year after year graduates of the
school established splendid records in the Chicago Normal College and passed into the classrooms of the public schools, [19]
thus setting a pace for others to follow. Chicago's southwest
side called for another such institution, yet no parish seemed
equal to the venture, leaving to the Sisters the risk and the
struggle. A central high school in that area would draw girls
from the parishes of Holy Family, St. Charles, Blessed Sacrament, Sacred Heart, St. Pius, St. Agatha, St. Bridget, Annunciation and St. Jarlath. Father Curran, S. J., of Holy Family
and Father Muldoon of St. Charles shared with Sister M. Hilary,

superior of the Holy Family Sisters, the vision of such an institution. When Sister presented the project to the motherhouse council she had the backing of the influential Sister M. Loyola, the Congregation's treasurer. That the plan of a central high school for girls, supported by a religious congregation, was without precedent in the entire country was not a matter of concern. The need was there and they believed they saw a way to meet it.

To Sister M. Loyola was assigned the task of locating a suitable building. This proved to be a three-story structure at the corner of Taylor and Cypress Streets. The lower two floors would serve for classes and the third would provide living quarters for the Sisters. The accumulation of dirt and neglect had first to be removed, and the Sisters from Holy Family spent the last weeks of the summer in drudgery - scrubbing the place and moving in the necessary furnishings and equipment.

Seventy-two girls appeared for the opening on the first September morning, all as first year students. In the large first-floor study hall, Sister M. Hilary assembled the girls for religion, Sister M. Columba Donnelly taught English and Latin, and Sister M. St. James Kinsella, physiology, physiography and art, while Sister M. Christiana Brown gave lessons in piano, mandolin and guitar in the several rooms of the second floor. [20] Each student paid a tuition charge of $1.00 a month, as much as girls were in a position to pay at a time for their fathers were earning only $1.00 to $1.25 a day with which to support their usually large families. That income sufficed to meet the rental cost. The music brought in added revenue, while the motherhouse agreed to send a monthly check to cover the deficit. Pressures were great, and the Sisters waited anxiously for the monthly check. On one occasion when it was delayed, the staunch Sister M. Hilary could express her frustrations only in tears.

By October 10 Mother's council had decided that the project gave sufficient promise of success to warrant building. Shortly after that, word went to each of the Chicago houses asking prayers, benefit programs and scholarships. Appeals were made to alumnae for their cooperation in these varied projects. Father Muldoon set himself the task of locating suitable property[21] on which the large two-story building was soon under construction; its address 1021 Cypress Street. Classes moved into the new building late in November, 1900. Thus a new pattern was set. Although the Catholic Education Association, established in 1904, was to give impetus to Catholic high schools St. Mary's nearest rival for the title of first was a central high school for girls opened in Philadelphia in 1912. [22] The fact that

St. Mary's opened without fanfare caused it to be overlooked in subsequent national studies.

A two-year commercial department opened in 1902 proved remarkably successful. The careful grade-school grounding in composition and spelling bore fruit, and graduates of the department found ready employment. The increased enrollment necessitated the adding of a third story to the building the following year.

Besides the high school courses offered, the girls were instructed in "religion and in gentle manners and in all that according to Catholic ideals constitute a refined and solid education. " Chartered in 1912, the school was not long in being affiliated with the Catholic University of America and approved by the Public Instruction Department of the State of Illinois. It was approved by the North Central Association of Schools and Colleges in 1933.

The first commencement exercises, held at the new Illinois Theatre on June 16, 1903, included the dramatic production "Ursula of Brittany. " The recently consecrated Bishop Muldoon, auxiliary of Archbishop Feehan, presented diplomas and certificates to the graduates, and gave the commencement address.[23]

At the suggestion of Bishop Muldoon, eleven of the school's first graduates applied to Chicago Normal College for entrance. As teachers, he pointed out, they could exert much influence for good. However, when, on their applications they gave the name of their school, the registrar said he had never heard of St. Mary's and refused to admit them. At this the Bishop presented himself to the Board of Admissions, reminding the members that as a public institution the Normal College could not arbitrarily reject any applicant. It was then agreed that the girls would be accepted if they could pass the entrance examination. Of the eleven who tried, nine passed. Little did the girls or the Admissions Board know that the Sisters spent the night before the examinations in prayer before the Blessed Sacrament.[24]

In 1915[25] two hundred of the five hundred applicants for the Normal passed the entrance examinations. Among those two hundred were forty of the forty-two St. Mary's girls who had made application.[26] The large proportion of Catholic school graduates who were entering the Chicago public school system was less than pleasing to the superintendent of public instruction, Ella Flagg Young. She attempted, though without success, to require that admission to the Normal school be on a quota basis. The Irish public school teacher became a familiar figure - a stereotype - if you will, in a city noted for its Irish police force and fire department. In 1920 Archbishop Mundelein explained the phenomenon in this way.

> . . . It will always redound to the credit and glory of the
> Irish immigrants and early settlers there, that wherever
> they could and where they had the schools under proper
> auspices, they always gave their daughters the chance of
> a better education. The father may have been only a laborer
> in the trenches, the mother without an education, but where
> the daughter showed signs of ability and a desire to study,
> they brought any and every sacrifice that she might have
> intellectual advantages if they could not give her material
> ones. That may explain the large number of Catholic girls
> with distinctly Irish names who are teachers in our municipal
> schools. I am told that 70 per cent of the teacher in the pub-
> lic schools are graduates of the Sisters' schools. . . . [27]

Many priests and religious came to visit the school to study
the plan of operation. When Archbishop Mundelein came into the
archdiocese in 1915, he saw in the regional central high school
a plan for the future development of the Chicago Catholic school
system and moved quickly in that direction. The opening in 1921
of the Immaculata, the B. V. M. high school for girls on the north
side, was a partial realization of that plan. Invited to give the
St. Mary's commencement address shortly after that opening,
the Archbishop said:

> When I came here from the East some years ago, I was
> unfamiliar with this type of school. We had academies. Oh,
> yes, - I had one in my own parish. I could never see that
> they meant much for scholarship, nor did they develop
> religious vocations. There was some non-Catholic atten-
> dance, but as for converts, a little parochial school con-
> ducted by the B. V. M. Sisters has more converts in a year
> than they ever had.

> But when I came here I found St. Mary's high school, a
> school where girls of all classes meet on an equal footing,
> where the only aristocracy is the aristocracy of brains.
> The methods of this institution are marked by briskness
> of attack. The girls are prepared for active service in the
> school, in commercial life, and in the home. The place
> neither gives nor asks odds of any other institution. You
> people may not know this, but it is due to the faculty of St.
> Mary's and of other similar schools, that admission to the

Normal for years past has been based on the results of
competitive examination, and not on percentage from the
schools. They have used their personal efforts with those
who had the decision of these matters to secure this result.
They have stood for the principle that the student should
prove her right to admission by her ability solely. The
faculty of this school have not only not feared, they have
challenged competition.

We are grateful for a school of this kind. We by no means
take it as a matter of course. In other places the diocese or
the parish has been put under contribution, but the Sisters
of the B. V. M. built and equipped their own school. To
furnish new missions they strip their various houses of all
but the barest necessities, and they do it cheerfully. As a
priest remarked to me the other day: "The Sisters of the
B. V. M. are not only poor individually, they are poor as a
Community. They have practised the utmost self-sacrifice,
and they have instilled the same spirit into their pupils.
For some time past, the girls and the Sisters here have
needed recreational facilities, yet they have cheerfully
yielded to the demands of the younger institution, the
Immaculata. It reminds one of an older sister, who, where
there is a pretty little girl in the house, gives up everything to make the little one as attractive as possible.

But St. Mary's did not give all to its younger sister. In 1924

Old St. Mary's, the alma mater of many of the pioneer
women of Chicago, and today one of the leading Catholic
High Schools for girls in the archdiocese, will open a new
auditorium and gymnasium building, February 19. . . .
The new building . . . comprises the gymnasium, science
laboratories, and art and music departments of the high
school as well as an auditorium which will seat 1, 200
people. [28]

The school was complete now with 22 classrooms, physical and
biological laboratories, four commercial rooms, domestic
science department, cafeteria, library and chapel.

The spirit of self-sacrifice which the Archbishop had remarked in the Sisters was indeed a heritage of St. Mary's graduates. The Alumnae Association, on the school's golden jubilee,
presented a check to Sister M. Aloysius, superior, for $500.00
to help provide a rest center for the Sisters in Tucson, Arizona.
The Association's larger purpose, however, was the purchase
of land for the transferral of St. Mary's to a more favorable

location. For this they had accumulated a fund of $20, 000. 00 when Cardinal Stritch refused permission for the move because of the need he saw for the school at its original site.

By the time of St. Mary's golden jubilee in 1949, four hundred young women among its 4, 948 graduates had entered the religious life, the others serving in various careers, including that of wife and mother. By that time shifts in population and the accompanying deterioration of the area raised the question of safety for the girls required to travel through it. The resultant falling off of enrollment led to a final decision to withdraw from the operation of the high school in June 1973.

In September 1973 the school opened for the first time under other auspices. It was operated as St. Mary Center for Learning by a private corporation, through a Land Trust Agreement with the B. V. M. Congregation. Effective August 1, 1973 the University of Illinois Medical Center leased the convent, built by the St. Mary's Alumnae in 1958, for the recently established School of Public Health. However, despite the fact that use of the building and equipment was free and subsidies were provided by the archdiocese, the Corporate Board operated the Center only until June 1976. All records were turned over to the University of Illinois, Circle Campus, which had taken a particular interest in the experiment. The property on which the buildings stood was then transferred to the State of Illinois to compensate for their demolition.

The desirability of perpetual vows had begun to concern the Sisters, and early in 1897[29] Mother Cecilia communicated with the Reverend Michael J. O'Connor, S. J. , of Xavier College, Cincinnati, regarding the canonical aspects of such vows. He responded with a careful discussion of the subject. In January 1899 Mother decided to confer with Archbishop Hennessy regarding the feasibility of so formalizing the Sisters' permanent commitment. The time seemed propitious, for the abbot of the Trappist monastery, the Reverend Louis Carew, OCSO, was in Rome, and he had expressed his willingness to lay the matter before the Congregation of Religious. However, the Archbishop, too near the end of his days to be greatly concerned, thought it best not to make any change.

Study sessions were scheduled again in the summers of 1898 and 1899, [30] following the pattern of that held in 1894. In addition to the institute at Holy Family, Chicago, and the several academies, there was a series of lectures on each of the summers given by the Right Reverend Monsignor Conaty, rector of Catholic University, for the novices and professed Sisters at Mt. Carmel.

On December 28, 1899, with the end of her second term of office near at hand, Mother Cecilia addressed the following letter to the Sisters.

My dear Sisters,

How much I have to thank you for your good will, your loyalty, and your devotion to the interests of our beloved congregation. I know all this will be just the same under another Superior, for it is given not to the individual but to the office; and no matter who may be placed there, you will give yourselves to her, or rather to God, with the same exactness and simplicity.

May God bless you all in the New Year, and may His unfailing love keep us united in heart and in soul and give us that exceedingly great reward which is promised to the faithful religious beyond all time and change.

Your affectionate
Sister M. Cecilia, C. B. V. M. [31]

The Archbishop's announcement in January 1900 of Mother Gertrude's return to the office of superior-general came as something of a surprise to the Sisters. The two other names proposed for the office were those of Sisters M. Gonzaga McCloskey and Maurice Duffy. Many of the Sisters must have grown weary by that time of the repeated rotation in office which had characterized the government from its first election in 1877. They were free to write in any names they wished, even that of Mother Cecilia, though her immediate reelection would have required confirmation by Rome. A clear majority for the seventy-three-year-old Mother Gertrude was then not readily predictable. Unfortunately, no tally of the votes remains.

The six names the consultors had proposed for their successors in office were: Mother Cecilia Dougherty and Sisters M. Agatha Hurley, Veronica Dunphy, Josephine Clarke, Basil Healey and Loyola Rutherford. The Sisters' vote placed Mother Cecilia first, followed by Sisters M. Loyola, Agatha and Josephine in that order. As new consultors, their first official action was the selection of Sister M. DeChantal O'Regan, treasurer, Sister M. Pulcheria McGuire, secretary, Sister M. Octavia Burke, visitor, and Sister M. Maurice Duffy, novice mistress, with Sister M. Gonzaga named as Mother's assistant.

A second surprise to the Sisters, at home and on the missions, came with the word that Mother Gertrude had assigned

Mother Cecilia, her first consultor, to the teaching of music at the Immaculate Conception Academy in Davenport.

CARRY-ALL TAKING SISTERS TO A PICNIC AT THE OLD MOTHERHOUSE

Notes

1 The Sisters who went in 1896 to staff St. Mary School, Iowa City, were: Sisters M. Etienne Fleming, Humbaline Solon, Girolamo Collins, Genoveffa Reinmann and Josita Waters.

2 On such occasions Sister M. Cecilia had exchanged her veil for a pink bonnet and donned a pink apron in place of her black serge, a change which had delighted her novices.

3 As late as November 28, 1913, Mother Ascension sent a letter to the Sisters in which she said: "The Sisters are hereby forbidden to take lessons from laymen in any branch of study; laymen should not be brought in to teach either Sisters or pupils. This restriction is in accordance with directions from the Holy See. "

4 St. Joseph's was a very poor parish at the time, and the Sisters were living in a kind of combination church and convent. The first Sisters stationed at St. Joseph's were: Sisters M. Cilinia Thompson, Scholastica McLaughlin, Lewis Kennedy and Felix Burns.

5 The Sisters originally stationed in LeMars were: Sisters M. Cortona Finley, Aloysius Curtin and Beata Griffin.

6 The Custom Book compiled in 1899 "by dispensation of the Mother General" granted permission for recreation at dinner and supper for all the major feasts and holidays. However, the strict constructionists regarded this as an abuse of power and Mother was obliged to rescind the privilege. After some years it seems to have been restored.

7 See Sister Mary Innocenta Montay, CSSF, MA, The History of Catholic Secondary Education in the Archdiocese of Chicago. (Washington, D. C. : Catholic University of America, 1953), p. 199f.

8 The Religious of the Sacred Heart conducted on Taylor Street, besides their academy, a parish school for small boys and for girls, with an enrollment approximating a thousand pupils.

9 Bessie Louise Pierce, A History of Chicago, Volume III, The Rise of a Modern City, 1871-1893. (Chicago: University of

Chicago Press, 1957). P. 42ff. deal with the immigrants in this area.

10 James W. Sanders, The Education of an Urban Minority: Catholics in Chicago, 1833-1965. (New York: Oxford University Press, 1977), p. 91.

11 However, not all the old glory had gone if we are to judge from an account in the New World for May 17, 1902. The occasion was the first Confirmation ceremony to be conducted by the newly consecrated Bishop Muldoon, auxiliary to the Archbishop of Chicago. The procession, led by a grand marshal and kept in line by his twenty-six assistant marshals, had its full panoply of bands and badges and banners, a cordon of police, and all the hundreds of children of the various Holy Family schools lined up in martial order. Meeting the carriage of the Bishop and his attendants at strategic places, suitable personages presented him with offerings of flowers, his carriage the first of a series of coaches for clergy and the press. The Confirmation service itself must have been something of an anti-climax.

12 The New World, April 14, 1900.

13 The Religious of the Sacred Heart purchased in 1901 a 45-acre tract of woodland in Lake Forest, Illinois, and in 1904 they transferred their boarding school to that site, the future location of Barat College. They continued their work for the parish girls and small boys for some time longer, until the Jewish community bought the property for a community settlement house. The new owners turned the chapel into a dance hall, while Jewish lads of the neighborhood tore down the highboard fence which surrounded the property for fire wood. In 1910 the buildings were destroyed by fire, apparently at the hands of arsonists.

14 Brother Thomas M. Mulkerins, S. J. , Holy Family Parish, Chicago, Priests and People. (Chicago: Universal Press, 1923), p. 480ff.

15 Ogden Avenue at that time was a plank road with toll gate at Crawford, now Pulaski.

16 This and neighboring parishes would bear the tragic loss when the Western Electric Company excursion on the fatal East

ended before it began. A rush of passengers to the dock side of the boat to bid goodbye to the crowd of spectators watching its departure caused the boat to overturn, and more than a thousand perished in the Chicago River within feet of the dock. The date of the tragedy was July 24, 1915.

17 The Sisters who opened Blessed Sacrament School were: Sisters M. Matilda Lahiff, Chrysantha Driscoll, Agrippina Hynes, Virginia Mulcahey, Francis Fitzgerald and Ursula Kenneally.

18 The Sisters who pioneered at St. Agatha's were: Sisters M. Evangelista Meehan, Constance Kelly, Seraphica Nagle, Sylvester Griffin and Servula Culligan.

19 Montay, p. 212f.

20 The fifth member of the little community was Sister M. Aquilina Hess, housekeeper.

21 The property owned by the Congregation in Presentation Parish was not regarded as suitable for the purpose of a high school.

22 See Thomas J. Donaghey, FSC, Philadelphia's Finest, a History of Education in the Catholic Archdiocese, 1692-1970. (Philadelphia: American Catholic Historical Society, 1972), p. 162f. Also see the Reverend J. A. Burns, Growth and Development of the Catholic School System in the United States. (New York: Benziger Brothers, 1951), p. 368. And Edward F. Spiers, The Central Catholic High Schools, A Survey of Their History and Status in United States. (Washington, D. C. : Catholic University Press, 1951). "A central high school for girls was finally opened in Philadelphia in 1912. Except for this experimentation, there had been no other activity in the central high school movement. " p. 32. The Philadelphia high school was financed by large benefactions and made use of the services of several different religious congregations.

23 St. Mary Golden Jubilee Booklet. A general source for the history of the school is the master's dissertation of Sister M. Anna Rose Callan, B. V. M. , The Sisters of Charity of the Blessed Virgin Mary and Their Schools in Chicago, 1867-1940, Loyola University, 1941. Chapter IV.

24 Details furnished by Sister M. Gonzaga Foley, B. V. M.

25 "By 1908 second generation Irish girls alone accounted for almost a quarter of all Chicago teachers. " Sanders, p. 121.

26 Callan, quoted from St. Mary's Annals, p. 131.

27 Ellen Skerrett, "Irish Catholic Parishes in Chicago, " read before the Midwest Conference of Irish Studies held at Loyola University, October 16, 1976.

28 Chicago Tribune, February 14, 1925, quoted by Callan, p. 133.

29 June 19, 1897 marked the death of Sister M. Baptist Seeley. After the death of Sister's father, her mother had made her home with the Sisters and continued to do so after Sister's death. Mother and daughter lie in adjacent graves in Mt. Carmel's Cemetery.

30 Sister M. Xavier O'Reilly's death on March 10, 1899 closed a long career of able service. A woman of unusual talents, the routine of the day's work and the want of opportunity for study had left her unfulfilled and lonely.

31 The Custom Book of 1899 directed the Sisters to use the initials "CBVM" after their names in all correspondence. It requested also that the Sisters refrain from referring to themselves as "the B. V. M. 's. " Later printings omitted these directives.

Chapter Nine

GREEN EYES AND GROWING SCHOOLS

The death of Archbishop John Hennessy on March 4, 1900 closed an episcopacy of thirty-five years. The funeral cere- monies brought many members of the hierarchy and of the clergy to Dubuque, Cardinal Gibbons[1] and an entourage coming by private car from Baltimore. The body of the Archbishop, in full episcopal vesture, lay in state in his cathedral, his casket of mahogany lined with copper, its handles mounted in gold.

After the impressive ceremonies attendant on his burial, the body was laid to rest in the cathedral's mortuary chapel, beside those of his predecessors, Bishops Loras and Smyth.

Hennessy died a wealthy man, his wills, as enigmatic as his life had been, assigning many generous bequests: burses to the American College in Rome and to the Catholic University of America; an endowment to the religious congregation he had founded, the Sisters of the Holy Ghost; and a large allotment for the construction of an archdiocesan theological seminary, the foundation of which he had laid many years before on the high bluff above the cathedral. A second will disposed of the large estate of his brother David, who had been his business agent. Apparently David, prior to his death, had entrusted to the Archbishop his entire holdings, inheritances from it to be assigned to their various relatives both in Ireland and in America. It would devolve upon Hennessy's successor to discern as best he could where personal wealth and diocesan resources began and left off.

The appointment of Bishop John J. Keane as successor to the see brought joy to clergy and people, a joy which was manifested by the thousands who greeted his arrival in Dubuque on September 27, 1900, and again in the plans of his clergy for his investiture with the pallium of the archbishop on April 17, 1901. Leaders in these latter preparations were Fathers John J. Toomey whom he

had appointed rector of the cathedral, and Roger Ryan, his and
his predecessor's vicar general. That occasion brought to
Dubuque four hundred priests, twenty-two bishops and five archbishops, as well as Keane's long time friend, Cardinal Gibbons.
Many among those present, not the least John Ireland, realized
deeply and rejoiced proportionately with the new Archbishop in
the ecclesiastical honors which lifted the shadows that had
gathered about his name. [2]

John Joseph Keane, a native of Ballyshannon, County Donegal,
Ireland[3], was born on September 12, 1839. His several sisters
had died in infancy, and his two brothers, Terrence and Thomas,
like him, were never rugged. Both died young, Thomas by
drowning in 1853. The imminent threat of famine added to the
harsh struggle for a livelihood led Hugh Keane, their father, to
bring his family to America in 1846, settling them first in St.
John's, New Brunswick, and then in Baltimore, Maryland. There
John was confirmed by Archbishop Eccleston, the first of several
Baltimore archbishops to be associated with his career. He received both his elementary and his secondary education from the
Christian Brothers. Encouraged by Father Thomas Foley, then
secretary to Archbishop Kenrick and later Bishop of Chicago,
he entered St. Charles College on September 2, 1859 in remote
preparation for the priesthood. Completing his studies there,
John entered the St. Mary Seminary, Baltimore, conducted by
the Sulpician Fathers. He was graduated with the degree bachelor
of arts, summa cum laude, and was ordained on July 2, 1866, in
the seminary chapel. Assigned by Kenrick's successor, Archbishop Martin Spalding, to St. Patrick Church, Washington, D. C.
he directed the activities of the young men of the parish, including the Father Matthew Total Abstinence Society. Having
himself taken the pledge from Father Matthew, he would continue
throughout his life to promote total abstinence, or at least temperance, in the use of alcoholic beverages.

When Archbishop James Roosevelt Bayley of Baltimore secured as his coadjutor James Gibbons, Bishop of Richmond, in
late March 1878, Father Keane was named by the newly elected
Leo XIII to succeed Gibbons in the Richmond diocese. Here he
proved a zealous bishop and an able administrator.

Participating in the Third Plenary Council of Baltimore in
1884, Keane took an active part in its deliberations. One of its
enactments was to change the course of his life - that authorizing the establishment of the Catholic University of America.
The story of his years there and of a subsequent period in Rome
is told elsewhere. [4]

Established now in his new see, the Archbishop visited the

Postulants in sunbonnets
worn to chapel and parlor

Same group on reception day
Front: Sisters M. Alberdetta, Mona, Felician,
Cypriana, Geralda
Back: Gerontius, Sebastiana, Julius, Bonita

many schools and religious houses[5] in and about Dubuque, then
set himself the task of making a visitation in the course of which
he would administer the sacrament of Confirmation in every parish
in his large diocese. During his first tour to country missions in
the area about Dubuque, though he was pleased with local conditions
generally, he was disturbed to find that the sacrament had not
been conferred in some of the parishes for as much as thirteen
years. He rejoiced when the responsibilities of his extensive
diocese were lessened by the establishment of the diocese of
Sioux City in 1902. Especially happy for him was the choice of
Philip J. Garrigan, vice rector of Catholic University and a
close friend, as its first bishop.

Keane's deep interest in education led him to focus attention
at once on St. Joseph's - later, Loras - college and seminary in
Dubuque, and on the opening of schools "wherever thirty or forty
pupils could be gathered together."[6] It extended also to Mt. St.
Joseph Academy where he encouraged Sister M. Bertrand Foley,
then superior, in her arrangements for raising the school's post-
graduate department to the status of a three-year college. [7]

Dubuque, at the time of Keane's coming, was a wide-open
town, with its officials profiting by corruptive influences. Keane
was to fight unrelentingly against the situation, through temperance societies within the Church. Later he received the support of other clergy of the city and of the newspapers, and was
able to take the fight into the courts. By 1907 he had won a decree
which, besides other limitations on their operation, enforced
the closing of the saloons of Dubuque on Sunday "for the first
time in fifty years."[8] But his health was not to stand the strain
of his varied labors much longer.

While the Archbishop was always gracious to the Sisters, we
catch something of his wry humor on the occasion of Mother
Gertrude's visit with him in May of 1904. The purpose of her
call was to seek his advice on the matter of a cardinal-protector[9]
for the Congregation. Sister M. Pulcheria, her companion, sums
up his comments as follows: "Doesn't approve. Says no one will
ever interfere with our community as we have approval of Holy
See. Does not see what a cardinal-protector would be of any use
to us. Like putting a purple ribbon around the neck for show.
That if we received Cardinal Martinelli, or any other Cardinal,
we would be required to write a sweet letter once or twice a year
and enclose a stipend. They, the Cardinals make their living
that way."[10] Sister adds: "He was nice, kind and paternal. Left
everything in Mother's hands after he had said all that against
it."

Mother Gertrude was too practical to meet the price tag on

purple ribbons, but seven years later, Mother Cecilia, again in
the office of superior-general, was less pragmatic. Having pursued the issue of a cardinal-protector, she secured the protection of the busy Cardinal Merry del Val, secretary of state
to Pius X. In a letter in which she made inquiry as to the Congregation's duties toward its cardinal-protector, she enclosed
a check for $500.00. His letter of thanks brought with it a
blessing from the Holy Father, a large portrait of himself
and a copy of his coat-of-arms.

Mother Gertrude's six quiet years as novice mistress were
over. With so large a portion of the novices assigned to the missions, she had virtually conducted a novitiate by mail, her letters brief but encouraging. As we follow her through the next six
years, we are amazed at her renewed energy, the boldness of
her enterprises, and her resiliency and endurance.
The erection of a suitable building for the new Chicago high
school was a first priority, but a close second was the construction of a large addition to Mt. St. Joseph to include chapel,
library, dining facilities, gymnasium and living quarters. The
academy was in the process of adding a college department, and
expansion of facilities was imperative. Enrollment had considerably increased at the downtown St. Joseph Academy in Dubuque
since its offer for sale in 1895. Plans were soon made for the
construction of a three-story brick school building to accommodate the increase, with the hope that "the people would help
pay for it." Additional construction awaited at All Hallows in
Wichita and St. Joseph, DesMoines, projects which Mother
Cecilia had feared to attempt. Then there remained the unfinished chapel at Mt. Carmel.
Within the next six years Mother was to open in Chicago
elementary schools at Holy Cross and St. Lawrence parishes
on the south side, Our Lady of Lourdes on the north, Our Lady
of Angels on the west, and Holy Name and St. Dominic on the
near north side. To these she would add St. Mary's, Pontiac,
Illinois, St. Mary's, Riverside and Sacred Heart and Corpus
Christi, Fort Dodge in Iowa. Her situation was eased somewhat by the closing of small missions at St. Patrick's, Burlington, Iowa, St. Anthony's, Weir, Kansas, and Annunciation near
Streator, Illinois where the pastor was demanding that the Sisters add the work of altar and sacristy to their teaching duties.
Though Mother Gertrude met the demands of so many pastors,
there were many more she was obliged to refuse. To these she
suggested in her matter-of-fact way that if they could send her

postulants she would be in a position to supply their needs. When Bishop James Davis of Davenport complained that the academy there was drawing girls from the parish high school, Mother reminded him that such duplication of high school classes was a waste of teachers, and that pastors in larger cities saw the advantages of centralizing the secondary schools.

At the persistent importunity of the Reverend D. D. Hischen, pastor of Holy Cross Parish on Chicago's south side, Mother Gertrude assigned nine Sisters[11] to the new mission, with Sister M. Euna Burke as their superior. The school having opened in 1901 with three hundred pupils, both student body and faculty grew quickly to a peak enrollment of 1,100. Sister M. Orestes Boland, one of the initial staff, continued at Holy Cross to the time of her retirement sixty years later, serving as superior or eighth grade teacher during those many years. The rating of the school was always high, but to Sister especially was due the success of its graduates in competition for scholarships to the growing number of Catholic high schools in the city.

Father Hischen's success in obtaining Sisters encouraged the Reverend Sylvester Maloney at the adjoining parish of St. Lawrence to try the same tactics in the interests of the Irish in the Grand Crossing area. His call at the motherhouse at least left him with the impression that he was free to use the earnings of the music teachers to help with his payment of the classroom teachers' salaries! Eight Sisters opened the new mission[12] with Sister M. Theodore McCarthy as superior. When Mother Gertrude called on Father Maloney in 1903, he told her that the happiest years of his life had been those since the Sisters came. Yet there was trouble ahead.

In 1900 the B. V. M. Sisters accepted the invitation of the Reverend James J. Jennings to staff his school in Presentation Parish, Chicago, then just two years old. His first church faced a country road in an area which today teems with industry and a population largely Black. Sister M. of the Angels O'Connor as superior[13] opened the first four grades of the new school to 124 children in September 1900. By 1920 the eighty-five original families in the parish had increased to 1,368, and there were a thousand children in attendance at the school. Father Jennings wasted no time in providing the necessary buildings, laying the cornerstone of a convent in 1901 and of a church two years later. His compact plant soon included a church, rectory, boys' school, girls' school, convent and auditorium, all in brick and stone. Changes come fast in Chicago's urban areas. Presentation, like so many other parishes, rose quickly, saw its day of glory, and then, almost as quickly, fell into decline. By 1970 deterioration of the area and unfortunate circumstances led to the withdrawal of the Sisters.

In 1900 St. Mary Parish in the rural town of Riverside, Iowa was also looking for Sisters. They were to replace a community of Franciscan Sisters who were withdrawing from the school. The pastor, the Reverend S. J. Wieland, having known the B. V. M. Sisters in Lyons, Iowa, appealed to Mother Gertrude, and she responded by sending Sisters M. Delphine Conway, Vincentine Hackett, Edwina Philips and Nazareth Geohegan to teach the one hundred pupils enrolled in the school. In 1907 when the Reverend Bernard Jacobsmeier, succeeding to the parish, turned the first spadeful of dirt for the erection of a new school, four of its prospective pupils participating in the ceremony would before many years be known in religion as Sisters M. Reparateur and Bernadette Yeggy, and the twins, Sisters M. Clarissima and Clotildis Walsh.

While bad weather and unpaved roads caused many absences, the usual school attendance was about two hundred. Sisters and parish members grew close, the Sisters paying frequent visits to the sick and the sorrowful, and the people responding generously to their needs. School reorganization which called for consolidation led to the closing of the school in 1969.

Mother Gertrude returned from an extensive visitation tour in time for the reception ceremonies at Mt. Carmel on December 9, 1900. These were attended by many relatives and friends of the new novices, and by the senior students from Mt. St. Joseph Academy. "All were deeply affected and impressed for good. " The following day brought Mt. Carmel's new chaplain, the Reverend Arthur M. Clark, [14] who was to serve in that capacity for the next eighteen years. He immediately announced his plans for lecturing twice a week to the novices, his talks on Tuesday to be of a religious nature - scripture, church history, etc. - and on Thursday, on practical subjects. For New Year's eve he arranged a midnight Mass, adoration of the Blessed Sacrament to continue through the night until noon, closing with Benediction. The rest of the day Father spoke to Sisters and novices on the city of Rome, its customs, churches, etc. , all illustrative of his zeal.

The motherhouse was still unfinished. The young Sister M. Teresita Butler from Iowa City, whose failing health required her to give up her Latin classes with the novices, was by 1901 confined to her bed in the infirmary. Assured of a comfortable inheritance, she begged that it be used for the completion of the chapel. On May 7 she was gladdened by the sound of saw and hammers. Seven days later death claimed her at the age of twenty-seven, after just three years of religious life. Dedication of the completed chapel on the feast of Our Lady of Guadalupe, December 12, brought many guests, priests, friends and relatives of the Sisters, and school children from the city.

Meanwhile the Reverend Edmund Heelan, pastor of Sacred Heart Parish, Fort Dodge, Iowa had requested Sisters for an elementary school, and on February 2, 1902 his school was opened. Sister M. Chrysantha Driscoll was assigned as superior the five Sisters[15] including among them a music teacher and a housekeeper. Of the 112 pupils in attendance, twenty-nine enrolled for music lessons, providing a principal source of income for the Sisters. The school Sisters were to receive the tuition in lieu of salary. [16] This Father Heelan promised to supplement with a check of $100.00 at the end of the year.

The following August Bishop Garrigan of Sioux City, having come to Dubuque for a Temperance meeting, visited Mt. Carmel to request Sisters for a second parish in Fort Dodge, that of Corpus Christi. Forty years before the Sisters had staffed a school in that parish under the kindly Father John J. Marsh. His premature death had led to their departure after just three years. The Sisters of Mercy had followed them, building and conducting an academy. It burned down in 1900 and the Sisters withdrew. The parish now promised to furnish utilities and equipment for both school and convent, while the Sisters were expected to meet all other needs out of tuition collected. Music income supplemented the tuition collected. The school opened the following September with ninety-nine boys and girls in attendance and Sister M. of Agreda Cauley as superior.

Meanwhile work had progressed on the beautiful Sacred Heart chapel building at Mt. St. Joseph Academy and College in Dubuque, and on May 2, 1902 dedication ceremonies conducted b Archbishop Keane drew many admiring visitors. College it had become, for in 1901 the state of Iowa had granted to the academy a charter permitting it to confer degrees as a three-year college It would grant its first such degree in June of 1904.

Mt. St. Joseph College and Academy - now Clarke College - traces its lineage back to the frame school building on Cathedral square to which the B. V. M. Sisters came in 1843, and which they named St. Mary Academy. Its removal to St. Joseph Prairie in 1846, then back to town in 1859 to share quarters with the Sacred Heart elementary school on the Fourteenth Street hill was followed in 1869, with its establishment in the recently purchased Wellington mansion to which the name St. Joseph

Academy was again applied. Not until 1881 did the school find a permanent home on the triangular area between the present Seminary Road and Clarke Drive. The school attained the level of a four-year college in 1912 and was enrolled as a member of the North Central Association of Schools and Colleges in 1918. [17] Sister M. Chionia Cavanaugh was then superior and Sister M. Antonia Durkin, dean. In 1928, having phased out the academy, the school, now a thriving institution, changed its title to Clarke College in honor of the foundress of the Sisters of Charity, B. V. M. , Mother Mary Frances Clarke.

The appointment of the able and far-seeing Sister M. Bertrand Foley as superior of the Mount in 1899, after her eight years' involvement in the academy, was a long step in the direction of college status. Academy graduates had been returning since 1895 for "post-graduate" courses, and Sisters were pushing their own educational frontiers to meet the new demand. On being named superior, Sister M. Bertrand went east to consult with educators at Columbia and Catholic University, and contacted several early colleges for women in the east and south. She "sent her most promising teachers to eastern colleges and universities, " wrote Sister M. Agatha Farrell, a pupil at the academy at the time, and later a prefect there. Sister added: "At the risk of being dangerously progressive, she /Sister M. Bertrand/ had Sisters trained in mathematics and the 'natural sciences' . . . in New York by teachers then on the faculty of Columbia University. "

The early faculty included Sister M. Clara Russell, gifted as a writer. Sister received some portion of her education at the University of Wisconsin probably as a girl and was granted a master's degree at the Catholic University of America in 1916. Sister M. Resignata Metzler, one of those tutored by Columbia professors, taught mathematics and science. Sister M. Clemenza Leahey, a graduate before her entrance from the normal college of Minnesota University, was instructor in pedagogy and teacher-training, courses which she later supplemented at Loyola University in Chicago. Sister M. Crescentia Markey, of whose earlier education no record remains, taught logic and the classics. Sister was awarded a master's degree at the Catholic University in 1914. Sister M. Basiline Bates, teacher of philosophy, was also tutored at Columbia. Sister received a doctoral degree in philosophy from the University of Colorado in 1922. The only lay woman on the faculty was Aurelia Williams, teacher of French. Sister M. Ernest Bowden, who entered from California in 1904 after some years of study at Berkeley, joined the faculty as teacher of modern languages and history. That they were supplemented by priest teachers from the men's college, at least for religious studies, can safely be presumed for that arrangement is known to have persisted from very early years.

Sister Mary Bertrand (Elizabeth) Foley was born in Mallow, Ireland on December 8, 1855, her parents, William Foley and his wife Mary Wall. This we learn from the school register of the Sacred Heart Academy, conducted by the Religious of the Sacred Heart on Taylor Street, Chicago. Here as "L" - probably "Liz" - Foley she remained for just one year, during which she received her First Communion and was confirmed. No further record of her remains there. That she taught for a time in the Holy Family boys' school we learn from Brother Mulkerins, S. J. 's listing of the school's teachers, and from an account of Sister written by Sister M. Borgia Walsh who knew Sister for many years at Mt. St. Joseph. No record remains of further opportunities for education, though the scope of her interests and the extent of her accomplishments suggest an enriched background. Elizabeth entered the Sisters of Charity on May 24, 1879 at the Prairie motherhouse, at the age of twenty-three.

It seems incredible that the one brief year with the "Madames" as the Religious were then called, and a year in which she could have been scarcely more than a child, would have been sufficient to mark her so strongly as her later life indicated. The lineaments of their training are clearly manifest in the practices she introduced at "the Mount." Her devotional talks, the etiquette hours she conducted each Sunday morning, and the "academy assemblies" or honor convocations which she so gravely solemnized, seem all to have been reflections of a considerable experience. Her devotion to the Blessed Virgin and especially to the Sacred Heart which they had instilled characterized her thought and her life.

The direction which Sister gave to novitiate studies even when she was herself a B. V. M. novice suggests the possibility of her having experienced a time of training in a well established novitiate prior to her coming to the B. V. M. 's, though no other evidence of such is presently available. [18] There are many indications of the high regard in which she was held by the Sisters who knew her in her active years. After her retirement to Mt. Carm Sister was called upon a number of times to give pre-reception retreats to the postulants. Though these are held to have been marked by a deep spirituality, the idiosyncracies which she had acquired through the years tended to distract the attention of the young from matters of deeper import.

IMMACULATE CONCEPTION ACADEMY

Sister M. Adora with Minims

Calisthenics Class

Sister M. Antonia with Seniors

The assignment of Mother Cecilia to the teaching of music at the Davenport academy, despite the choice the Sisters had made of her as the first general consultor, brought repercussions among those who had loved her dearly, both as novice mistress and as their highest superior. Here she was subject to Sister M. Editha Flanagan as superior. Sister was a close friend of Mother Gertrude, and an able musician, but also a determined woman.[19]

While, during her term of office, Sister M. Cecilia, in her correspondence with the Sisters, had never made use of the title "Mother, " yet that title had followed Mother Gertrude after her time in office, and an ingrained respect seemed to demand it. However, on Mother Cecilia's return to Davenport, the Sisters were forbidden to use it.[20] Mother's place among the consultors was assigned to Sister M. Maurice Duffy, an unprecedented action and certainly not canonical.

While it was customary for a local superior when her term of office had expired to return to the ranks in all respects, the case was scarcely the same in regard to a former novice mistress and superior-general whose correspondence and personal contacts should have been privileged as one who had received many confidences. However, Mother's letters were subjected to the same scrutiny as those of the youngest Sister, and she was held to the observance of a partially outmoded regulation requiring a companion for the entertainment of guests in the parlor, and of observing a limit of half an hour for such visits. A story persists of a bishop who, on calling to see "Mother, " was told that "Mother is in Dubuque. " When he learned on arrival at Mt. Carmel that Mother Cecilia was in reality in Davenport, he left the Sisters there with no uncertainty of his scorn for such pettifogging.

Assigned the beginners in music, Mother was given the humble tasks of the household and required to sleep in a dormitory with the little girls.[21] Though she was heard to utter no word of complaint,[22] the Sisters who loved her were scandalized by the treatment accorded her and them when they found their visits to her discouraged. Resentments built and it was not long before thought turned to the election which had returned Mother Gertrude to office in 1900. Those most actively concerned seem to have been the Sisters at Annunciation Convent in Chicago and at St. Francis Academy, Council Bluffs where Sister M. Antonia Durkin was directress. Those immediately at hand were Sisters M. Regina Lynch, Adora Caverly and Blanche Fosselman, all deeply devoted to Mother. In quiet determination these Sisters laid the groundwork for a separation and the forming of another congregation with Mother Cecilia at its head.[23] However, when word

of the plan reached Mother Cecilia, she renounced it with all
the strength of her being. "Never! This is where I entered, and
this is where I remain, " was her declaration of unswerving
fidelity to her Congregation.

Whatever responsibility Mother Gertrude may have had for
the treatment accorded to Mother Cecilia at the academy, when
rumors came to her that the Congregation itself was endangered,
she moved quickly. Sister M. Editha was replaced in 1902 by
the gracious Sister M. Adora Caverly. Mother Gertrude made
it her business to come to Davenport for the purpose of conferring with Mother Cecilia and of entrusting to her business affairs in that area. In 1903 she named Mother Cecilia to the
superiorship of St. Francis Academy, Council Bluffs, and accompanied her to her new mission. There the children were
carefully instructed to call her Mother, and as they soon came
to love her, they appreciated the appropriateness of the title. [24]

Mother Cecilia's term of office in Council Bluffs was no
sinecure. A difficult pastor, pressures of debt, maintenance
problems in a badly constructed establishment, and an epidemic
of scarlet fever which resulted in the death of one child, all took
their toll. Health hazards for children were many and especially
to be dreaded in the close quarters of boarding schools, as they
would continue to be also with older persons. Diphtheria, scarlet
fever, measles, etc., the bane of children, were paralleled by
typhoid, pneumonia, erysipelas among their elders.

The spring of 1902 brought word of Sister M. Agatha's grave
illness. Though she herself was scarcely recovered from a
grave illness, Mother Gertrude traveled to Chicago three times
during the month of April. On the second of these trips she took
with her a Sister-nurse from the infirmary to relieve the busy
Sisters of care for the sick woman. Death came on May 5, 1902.
The visitation in the Sisters' convent and the funeral services
in the Holy Family Church gave fitting recognition to Sister M.
Agatha's forty years of strenuous service in the nurturing of
Catholic education in the city. Burial was in Dubuque, in Mt.
Carmel's own cemetery.

Mother Gertrude was soon off on her busy round again. With
fifty-nine houses, including eight boarding schools, three high
schools, and the academy of Mt. St. Joseph in the process of
becoming a college, she had much to plan for. Her extensive
religious family included 729 professed religious, 96 novices
and six postulants, each with her needs and talents, and each
with a work to do. While Sister M. Octavia Burke was official-

ly designated as visitor for all the houses, her role was that of
giving comfort and encouragement to superiors and Sisters, of
visiting the classrooms and making such helpful suggestions as
she could to the busy teachers. Necessary changes of personnel
she could only refer to Mother Gertrude.

Mother's aim was to visit each of the widely scattered houses
at least once in each three-year term of office. Those for which
she had direct responsibility for building and financing she would
visit as many times as the situations seemed to warrant. Direct
contact with bishops and pastors helped to assure them of a hearing and a clarification of issues, thus preventing misunderstandings and winning cooperation. All this meant almost incessant
travel with all the accompanying inconveniences and delays: to
Wichita for the purpose of making secure the new mollified
Bishop Hennessy's promise of land; to Sioux City to gently persuade Bishop Garrigan to close the Marcus boarding school and
to dissuade him from the idea of a boarding school in Sioux City;
then on to Council Bluffs in an effort to placate the pastor who
was calling down Irish curses on the Sisters for having cut the
sunlight off his favorite porch with their new auditorium. There
were the usual personality clashes among the Sisters and with
pastors. These she must resolve, making such changes as
seemed warranted. There were the sick and the mentally disturbed to provide for, architects, bankers and canonists with
whom she must confer.

From all this, however, the thoughts of Mother and the Sisters were abruptly turned to the tragic fire which took over six
hundred lives in the midst of the Christmas holidays in 1903.
The Iroquois Theatre[25] in Chicago was crowded with children and
young people enjoying the production of "Mr. Bluebeard, Jr."
when a scenic curtain against a backstage spotlight started the
conflagration. Panic struck and a rush for the doors which
jammed the exits led to death by suffocation for great numbers.
Among those lost were several young people whom the Sisters
had taught in the parish schools and St. Mary's, and even Mt.
St. Joseph Academy in Dubuque, home for the holidays.

Chicago parishes were again clamoring for Sisters. Our Lady
of Lourdes, the mother church of six later churches on the upper north side of Chicago - St. Jerome's, St. Gertrude's, St.
Andrew's, St. Ita's, St. Mary of the Lake, and St. Thomas
Canterbury - had been established in 1891 with the Reverend
John Coughlin as pastor. The Ravenswood area was then a
sparsely settled woodland and the elevated line was yet to come.
It was in response to the appeal of a group of women that Archbishop Patrick A. Feehan waived the requirement of one hundred

families in favor of ninety whose cause they pleaded for the opening of a new parish. The first parish Mass was said in a rented hall on Easter 1891. The following year a large frame church at Ashland and Leland was dedicated. The Reverend Francis N. Perry, having then succeeded to the pastorate, requested Sisters.

The school was opened in September 1903 with three hundred pupils and a staff of nine B. V. M. 's, [26] Sister M. Charlotte Stackhouse the superior. In 1906 high school classes were inaugurated with an enrollment of twenty-six girls and Sisters M. Constantia O'Leary and Emily Whalen as teachers. Before Lourdes High School closed[27] in 1922, it had graduated 320 young women, many of whom entered Chicago Normal.

In 1914 Father Perry began the construction of a beautiful Romanesque church, but his death that year left the work to be completed by his successor, the Reverend James M. Scanlan. When plans were made for the widening of Ashland Avenue, it was apparent that many feet would be cut off the church structure, already too small. This situation led to the accomplishment of a remarkable engineering fete: the moving of the 10,000-ton church across the street, turning it a full ninety degrees, and dividing it for the sake of lengthening the structure. The enlarged church was rededicated in 1929.

In 1944 Monsignor John P. Campbell, then pastor, having renovated the school following a fire, built a large and commodious convent for the Sisters.

Our Lady of Lourdes was an active and prosperous parish for many years. Today its faculty of six B. V. M. Sisters faces a greatly reduced enrollment, the area being now largely populated by Appalachians, Spanish-Americans and Chinese, large numbers of whom are non-Catholic.

The parish of Our Lady of Angels, established in 1894 with the Reverend James A. Hynes as pastor, opened on Chicago's west side in a church-school-convent combination containing eight classrooms. Sister M. Louise Clarke was chosen as superior of the new enterprise, and with her went Sisters M. Justa Finnegan, Elias Cassidy and the newly professed Anna Sweeney. In the course of that first school year of 1904-1905 there were 354 pupils enrolled.

Father Hynes' death in 1936, after forty years of service, led to the appointment of the Reverend Joseph F. Cussen. The year 1947-1948 witnessed a peak enrollment of 1,157 pupils with 113 kindergarten children in half-day sessions. Sister M. St. Florence Casey was superior at that time.

It was the unhappy lot of Father Cussen and Sister M. St.

Florence to bear the burden of the tragic fire on December 1, 1958 which destroyed the school and snuffed out the lives of ninety-three children and three Sisters - M. Canice Lyng, Seraphica Kelley and Clare Therese Champagne. The fire, apparently touched off in trash cans near the basement stairs, quickly cut off exits. Among those who escaped there were three Sisters and many children who suffered burns and other injuries, some of whom were doomed to long months of hospitalization.

Albert G. Meyer, then Archbishop of Chicago, responded heroically, redeeming all losses that were redeemable, and at first bussing the surviving children to Our Lady Help of Christians parish school for half-day sessions, [28] then renting vacant classrooms in the public schools for the accommodation of all classes. In addition, the Archdiocese met damage suits in the millions for losses for which no money could compensate. A new and modern school was ready to receive the children again in September 1960.

As Mother Gertrude's three-year term of office was drawing to a close, an accounting of financial status was in order, and it was formidable, showing the total indebtedness to the motherhouse of all the houses which were community-owned, in addition to Mt. Carmel's own indebtedness:

Mount Carmel	40, 466. 89
St. Mary High School	26, 500. 00
Our Lady of Angels Academy	32, 300. 00
St. Joseph's, Des Moines	26, 452. 96
Mt. Carmel, Wichita	27, 000. 00
Holy Angels Academy	41, 000. 00
St. Joseph, Dubuque	29, 437. 29
I. C. A. , Davenport	20, 000. 00
Mt. St. Joseph	56, 000. 00
St. Francis, Council Bluffs	6, 700. 00
	$305, 857. 14

A consultors' meeting proposed the names of Mother Gertrude Regan, Sister M. Seraphina Short and Sister M. Esther Warren as suitable candidates for the office of superior-general. The six names they submitted as their possible successors were: Sisters M. Gonzaga McCloskey, Mother Cecilia Dougherty, Maurice Duffy, Bertrand Foley, Annunciation Hannon and Chioni Cavanaugh. On January 27 the Reverend M. Barry, chancellor of the Archdiocese, announced the results of the election which confirmed Mother Gertrude in the office of superior-general. Th consultors chosen were: Sisters M. Bertrand and Gonzaga, Mother Cecilia and Sister M. Maurice. Sister M. Gonzaga was again named as assistant to Mother Gertrude, Sister M. Maurice Duffy as novice mistress, Sister M. DeChantal O'Regan as procurator, and Sister M. Pulcheria McGuire, secretary.

The question of teaching boys in the upper years soon became pressing as the result of an unfortunate experience. A young music teacher, having apparently formed an attachment for a youth she was instructing in piano, then becoming disenchanted with the religious life, had departed without ceremony. Though she soon applied to her bishop for dispensation from vows, and Mother knew that she was safe in her own home, the anxiety for others so placed called for action. Indeed so did the good name of the Congregation, for the newspapers were making the most of the situation. At a meeting of the consultors it was decided that henceforth the Sisters would not be required to teach boys beyond their eighth grade in school or beyond their fourteenth year as music students. To insure the cooperation of the pastors, Mother Gertrude set out to visit each Iowa pastor, for it was especially their small parish high schools that were involved. Their reception was kindly and understanding, yet they expressed regret for the high school boys and those in commercial classes.

At the end of one such round as she was leaving the convent in Washington, Iowa she sustained a heavy fall. Although the effects of it were with her for many weeks, she managed a trip also to St. Mary's, Moline, Illinois, where the Sisters had served for the previous twenty years. There the pastor was so convinced of the need for keeping his boys in the parish school, that, with the support of Bishop Spalding, he replaced the B. V. M. Sisters with Sisters of Mercy from Ottawa, Illinois. Had the change been delayed until fall, it probably would not have taken place, for the following letter from Archbishop Keane led to concessions for small schools where the boys would be left with no other choice than attendance at the public school.

Vinton, Iowa
Oct. 19, 1904

Dear Mother Gertrude:

There is an important matter that has concerned me much of late, and about which I wish to confer with you.

When I agreed with you in regard to refusing boys for high school grades, I did not foresee what trouble this would cause in our poor parishes. Priest after priest has protested to me against being compelled to send their boys of only 13 or 14 years of age to the secular high school, at the very age when religious influences are most necessary for them, -- while their sisters can still go on in the Catholic school, though they stand far less in need of its good influences than the boys do.

They argue that, while there is evidently good reason for refusing to teach such boys music, which leaves secular and teacher alone, the same reason does not hold for the ordinary "high school branches, " which are taught in classes.

I acknowledge that the more I reflect, the more I am impressed with the weight of their reasons and the greatness of the interests involved. And I fear I shall have to join the priests in pleading with you, to hold fast to your rule in cities like Chicago, where Catholic high school facilities are abundant, but to relax it to the extent above indicated in our poor parishes that have no such facilities. -- Let me ask you to come and see me in regard to it, at my house in Dubuque, Friday forenoon.

Yours in X
+J. J. Keane

The appointment settled the matter for the smaller and more remote high schools.

Quite apart from the strain of meeting such situations, there were the difficulties involved in the travel itself. On one occasion, half sick with anxieties over vacant classrooms and ailing Sisters, Mother Gertrude and a companion set out on a December day by carriage for Cascade, Iowa, twenty-five miles away, then on eight miles further, to Garryowen, returning to Mt. Carmel over rough country roads, all in a single day. That she returned with a heavy cold from which she was many weeks recovering is not surprising.

Anxious about the condition of Sister M. Vincentine Hackett in Riverside, Iowa, Mother and Sister M. Pulcheria took the Illinois Central train from Dubuque at 7:27 on a May morning to Cedar Rapids, changing trains there for Iowa City. Then traveling via Rock Island lines, they arrived in Riverside at five o'clock, having covered an actual distance of one hundred miles. Satisfied that Sister's needs were being met, Mother set out with her companion on the return trip at seven the next morning. The Sisters somehow took the wrong train. Realizing their mistake, when they reached a small town eight miles out of their way, they dismounted, caught a freight train and enjoyed the accommodations of the caboose as far as Iowa City. There they spent the night with the Sisters at St. Agatha's, leaving at five o'clock

the next morning for Cedar Rapids by interurban. An eastbound
Illinois Central train at 7:30 brought them home in time for their
noon lunch.

Chicago visits were scarcely less hectic, though distances
were much shorter. Calls at six or seven widely scattered convents and a hospital or two in a single day constituted a not unusual schedule. Horse cabs were standard travel where street
cars and the recently constructed elevated lines failed to offer
convenient service.

After a series of such experiences, Sister M. Pulcheria
felt moved to note in the community's log, the Record of Events:

It is wonderful how Mother Gertrude can stand so much
fatigue and overwork at her age /then seventy-seven/.
God surely sustains her in her labors for His honor and
glory. Many times her companion, completely exhausted,
would complain were she not ashamed to mention her weari-
ness when looking on the zeal of little Mother Gertrude.
Everywhere she goes she brings a blessing. In her gentle,
religious way she makes crooked paths straight and leaves
peace and happiness and renewed courage to the members.
May God bless her and spare her to the Community for
many years to come.

Being relatively free from local responsibilities, Sister M.
Pulcheria sometimes served as companion to others than Mother Gertrude. On one such occasion, she was accompanying a
novice to Chicago to the bedside of her dying father. Within a
half hour's ride of the city, the coach just ahead of theirs was
torn frightfully all along the side on which they were sitting,
by a flying door from a passing freight train. Every window on
that side in the coach in which they were riding was broken except the one beside them. A large bar of iron flew through the
window in front of them. The passengers were covered with
shattered glass and all was excitement for a time. When calm
was restored, the Sisters' fellow-passengers were startled and
curious that one window only, and that in the middle of the coach,
had not even a crack. The Sisters, on their part, were gratefully
recalling that they had just finished the recitation of the rosary
for the souls in purgatory when the accident occurred.

At the request of Bishop Spalding of Peoria, Mother Gertrude
sent Mother Cecilia and Sister M. Adora Caverly to Pontiac,
Illinois to discuss with Father Lyons, the pastor, the advisability

of opening a grade school in the St. Mary Parish. As a result
of their visit, Mother appointed Sisters M. Verena Griffen,
Norberta Lynch and three young professed Sisters, Salvius
Cunningham, Tarcisius O'Shea and Adriano McDonnell to open
the first three classrooms in the fall of 1903. The higher grades
were opened in succession. Father Lyons, setting out in 1910
on a trip to Ireland, died on shipboard. His successor, Father
Cannon, who was shortly made pastor, did much to improve the
plant. Sister M. Henrietta Motie, named superior in 1912, celebrated her golden jubilee in 1917, an occasion which the parish
chose to share with her and which brought Mother Cecilia and
other Sisters as guests. The large school building of 1902 was
razed in 1965 with the coming of the Reverend John T. Shields,
and a new parish plant put under construction. The school is
thriving today with six B. V. M. Sisters involved.

Meanwhile Bishop Muldoon had requested Sisters to teach
religion to the boys at John Worthy Reform School in Chicago.
For this Mother called on Sisters at St. Mary High School,
since they were free of weekend parish responsibilities. Many
of the boys had not finished fourth grade, and those who were
Catholics had been baptized only. The Sisters continued the
work through several years, preparing the boys for the sacraments of Penance, Holy Communion and Confirmation, and a
few who sought Baptism.

On May 30, 1903 the Sisters' chaplain, Father Clark, went
east to Boston, then for a visit with his sister at Framingham,
Massachusetts. From there he attended the ordination in New
York of a young man, whom as John Smith Father had adopted
at the time of the death of the boy's mother. The lad was then
only nine. The young priest returned with him to Dubuque for a
time. A new home had by then been built for the workmen,
leaving Father Clark in full possession of the brick house they
had previously shared.

Father had assumed the direction of the novices, leaving
their mistress in something of a quandary over the methods he
used to test her training. Practices he introduced occasionally
approached the bizarre as when he led the novices in the rosary
by moonlight in the graveyard as a way of celebrating the feast
of All Souls' day. His services were interrupted at intervals
by accidents or ill health. He found it necessary on one occasion to go to Chicago for treatment of an attack of rheumatism
An unfortunate accident with a steam valve there resulted in a
bad scald which took many weeks to heal. In 1903 he planned for
a small reliquary altar near that of St. Joseph in the motherhouse chapel. At the time it was installed and blessed, fifty of

the older Sisters carried in procession with Father Clark and
attendants the many first-class relics to be enclosed in it.
Among these were the remains of St. Justinus which Father
Donaghoe had brought back from Rome. This was contained in
an especially made cedar box and veiled with red silk.

An occasional note in the secretary's Record of Events indicates an illness or a fall. On February 6, 1907 an entry tells
of his return from the hospital where he had been confined for
seven weeks. He was still unable for duty, however, and to
enable him to say his daily Mass without the effort of climbing
the stairs, the Sisters moved the infirmary chapel to the ground
floor. On February 28 of 1908 the secretary recorded wryly:
"Father Clark again laid up. Fell and broke his thumb. Will stay
at college till better. " So the years went by with the priest growing each year a bit more helpless and difficult. In his later years,
after his lectures in the novitiate, two novices dutifully led him
back to his residence, a new and pleasant cottage beyond the
spacious infirmary which had been erected meantime.

The spring of 1904 witnessed the destruction of the old adobe
chapel, the frame infirmary building from which Mother Clarke
had long directed the Congregation, and the quaint stone structure
which had served for motherhouse and novitiate on the Prairie.
Only the original parish house and Father Donaghoe's residence
which had been adjoined to it remained. Sister M. Josephine
Clarke expressed the sorrow of many when she wrote to a Sister friend:

> I send you photos of the old home. You will prize them
> doubly as they are to be torn down. Even the pleasure of
> seeing the remains of what was once so dear will be denied
> us. I never thought Mother Gertrude would be the one to do
> such a thing. . . .

That year also the Sisters learned that the land across from
Mt. St. Joseph Academy was to be occupied by a dairy. Despite
a debt of $88,000 on their new chapel, they arranged for the
immediate purchase of the property.

It was August 4, 1903 that the great bell brought from the old
motherhouse range jubilantly proclaiming the election of a new
pope, Pius X. On his return after the conclave Archbishop Keane
earnestly advised Mother Gertrude to hold the novices at Mt.
Carmel at least through their canonical year. However, the
pressures were great, the most urgent of these coming from
the Reverend M. J. Fitzsimmons, pastor of the Holy Name
Cathedral Parish, Chicago. His request was earnestly advanced

by his friend Bishop Muldoon.

Shortly after Archbishop James E. Quigley of Chicago assumed his duties in 1903, he effected the division of Holy Name Parish, establishing the parish of St. Dominic to serve its western section. The description given in a recent study is as applicable to the Cathedral Parish today as it was then and even earlier:

> The old cathedral parish of the Holy Name on the near north side, after 50 years of serving first Irish immigrants and then a cosmopolitan hodge-podge of slum dwellers and transients, by the 1890's bridged both the slum of the west, and the Gold Coast then developing as the City's most prestigious area to the east. Most parishioners came from very modest or worse circumstances, though "the principal pews were regularly filled by many of the wealthier people of the city, who preferred a residence in the parish."[30]

In 1876, five years after the Chicago fire had wiped out the entire area, Bishop Foley had invited the Religious of the Sacred Heart to make a foundation in the Cathedral parish, transferring to them a piece of property at the corner of State Street and Chicago Avenue, adjacent to the Cathedral. Here they built a four-story brick academy for girls into which they moved in December 1878. Their services were requested also for the parish school when it opened in January 1880 with an attendance of two hundred children. Here the Religious taught both boys and girls until 1883 when the Viatorian Brothers opened a school for boys in a narrow, three-story brick structure on Sedgwick Street just off Chicago Avenue. Thenceforth the Religious taught only the girls, while preparing many other children of the neighborhood for their First Communion and Confirmation.

In 1904, when difficulties arose regarding the title to the property on which the academy stood, the Religious left the parish, reopening their academy in a residence on north Clark Street. A second move to larger quarters on Pine Grove preceded their permanent settlement at 6250 North Sheridan Road, where they continue to the present.[31]

In that same year the Brothers gave up the Sedgwick Street school and the pastor, the Reverend M. J. Fitzsimmons, then turned to the B.V.M. Sisters for the staffing of the parish school, now to be coeducational. Sister M. Chionia Cavanaugh, assigned as its first superior, began her labors with the purchase of furnishings for as much of the gaunt and empty forty-room building as would be needed for convent purposes. She then returned to Dubuque for the "six school teachers, a music teacher and a housekeeper" which Mother Gertrude had promised. On August 25 the nine Sisters[32] were setting out for Chicago with their tickets and a ten-dollar bill in the superior's pocket. At the last moment, Mother decided to send with them a Sister intended for St. Dominic's, the cost of her ticket cutting their financial resources in half. Realizing the many needs they would have before the opening of school brought in tuition, the Sisters at Blessed Sacrament and St. Vincent's opened their household purses for the newcomers.

The school doors were opened on September 6. This brought a deluge of children: the girls of previous years, boys from the "Brudders, " and both boys and girls from the public schools of the neighborhood. Sisters M. Balbina Durkin and Columbière Hagerty were each confronted with a hundred pupils, and Sister M. Rosella Eulberg, a novice who had been assigned the beginners, "counted as many as one hundred twenty-five, but could not say how many more. "[33] Cathedral School proved popular!

Father Fitzsimmons was soon on his way to Dubuque, returning with Sisters M. Maurice Duffy and Octavia Burke, who removed a Sister from each of four other schools, St. Vincent's, Holy Family, Sacred Heart and St. Pius, to meet the emergency. The following fall brought requests from the pastor for more grade and several high school teachers, his letter impressing Mother with "the importance of our school, " and requiring that "/you/ do your part for the equitable fulfillment of our contract. " He added emphatically - and arbitrarily - "I cannot consider the matter of employing lay teachers; after the close of the present term they will have to be excluded from our teaching staff. " The day would come when pastors had no choice.

The high school department, opened at such an early date, was closed in 1922 with the opening of the Immaculata High School on the north side. High school courses were offered again, however, in 1942 at the wish of Cardinal Samuel Stritch for the first and second year students, and in 1944 for the upper two years. The tuition charge of $1. 00 a month indicates the Cardinal's wish that it serve young people who could not otherwise have a Catholic education.

Not until 1958 was the decaying and long inadequate school building replaced with the present substantial structure on State Street and Chicago Avenue. There it serves as elementary school, a more recent addition providing the facilities of a modern high school, both of which continue to be served by the B. V. M. Sisters.

On the heels of Monsignor Fitzsimmons' first request for

Sisters in 1904 there came a similar plea from the Reverend
E. M. Griffin, addressed from the Annunciation rectory, to
meet the needs of the new St. Dominic Parish of which he had
been named pastor. His request was for "about ten, but will be
satisfied at the beginning with a smaller number, whatever you
send. " They would be established in the "fine school building"
on Sedgwick Street just vacated by the Brothers. He reminded
Mother that "I have, as you know, always been a friend of the
B. V. M. 's and have sent many a worthy subject to Dubuque
since I came to Annunciation, and now you have an opportunity
to repay me. . . . The Sisters will have an excellent field and
will be taken good care of. "

The predicted attendance proved to be large and nine Sisters
were assigned to St. Dominic School that fall with Sister M.
Casia O'Connor as superior. [34] These were supplemented by
four secular teachers. Two frame houses were rolled from Oak
Street down the passageway back of Sedgwick Street to be fused
into a single dwelling to serve temporarily as convent.

Residences in the area were clean and neat, the homes of
Irish, Swedes and Germans. Two blocks to the west was a growing "Little Italy" in the St. Philip Benizi Parish which had no
school. St. Dominic School was sufficiently Irish that both Irish
history and Irish dances became an early part of the curriculum,
and St. Dominic's was regarded for a brief time as a model
Irish parish.

By the time of Father Griffin's death in 1910, however, the
neighborhood was changing rapidly. Factories and Italian immigrants were moving into the area as its original inhabitants
moved away. A parish of one thousand families, by 1916 the
number had dwindled to two hundred fifty. After a relatively brief
pastorate of Father Scanlan, the Reverend Bernard D. Rogers
was made pastor. In 1917 he wrote to Mother Cecilia of a debt
of $83, 500. 00, referring to his new parishioners as "a class of
people who live around factories" with scarcely three hundred
English-speaking families among them. There were fifteen
hundred Italian children in public schools in the St. Philip Benizi
Parish, though the Mantellate or Servite Sisters had come in
1916 to serve them. The problem of caring for the Italian children, not only here but in other parts of the city was becoming
acute, a situation indeed of city-wide proportions.

Of all the ethnic groups to settle in Chicago, the only one interested in establishing neither church nor school of their own
was the Italians. [35] Coming in great numbers after 1890, all
were at least nominally Catholics. A few Servite priests had
entered the city by 1870, and in 1881 established Assumption

Parish on the near north side. Here by 1899 Mother Cabrini had
opened a school. It, however, could serve but a limited area.
By the time the number of foreign-born Italians in the city had
risen to 16,000, Protestant ministers and settlement workers
had become active among them. Catholic women opened Sunday
schools for them, and to save them from the well-meaning but
non-Catholic influence of Jane Adams' Hull House, Mary Amberg,
daughter of a philanthropic family, and her friends established
Madonna Center[36] in the same area. By 1903 Guardian Angel
Mission, formerly taught by the B.V.M. Sisters as a neighborhood school of Holy Family Parish, now with one thousand families, was established as a separate parish.

It became apparent that Italian parents would not send their
children to parochial schools if they had to pay tuition for them.
Archbishop Quigley took action, and by 1916 there were nine Italian
parishes in the city, all subsidized by the Archdiocese. However,
only one had a school. In 1913 the Archbishop reported the problem to Rome, adding: "the Italians from Southern Italy and Sicily
are unexcelled in their ignorance of religion." When in 1917
Cardinal Mundelein appealed to Mother Cecilia to contribute the
services of some of her Sisters to the cause, she promised
six. Two of these would serve the Italians now settled in St.
Dominic Parish, and the others the Holy Family area, staffing
St. Callistus School after 1925.

In 1918 Cardinal Mundelein responded to the appeal of Father
Luigi Giambastiani at St. Philip Benizi and allocated $65,000
for the building of a school which opened in 1920 with the Sisters
of St. Dominic of Sinsinawa in charge. [37] The experience of such
lively and undisciplined children was an unique one for the Sisters.

In time the "fine school building" as well as the dwelling of
the Sisters became virtually uninhabitable. On July 30, 1918 the
Sisters wrote to Mother Cecilia, stating bluntly, "We want to
leave," adding that "the house is unsafe; its walls threaten to
fall." As for the school, "the sanitary conditions are intolerable.
There is no janitor to sweep or take care of other places. There
is no proper heat in winter. Rats swarm about even in the day
time." The letter recalls that when the Sisters came in 1904,
it was promised that a house would be built for them immediately. As for the children, it was unfair to keep them in such a
school when there were other Catholic schools nearby.

Little had been done to improve the situation when in 1941
Sister M. Assunta Foley died of pneumonia in the house. Visitation brought many relatives and friends. A porch board gave
way under one of the guests, necessitating repairs that night.
For this the material nearest at hand was used, the ends of a

fruit crate. While they could do little regarding the property,
a group of Irish graduates of the early school had formed the
Casia Club, named in honor of the first superior. It had supplemented the Sisters' meager income from the parish, providing many of the Sisters' daily necessities. It continued its
services until the closing of the school in 1959.

It was not until 1945 that the Archdiocese moved to acquire
possession of an abandoned but well-built public school nearby.
Two years later, under Cardinal Stritch, a neat brick convent
was built next door, and the transfer was made under the superiorship of Sister M. Patrize Mullaney. Available space in the
school building suggested to the Cardinal the need of many
young people who could not afford the tuition charges in private
high schools. He asked that classes be opened for those in the
new situation. Twenty-nine freshmen enrolled the first year.
Twenty-two of these survived to graduate in 1949, the Cardinal
himself conferring diplomas. Enrollments grew steadily.

Meanwhile a public housing project was changing the face
of the neighborhood, and its shifting population brought in an
increasing proportion of Blacks, making St. Dominic's the most
totally integrated of the city's Catholic schools.

The end came quickly when the tragic fire at Our Lady of
Angels elementary school alerted the Archdiocesan Board of
Education to the hazards of fire which the school building pres-
ented. June of 1959 witnessed the closing of the high school.
An offer of vacant rooms at the nearby St. Philip Benizi
School gave the elementary grades of St. Dominic's a one-year
lease on life.

On April 28, 1904 Mother Gertrude wrote to Bishop Garrigan
of Sioux City in a troubled state of mind:

Rt. Rev. Dear Bishop,
We have heard from a reliable source that you have invited Sisters of your own choice to take charge of the schools
in your diocese. Will you kindly inform us at your earliest
convenience if we may consider ourselves at liberty to place
our Sisters elsewhere next September? . . .

Whatever her source of information, the Bishop made no delay
in refuting it:

Sioux City, Iowa, May 1, 1904

Dear Mother Gertrude,

Your note of the 28th ult. came duly to hand, and not only surprised me, but astonished and pained me. That some one whom you regard as a "reliable source" should misrepresent me, and even falsify me, is beyond my comprehension. I fear also that you have been disturbed and made anxious by this false statement. No, it never entered my head to make such a change, nor for that matter any change; and I have never approached any Community in the East or elsewhere on this subject. I could not do it if I wanted to; it is an impossibility; and it would be against my conscience, as I cannot be ignorant of the great injury it would be to our schools and religion. God forbid that I should ever attempt a move so cruel and unjust as that would be! No, even the thought of it never came to me. I am well pleased with your Sisters and hear them well spoken of everywhere they are engaged in the diocese. Here in my own schools, I find your children good teachers, and good religious, and very easy to get along with. Why should I deprive my diocese of such a body of noble religious women? No, no, I never thought it, never said it. Now this is all I need say, I trust. I only request you to give me the name of this "reliable source, " in order that I may vindicate justice and punish malice. With the expression of sentiments of esteem for yourself and your Community, I remain,

Yours very truly in Christ,

P. J. Garrigan

Bp. of Sioux City

Happily no changes were made and the B. V. M. Sisters continue in Sioux City to the present, teaching in the modern Heelan High School and in the St. Joseph elementary school.

Mother Gertrude's concern turned next to the Sisters, and on November 1, 1905 a circular letter called their attention to departures from the acceptable in dress and conduct.

The wearing of "deep collars" she deprecated, observing that "the Sisters' necks are no longer than when they were received. " Some Sisters, she had noticed, were making their night dresses "with yokes and ruffled sleeves, " while others "go so far as to powder their faces. This I can scarcely believe, " she added. Superiors were warned against the purchase of "fancy soaps, talcum powder, etc. " The Sisters were to wear "no fancy or tipped shoes" and were not to be seen on the street after dark. And, in another vein, "some of the Sisters have even gone to the theatre. "

She reminded them of the rules and customs with regard to seculars, indicating the offenses of some of them who were "spending too much time with them, riding out frequently with them, sailing on the lake with them, etc. etc. "

Sisters changed from one mission to another were reminded to "go quietly, without even mentioning the fact to any of their pupils or any seculars, and none of the Sisters should make the change known until after the Sister is gone. " Further, "they shall not keep up a correspondence with the Sisters or with children or any of the people. " The Sisters were not to entertain the priest at his breakfast, ordinarily taken in the convent parlor after Mass, or to invite him to their table. Carrying their exclusiveness still further, Mother wrote:

> The Sisters should never be permitted to attend public places for instruction of any kind, that is, pertaining to school work. There are in many places institutes where the public school teachers go for instruction in certain branches. Some of our Sisters would go there also, but they should not be permitted. If they need help in any branch, they should make it known, and an opportunity will be given them to get help from their own Sisters. We should be more willing to receive help from our own Sisters than from persons outside the Community.

Each evening at eight o'clock recreation was brought to an end by the ringing of a small bell. Then, for half an hour before night prayers, one of the Sisters read aloud from a spiritual book for the edification of all. At the end of a strenuous day, to sit idle, lulled by the drone of a tired voice, was to invite sleep. Besides, there was mending that cried to be done and borders to quill. Hopefully, a proposal sent to the motherhouse would solve both problems. The change, however, did not prove acceptable.

Then in November 1905 the pastor at Holy Rosary, Milwaukee, in need of all the pew rent he could get, wrote to request that if the Sisters must attend the high Mass they sit in the gallery for it. Since that arrangement would defeat the purpose of their attendance - that of giving edification to the congregation - Mother compromised by suggesting that the less desirable seats on the side aisle serve the Sisters, instead of the more lucrative front pews.

But from time to time tragedy brought a deeper sense of reality. An explosion of a boiler in the heating plant at Mt. Carm Academy, Wichita, at Christmas time in 1905 resulted in the suc

den death of Patrick Kennedy, engineer. The anguished wife
was left with four young children, the oldest just seven and the
youngest an infant of fifteen months. With an insurance benefit
of just one thousand dollars to depend on, Margaret Kennedy
wrote Mother Gertrude asking as recompense a second thousand.
Mother promptly sent a check for $1,200.00, and Sister M.
Isabella Kane, then superior of the academy, offered to educate
the little seven-year-old girl, Mary. It seems small compensation to us now, and as the child grew up in the academy, outside
her own family circle and subject to the narrow restrictions of
boarding school life, she must have often felt it so. Mary, nonetheless, entered the Congregation, and as Sister M. Adella has
spent her years as a music teacher in its ranks.

The last of the parish schools to be opened under the superiorship of Mother Gertrude was that of St. Jerome's, Rogers Park, in
Chicago. A little country parish, it had its beginnings as a mission church in the day of the horse-drawn street car. Services
were held in a store building at Lunt and Ravenswood until in
1895 the Reverend Arthur Lonergan undertook the construction of a
church for its eighty-nine families. His untimely death resulted in
the appointment of the Reverend James L. Callaghan who served
until the Reverend P. A. McLaughlin was appointed in 1901. Father McLaughlin was anxious to establish a school, but many of his
parishioners failed to see the need. However, after completing
the first section of the present school in 1905, he engaged two
B.V.M. Sisters, Mary Catherine McCarthy and Agnese Gibbs, to
open the first four grades. For the first year the Sisters lived at
Our Lady of Lourdes convent, traveling by street car to Devon
and on foot the last mile of the way. Only in 1909 were a sufficient
number of parishioners willing to support a school to permit the
pastor to purchase a house for the six Sisters who would serve
the school. [38] Sister M. Cherubina McQuaid came as first superior. On the death of Father McLaughlin of pneumonia in 1913,
his successor, the Reverend Thomas F. Farrell, immediately
set about the construction of a new church and additional classrooms. When Monsignor Daniel Frawley took over in 1931, his
first concern was the building of a larger convent for the Sisters
which he situated at 1700 Morse. In August 1941 he began exca-
vations for the present school. The parish today faces the devolu-
tion which has been the common fate of urban parishes. The
school continues to operate but with only a small nucleus of
B.V.M. Sisters.

The election which closed Mother Gertrude's final term of office as mother-general on February 2, 1906 brought Mother Cecilia Dougherty into that position again. She was then superior at St. Francis Academy in Council Bluffs, and it was necessary for her to close up affairs there somewhat hurriedly in order to be in Dubuque in time for the traditional date of installation, February 2. Sister M. Loyola Rutherford had been named her assistant, Sister M. Lambertina Doran, secretary, Sister M. DeChantal O'Regan, treasurer, Sister M. Esther Warren, novice mistress, Sister M. Octavia Burke, visitor. Those elected as consultors were Mother Gertrude and Sisters M. Bertrand Foley, Seraphina Short and Maurice Duffy.

Mother Gertrude's strenuous years were over. She was now seventy-nine and deserving of a rest. But Mother Gertrude had never learned the knack of resting. There were to be thirteen years ahead of her, though they would be hers only a day at a time and each day found her busy. Besides her duties as consultor, she undertook the keeping of the motherhouse accounts, and on laundry days lent a hand along with the youngest postulant.

ST. MARY HIGH SCHOOL. FARTHER BUILDING CONSTRUCTED IN 1924

Notes

1 The Cardinal, attended by Archbishop Ireland and Bishops Cosgrove and Scannell (Omaha), were entertained at Mt. Carmel as dinner guests.

2 See "A Critical Era in American Church History, " Appendix I.

3 Biographical data on Archbishop Keane has for its source Patrick Henry Ahern's Life of John J. Keane, Educator and Archbishop, 1839-1918. (Milwaukee: Bruce Publishing Company, 1954).

4 See Appendix I.

5 From the handwritten diary kept by Keane through the years in which he served the Archdiocese of Dubuque. It is to be found in the archives of the chancery office there.

6 Ibid.

7 One problem that faced the new Archbishop was that of the Sisters of the Holy Ghost. The pastor at Rockwell, Iowa had undertaken to build a motherhouse-school for the Sisters, calling on the Archdiocese for their share of the Hennessy estate. However, the Sisters repudiated his action. "Their school in the Cathedral parish, " Keane wrote in his diary, "having proved a sad failure and being a detriment to the sisterhood through its contrast with the flourishing schools of the Sisters of Charity, I have agreed to its being closed. Their only remaining foundation in Dubuque is their school in St. Anthony parish. " His diary states further: "Sunday, Oct. 28, /1900/ dedicated the new church of St. Anthony, West Dubuque, and preached. . . . Father O'Malley has built a beautiful church and is striving vigorously to resurrect the parish. A mission by the Paulist Fathers opened on Sunday. "

8 Ahern, p. 331.

9 Mother had previously discussed the matter with the Very Reverend Joseph Grimmelsman, S. J. , Provincial of the Missouri Province, with regard to requesting a cardinal-protector. He had tended to encourage the action, suggesting Cardinal Martinelli as a good choice since he spoke English and would be understanding of their needs.

10   See <u>Record of Events</u> for May 1904. Sister M. Pulcheria was secretary at the time, and as such recorded all matters of particular significance in a large hand-written book in the B. V. M. archives.

11   The first Sisters at Holy Cross were Sisters M. Anna Burke, Evangelista Meehan, Alphonse Doyle, Orestes Boland, Anastasius McLaughlin, Petronia Doyle, Nathalie Jones, Justine Whelan and Jarlath Fitzgibbons.

12   Those assigned to St. Lawrence were Sisters M. Theodore McCarthy, Demetria Fitzgibbons, Sylvester Griffen, Adelbert McGuire, Vestina Higgens, Meinrad Thornton, Melania Sullivan and Rachel Eppel.

13   The first Sisters assigned to Presentation School were Sisters Mary of the Angels O'Connor, Emerentiana McKinnon, Agnesita Ineichen, Aloyse Moran, Dominic Power and Concepta Ryan.

14   Father Clark, a former Paulist, came to the diocese from the Paulist mission in San Francisco. His own backgrounds were eastern.

15   The Sisters who opened the Sacred Heart mission in Fort Dodge were: Sisters M. Chrysantha Driscoll, Placentia Fitzgerald, Tarasius Kehoe, Stanislaus McNeill, Anna Sweeney and Darena Hennessy.

16   Terms for music lessons at the time were $10. 00 a quarter for 24 lessons for children attending the school and $12. 00 for others. School tuition rates were a dollar a month for the upper grades, seventy-five cents for the intermediate, and fifty cents for the primary.

17   It was the able president of the College of St. Catherine in St. Paul, Sister M. Antonia McHugh, C. S. J. , who had urged Clarke's dean to apply for membership.

18   The archivist for the Religious of the Sacred Heart, Sister Helen Sheahan, RSCJ, having thoroughly searched their records, states that when Elizabeth Foley spent a year in their academy she was sixteen years of age, and that she may have graduated that year. Sister suggests that Elizabeth may have kept in close touch with their Sisters through sodalities, and in the cour

of these associations have imbibed much of their tradition and spirit.

19 Sister M. Editha Flanagan entered the Congregation from St. Agatha Academy in Iowa City at the early age of fifteen, but already an accomplished musician. She was assigned to the Davenport academy as a novice, at the time that Sister M. Cecilia was in charge of the boarding students and was teaching piano there. Sister M. Gonzaga, superior at that time, gave the talented young woman every advantage, taking her to Chicago for the concerts of artists and securing for her the best instruction. Quite naturally, the more advanced and talented of the students were assigned to her, and with the stress which Sister M. Gonzaga placed on music, the preparation for recitals, etc., took precedence over classwork or other assignments. Sister was a composer of merit, as well as a teacher, especially in the composition of choruses on religious subjects. Unfortunately, little of her work has been published.

20 The only apparent authorization for deleting the title would seem to have been that which appears in Common Observances as issued some years later in 1906, p. 46; even that would have called for only the strictest construction: "In the Congregation, the Superior General is spoken of as Mother. . . . "

21 Sister M. Evangela Henthorne was a student at the academy at this time, and was old enough to be alert to relations among the Sisters. It is she to whom these details are largely attributed in the notes of Sister Doris Mary Walsh, who gathered many data on the lives of Mothers Cecilia and Gertrude. Sister M. Evangela is now deceased.

22 A slight hint of Mother's feelings is manifest in a consoling letter written to a Sister who was grieving over a change from St. Joseph Academy, DesMoines: ". . . Don't be lonesome, child, nor heartsick either; these changes are not worth a sigh or tear of ours. . . . Remember you and I are where God wants us to be and that is enough; we should want nothing more. . . . He watches over us, directs and presides over these changes - and His holy will is that we submit with good grace, lovingly and cheerfully. That's what I'm trying to do, and now it's your turn to help me. "

23 Sister M. Antonia Durkin, able and highly thought of, lost her sight in her later years. Sister M. Robert Hugh Pendergast

used often to read to her, and at times Sister grew reminiscent. On one such occasion she spoke of the "skullduggery" in the election of 1900, and told of the fully developed plan in which she had shared for a break in the community if Mother Cecilia would give it her consent. A Sister whose duties brought her in close contact with Mother Gertrude during the latter's last days was aware of Mother's efforts to make reparation for some aspects of that election best known to herself.

24 Sister M. Eileen Curran who was then a child at the academy spoke with warmest affection of Mother Cecilia as superior there.

25 A brother of Sister M. Cherubina Powers, then deceased, was one of the owners of the theatre, and the Sisters shared the family's deep grief in the tragedy.

26 Sister M. Charlotte's companions in the opening of the school were: Sisters M. Lillian Carney, Auxilia Kelly, Pionia Clarke, Emma Healy, Wendelin Fitzgerald, of Mercy McGuchen, Euphemia Finn and Paschalina Masterson.

27 The opening of the north side central high school for girls, the Immaculata by B. V. M. Sisters resulted in the closing of Lourdes, Holy Name and DePaul high schools in 1922, their faculties generally being absorbed by the new school.

28 Monsignor Kelly of Our Lady Help of Christians planned with the Sisters there for half-day sessions in order to accommodate the children from Our Lady of Angels. Until February 3, 1959, nineteen buses arrived at noon each day, the children moving quietly into their borrowed classrooms.

29 It seems ironical that Father Cussen should have been visited with so great a trial. When the B. V. M. infirmary burned in 1955, he responded with great magnanimity to the Sisters' loss.

30 James W. Sanders, The Education of an Urban Minority, Catholics in Chicago, 1833-1965. (New York: Oxford University Press, 1977), p. 96.

31 Data furnished by M. Fitzpatrick, RSCJ.

32 The first Sisters to staff the Holy Name School were:

Sisters M. Chionia Cavanaugh, Bonita Driscoll, Columbière Hagerty, Lourdes Brophy, Balbina Durkin, Augusta Hannaher, and four novices, Herbert Rogers, Harriet McNerney, Eulalia McSwiggin and Rosella Eulberg.

33 Louise Callan, RSCJ, The Society of the Sacred Heart in North America. (New York: Gongmans, Green and Co., 1937), p. 82.

34 Besides Sister M. Casia, the Sisters sent to St. Dominic's in 1904 were: Sisters M. Theodora McCarthy, Theodosia Stiles, Louise Collendar, Placidus Doyle, Priscilla Ryan, Assumption Lyons, Timothy Hurley and Venantia Gaffney.

35 Sanders, p. 67 ff.

36 Rev. George A. Lane, S. J. , editor, Madonna Center. (Chicago: Loyola University Press, 1976).

37 Sister Mary Eva McCarty, OP, The Sinsinawa Dominicans: Outlines of Twentieth Century Development, 1901-1949. (Dubuque: The Hoermann Press, 1952), p. 130.

38 Other members of the St. Jerome household were: Sisters M. Agnese Gibbs, Gerena Guilder, Mildredine Mott, Roderick Burke, and their housekeeper, Sister M. Helen Donovan.

CAMPUS OF MT. ST. GERTRUDE ACADEMY, BOULDER
FLATIRONS IN BACKGROUND

Chapter Ten

TWO KEANES AND A PROBLEM OF BOYS

When Mother Cecilia resumed the office of superior-general
on February 2, 1906 it was a triple occasion, being also her
sixty-eighth birthday and her fiftieth anniversary in religion.
But her new responsibilities were her first concern, and of
these finance was to prove her greatest source of anxiety. It
was reassuring to see that the outstanding debt against the motherhouse had been reduced to $35,000 during the previous year.
Listed receipts for that year had totaled $90,942.07, the prin-
cipal sources being $40,589.88 from the mission houses,
$4,214.19 brought by the novices, $6,810.88 as returns from
Sisters' estates, and $33,612.72 from the rental and sale of
lands. Owing still at interest rates varying from 4% to 5% was
$79,000, while the total indebtedness to the motherhouse from
St. Mary High School and six boarding academies equalled
$108,232.30. Figures always frightened her but they were none-
theless unescapable. From them other worries would prove a
distraction.

Great dismay struck Mt. Carmel when the word was flashed
across the nation on April 18, 1906 that an early morning earthquake in San Francisco had taken hundreds of lives, left many
hundreds more injured and done an incalculable amount of damage
leaving thousands homeless. After-shocks continued for days,
fifty-two in all, breaking gas and water mains and starting new
fires which couldn't be checked for lack of a water supply. Five
days of anxious waiting passed without word of the fifteen
B.V.M. Sisters at St. Brigid's. It finally came on the sixth day
that all were safe, though all but 150 of the 800 houses in the
parish had been demolished. Sister M. Basil Healy, superior
at Petaluma, had at last been able, despite twisted rails, to
come by train, crossing the Bay on a barge to bring a basket
of food to the Sisters if happily she found them alive. Making

Archbishop John J. Keane   Archbishop James J. Keane

Msgr. E. A. Pace, PhD

her way to the Praesidio where the army had set up a great tent
city at the site of its own barracks, she found all thoroughly
employed. Barges were arriving daily from towns along the
coast bringing food and supplies. The Sisters were involved in
distributing milk, butter, bread and coffee to mothers and their
children from the headquarters of the army chaplain who had
put it at their disposal. Others shared in the making of a nourish-
ing stew on outdoor stoves to feed the hungry thousands. Gathering up as many as they could of the restless, wandering children,
the Sisters were conducting classes in a large tent. Though at
first the children were an unruly lot, reasonable order prevailed
in time and lessons went forward. This was the word which went
back to those anxiously awaiting at the motherhouse.

Meanwhile all the able men and boys were clearing the streets,
repairing water mains and gas lines, and providing sanitary facilities to safeguard the city against typhoid and dysentery. Grief
for lost lives and destruction of much that was dear to them
brought many to the Sisters for comfort, and for weeks they
held evening prayer services - the rosary, hymns and a reassuring discourse by one of the Sisters. Finally in June when the
number of homeless had been reduced from 300,000 to 50,000,
the Sisters were able to return to the frame building that served
as school and convent. While fire had raced down both sides of
Van Ness Avenue, it had skipped the parish plant, confining itself to one side of the street for that one block. The Sisters'
quarters on the top floor were in an unsafe condition necessitating the building of a convent. Statues and other breakable articles were scattered about the classrooms but there was no serious damage and school was resumed shortly.

The Sisters could then look back on their experiences - how,
fortunately, they were up and dressed when that first heavy
tremor came; how Sister M. Consolata, kneeling at the altar
railing, had found herself bathed in warm oil from the sanctuary
lamp when it swung violently; how Sister M. Robertine had tossed
all available bedding from the upper windows after they had
watched the cross from the church steeple come tumbling down
and knew their situation was not safe; how Sister M. Conradine,
always alert to the needs of others, had helped the injured,
transporting them to improvised hospitals. It was an experience
they would never forget.

But all was not over. An infestation of rats brought cholera
to the beleaguered city in the early winter, with sixty-five deaths
in a single day. Coffins were not to be had, the bodies being
wrapped in sheets for burial. [1]

Believing that it would be impossible to reopen the schools

for sometime, Mother Cecilia had invited the Sisters to come
home, and had promised to staff a new school in St. Louis with
their assistance. Only four returned, but they would make the
new mission possible. Meanwhile Dubuque's chancellor had requested funds for relief of the sufferers. Mother Cecilia pledged
$500.00 from the motherhouse, $100.00 from each of the academies, and $20.00 from each mission house, in addition to the
contributions of the children.

The Jesuit Fathers in St. Louis early established a parish in
connection with their university in the central part of the city.
After the Civil War the virulent anti-catholicism of the Know-
nothing Party made their situation there intolerable, and they
built a great Gothic church dedicated to St. Francis Xavier outside the city limits. The grade school of the parish was not
then, however, transferred to the new site. When the pastor,
the Reverend H. Bronsgeest, S. J., realized that many of the
children in the new area were going to the public school, he appealed to the university board of the consultors for the establishment of a school in the proximity of the church. An appeal to
the archdiocese for Sisters brought back word that there were
none available.

The Reverend W. B. Rogers, S. J., formerly of Gesu Parish
in Milwaukee and now president of the university, advised the
board: "When you get the finances worked out, write to the
B. V. M. 's in Dubuque and see if they can send you teachers.
They are working mostly in Iowa, Illinois and Wisconsin, and
have a reputation for running excellent schools. "

An unexpected bequest made possible the purchase of a large
residence on Pine Street for school purposes and the rental of
a nearby house for the Sisters. Sisters M. Bertrand Foley and
Seraphina Short went to purchase the necessary equipment, or-
dering its delivery in ample time for the arrival of the new community. Despite their careful planning, the Sisters came to an
empty house. Alerted by a neighbor, Father Bronsgeest managed
at least cots and bedding for the night.

The first community included Sister M. Seraphina Short, superior, and Sisters M. Angelina Guinan, Ruth Dooley, Benedetta
Riley, Ralph Degnan, Genese Hayes, St. Clare Carney and
Pelagia Liska. Furnishings and supplies came slowly, and for
years the Sisters managed with only the bare necessities, such
tuition as they could collect being their single source of income.

School opened in September with 190 children enrolled. However, many of the parishioners thought the introduction of a new
group of teaching sisters into St. Louis where there were already
several well-established orders was due to some eccentricity of

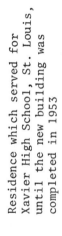

Residence which served for
Xavier High School, St. Louis,
until the new building was
completed in 1953

St. Francis Xavier Elementary
School, St. Louis, opened 1906

Sisters in summer shawls in
Lincoln Park, Chicago, 1906

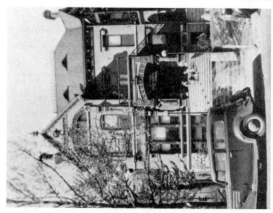

the Fathers, and for some years they paid little attention to the financial straits in which the Sisters found themselves. But time remedied that and eventually there were many loyal friends. As their school grew, a second residence furnished additional living space for the added faculty.

St. Francis Xavier today is a favored school, operating in a modern and substantial building and drawing from a neighborhood largely Black, with methods and curriculum adapted to the best interests of the children it serves.

But the Jesuit Fathers had soon raised their sights to include a high school for girls. It was not long after the crash of the stock market in 1929 that the pastor of the college church, the Reverend Patrick Burke, S. J., purchased the Grone home on West Pine, one of many large residences that were then up for sale. When his written request for B. V. M. 's to staff it met with a polite refusal, he took the train to Dubuque, and the twenty-five-room mansion was shortly opened as Xavier High School, with Sister M. Edith McGrath its principal.

Those were harsh days in which earning a living held top priority. Typing, shorthand and business machines shared the curriculum with the academic courses. In the school year 1933-1934 Xavier High received full accreditation from the State of Missouri, and in June graduated eighteen girls in ceremonies at the college church.

The story of the school's successes, its strenuous war efforts, its scholastic attainments, the memories built from participation in Father Daniel Lord's spirited summer gatherings of sodalists, the fun of sharing in the musical plays and pageants he both wrote and directed, all built a spirit that grew with the years.

The school had burst its seams before the modern Xavier High was built in 1952-1953 to accommodate its student body and provide suitable quarters for its many activities. Completely equipped with every facility expected in a modern high school, its capacity approximately five hundred students, it was to have a much too brief career. A greatly changed neighborhood had so reduced the student body by the seventies that the school was closed in 1974, and in 1976 the building was sold to the university which had long shared the facilities of its auditorium and gymnasium - a casualty to change. [2]

Even from the early twenties the Sisters in the grade school, several of whom are now retired at Mt. Carmel, attended the University extension course at the Sacred Heart Academy a few blocks west of their convent. During the superiorship of Sister M. Myra Liddle in 1928, twenty-one B. V. M. 's took summer

courses offered by the University, enjoying the convenience of
the Xavier High School Convent. Until its close the convent
served as residence for Sisters in study at the University.

Sister M. Pulcheria McGuire had used every spare moment
during her six years as general secretary and companion to
Mother Gertrude in the compiling of a book of recollections
which she called the Annals. For it she had drawn on materials
furnished her by Sisters M. Michael Nihill and Loyola Rutherford, and on the many reminiscences she herself had gathered
from the older members. In 1906 typed and hectographed copies
of its four hundred pages were sent to the larger houses where
they were read with great eagerness. Several copies of the
Annals are preserved in the B. V. M. archives and still afford
interesting reading. When Sister M. Lambertina Doran compiled
the Congregation's first published history, In the Early Days,
she drew rather heavily on the Annals, a fact which she acknowledged in her foreword. Her work, covering the years 1833-1887,
went into circulation in 1912. It seems to have been well received
for it went through three printings. More about it later.

Outlines for home study according to individual needs went to
the missions in early summer of 1907, with examinations by mail
planned at the end of the course. All the superiors were again
present for a brief session, June 24--July 6, except Sister M.
Basil, Petaluma, Sister M. Remberta, San Francisco, and Sister M. Clementia, DesMoines. Dr. Thomas Shields of the Catholic University gave a series of lectures, his general subject,
educational methods as demonstrated by Christ, the Teacher. He
greatly deplored the method being generally used of teaching
religion by rote recitation of the Baltimore Catechism. Unfortunately, he pointed out, the catechism had been compiled by
theologians who knew little or nothing about the laws of learning,
its content having been directed toward teachers, not pupils.
Shields was himself pioneering in a system of Catholic education
based on the laws of learning and the principles Our Lord had
made use of in his instructions. During the session Sister M.
Lamberta Fitzgerald demonstrated the use of physics apparatus.
Toward the end of the assembly Mother Gertrude, then first
consultor, became very ill, and on July 27 being thought near
death she was anointed. Recovery was slow.

On August 15, profession day, guests were present for the
ceremonies. As Sister M. Lambertina recorded: "Thirty-five

Infirmary Chapel on Christmas, 1954, and the view of it after
the fire of July 28, 1955. Note the bent candlestick with
the unmelted candle at the far left. The statue stands today in
in a niche of the first floor recreation room in Marian Hall,
the present day infirmary.

seculars here for breakfast. The house a scene of confusion all day. " Doubtless a happy sort of confusion, but one which apparently weighed too heavily with some of the older Sisters, for the practice of closing the house to all visitors on such occasions was soon the order of the day.

The Sisters' infirmary in the cell wing of the new motherhouse was very inconvenient and was being taxed beyond its limits. When in 1907, Sister M. Arthur Danahey received a sizable inheritance, she asked that it be used for the construction of a new and well equipped infirmary separate from the motherhouse itself. Mr. Henry J. Schachts, who had designed the chapel building at Mt. St. Joseph, was chosen as its architect. The design of the building was unique. The semi-circular chapel was the focal point of the structure. A half-circle of ten rooms lay just beyond the narrow corridor which separated the rooms from the chapel. Glass walls permitted the bed patients to be present for the celebration of Mass or for Benediction, while the drawing of shades in their rooms at other times provided the necessary privacy. It was a two-story structure with a large sun deck and spacious private rooms for all the ninety patients. Ground was broken on August 1, 1907, and the building was ready for occupancy by the following fall. For forty-eight years it sheltered the sick and the aged where, tenderly and efficiently, their every need was met.

On a hot summer evening in 1955 a fire which began in the overheated attic had gotten much headway before it was discovered at about 9:30. The patients included many who had been bedridden for a number of years. Despite the failure in the lighting system and the rapid advance of the fire, everyone was brought out in safety. The presence of a large number of tertians home for final vows was providential. They moved in like a drill team, carrying many out on mattresses and walking others out, many of whom had not been ambulatory for years. Without panic the work proceeded, the patients being placed at a distance on the lawn far out of the way of the great number of helpers who streamed in from every side. The hospitals and nursing homes of the city called to offer every possible assistance. A new wing at Mercy Hospital had not yet been occupied. A large number of patients were taken there by ambulance, while others were cared for by the Sisters of St. Francis in their Xavier Hospital or were provided for in other situations, the infirmary staff transferring to these sites as needed. A crew of nurses came from as far away as Davenport.

Fire threatened to cross the bridge that joined the infirmary and motherhouse, but firemen quickly demolished that structure. The original infirmary building was leveled to the ground. Fortunately a section which had been added in the thirties was provided with heavy fire doors and so was left in safety.

The accompanying photographs tell their own story. The untouched statue of the Blessed Virgin and the unmelted candle beside it were sources of wonder to many. The statue today occupies a niche in the first floor recreation room of the new and much larger infirmary building entitled Marian Hall.

It was not only to the B. V. M. 's that trouble came in 1955. The Sisters of the Visitation were feeling keenly the inroads among them of tuberculosis, threatening the future of their school as well as their community. They had grave need of help to build a new wing. In view of their necessity, Archbishop Keane contracted with the Sisters to meet, with a loan bearing no interest, whatever remained of its cost when they had done what they could. [3]

While it seems remote from the Sisters, they were not wholly insulated from the general feeling of insecurity which pervaded the Church in the first decades of the twentieth century. In 1864 Pius IX's publication of a Syllabus of Errors, listing many dangers which he regarded as threatening orthodoxy in a fast changing age, had sent a tremor through the more forward looking of the clerical scholars. Inspired largely by the more conservative among the churchmen, in 1907 Pius X went a step farther with his encyclical on Modernism. It was followed by an intransigent search for any possible evidence of modernistic trends of thought or teaching. [4]

Cardinal Merry del Val, the papal secretary of state, was especially zealous in this search. A message from him to Archbishop Keane in 1907 spoke the appreciation of the Holy Father for the expression of loyalty on the part of the bishops suffragan to Keane in their full acceptance of the encyclical. The following year, in keeping with directives from Rome, the Archbishop established a comitatus vigilantes which was expected to warn the Holy Father of any trace of modernism to be detected in the archdiocese. Keane reports in his Diary that they "could not find a vestige among priests or people. "

The effects of such a search on the mentality of the times was to cast suspicion on any new or original thought. The Sisters did not escape this pervading fear of the new. The oft-repeated caution to make no departure from established practice "even though it might seem to be much better, " long stood in the way of helpful innovation and a healthy resourcefulness.

Our Lady Help of Christians in Austin, a subdivision of Chicago, began as a mission church from St. Catherine's. From there Mercy Sisters came regularly to instruct the children. When in 1901 Archbishop Feehan established it as a separate parish, it had no boundaries north or west, but stretched away into prairies and cornfields. The Reverend Joseph O'Reilly was named pastor for the 150 families, largely Irish, in the area. By 1907 Father O'Reilly had constructed a combination building which provided for a church, a school, an auditorium, a convent and a parish hall. There came that fall Sisters M. Remi Wallace, Delphine Conway, Hildabert Kinsella, Leola Sheedy, Thecla Carroll and Mark Mulick to staff an elementary school.

The parish grew rapidly and on the occasion of its golden jubilee in 1951 it could boast of 2, 500 families whose 1, 310 children were enrolled in the parish school under the care of twenty-five B. V. M. Sisters and three lay teachers. The school could count among its graduates twenty-five priests, one brother and twenty-one seminarians. Forty-one of its girls had joined the B. V. M. 's and ten had gone to other orders.

Father O'Reilly built the present church in 1927 and that year the first graduate to be ordained, the Reverend William O'Connor, later Bishop of Springfield, said his first Mass.

The school's peak enrollment was 1, 600 children, the girls in blue serge uniforms with white collars and cuffs, and long black stockings, the boys with dark trousers, light shirts and ties. Today the parish is almost entirely Black, with but few Catholics among them. The parish team of priests and Sisters strives to meet such needs as it humanly can, both in school and church.

It was largely as a result of pressure for teachers in the parish schools that the council in its meeting of July 12, 1907 resolved to dismiss all boarders from the schools at Petaluma and Marcus and the St. Mary Academy in Elgin. In order that the Sisters at Mt. St. Gertrude, Boulder, be free for their avowed work in the classroom, it had become imperative that they be relieved of the excessive demands made by their "parlor-boarders, " invalided ladies and vacationers whom they had taken in for the sake of the revenue these promised. The mother house planned to compensate for any financial loss. The final

decision regarding Petaluma and Marcus, however, rested with
the respective bishops, and they yielded only slowly.

A second matter given much consideration in that meeting was
the formulating of a contract for remuneration expected from
schools to be opened in the future. It contained the following
conditions:

1. The Sisters would accept what they could collect in tuition
money and keep the income from music, or

2. Each Sister would be paid $25.00 a month, instead of the
$20.00 heretofore agreed upon, the Sisters to keep the music
money.

3. Where contracts already exist, the stipend paid the Sisters
be raised from $20.00 to $25.00 for each school and music
teacher, and only one music teacher would be assigned to
any school which claimed the music money. (The music
teacher taught sight-singing and trained the children's choir
in addition to the giving of private lessons.)

4. There must be some provision for the Sisters' livelihood
during the months of vacation.

This new contract was sent to the Chicago pastors, Bishop
Muldoon, and Fathers Jennings, Hynes, Hischen, Dunne, Maloney,
Conway and Fitzsimmons, and to Father Sullivan of Cedar Rapids,
Father Donlon of Cedar Falls, Father McCann of Elgin and Father Sueppel of Washington, Iowa. The pastors seem not to have
taken it too seriously for it was five years later that decisive
action was taken.

It was decided further to send a draft for $1,000 to the Holy
Father Pius X in honor of his jubilee. The meeting closed with
the reading of letters from four canonists, doubtless regarding
a contemplated division into provinces and the nature and advantages offered by perpetual profession.

On September 9, 1907 a visit paid to the motherhouse by the
Apostolic Delegate, the Most Reverend Diomede Falconio, [5]
and his entourage, caused no little excitement and concern.
Mother Cecilia was in Davenport at the time. Father Clark and
such officials as were at home accompanied His Excellency on
a tour of the motherhouse. Twenty-nine postulants had come just
the day before. Besides these there were twenty-three novices

and three postulants in residence. All were assembled in the novitiate to meet the delegate. He expressed surprise that so large a congregation should have so few novices, whereupon Father Clark assured him that there were more, the rest having been assigned to classrooms on the missions. The Cardinal then inquired as to whether they wore the white novice veil in the classroom. Father hastened to assure him that their veils were black, a bit of information which proved less than satisfactory. He must see the mother-general.

When Mother Cecilia returned from Davenport the next day, the delegate spoke gravely: "You must bring your novices back from the missions. Their vows will not be valid unless they have a full year of uninterrupted novitiate here at Mt. Carmel. "

It was a frightening thought: that all those vows made without the Sisters having fulfilled the full year requirement were invalid, including even those Sisters who now held office and whose official acts would then likewise be invalid. What could possibly be done about it now? Falconio then proved reassuring. A petition addressed to the Holy Father with a full explanation of circumstances would doubtless bring a sanation, a decree validating all vows made in ignorance of the law. As for the thirty-two novices now on the missions - that must be corrected and novices were thenceforth to be given their two full years of novice training.

Carrying out the delegate's instructions called for the return of thirty-two black-veiled novices to the motherhouse. To ameliorate the classroom problem, half could be brought home at a time. The twenty-three presently at home could not go out until their full two years of training had been completed. Thus pastors were involved and must be notified. There was one other recourse - the closing of the less viable academies thus releasing a number of teachers for parish schools. So it was that on the following June the boarding students from St. Francis, Council Bluffs, were transferred to St. Joseph Academy, DesMoines. St. Agatha's[6] enrollment, largely day students, was absorbed by the St. Mary High School, Iowa City, and the school at St. Patrick's was made coeducational. St. Cecilia's, Holden, Missouri, was simply closed.

The official document validating all earlier vows came on December 7 to the relief of all. On December 28 Mother Cecilia and companion visited Falconio in Washington for further clarification of her duties. On their way home the Sisters stopped in Philadelphia to pay a visit to Old St. Joseph's where the first five Sisters had found themselves in friendly hands on their arrival in the New World. The Apostolic Delegate, having received Mother with great graciousness, kept a promise of books on canon law, his package arriving on January 17, 1908.

Meantime, other religious congregations were being faced with the same problem - that of vows without adequate novitiate training - and the word had gotten around. Mother Cecilia suddenly became something of an authority on the subject and was called upon to answer inquiries from a number of other mothers-general. She was thus able to prepare them to take the initiative in their own cases. As for the black-veiled novices brought home from the missions, return to the status and routine of novice life was not an easy experience.

The teaching of boys by the Sisters seemed to present a perennial problem. In 1885, when Mother Clarke was seeking the final approbation of their Rule, she requested that the Sacred Congregation "allow us while the necessity of the times require it, to teach boys up to ten years of age but no older. " When the approved Rule came in 1887, the English translation which she received read, "They are to teach children. " In 1908 when the Apostolic Delegate reviewed the Sisters' Rule in its original Latin, he found that they were authorized to teach only "puellae. " Translating the word more literally than had the Jesuit Fathers, he made it clear to Mother Cecilia that the Sisters had no authority for the teaching of boys. This in the face of the fact that they had taught the younger boys from the earliest days and were then teaching boys even in a number of smaller high schools and commercial classes. He advised Mother to apply for a sanation from past operations, and for a rescript permitting them to continue the teaching of boys. On his part Falconio seconded the Sisters' request and suggested that they take no action in the schools until word came from Rome.

Needless to say, even the possibility of losing the services of the Sisters for the boys made a mighty stir among bishops and pastors. Archbishop Keane was away for a protracted rest at the time. On his return to Dubuque in March 1909, he noted in his diary that the Apostolic Delegate had advised him of a recently received rescript, permitting the Sisters to teach boys through their twelfth year. (It added, however, that boys and girls must be taught in separate classrooms.) "But unanimously it is urged, " the Archbishop wrote, "that this must be extended to fourteen years, as between twelve and fourteen there is no place for them in the public school. I have today written in that sense to the Apostolic Delegate, also to Archbishop Quigley of Chicago, who has expressed himself strongly likewise. " A month later, Keane forwarded to Falconio strong letters on the subject from Bishops Bonacum of Lincoln, Garrigan of Sioux City, and Davis of Davenport.

While the Sisters awaited the outcome of the Bishops' appeal, those who taught boys were inclined to join their sentiments with those of the pastors, at least until Mother Cecilia wrote to their superiors: ". . . it will be well to remind them that we willingly conform to any directions received from the Holy See, and that no Sister is at liberty to criticize such directions or to suggest improvements. " Sister M. Lambertina noted mildly in the Record of Events, ". . . restrictions regarding our teaching boys have aroused much disfavor in pastors and even some Sisters. "

In early April 1910 Bishop Garrigan, apparently at the request of the seriously ailing Keane, went to Washington for an interview with the Apostolic Delegate, calling on Mother Cecilia on his way. Garrigan's visit with Falconio had a second purpose, that of impressing him with Keane's critical need of a coadjutor. Mother Cecilia had provided the Bishop with ammunition for his attack on the unfortunate delegate. This included the reminder that many of the children in the Sioux City Diocese were of Bohemian, Slavic, Italian or Lithuanian parentage, who must be taught to understand English before they could be instructed in the truths of religion. It was the teaching of the children which kept the parents in the church. Where pastors had sought religious who were free to teach boys they had had no success. 'If we abandon parochial schools, " Mother wrote, 'to other orders of women, the main object of our foundation will be defeated. . . . Already we have been asked why we cannot continue to do what other Sisters are permitted to do. " Mother then presented the problem of expense for small schools of the additional teachers, classrooms and costs involved in the teaching of boys and girls separately.

The visit revealed that a second rescript had come permitting the teaching of boys through their fourteenth year. But this had not yet solved the Bishops' problems, for many boys, especially those of foreign parents, were considerably beyond their fourteenth year before they had finished their elementary schooling.

Faced with all this, Falconio followed their visit with a letter to Garrigan:

> After all I had to do to get permission for them to teach boys not over fourteen years of age, [7] I think it would be very unwise for me to ask the Sacred Congregation a general permission. . . . Therefore, let the Sisters have recourse to the Ordinary of their respective diocese who shall judge in such particular cases according to his prudence and conscience. If the permission be granted, the Superior should see that

the case of such young men be entrusted to elderly and
proved Sisters.

Regarding coeducation, the decree was to be obeyed for boys
over fourteen, with some allowance made where necessary for
those under that age. For boys under seven there was no requirement.

It did not take the bishops long to pursue the advantage presented them. Archbishop James J. Keane, who had meantime
succeeded the retired Archbishop of so nearly the same name,
wrote Mother Cecilia:

> The Holy See has been pleased to grant certain dispen-
> sations from the provisions of your Rule, enabling you to
> resume the teaching of boys. His Excellency, the Apostolic
> Delegate, refers you to the Rt. Rev. Ordinaries for the
> interpretation of such dispensations.
>
> I have exhorted the priests to employ where possible a
> man to control and teach as far as he may be able the high
> school branches to boys where there is no high school. When
> the aforesaid provision cannot be made, the Sisters shall
> admit boys to high school classes that they may not be ex-
> posed to the danger of losing their faith in non-Catholic
> schools.

Just one week in office, the new Archbishop made it clear to
his priests that the Sisters would teach boys through the high
school years. Mother Ascension having by then succeeded to
the office of Mother-general called on the Archbishop in company
with Mother Cecilia. They requested that he furnish them with
his written authorization for that exemption from their Rule. At
that time also they received his approval for a remuneration to
be asked of the pastors of $35. 00 a month for high school
teachers.

Other bishops quickly followed suit, as the following agreeable letter from Bishop Austin Dowling of DesMoines indicates:

September 2, 1912

My dear Mother Ascension -

I received your letter à propos of teaching boys in the
High School grades, and now that I know your position I
wish to say that in my opinion it would be a good thing for
our schools if they are to develop and do their work that
your Sisters should for the present teach boys of these
grades in this diocese.

Of course it is desireable /sic/ that men should teach
boys of that age, but you know as well as I that it is impossible to find them and our boys therefore pass from our
schools to other schools where women are their teachers
till the High School course is over. /illegible/ we lose
them as is abundantly evident in DesMoines. I should be
the first to oppose this modification of your custom did I
anticipate any of the abuses that suggest themselves to
those unfamiliar with our conditions or the veneration in
which our children hold the religious garb.

I dream of a high school for boys in DesMoines, but it
is as yet a vision by night which fades when the sun is up.
Till my dream comes true, [8] I wish that your Sisters would
teach the boys of the High School grades in this diocese
when pastors request them to do so. . . .

Diomede Falconio, OFM, as Apostolic Delegate, had done
much more in 1908 than interpret the B. V. M. rule on teaching
boys. He had that year secured for the United States a release
from the subordinate status of missionary country, and religious orders and congregations had been removed from the
jurisdiction of the Propaganda Fide and placed under the direction of the Congregation of the Affairs of Religious (now the
Congregation of Religious and Secular Institutes). Having been
raised to the cardinalate in 1911, he was made prefect of that
Congregation, and as such was most helpful when the Sisters'
petition for perpetual vows and provincial government was
presented to that body. Cardinal Falconio proved a gracious
friend to the Sisters, and for his many services he sought no
recompense save the satisfaction that they were engaged in a
great work. Had he been cardinal at the time during Archbishop
Keane's protracted illness when the Sisters were facing many
problems, he would doubtless have been their choice as Cardinal
protector. As it was, he performed for them services for which
Merry del Val, as Secretary of State to Pius X, had neither the
time nor the inclination. On his death on February 7, 1917, a
high Mass of requiem was sung for him in Mt. Carmel's Chapel.

Meantime life had moved along at the motherhouse. On September 25, 1908 great was the satisfaction when the electric
light system went into operation. And on November first the
Congregation celebrated the diamond anniversary of its founding
in Philadelphia. This was quickly followed by the dedication of
the new infirmary. On November 12, 1908 the Blessed Sacrame▶

was carried in procession to its new chapel, and its first eight patients were established in its rooms. They were: Sisters M. Paul Scanlon, Euphemia Finn, Avellino Boyle, Walburga Shebler, Carmella Bowden, Bathilda Lane, Wenceslaus Shea and Roche Guihan, all elderly. Sister M. Ascension Lilly was named the administrator for the new venture, and she with a small staff of Sisters shared the many duties involved. Before Christmas they had witnessed two surgical operations in the room especially equipped for that purpose.

The Archbishop's health, never robust, had been under heavy strain for many years. By the end of 1908 he had begun to report in his diary occasional lapses into partial unconsciousness which he attributed to a long-standing "valvular lesion of the heart. " That winter he went to New Orleans and San Antonio to escape the rigors of the Iowa winter and to rest. He was unable for the Holy Thursday services in 1909, calling on Bishop James J. Keane of Cheyenne for assistance and for his replacement on the confirmation-visitation tour for that year. By the end of May he noted the additional symptom of "a very serious impairment of memory. "

By August Keane had determined on asking for a coadjutor with right of succession, communicating his wish through the Secretary of State, Cardinal Merry del Val, and sending a second letter through the Apostolic Delegate. This was the first of a succession of pleas made directly or through Bishop friends. Then when finally he was advised by Cardinal Gibbons that he would have been successful if he had asked for an auxiliary instead, he did that, only to learn through Falconio that Rome had declined that also, "trusting that I can get along with the aid of neighboring bishops. " Meanwhile Keane had dutifully sent through the Apostolic Delegate the Archdiocesan Peter's Pence, amounting for the year to $3, 647. 82.

Rome seemed determined to act on nothing short of Keane's resignation, an act which would throw him on the charity of his successor. On March 8, 1911 he instructed Falconio to forward his resignation to the Holy Father. On April 27 he wrote: "Have today received from the Most Reverend Apostolic Delegate word that the Holy Father has accepted my resignation of this see, and that I am no longer Archbishop of Dubuque; from my heart I adore and welcome the will of God. " He spoke then of the senior Bishop of the Province, Bishop Scannell of Omaha, as the person designated to take steps toward the election of the new Archbishop, adding: "Thanks be to God for the ten happy

years that I have spent as Archbishop of Dubuque. May His
Divine Providence direct and shape all my future, and may He
soon take me to our Eternal Home. "

Then one final message came. He was no less an Archbishop,
and so he must be provided with a see, but one which continued
to exist only on the pages of history. So Keane took pen again to
write the final entry in the diary which told in greatest charity
the story of those "happy years":

> June 29, 1911. Received notification from the Sacred
> Consistorial in Rome that my Bulls as Archbishop of Cio
> were ready and would be forwarded on receipt of 2000 lire.
> I have today sent $400.00 to Monsignor Kennedy, rector of
> the American College, asking him to settle for and forward
> the Bulls.

Two days earlier Sister Mary Pulcheria had noted in her
Record of Events:

> Archbishop Keane came yesterday, intending to stay during
> the hot weather. He finds he cannot stand the noise of the
> trains. Went home this A.M. It is sad to see his weakened
> condition of mind and body. The doctors say he has senile
> epilepsy.

Thus it was that on August 11, 1911, another Keane - a different Keane - became the new Archbishop of Dubuque.

James Keane, the son of John Keane of County Clare and
his wife, Margaret Connor, County Galway, Ireland, was born
August 26, 1856 on a farm near Joliet, Illinois. John Keane
had first settled with his wife and their children, Dennis,
Bridget and Joanna, on land he had purchased in the heart of
present Chicago. The threat of ague in that swampy area had
led to the move. James' twin brother, John, died in infancy.
James later took his name in Confirmation.

A second move in 1858 took the family to a Minnesota land
grant twenty miles from Rochester, where they attended Mass
when conditions permitted. On occasions Mass was said in the
Keane home as a mission station.

After four years of successful study in St. John University,
Collegeville, James attended the Grand Seminary of St. Sulpice
in Montreal. He was ordained on December 23, 1882, for the
diocese of St. Paul where he served for two years under the
Right Reverend Thomas L. Grace, OP, and for eighteen years
under John Ireland, coadjutor and successor to Grace. His

great admiration for Archbishop Ireland was a strong influence in his later years.

Serving in parishes until 1885, the young priest was then made bursar at the newly established St. Thomas Seminary and College. He was named president of the college in 1887 and continued in that office until 1892. His position there brought him into contact with students from many parts of the world. Indeed, when Cardinal Gibbons visited St. Paul in 1887 greetings were extended to him in fourteen languages. Made pastor in 1892 of the Immaculate Conception Church, Minneapolis, Keane became known as the priest of the confessional from his dedication to that priestly duty.

The Right Reverend Thomas M. Lenihan, second Bishop of Cheyenne, suffering from a heart ailment had for some time before his death in 1901 directed his diocese from his home in Dubuque. Keane, then named his successor, was consecrated in company with the Reverend John Stariha, first Bishop of Lead, by Archbishop Ireland in the St. Paul Cathedral on October 28, 1902.

The state of Wyoming, where Keane found himself a pioneer missionary, was rich in minerals but poor in priests, churches, and the means to support both. As Cheyenne was part of the province of Dubuque, he was shortly called by the Archbishop to consider a division of the province. It was hoped that so remote an area as Wyoming might be joined with Nebraska, Omaha to serve as metropolitan see. The same conference considered the establishment of the see of DesMoines. While the second plan was accepted by Rome on August 12, 1911, the time was not considered ripe for establishing Omaha as an archdiocesan see. [10]

Keane remained nine years in Cheyenne, conducting hundreds of missions and delivering numerous lectures, traveling to remote areas by stage coach or on horseback. To raise money for his diocese, he engaged in lecture tours under the auspices of the Knights of Columbus, speaking to turn-away crowds in Milwaukee, Buffalo and in Boston. There Cardinal O'Connell followed his talk with a request for a collection which netted him $20,000 for the needs of his diocese. He drew large crowds in Houston, Denver and Los Angeles, and in 1908 gave the prayer at the Democratic convention in Denver. Called on to give the priests' retreat in Dubuque in 1904, he twice made the Confirmation-visitation tour of the diocese for the ailing Archbishop. Before leaving Cheyenne, Keane had built a cathedral and a rectory, and established a fund for the conduct of the diocese.

After such close association with the Dubuque Archdiocese, it is not surprising that on August 11, 1911 he was named the third Archbishop of Dubuque. [11] He seems not to have relished the new assignment for he declared in his first address to the people, "I've been transplanted and there is little hope that I shall take root. " But, rootless or otherwise, he administered the Archdiocese until his death on August 2, 1929. [12]

On April 22, 1909 the Sisters purchased a handsome pair of shiny black horses for $485. 00 and an old team they no longer deemed suitable for the convent carriage. The horses shortly ran away with driver and Sisters who narrowly escaped injury. However, the accident proved something of a blessing, for it rubbed off enough of the shiny black to alert the Sisters to the fact that the team had been given a coat of glossy black paint. Faced with the fraud, the horse trader paid back $500. 00, with which they made a much wiser purchase.

A new residence for the chaplain was erected that year, a trim cottage north of the new infirmary. The brick residence was then used for an occasional case of contagion and as a residence for the infirmary nurses. It was in this new and comfortable cottage that the ailing Archbishop had hoped to find some respite.

In October 1909 the Council decided on the transfer of all the bodies from the cemetery on the Prairie to the new graveyard at Mt. Carmel. An order was shortly placed for 152 uniform wooden boxes for that purpose. John Brady, for many years in charge of the motherhouse farm, with his brother James, was entrusted with the task. Into each box with the remains of a Sister went the iron cross that marked her grave. Five wagon loads of this strange cargo completed the transfer in the course of the next year or so. Then the reburial process began and the iron crosses were set in place again.

In 1898 the iron crosses marking the graves of Father Donagho and Mother Clarke were replaced by monuments - for him a substantial granite, and for her a marble shaft, each surmounted by a cross. Fixed to the iron cross which had till then marked Mother Clarke's resting place was a heavy metal plaque, edged with ivy leaves and bearing the legend

IN MEMORY OF LOVED MOTHER
M. F. CLARKE
FOUNDRESS AND SUP. GEN.
OF THE CONG.
OF THE SISTERS OF CHARITY, B. V. M.
DIED DEC. 4, 1887.
AGED 84.
MAY SHE REST IN PEACE

The memory of that plaque had died with the last Sister who saw it before the erection of Mother Clarke's monument. But not with John Brady who had managed the farm in her last years. When the Sisters moved into Dubuque John had moved there also, making his home but a short distance from the new Mt. Carmel. There he continued his labors for the Sisters. Until his death his reverence for their foundress had led him to keep a candle burning before the stand on which he had enshrined the precious memento. This he revealed to a future B. V. M. when, [13] on a visit to her novice-Sister, she had taken lodging in the Brady home. That was back in 1916, and the memory had faded for her too. Members of the Brady family had died or scattered, and the home was passed on to other tenants.

Eighty years after the iron cross and its plaque had been replaced, sixty-two years after the future postulant had viewed it, the same metal memento, whole and untarnished, came to light in the spring of 1978 in a scrap metal pile in the yard of the Ecology Control Corporation in Dubuque. Proprietor of the yard, Philip Mihalakis, was not slow to recognize its significance, presenting it at once to the Congregation's officials at Mt. Carmel. There it will occupy an honored place in the Heritage Room of the motherhouse, along with other mementoes of a treasured past.

Another historic event was now to take place. The graves of Father Donaghoe and the original five Sisters, all clustered near the entrance of the Prairie Cemetery, awaited the completion of a mausoleum at Mt. Carmel in which their remains would rest. On May 25, 1910, at an early hour, a solemn group, including Mothers Cecilia and Gertrude and thirty others of the Sisters, with Father Clark and the necessary workmen, gathered in the graveyard for the exhumation. The wooden coffin in which Mother Clarke had been interred had deteriorated through dampness and decay. What remained was carefully wrapped in linen cloth and placed in a metal lined cedar chest. It was necessary to use pulleys to raise Father Donaghoe's metal casket to the surface, for it had filled with water which must then be drained away. His remains and those of the other four Sisters were then encased each in its small wooden casket. All were placed in a hearse for the trip back to Mt. Carmel.

At the convent gate the procession of carriages passed through a double file of Sisters, novices and postulants, who followed it to the cemetery. Here, after the blessing of the mausoleum, each was placed in its proper niche, and as the masons sealed the compartments the Sisters sang their favorite hymns. There the bodies await the general resurrection. Later mothers-general have been interred in the area on either side of the mausoleum.

A decree received from Rome on November 3, 1909 required that each house have two local councillors who were especially responsible for the financial administration of the household. The decree warned that "the conscience of superiors is gravely burdened if she conceals from her consultors goods, income, money in any form, even personal gifts to the superior. All must be committed fully and exactly to the examination and approbation of the councillors. . . . " The consultors were required to affix their signatures monthly to the house account book, and to the quarterly report sent to the motherhouse.

The triennial election which took place in January 1909 resulted in the replacement of Sister M. Octavia Burke by Sister M. Esther Warren as Mother's assistant, and of Sister M. Esther as novice mistress by Sister M. Angela Fitzgerald. The elected consultors were Mother M. Gertrude Regan and Sisters M. Loyola Rutherford, Ascension Lilly and Octavia Burke. Announcement of the election results called for the unusual concession of recreation at meals that day. At a meeting of the council held on February 2, installation day, it was decided that the Sister-visitor could no longer satisfactorily conduct annual visitations to the great number of houses with their wide geographical distribution. Her duties must now be shared when necessary by the consultors.

Account book entries for 1910 and 1911 give insights into reading matter available to the Sisters. They include a check for $100.00 to the American Historical Society, and subscriptions to periodicals: the Milwaukee Citizen, Catholic World, Ecclesiastical Review, Extension, Sacred Heart Messenger, World Events, School Journal, Historical Records, America, Iowa Annals, The Missionary, Catholic Citizen, True Voice, Western

Watchman, The Leader, and the historical studies, A History of Iowa, and The Catholic Church in the United States. With the Catholic Encyclopedia in the planning, an advance order was given in 1906 at a price of $96.00.

Loved as Mother Cecilia was, her official acts from time to time brought sharp remonstrances or at least much muttering. The closing of the several boarding academies that had held happy associations for many of the Sisters was one of those actions. Another was her action in removing six Sisters from active service to send them for study. Not only the "waste" of taking them from the schools when there was so much pressure for teachers, but the expense to be involved in their months of study gave cause for complaint. The $6,000.00 budgeted for their education, it was commented, was equal to the salaries of thirty teaching Sisters! And as for the Sisters chosen, why those? She must sometimes have envied her predecessor, retired now to the position of first councillor.

Despite her several duties, Mother Gertrude had time for friendly correspondence with the Sisters and others. To one she wrote, "Thanks a thousand times to God for permitting us to go daily to Holy Communion." To Father Cottle in San Francisco went the hope that he "will be able to use his lovely church in December. I hope it will be many years before such an earthquake shock will be seen or felt again." Regarding the death of an old friend in Davenport, the Reverend A. A. Lambert, a former Jesuit, she wrote on January 18, 1909: "Many Sisters had hoped he would beg to be taken to his own Fathers before he died. Thank God he was prepared to meet his Lord." On December 15 of that year she commented that "Father Dumbach[14] had been laid to rest." She spoke of word that Sister M. Carmelita Ring was gradually improving from the burns she had sustained at Mt. St. Joseph Academy when a turpentine-wax cloth she was using had caught fire. And again: "Mother Cecilia has not been well at all."

Mother Cecilia's letters express a more involved concern. To a sick Sister she wrote on November 20, 1907:

No time to write since my return from Chicago meeting with superiors from the missions - all in trouble of every variety, some physically, some mentally, and some morally. God help us all! We are well kept only in his holy keeping.

Then on March 4, 1908 she wrote to another after she herself had sustained a bad fall:

I am not myself at all and you must explain for me and give each my grateful love, with one of the pictures enclosed. I am so miserable today owing to the general shake-up of my seventy-year-old body by that unfortunate fall that I am good for naught but to go to bed. Your own loving old S. M. Cecilia.

Sister M. Louise Clarke was seriously ill at St. Mary's, Iowa City. To her in early 1908, Mother wrote:

How sorry I am to hear of your serious illness. You must brace up, Dearie, don't dare go and die now even if you are sure of stepping right into Heaven, for I can't replace one of you, and I'm nearly wild with all the anxieties that are cropping up - just one thing and then another. Now, be brave, my Sister. I know Our Lord will spare you to us. We are praying for you and all our poor sick. Now don't go to Heaven.

To Sister M. Irma Cooper recuperating at Boulder, Mother wrote on November 3, 1909:

Remain as long as your health requires and be free from all restrictions and duties.

And to Sister M. Matilda Lahiff, exhausted from her duties as superior at Holy Family, she wrote on July 12, 1911:

We have placed you at Our Lady of Angels with sixth grade girls. It is lovely out there. Everything about the place. I was out there during the convention, and was amazed by all the improvements. I feel you will enjoy it.

Sister M. Gervase Tuffy, superior at the newly established St. Joseph's in Butte, Montana had just been through the ordeal of a fire which had destroyed both church and school. Very shortly after that the pastor, Father Thompson, was hospitalized His death came at the time the new church was ready for use. Mother wrote:

By all means send Father Thompson a check for $50. 00. Send it from yourself. I wrote him from the Bluffs to the hospital and did long to put some money in the letter, but hadn'it it, nor have I it now. We are in awful straits for money these times. Can't even pay our coal bill. . . .

Two weeks later she wrote in response to an appeal from Sister:

About your clothes, Sister dear, I could not get an atom worth sending on account of the crowd of youngsters we have here to support and clothe - 43 postulants, 74 novices. Sister M. Antonina uses every rag she can scrape up to save. And honestly we have no money. You heard about our fire - in the bungalow, but the insurance covers most of that loss. I hope you will let the Sisters who lost their clothing write to their relatives for help. [15] We have so much hired help, and their salaries so high that our income is considerably lessened. But God is good. We must trust in Him.

During these years, despite Mother Cecilia's money problems, there appear among the motherhouse accounts the following gifts and donations:

St. Joseph College	$230. 00
Quebec Fathers	22. 00
Paulist Fathers	30. 00
Charity, Priests and Servants	25. 00
Carmelites, New Orleans	10. 00
Ursulines, Canada	10. 00
Poor Clares and Ursulines	20. 00
Charity to Rev. J. J. Thompson, Butte	300. 00
Charity to Denver student	10. 00
Present to Father Tihen	100. 00
Most Reverend Keane	300. 00

These in addition to the offering of $500. 00 to the Sisters' new Cardinal-protector.

Although Mother Cecilia's term of office had expired three weeks before the writing of this letter on February 24, 1912, she was sufficiently involved as a first consultor to Mother Ascension to continue the story of Sister M. Gervase's troubles at St. Joseph's, Butte. Her great concern now was for a young Sister ill with tuberculosis.

My own dear Sister,
Yours received yesterday and, oh dear Lord! how bad
& sad it made me feel! Poor St. Joseph's! the Cross keeps
close to it right along! But, "in the Cross is life" -- let us
not lose heart. You won't, I know, for your dear Mother
made a good Catholic of you.
Poor Cyrilla! I can't realize that we are going to lose
her too. Your letter of today has raised my hopes again --
she may fight this too -- she has fought so much and lived.
Do you know, I fear our Community is going to bear the
cross of tuberculosis again? we have 6 or 7 young members
fighting it now -- all ordered to Boulder, and no place for
them there. May God help us! Is Sr. M. Cyrilla in the
Hospital? or in the Convent -- which? If in the Convent,
how do you manage for room? for she should sleep alone,
be well covered, and have her windows open all night, no
matter how cold. As to replacing her -- or giving her help
in March -- I could not do it if my eternal salvation depended
on it. In August next we will have one music teacher -- just
one: and if our dear Sr. Cyrilla must give up -- we can
keep that one for you so there we are, Gervase dear.
I saw poor dear Fr. Thompson's new church railing &
two confessionals -- after he was laid to rest! The foreman
at the Altar Co. did not know that God had taken our Father
Home -- until I told him: he was shocked.
Your anxious old,
Sr. M. Cecilia

Even to consider the possibility of Sister M. Cyrilla's continuing to teach music and so coming into close contact with
young children is frightening to us today.

Opened in 1906, St. John School in DesMoines had Sister M.
Coletta Farry for its first superior and the Reverend D.
Mulvihill its pastor. The school continues to the present. It
is regrettable that no account was left of its beginnings save
the names of its first staff. These were: Sisters M. Casimir
Weldon, Olympia Sullivan, Faber Montague, Etheline McCann,
St. Elizabeth Marshall and Fides McDermott.
In 1907 St. Vincent School, Kansas City, was opened under
the direction of the Vincentian Father F. X. Antill, with Sister
M. Emiliana Macaulay as its superior. [16] Father Antill had
met two B. V. M. Sisters as they emerged from a visit to his
church many months before. He greeted them warmly and

asked that they cross the street and bury a small statue of St. Joseph and a miraculous medal in a desirable plot there, later the site of St. Vincent Academy. The Sisters produced the desired articles from voluminous pockets. They were asked to add to their action a letter to Mother Cecilia urging her to provide Sisters for the school he planned. Within six months he had purchased the property and obtained a promise of Sisters.

Upon the death of Father Antill from pneumonia in January 1920, Father F. X. McCabe from DePaul University succeeded to the pastorate. A new church, built in 1922, was described as "monument in stone and debt." However, the parish prospered, and the Sisters continued to serve St. Vincent Academy until the summer of 1977.

In 1907 the B. V. M. Sisters also took charge of two schools in Butte, Montana, that of Immaculate Conception under Father O. D. Barry and St. Joseph's under Father A. Lenihan. Sisters M. Florence Clowry and Leandre Swift were the respective superiors. [17] The Sisters traveled west by way of St. Paul where they were met by Bishop John Carroll of the Helena Diocese, and formerly of St. Joseph College, Dubuque, who was there giving the priests' retreat. He conducted the Sisters to St. Catherine Academy, where the Sisters of St. Joseph proved gracious hostesses. The Bishop then accompanied the Sisters on the train as far as Livingston, Montana, where he was engaged for services, having treated them royally on the way. The pastors were at the train to meet them.

Construction at the Immaculate Conception School had been delayed by a strike, then ended. The Sisters, whose convent was to be the third floor of the school, were given the home of a friendly Civil War veteran, Judge William Clancy, who proved a genial landlord. Plans for three classrooms were quickly modified with the hiring of a lay teacher for a fourth room when two hundred children enrolled for school.

The copper mines had been closed since the previous fall, and as a result the mining families were suffering. The Sisters realized only later at what sacrifice the people had responded to their needs. It was the following May when a mine official, John Ryan, on his return from a directors' meeting in New York, was met miles east of Butte by a group of anxious miners. They wired back the joyful news, "Mines to open." Jubilation was unbounded.

Bishop Carroll was a frequent visitor to the schools. His great delight was to be present at the August institutes where the Sisters demonstrated new and approved methods of teaching and discussed the papers he had assigned to the different orders of Sisters.

A decreased enrollment and a shortage of Sisters forced the closing of Immaculate Conception School in 1976, and the merging that same year of St. Joseph School with St. Ann's and St. John the Evangelist. These had been outschools to St. Joseph's since their establishment in 1917.

With the closing of St. Agatha Academy in Iowa City in 1909, a coeducational school was opened in St. Patrick Parish where the Reverend F. J. Ward was pastor. Sisters from the academy had taught the boys of the parish since 1874 or 1875. Sisters M. Etienne Fleming and Adelaide O'Neil instructed eighty boys that first year in the eight elementary grades, while a Sister came from the academy twice a week for music. Now in 1909 Sister M. Anacleta, the academy's last superior, was assigned the same position in the new situation. With her came Sister M. Faustina Kirk and the highly revered and long remembered Sister M. Innocentia McCarthy, to be followed shortly by Sister M. Maxima Donlan for the seventh and eighth grades and the teaching of some high school subjects. There were no boys in the high school until 1912, but soon boys and girls were about equal in number. Two additional classrooms brought Sisters M. Petra Slattery and Martinian Dunnwald as teachers. The school hall at St. Patrick's was the scene of many gatherings of university students for debates and exercises in oratory.

Both St. Patrick's and St. Mary's High Schools continued until the opening of the central Regina High School in 1958. The following year the grade schools merged into Iowa City Catholic, using the facilities of the St. Patrick School with its gym and auditorium. The Sisters now reside at Regina Convent.

The Sisters at Gesu, Milwaukee, were provided with their own convent in 1911, having to that time made their residence at the Holy Angels Academy. The Sisters who constituted its staff were: M. Ildephonse Kennedy, Devota Ennis, Pancratia Coyle, Urbanita Stapleton, Benezetta Fosselman and St. Peter Tansey.

Rising educational standards threatened the existence of the Catholic school system in the first decade of the 1900's if some source of higher education for its teachers were not made available to them. A few colleges conducted by the Sisters were coming into being, though their faculties, largely inbred, were generally weak and their resources limited. Such Catholic universities as existed were exclusively male. The pattern of summer sessions so familiar in later years was quite unknown. Not only religious teachers but women in general were awakening to the advantages which college training opened up to them.

While the National Catholic Education Association took shape during the years 1899-1904, it was not until 1906 that the first allusion was made to the higher education of women. A Jesuit speaker at that year's convention, foreseeing a demand for degrees for those engaged in the teaching profession, spoke of the necessity for the admission of women to the Catholic University of America to fit them for college teaching. The Jesuits themselves were not authorized to teach women, and in general did not favor coeducation. The Catholic University had initiated correspondence courses in 1905 and many had begun to take advantage of these. With Dr. Shields and Dr. Pace, the vice-rector, Dr. Conaty, the rector of the University, and Maurice Francis Egan of the English department all available for summer lectures or institutes in various parts of the country, the Sisters grew eager for closer contact with the university itself. This would be slow in coming.

The problem of women's education posed a challenge to rising universities conducted by orders of men and to the Catholic University of America, under the direction of the hierarchy. As Marquette in Milwaukee advanced from college status to university in 1907, it faced the problem of coeducation which the Fathers looked upon as a threat to the Jesuit educational tradition. One young woman had been awarded a B. S. that year, the result of work she had somehow taken in the college. It made news as, "the first college degree conferred on a woman in the history of the Jesuit order. " As the University acquired independent professional schools - Medical, Dental and Law - it acquired also an occasional woman student, the first of these being granted a law degree at the 1910 commencement. However, Jesuit colleges had traditionally served only male students, and many of the Fathers preferred to keep it that way. A means of doing this, they hoped, was to induce a congregation of women to open a Sisters' college under the auspices of the University, which would hold itself responsible for the granting of degrees and the sharing of faculties. This presented a dilemma, however, for to get women's colleges they would have to open the doors to coeducation by admitting religious women to their classes. A visitor to the campus, the Reverend Cornelius Shyne, S. J., proposed a solution.

The nuns would be best able to study during the summer recess, while free from their grade-school teaching duties; none of the boys would think of spoiling their vacation by taking classes at that time. Therefore, bring in some willing Sisters when the campus was ordinarily deserted, rush them through their training, let them start the colleges for women and the problem would be solved.

And so an eight-week summer school for the purpose was scheduled to commence on June 28, 1909. However, when the nuns came, other women came also, to the great distress of the Father-provincial of the Mid-America Jesuits, who suggested canceling the classes. These went forward, however, while an appeal was made to the Father General in Rome.

No other Catholic school had previously held a summer session. This innovation was vigorously protested by many of the Jesuits, as was the idea of women on the University campus. However, the summer of 1910 arrived ahead of any word from Rome, and the women came again. The University had meanwhile affiliated with the Wisconsin Conservatory of Music with its many women students, and the doors squeaked open a little wider. When finally in the spring of 1912 word came from Rome it gave permission for "ladies and even nuns to attend. " Women had come to stay. [18]

The minutes of a council meeting at Mt. Carmel on February 12, 1911 indicate that Mother Cecilia and her consultors had for some time discussed among themselves the feasibility of accepting an invitation from Marquette University, and one also from DePaul University in Chicago, to establish a woman's college affiliated with each university, and thus make their own contribution to the higher education of women, and especially of Sisters. The minutes indicate that a tentative agreement had been reached for the Milwaukee venture, with the added note that the Sisters had been studying to that end[19] and would be ready in September of that year. Regarding the DePaul proposition, it was decided that a second college that same year would add too great a financial burden and that there were not enough available Sisters to open two colleges in the same year.

On February 19 the council gave permission to purchase the necessary property in Milwaukee at a cost of $50, 000. 00 on which a building would be constructed for approximately $35, 000. The debt thus incurred would be partially set off by the "sale of property now occupied by the Sisters. " There is no indication of the property intended for sale. A vote was taken with Sisters M. Loyola, Octavia, Ascension, Esther and De Chantal favoring the project, and Mothers Cecilia and Gertrude and Sister M. Lambertina opposing. It was therefore determined to proceed with the project. [20]

Then followed a reassessment of the situation. By giving

themselves another year of preparation, the Sisters could open the two proposed colleges, depending on the faculties of the universities to supplement their own teaching staffs. With this thought Mother Cecilia wrote to a Sister friend, evidently a superior, on April 23, 1911:

> We have affiliated with Marquette and DePaul universities and are to open a woman's college in connection with each a year from next September. We are sending six Sisters, three for each college, to Trinity College, Washington, for one year to prepare for this college work; the degrees are to be conferred by both universities. Now what think you! We should have made this move toward higher education long ago, but let you all pray, we may catch up - for God's greater glory and the good of souls. . . . You may tell the Sisters all this and let them pray fervently. . . .
>
> Your own anxious old
> Sr. M. Cecilia

Fortunately word had come meantime that Dr. Thomas Shields, head of Catholic University's education department, planned to conduct a normal institute in Washington, D. C. , beginning July 1, 1911. The Sisters promptly engaged a house conveniently located to the campus and belonging to Dr. Henry Hyvernat, founder of the Institute for Christian Oriental Research and long-time professor at the University. With this entrée, Mother Cecilia addressed herself on May 20, 1911 to the rector of the University, the Right Reverend Monsignor T. J. Shahan. [21] However, she made no mention of so ambitious a project as the simultaneous opening of two colleges.

> Our Congregation, the Sisters of Charity, B. V. M. , has been called upon to open a woman's college in Milwaukee, and we are necessitated to prepare six of our Sisters for the work. We have agreed to open the college in October, 1912, and the teachers should have degrees by that time.
>
> Several of the Sisters, intended for teachers in the new college, have carried college work in some branches and hold credits for same. Others have covered the ground work, along certain lines, but have no credits for the work; these latter are willing to take the University examinations in order to receive the necessary credit.
>
> To afford the Sisters a home during the required year's residence, we have secured Dr. Hyvernat's house in Washington. The Sisters will attend the Normal Institute,

beginning July 1st, and could do work in the elected courses during the interval before the opening of the fall session of the University. The Sisters will require instruction in the Languages, Science, Mathematics, Philosophy, Religion, History, Sociology and Education. They are prepared to do heavy work.

We are confident that you are in sympathy with the higher education of Catholic women and feel certain that you will be interested in the exigencies of the present case. Besides the State University of Wisconsin, at Madison, which draws its quota from our Catholic population of the Middle West, we must compete with a long established sectarian college, the Milwaukee-Downer in Milwaukee, which has a large enrollment of Catholic young women.

Friends of Catholic education, whose opinion in the matter has weight, have advised us to seek the necessary instruction at the Catholic University, as it represents the highest standard of Catholic education. Then, too, degrees from the University will give the prestige necessary for the successful establishment of the college in Milwaukee.

We appeal to you, Rt. Rev. Monsignor, and we feel confident that you will aid us in this movement toward furthering the higher education of Catholic women. May we ask the favor of an early answer. . . .

The response having been favorable, the six chosen Sisters set forth June 29 at the close of a June meeting of the National Catholic Educational Association for Washington. They were: Sisters M. Crescentia Markey, Antonia Durkin, Columba Donnelly, Regina Lynch, Justitia Coffey and Evangela Henthorne Having hired a cook they were "prepared to do heavy work. " As Mother Cecilia had predicted, four of the six received B. A. degrees by the close of the summer session in 1912 - Sisters M. Columba, Antonia, Regina and Crescentia. Sisters M. Urban Bermingham and Justitia Coffey received bachelor degrees in 1913, and Sister M. Lamberta Fitzgerald in 1914. Sister M. Urban continued her studies in 1914-1915 doing graduate work. Sister M. Josephina Malone, whose prior studies had been made at Mt. St. Joseph which by that time was a four-year college, and Sister M. Antonia,were granted master's degrees the next year, and in 1914 Sisters M. Crescentia, Regina and Basiline Bates received their master's. [22]

The education of these first Sisters was not without a price to them, however. Not even during the weeks of the summer were the Sisters admitted to the then deserted University campus

A temporary arrangement with the Benedictine Convent served for the normal institute as a first step in the direction of Dr. Shields' proposed Sisters' College. Besides B. V. M. 's for the institute[23] there were "five Sisters from St. Mary of the Woods, one Sister of Humility, a Sister of Mercy from St. Xavier in Chicago, two Dominican Sisters, two from the Incarnate Word of Texas, and several Benedictine Sisters from the school whose classrooms we used, and those Sisters of Providence who kept house for Divinity Hall. "[24]

Besides the normal institute sessions, the six B. V. M. Sisters were taking all the tutorial courses they could crowd in. "Five days a week courses were conducted in the Benedictine classrooms (hour periods) at 8, 12, 3, 4, and 5 o'clock. Besides that, second year Greek and Latin Philology (small groups) were taught in a music room each day at nine. "[25] Then there were French lessons available in the evenings.

The summer session over, the Sisters remained on through the school year and until the end of July of 1912, during which time they were tutored by Dr. Shields and Dr. Edward Pace[26] of the University. Checks covering their services are included in the many remittances to cover the needs of the Sisters, all of which totaled approximately $3, 885. 00, certainly much less than the cost the council had estimated of $6, 000. 00. Among these many items was one for $40. 00 charged by the pastor of the nearby church as pew rent during the Sisters' stay in Washington.

But the best laid plans often go awry. Dubuque's new archbishop did not hesitate to remind Mother Cecilia that Mt. St. Joseph, Dubuque, had need of all the degrees it could get. Both engagements were thus necessarily broken.

Disappointed in his plans for the B. V. M. Sisters, the Reverend F. X. McCabe, C. M. , turned to the Dominican Sisters of Sinsinawa[27] in the hope that they might attempt a woman's college in affiliation with the University. DePaul was a young and ambitious institution at that time, having been chartered as a university only in 1907. After much weighing of the matter, the Sisters were prepared to accept the offer. However, by that time the Vincentian superiors decided that the move was untimely. Efforts to enlist individual B. V. M. 's for the University faculty also failed. However, hope died hard with Father McCabe, and we find resonances of plans for a Jeanne d'Arc College for Women as late as 1917. Sister M. Lambertina Doran, who was then in charge of the DePaul High School for Girls, he planned to make dean of the proposed college. In order that she might be properly endowed for the position, he presented her with a doctoral degree in that year. [28]

Catholic women, teachers in the public schools, were anxious
to advance themselves through furthering their Catholic education. A group of them waited on Archbishop Quigley in early 1911
to lay their case before him. He in turn appealed to DePaul University, and plans were quickly under way to offer a full program
of summer courses. With a tuition charge of $15.00 for the sum-
mer, classes in a broad range of subjects were held for four
hours each day - 9:00-11:00 and 11:30-1:30. The success of the
summer session led to the opening of extension courses throughout the school year, in three late afternoon sessions a week. [29]
It was strenuous living for the Sisters and teachers who, after
a full day in the classroom, journeyed by public transportation
to Fullerton and Sheffield for two-hour evening classes. Yet
early catalogs indicate that sixty B.V.M.'s attended classes
at DePaul between 1911-1916.

Sister M. Lambertina Doran, as secretary general, 1906-
1912, compiled the Congregation's first official history, In the
Early Days, published in 1911 by Herder and Herder, St. Louis.
It is undocumented and shows little evidence of original research.
Years after the book's publication, many of Mother Clarke's
letters were found in Sister's office stowed away in shoe boxes
with miscellaneous materials and still enclosed in their envelopes.
As Sister admits, she borrowed much from the earlier anecdotal
Annals.

A peculiarity of the book in the light of more recent studies
is the marked preeminence given to the Reverend T. J. Donaghoe
as founder and superior-general of the Sisters of Charity. This
would seem particularly to reflect the mind of Mother Gertrude
Regan, which is not too surprising for she had received pref-
erential treatment from him from her earliest years as a
member. The force of her influence is shown in that her wish
prevailed in this regard, despite the much greater attraction
Mother Clarke had for Mother Cecilia who was superior-general
at the time the book was written. A certain pragmatism may
had led others to accede to Mother Gertrude in this. As a
congregation of educators, some doubtless felt its reputation
would be compromised by an acknowledgment of a simple woman
without more than a modicum of formal education as its founder.
The Paris-educated vicar general of a diocese, lifelong friend
of perhaps the most widely known prelate of his day, would certainly add more prestige in that role. His long years in the

dominant position and his own public claim to the honor certainly lent weight to their choice of Father Donaghoe as founder.

Sister M. Louise Clarke, who knew Mother Gertrude intimately in her later years and who held her in high regard, nevertheless declared her responsible for the slight consideration given Mother Clarke in the Early Days. She wrote:

> It is really Mother Gertrude who is responsible for our knowing so little about the hardships of those early days. Because Mother Clarke would never demand "our rights, " saying, "God knows, " Mother Gertrude crossed out all reference to the trials of Mother Clarke in our annals. The notes rejected seem to have been lost and we are without most of the details about Mother Clarke's crosses and ecstasies. [30]

The recent discovery of the plaque with which the Sisters marked Mother Clarke's grave at the time of her burial leaves no doubt that those who had shared her lot and knew her best had no doubt that she was their well-loved foundress. And it is for the rediscovery and renewal of her spirit and the charism which they share that the Sisters strive today.

Notes

1 Details of the San Francisco earthquake were furnished
to Sister M. Doris Marie Walsh by Sister M. Robertine Welch,
now deceased. They are a part of the copious notes furnished
the writer by Sister Doris.

2 Many of the details in the account of both the elementary
and the high school were taken from Jean Fahey Eberle's
"Xavier High, " a booklet issued at the time of the school's
closing.

3 Keane, Diary.

4 See Appendix L

5 Falconio was named a cardinal in 1911. Meantime he had
the rank of bishop.

6 The building occupied by the St. Agatha Academy was
promptly sold to the University for student lodging. That at
Holden remained idle until it was finally given in trade for Florida
land. St. Francis was sold to the parish for parochial school purposes. The asking price was $30,000.00, but when the pastor
pled inability to meet that figure, the Congregation remitted
$10,000.00 and settled for the balance. The boys at St. Patrick's
had for some years been taught as an out-school from St.
Agatha's.

7 Falconio's first application made to Propaganda Fide had
received the following bit of circumlocution: ". . . not wishing
with their authority to approve that religious women should
devote themselves to the instruction of pupils of the masculine
sex. . . /Propaganda/ abstained prudently from imposing formal
prohibition, leaving to some Ordinary the responsibility of what
would happen in the course of doing it. . . . In its Decree of Approval it would set a practice of which it did not approve. "
Falconio had obtained the concession of teaching boys not over
fourteen by citing the case of a recently approved constitution
permitting a community of Franciscan Sisters in Philadelphia to
teach boys of that age.

8 After many years as a successful boys' school, Dowling
High School in DesMoines opened at a new site in West DesMoine
in 1972. Here it operates in connection with the St. Joseph Acad

which served the girls of DesMoines for eighty-seven years.

9 <u>Our Herald,</u> April 1917, Vol. V, No. 2, p. 105.

10 The Dubuque Province remained intact until November 15, 1941, when the diocese of Cheyenne became suffragan to the new Archdiocese of Denver. Omaha did not become an archdiocese until 1945.

11 The new Archbishop was gracious to his predecessor, insisting that he maintain his suite in the cathedral rectory. This, however, John Keane declined, though he continued to make his home in a less auspicious part of the dwelling. At the time of his first diocesan synod the clergy presented James Keane with the deed to the former Stout residence, a spacious sandstone structure which had been furnished throughout by an unnamed benefactor. When the retired Archbishop bestowed the pallium on his successor on January 21, 1911, Archbishop Ireland spoke. The occasion was otherwise without show or pomp though many bishops attended.

12 The above details have been drawn almost entirely from <u>A Sketch of the Most Reverend James John Keane, Third Arch-</u><u>bishop of Dubuque, 1856-1929.</u> Master's dissertation of Sister M. Rosinda O'Neill, B. V. M. , submitted to the Catholic University of America in 1947.

13 Sister M. Aurelia LaBelle, now a patient in the Marian Hall infirmary, recounted the incident on seeing the recovered plaque. Her novice-Sister was Sister M. Innocent. As children they had attended St. Francis Academy, Council Bluffs.

14 The Reverend Henry Dumbach, S. J. , initiated the establishment of Loyola University. He was responsible for the purchase of the North Shore Campus. One of the early buildings bears his name.

15 This was quite an unheard of directive, for the Rule required that the Sisters be provided for in all respects by the Congregation after they had taken vows. Mother Gertrude would not have hesitated to take out a loan for such needs.

16 The St. Vincent household included besides the superior, Sisters M. Alma Sheedy, Rosina Harrigan, Agnella Broderick, Immaculate Reidy and Seratina Mulick.

354

17 Besides the superior, the staff of Immaculate Conception School included Sisters M. St. Joseph Crennan, Agnita Smith, Aquinas Callaghan and St. Mel McCarthy. Those at St. Joseph's were Sisters M. Adolpha Durkin, Ricardus Herlehey, Basil Healy, Richard Bordeaux and Martina Britt.

18 All the above data are derived from a xeroxed copy of extracts from The Story of Marquette University by Raphael N. Hamilton, S. J. (Milwaukee: Marquette University Press, 1953), furnished the writer by the Reverend Robert Callen, S. J. , university archivist.

19 The fact that the B. V. M. Sisters were teaching in three Milwaukee schools and that twenty-three B. V. M. 's had received degrees from Marquette by 1918 would seem to indicate that they had taken advantage of the earliest classes available to them at Marquette.

20 While a matter of this proportion might well have called for a deliberative vote of the council, Mother Cecilia seems not to have understood the difference between a deliberative and a consultative vote. This could well have left her subject to the vote of her council at times when the final decision was within her power.

21 It is believed that Mother Cecilia was greatly encouraged in this action by Sister M. Antonia Durkin, then on the faculty of Mt. St. Joseph College. Sister had taken correspondence courses from the University in 1908 and 1909 and thought it high time the University take a forward step in providing educational opportunities for women.

22 Data furnished by Rosabelle Kelp, archivist, Catholic University of America.

23 It is not clear whether these stayed on for further study.

24 Notes of Sister M. Evangela Henthorne.

25 Our Herald, Vol. IV, No. 1, January 1916, p. 69. (Henthorne notes).

26 Monsignor Edward A. Pace was founder and first director of the Institute of Pedagogy at Catholic University. This later developed into the Department of Education. He established the

psychological laboratory there, the second in the country. He was editor of the Catholic Encyclopedia, 1907-1914, first president of the American Philosophical Association, and in the years 1925-1936 he served as the vice-rector of the University.

27 McCarty, Sinsinawa Dominicans, pp. 181-183.

28 Data provided by the Reverend Patrick J. Mullins, C. M. , archivist of DePaul University, among which were the early university catalogs. Sister M. Lambertina had received a B. A. at the University in 1913, and there is some indication that she was granted a master's degree by the University of Wisconsin with her study In the Early Days offered to the department of English as her dissertation.

29 Ibid.

30 See Mother Gertrude's biographical file in the archives.

Chapter Eleven

A TIME OF CHANGE AND CHALLENGE

The election of January 1912 showed for the first time the weakness of the Congregation's method of choosing its highest officer. The majority vote required for the office of superior general would become increasingly difficult to obtain as numbers grew and its missions became more widely scattered. It was only a plurality vote which singled out Sister Mary Ascension Lilly for that office. The word of that vote reached her in the midst of humble household chores in the new infirmary. Confirmation of the election would have to come from Rome. Meanwhile Mother Cecilia and her consultors, as well as their appointees, would remain in office until the confirmation came. It reached Dubuque on March 26 in a letter from the Apostolic Delegate. Mother Ascension was then installed by the new Archbishop, together with her four consultors, Mother Cecilia and Sisters M. Loyola, Octavia and Lambertina. Sister M. Basil Healy had been chosen as assistant to the Mother, while Sisters M. Angela Fitzgerald, Octavia Burke, Lambertina Doran and DeChantal O'Regan retained their respective offices of novice mistress, visitor, secretary and procurator.

Mother Mary Ascension Lilly entered the Congregation from her home in Burlington, Iowa on December 13, 1867, at the age of twenty-two. Louise Lilly, the older of two daughters of Thoma Lilly and his wife Mary Cecilia Wetzler, was born in Lancaster, Ohio in 1845. Her father was a descendant of colonists who came from England to Maryland with Lord Baltimore. Her mother, a convert to the faith, was among the early Dutch settlers of Pennsylvania. On the early death of the father, the little family moved to Burlington, Iowa in 1852 where Mrs. Lilly's mother, brothers and sisters had settled. Here Mrs. Lilly was responsible for their conversions.

Louise attended St. Paul School, taught then by laymen, wher

an uncle was among the teachers. When in 1857 five B. V. M.
Sisters came to Burlington to take charge of the school, she
felt quite at home with them, particularly with Sister M.
Antonia O'Brien, her music teacher. At the time of her
entrance the young woman's courage failed her as she stood
on the station platform at a change of trains enroute to
Dubuque. In a wave of loneliness she decided that if the train
for Burlington came next she would take it back to her home.
Fortunately, it was headed to Dubuque.

Sister's first mission as a religious was in Elkader, Iowa
where, as a novice, she went with her superior, Sister M.
Clotilde Walsh, and two other novices, Sisters M. Loyola
Rutherford and Benedict McLaughlin. Here, after their day's
work in the classroom, the four often sewed well into the night
making veils and dresses for the girls in the First Communion
class and doing such other needlework as they received orders
for.

Sister's next assignment was to the free school in Iowa City
which the Sisters taught gratis in fulfillment of a pledge to
Father Emmonds. Here Sister was faced with nearly a hundred
boys and girls of varied grades and ages. Two years later she
was assigned to the eighth grade boys at Annunciation School,
Chicago, an assignment which she shared with Sister M. Loyola
with whom she had formed a fast friendship in their strenuous
years at Elkader.

In 1883 Sister was assigned as superior at the new St. Vincent
School in Chicago. From there she went in 1890 with the first
group of Sisters to St. Theresa's, the Cathedral school in downtown Lincoln, Nebraska. Lincoln was mission territory at that
time under its first bishop - Thomas Bonacum. Many of the
parents as lapsed Catholics were quite uninterested in a Catholic
school for their children. Sister, in company with her superior,
Sister M. Constantia O'Leary or the ample Columba Heffernan,
trudged the muddy streets or crossed fields rough with corn
stubble, wherever children were likely to be found. The situation improved quickly. In 1895 St. Theresa's enrollment listed
142 boys and 98 girls. Sister M. Ascension maintained a firm
but considerate discipline over her classroom of seventh and
eighth grade boys and they formed a deep regard for her.

In cooperation with the priests, Sister was able to have a
number of irregular marriages validated, and so to bring the
couples back to the sacraments. When Bishop Bonacum initiated
a drive for the starving people of Nebraska and the Dakotas in
a year in which their crops failed, Sister and her pupils pack-
aged a large number of relief items. Sister urged the opening

of a mission as a means of renewing the faith of the people. "In her own way, " a former student remarked, "Sister Mary Ascension really brought Catholicity to Lincoln. "

Gradually high school subjects were added to the curriculum and vocations began to appear. Among the girls to enter the Congregation were four: Sisters M. Generosa Barton, Hermana McGinley, Leon Weckbach and Rosalita McLaughlin. In the course of her teaching, Sister had the privilege of encouraging twenty young men in their vocations to the priesthood.

In 1899 Sister was transferred to Gesu School, Milwaukee, returning to Lincoln in 1902 as superior. Here she was able to achieve excellence in studies and curricular activities, so that Cathedral School in Lincoln was outstanding in the state for its level of scholarship and accomplishment. There was no program of sports - chores and long hikes to school consumed any excess energy. The one big event of the year was the picnic on Sister Mary Ascension's feast day. A hayrack ride to the park for a day of games and a bountiful lunch made a joyful occasion for the Sisters as well as the children.

When the six years of her superiorship were up Sister Mary Ascension returned to Mt. Carmel as administrator of the new infirmary. Four years later she became the fourth Sister to serve the Congregation as its mother-general. [1] The problems that faced her were many but she had served a strenuous apprenticeship.

One of these problems was, as usual, financial. In addition to the grave needs which had persisted through the years, there was a new challenge to meet as Catholic universities opened their doors to women. The desire for excellence in their teaching, as well as the rising demands for certification and degrees, pressed not only on the beginning teacher but on all those engaged in the business of educating the young.

Income from the fifty-nine parochial schools was falling far short not only of the Congregation's needs but of the salaries contracted for. In the year just prior to Mother Ascension's election, twenty-four of these fifty-nine missions failed to pay the full $200. 00 per year salary for each teacher. The total receipts from those missions for that year equaled $28, 604. 89, an average income of just $125. 43 for each of the 228 classroom teachers, leaving a total deficit of $16, 995. 11. The presence of an uncompensated housekeeper and at least one music teacher[2] on each of these missions, both essential to the operation of the mission, reduced the average income to $103. 63 a year for each Sister.

On a broader scale a random sampling of fourteen schools

for three-year periods between 1896 and 1922, which compared household expenses of the Sisters living in great frugality with the income they received from the schools for their services, revealed a deficit in each instance save one, with a total deficit of $35,355.43. In that one instance the pastor had claimed the full earnings of the music teachers in his school, using as much of these as were needed to pay the ten members of the teaching staff their total three-year salary of $6,000.00. The Sisters' household expenses for those three years left a balance of $262.41, their sole possible contribution to the needs of the motherhouse.

It is small wonder that Mother Ascension wrote promptly to the superiors that she could meet only one-third of the mother-house expenses with the remittances from the missions.

We may well ask: how did the individual missions meet their deficit? and how did the motherhouse maintain itself if the body of teaching Sisters could contribute so little to its support? On the local mission the earnings of the music teacher, supplemented by the commission on books and school supplies and an end of the year entertainment – where the pastor permitted the Sisters to retain these – and such personal gifts as the Sisters received, chiefly from their own families, made up for the differential between school income and their household expenses.

As for the motherhouse, music income from the missions provided the greater part of the one-third of which Mother Ascension spoke. The other two-thirds of motherhouse costs were met by the dowries, large or small or entirely lacking, which the novices were able to bring, and which the Sisters later learned canon law required be invested. Then there were the returns from the motherhouse farm, and lastly, the sale of lands and the use of inheritances which came to the Sisters from their families, a consuming of community assets in day to day living.

But it was not only a matter of finances. Inadequate schools and convents, often in disrepair, without janitor service, badly lighted and poorly heated, added unnecessary burdens.

It was in the face of all this that in 1912 the council drew up a new contract to be presented to the pastors. It required that they

furnish and keep in repair buildings suitable for a parochial school, furnish janitor, fuel, light and water for said buildings; also to provide a furnished residence for the Sisters; to pay to the Directress /principal/ and each teacher of the primary and grammar departments a salary of $25.00 per month, and each teacher in the high school and in the commercial department a salary of $35.00 a month. As a means of support for the Sisters during vacation the proceeds of one entertainment prepared by the Sisters will be given them, or, if the pastor prefers, let twenty-five dollars per month for the two vacation months be paid to each teacher. . . . All revenue for music teaching will be retained by the Sisters as this is needed for the motherhouse with its infirmary and novitiate.

Sisters from the motherhouse were assigned to visit each pastor to introduce the contract. They were to make it clear that the practice of giving the music revenue to the pastor, where it existed, was to be discontinued. This condition brought a sharp reaction from the pastors who had been claiming the revenue - those of St. Lawrence, of Holy Cross, and of Holy Name. Monsignor Fitzsimmons of Holy Name who had been receiving $1,350 of the music money a year for the previous eight years threatened to get another order to teach his school. The Sisters must continue that payment or go.

Father Maloney of St. Lawrence Parish visited the mother-house on December 21, 1912 determined to retain all the music revenue. He presented a substitute contract which concluded with the sentence, "If this contract be rejected, kindly remove Sisters before December 28th." The Sisters' council met immediately and voted to stand by their own contract, and Father Maloney was so notified. He had stated in the course of his visit to Mt. Carmel that an order of Dominican Sisters from New York were willing to teach for him, give him the music revenue, and take care of altar and sacristy for $25.00 a month each. The letter addressed by the council on December 22 having informed him of their stand, the Sisters gave him several days to reconsider his stand while they quietly set school and convent in order. Then, packing their trunks, on December 28 they departed in silence, leaving Father Maloney to face an astounded and highly incensed congregation.

Three local superiors from Chicago houses, Sisters M. Lamberta, Petronia and Leo, visited Mt. Carmel on January 6 to report the extreme displeasure of the Chicago pastors. As a result it was first decided to withdraw the contract, but before doing so Sisters would be sent to Archbishops Quigley and Keane and Bishop Garrigan, hoping to be guided by their reactions. Sisters M. Lamberta and Leandre called upon Archbishop Quigle His advice was against a withdrawal of the contract. "It would not do, " he said, "to lay down your arms when the battle is half won. " He advised the Congregation before taking any school ther

after to secure a signed contract providing for all the Sisters'
needs. It was his practice, he said, when he gave a parish to
a priest to oblige the priest to sign a contract providing a salary
for school teachers. He discussed with the Sisters the contracts
of other teaching orders, and urged them to "keep hammering"
until they got what they justly deserved.

Bishop Garrigan indicated that the contract would bear heavily
on the poorer parishes, and hoped that for them it might be
modified. Archbishop Keane was content to let the contract
stand.

Father Hischen of Holy Cross evidently decided that discretion
was the better part of valor, for he subsided in silence. Monsignor Fitzsimmons did not yield so easily. While he conceded the
music money, the substitute contract he presented contained qualifications regarding provision for the summer, which the Sisters
agreed for the sake of peace to give a year's trial. [3]

The resistance of pastors gradually died down, and the Sisters
retained the music revenue, but the payment of stipulated salaries
continued to lag. [4]

On November 21, shortly before the balloting for the 1912
election, Archbishop James J. Keane followed a profession ceremony with a meeting involving Mother Cecilia and her consultors.
Topics he discussed with the Sisters included:

1. a necessary revision of their Rule.

2. his wish that the Sisters teach boys in the Archdiocese
   as long as they stay in school. While the Sisters should
   discourage coeducation, they must accept it wherever it
   could not be avoided.

3. that the Sisters should not consider the opening of more
   colleges for many years to come.

4. that the Congregation was too "Jesuitical, " and that the
   Sisters must get his permission before writing priests
   to give their retreats. [5]

A formal but undated communication from the Archbishop
is a clear mandate for the erection of provinces. It ends with
the admonition: "That all this may be wisely and satisfactorily
done, it would be well to represent the matter to your Congregation by a circular letter, and request the cooperation of
all the Sisters and an expression of their opinion. "

As early as 1897 Mother Cecilia had sought the advice of the

Jesuit Father, Michael J. O'Connor of Xavier College, Cincinnati in the matter of perpetual vows, and had received a careful analysis of their advantages and their nature. In 1907 she had raised with the Apostolic Delegate the question of division into provinces. Falconio had responded that the time was not yet ripe, and that no such step should be attempted without a canvas of the Congregation to determine the wishes of the Sisters. The difficulty involved in Mother Ascension's election convinced the Sisters that the time for action was at hand. Consultations with canonists and a careful study of the canon law treatises with which Falconio had provided Mother Cecilia prepared the Sisters in government for their roles under the new organizational pattern. To obtain the views of the Sisters on the missions, a list of points for discussion was mailed to each house.

Falconio was by that time a cardinal and head of the Congregation of Religious in Rome. Mother Cecilia continued the correspondence with him in the matter of provinces. His letter to her of May 2, 1912 provided instruction in procedures to be followed in order to obtain the necessary amendments to their Constitutions.

In a circular letter to the Sisters she assured them that Archbishop Keane was in full accord with the plan. It could not result in a cleavage, such as some of the Sisters feared. There would continue to be but one mother-general, one motherhouse and one novitiate. In a growing Congregation of 1,105 living members it was impossible for one person to know and meet the needs of so many. To obtain the reacion of the Sisters Mother Cecilia requested that by April 24 each house send to the motherhouse two papers, one listing the signatures of those who favored the necessary amendments to the Constitutions, and the other containing the sentiments of those not in favor of the changes involved. [6]

Mother Ascension followed this letter with one of her own adding her assurances. For the Sisters' comfort she quoted from a letter received from the Consultor of the Sacred Congregation of Religious:

> According as an Institute develops by the grace of God and extends its field of action more and more widely, it comes to pass that the bond which attaches it to a common center tends to become enfeebled. The houses being more left to themselves, relaxation can find its way in before one can apply salutary remedies. The S. Congr. proposes the creation of provinces as a means of providing better and more efficaciously for the necessities of administration.

Mother further reminded the Sisters that the question had
come up even in Mother Clarke's day as an issue that would have
to be met when the development of the Congregation called for it.
She then carefully explained the relations of a Sister-provincial
to the general government and to the Sisters. She outlined the
nature and functions of a general chapter which thenceforth would
elect the Mother and her council members. It would also discuss
and determine necessary action in the graver affairs of the Congregation. She listed the officers who would be ex officio members
of the chapter, and explained the method by which each of the
four proposed provinces would elect its two delegates to the
chapter.

On May 8 Mother Ascension reported that the returns from
the Sisters showed a unanimity favoring the changes in the Constitutions which provincial government would necessitate. [7] Only
thirty-three Sisters opposed the plan. Twenty-seven others
specified conditions under which they would favor it.

The next step was an assembly of superiors at the motherhouse in August 1913 to consider the suggestions given. Meantime, on July 13 Mother informed the Sisters that

> through the interposition of our Cardinal Protector, the
> great privilege of making Perpetual Vows will be granted to
> us. Not one of us, I am sure, ever made her holy vows with
> any other intention than that of being faithful to them until
> death. Still I wish to consult each Sister in regard to the
> favor in prospect.

Only those Sisters who had lived under vows for at least six
years were eligible for perpetual vows. No Sister was obliged
to make such a commitment, and for those who preferred to
continue as they had, renewing their engagement triennially,
their status in the Congregation would in no way be compromised.
They would be eligible for any office and would continue to have
the same voting rights as those who had chosen to avail themselves of the privilege of perpetual vows. These latter would
express their decision by adding their signature to the simple
formula: "I shall thank God for the privilege of binding myself
to His holy service by Perpetual Vows. "

The meeting held at the motherhouse August 17-26, 1913,
and referred to as a "general chapter, " involved governing officials, the superiors of all the local houses, and a number of
invited members, a total of 118 assembling. A secret ballot
favored the adoption of provincial government by a vote of 111
to 7. On a second ballot taken later in the day, only five Sisters

opposed the change. The assembly voted also that the new Constitutions would solve the "boy problem" by indicating the apostolate of the Sisters as "the work of Catholic education. "

Preparation of the materials for Rome took time, and more time was required before the modified Constitutions were returned and the new pattern of government instituted. All this involved two years of waiting.

Mother Ascension was now faced with the difficult task of assigning houses to the four future provincial superiors. The traditional pattern for provinces adhered to by the Church was territorial. The preponderance of Sisters in Chicago presented a difficulty. If all there were assigned to the direction of one provincial, that province might easily become a power unto itself. For the B. V. M. 's a territorial division would prove disastrous.

Mother Ascension pondered the problem for many weeks. The solution finally came as she knelt praying in the chapel. She emerged radiant, exclaiming to her consultors: "Chicago is a pie. We'll cut it! " Each province would include a number of the Chicago houses and the provincials would work together to preserve uniformity in their administration.

The cutting, in later years, involved the west coast too, an arrangement equally essential there for the west would have its own distinctive features. As a single province so far removed from the central government, it might in time go its own way. The plan proved also to have unforeseen merits, for it gave each Sister the possibility of serving in a wide range of geographical situations, thus broadening her experience and bringing a fresh outlook to each situation. In time then each province included a span of houses from Chicago to the far west. The assigning of new missions to the respective provinces, for convenience in travel, tended to follow the main railroad lines west. A Sister's need for a change of climate or health services could thus be met even within the province, while it lay always within the power of the superior-general to transfer a Sister from one province to another when family needs or other considerations made it feasible.

It was a plan, however, which called for careful explanation when it was presented to the Sacred Congregation of Religious. Thanks to the understanding of its Cardinal Prefect, Diomede Falconio, it was made acceptable to the other cardinals, and there was little delay in its adoption.

At last, on May 8, 1914, word came that permission was formally given "through the Most Reverend Ordinary of Dubuque for the erection of four provinces, those of the Sacred Heart, the Immaculate Conception, Holy Family and St. Joseph. The decree bore the signature: "Donatus, Archbishop of Ephesus, Sec. " A communication from Cardinal Falconio requested that the Sisters send a description "of your holy Abit. " This was partially complied with by a mailing of the photograph of Sister M. Agatha in outdoor dress, and a picture purporting to be that of Sister M. Catherine Byrne wearing indoor attire. [8]

Then in September Mother Ascension shared with the Sisters the letter from Cardinal Falconio in which he enclosed the long desired decree permitting the taking of perpetual vows. In the same mail he sent the revised Constitutions which were to be given a seven-year trial before final approbation.

All was now in readiness[9] for implementation. On December 31, 1914, following a triduum of prayer and instruction conducted by Father Conroy, S. J. , Mother Ascension made her perpetual commitment at a 5:45 Mass in the infirmary chapel, then received the vows of the other Sisters there. At 6:30 in the motherhouse chapel, she received the vows of seventy-five Sisters assembled for Mass. [10] Sisters on the missions followed a similar pattern.

On March 15, 1915, Mother Ascension and her consultors named the four Sisters[11] who would fill the office of provincial until the Congregation's first General Chapter in July. An equitable number of the seventy-four houses was assigned to each provincial, and the new system of government became effective on March 25, 1915. After their appointment, the four Sisters met together and with the Archbishop to consider the nature of their duties and to plan for the desirable uniformity in their manner of government. The alignment was as follows:

Sister M. Isabella Kane, Sacred Heart Province. Residence, St. Mary High School, Chicago. Missions: St. Mary's, Sacred Heart, St. Pius, St. Charles, Chicago; Mt. St. Joseph College, St. Joseph Academy, St. Raphael's, Dubuque; Cathedral and St. Joseph's, Sioux City; Corpus Christi and Sacred Heart, Fort Dodge; St. Mary's and St. Ellen's , Emmetsburg; Marcus, Ackley, Waterloo and Boone, Iowa.

Sister M. Edmunda Burke, Immaculate Conception Province. Residence, Immaculate Conception Academy, Davenport. Missions: Immaculate Conception Academy and Sacred Heart, Davenport; Our Lady of Angels and St. Irenaeus, Lyons; St. Patrick's and St. Mary's, Iowa City; Cedar Rapids, Cedar Falls, Garryowen, Cascade, Clinton, Muscatine, Iowa; Rock Island, Illinois; and Holy Cross, Queen of Heaven, Blessed Sacrament, St. Agatha's and Holy Name, Chicago.

Sister M. Adora Caverly, Holy Family Province. Residence, Mt. Carmel Academy, Wichita. Missions: Mt. Carmel Academy,

Wichita; St. Aloysius and St. Vincent's, Kansas City; Holy
Rosary, Holy Angels and Gesu, Milwaukee; Lincoln, Pontiac
and DeKalb in Illinois; St. Louis; Burlington, Washington and
Riverside in Iowa; and Our Lady Help of Christians, Our Lady
of Lourdes, Presentation, Annunciation and St. Vincent's in
Chicago.

Sister M. Benedicta Prendergast, St. Joseph Province.
Residence, St. Joseph Academy, DesMoines. Missions: St.
Joseph Academy, St. Ambrose, St. John's and Visitation, Des
Moines; Immaculate Conception and St. Joseph's, Butte, Montana;
Mt. St. Gertrude and Sacred Heart, Boulder; San Francisco and
Petaluma, California; Lincoln and Omaha, Nebraska; Council
Bluffs and Cresco, Iowa; St. Bridget's, St. Dominic's, St.
Gertrude's, Our Lady of Angels and Holy Family, Chicago.

The first official General Chapter of the Congregation opened
at Mt. Carmel on July 16, 1915, with twenty-nine members
present. After the Mass of the Holy Spirit, the first business
was the receiving of the delegates' credentials. Then followed
the election of the superior-general in the presence of the Archbishop. As its result, the aging Mother Cecilia was returned to
office. Members chosen for her canonical council were in order:
Mother Ascension and Sisters M. Bertrand Foley, Editha
Flanagan and Esther Warren. Sister M. Crescentia Markey was
again named secretary and Sister M. Urban Bermingham, treasurer. Their installation was followed by the Chapter of Affairs.

Mother Ascension named a financial committee and committee
for proposals, for education and for discipline. The financial
report was checked and approved, and the other committees
proceeded to their duties, the last two receiving the proposals
allotted to them. Nothing of great significance was involved in
this first chapter, save the confirmation in office of the four
provincials who were already engaged in their separate functions.
However, a beginning had been made and a pattern set, simple
as it was, for all future chapters.

Minor adjustments were involved in meeting the conditions of
the new Rule. It required a separation of the postulants and
novices. When September 8 brought forty lively young women
into the postulate, Mother Cecilia was given charge of the group
which would always thereafter be labelled "the Forty." For the
first time, the canonical dowry - $40.00 - was invested as a
small but secure cushion against possible eventualities. [12]
Chapter sessions were scheduled to begin on July 16, and terms
of office were likewise governed by that date. And, as a practica
rather than a canonical measure, the stiffly starched bonnets the
postulants had been wearing for chapel and parlor were replaced

for chapel wear with net veils. The ironing of forty bonnets with flat irons heated on wood stoves, each bonnet requiring a full hour, was too daunting a task to be undertaken. The few calls there would be to the parlor could well be provided for by a small "pool" of bonnets for ready use. Even these had been laid aside by 1920.

Like Mother Cecilia, Mother Ascension was an able and far-sighted school woman. The first summer's assignments she [13] handled by the simple directive: "The Sisters who attended the University /DePaul or Marquette/ may go again this summer also. Other high school teachers may attend the University or an institute held at St. Mary's High School, as the superiors will decide. " To meet the needs of the elementary school teachers, she set to work at once planning for a summer institute to be held June 24 to July 6 in Chicago. Similar institutes would be held with the boarding schools as centers. She committed the organizational details to Sisters M. Leandre Swift, Edmunda Burke and Rosina Harrigan The general plan followed much the same pattern as that which served under Mother Cecilia. The full program was to be carried out in each of four areas of the city, each of the sixteen convents involved to handle the subject matter for two grades. The Sisters were asked to reside in the center at which they were attending classes. Each session was planned to begin at 8 o'clock and close at 11:45, Monday through Saturday. All instructors were to be B.V.M.'s, except for the subject of English. All seventh and eighth grade teachers were required to attend a class taught every second day by an English specialist engaged for the session. The circular letter outlining plans stated that

> The main object of the Institute is to call forth devices and methods which the Sisters have found by long years of experience to be productive of the best results. Too much emphasis cannot be placed on the fact that reading must be taught correctly in the first, second and third grades. The child who does not learn to read in those grades will never become a reader. The principle is equally true in number work; speed, accuracy and efficiency in the four fundamental rules must be acquired before taking up the more complex.

Superiors met in the spring to select the Sisters who were deemed most capable of carrying on specific lines of work. These were notified in ample time for preparation. Subject matter covered the entire curriculum at each grade level, with special emphasis given to nature study, the use of the dictionary, letter writing, cleanliness, moral training and etiquette. The problems of absence, tardiness[14] and "general delinquencies" were to be considered. It was indeed a full program.

Saturday classes were resumed in 1913 and 1914, meetings to be held at St. Pius School two Saturdays out of three. The work that first year included sight-singing, drawing, primary methods and principles of education, all directed toward primary teachers. Special arrangements in the course of the year assisted third and fourth grade teachers with "Primary Work and Principles of Education. " Thus every effort was made to help teachers lay a firm foundation in the fundamentals.

Meanwhile there went to all elementary teachers carefully formulated methods of grading the children's work. For beginners in arithmetic, Mother wrote:

> The number work of the first grade includes all the combinations from one to ten (not one to twenty), so that all the results in addition, subtraction, multiplication and division are equal to 10 or less. This work should be done in concrete form in as many ways as possible. Lead the children to see that these operations are simply different modes of grouping objects.

Attention was directed toward the "conveying of meaning /as/ the most essential point in reading; this includes emphasis, pauses and inflection; with those must be included articulation and pronunciation. " Oral reading was an art at that time, as was penmanship.

Together with these directives, Mother Ascension sent printed forms for permanent records on which the Sisters were to indicate the courses they had included in their studies, one form to cover the academic, and a second the training the Sisters had received in the various aspects of music, instrumental and vocal, harmony and theory. These, she indicated, were necessary to enable her to place the Sisters in work for which they were best prepared.

Music and normal school certificates were issued to the novices at Mt. Carmel during Mother Ascension's years there, though no data remain regarding the subject matter actually covered in the normal courses. Sister M. Edwina, having had thirteen years of piano "and a generous dose of harmony, " returned for the archives a certificate she had received in music.[15]

The Sisters had found ways of preparing their own members
for ever better teaching in the elementary schools. Those at the
secondary level were not so well provided for. This condition
existed so generally that Archbishop James J. Keane negotiated
with the education department of the Catholic University of
America for an extension summer session to be held in Dubuque
in 1914. Before its opening Father Gorman, president of
Dubuque /now Loras/ College[16] which was to host the session,
wrote Mother Cecilia to learn how many of the Sisters they
could depend on for attendance. He was assured of twenty-five
to thirty.

Sisters came from Texas, Canada, West Virginia, Missouri
and the Dakotas, as well as Iowa. Among the professors were
Dr. T. E. Shields, Dr. E. A. Pace, Dr. William Turner and
Dr. P. J. McCormick[17] of the Catholic University. Sister M.
Clara Russell, B. V. M. , chairman of the English Department at
Mt. St. Joseph College, in an article in the Catholic Educational
Review for September 1914, wrote of the summer's work:

Fifty-two courses were offered, including professional and
academic subjects. [18] One of the most interesting was Psychology of Education by Dr. Shields; and, realizing its
supreme importance and necessity, nearly all the teachers
elected that. There was some difficulty in choosing from
the others. It was hard to pass by the lecture halls where
Dr. Turner was giving an exposition of Pragmatism or some
other form of modern philosophy, dealing fairly and broadly
with every thinker but leaving no doubt as to wrong principles;
where Dr. Kerby's class was intent upon an interesting socio-
logical problem; or where Father Carey was weaving into his
translation of some ancient classic all the beauty of the
Ildathach - it was hard to pass by all these and go down to
Sixth Grade English. But the immediate needs of the home
school had to be considered, and they must come first of all.
Yet when once the class had begun, and the psychology of
method revealed itself in the delight of the vital beauty dis-
coverable in the mind of a little child, in these more truly
pragmatic values one forgot all about the Many-colored
Land and the "new names for old ways of thinking. " Then,
too, one came to a fuller realization of the fact that, to quote
Dr. Pace, the normal relation between the University and
our Catholic schools is an affiliation which makes the child
in the grades no less than the graduate student a product of
the University in what is most essential for mental, moral
and religious formation. [19]

MT. ST. JOSEPH COLLEGE AND ACADEMY, DUBUQUE, 1915

The Reverend Dr. Turner and Dr. Costello, both teachers for the summer session, resided at Mt. Carmel that summer. The summer of 1915 brought Dr. McCormick of the University, and Dr. McEvoy of St. Francis Seminary, Wisconsin, as residents in the chaplain's quarters at Mt. Carmel.

The University extension courses continued through 1915 and 1916, but conditions during the country's involvement in World War I brought them to an end. [20] After their close, however, the college held a ten-week normal course for the training of elementary teachers, and followed this with summer sessions. It also welcomed the Sisters into classes during the scholastic year.

Dr. Shields wrote in 1914 urging that the Congregation establish a house of study for the Sisters in connection with the Sisters' College in Washington, D. C. The plan was not regarded as feasible at the time, and with the opening of opportunities for study nearer home, the proposal was never accepted.

Many of the B. V. M. schools had active alumni organizations dedicated to the interests of their own local situations and to the maintaining of warm associations among former classmates. There was no over-all organization until September 1912. At that time, Mrs. Jennie Kane McEniry, a graduate of the Immaculate Conception Academy, Davenport of the class of 1878, initiated, with the blessing of Mother Ascension, the National Federation of B. V. M. Alumni. Its purpose was to bring

into communication these various alumni associations, to compare methods of work, to promote unity of purpose and action, to encourage alumni scholarships, and to foster, not only school loyalty, but Community spirit, to the end that the colleges and high schools of the Sisters of Charity of the Blessed Virgin Mary may be sought by federation members who desire higher courses of study.

The remarkable loyalty of many local alumni associations took hold of the larger body. Biennial conventions held in various sections of the country focused efforts toward and deepened interest in major projects of the Congregation: scholarships, a college endowment, necessary building enterprises, the needs of the Sisters' infirmary and their retirement program. The list of distinguished women who followed Mrs. McEniry in the office of president included: Margaret O'Connor, St. Aloysius, Chicago; Elizabeth King, St. Joseph Academy, DesMoines: Mrs. Frank McNichols, Mt. St. Joseph, Dubuque; Ada K. Gannon, Immaculate Conception Academy, Davenport;

Elizabeth Morris, Council Bluffs, Iowa; Marcella O'Neil, Immaculata High School, Chicago; Marion Vastine, Davenport Chapter; Mrs. Charles J. O'Neil, Mundelein College, Chicago; Ruth A. Stockman, Xavier, St. Louis; Mrs. Mabel Henry, Mt. St. Gertrude, Boulder; Mary Ellen Maloney, St. Mary High School, Chicago; Mary Carroll, Kansas City Chapter and Mary Lois Walsh, Immaculata High School, Chicago.

The core of faithful workers who helped bring to success the various projects of the Federation included: Margaret Allen and Hilda Burke, Kansas City; Rita Mae Tharinger and Margaret Lawlor, Milwaukee; Betty and Bernice O'Farrell, Chicago; "Red" Spillane, San Francisco; Janann Spahn and Bernice O'Farrell Briggs, Dubuque; Clara Mangan, Davenport; Cecilia Wascisco, Mundelein College; Mrs. Tim Kuizenga and Alma Nichols, Our Lady of Angels Academy, Clinton; Jim Brady and Marie Petras, Cedar Rapids.

Federation scholarships were made available to B. V. M. high school graduates through the years. In 1916, under the presidency of Elizabeth King, the Federation directed its efforts toward scholarships for the Sisters at the Catholic Sisters College, affiliated with the Catholic University of America in Washington, D. C. Later efforts extended these scholarships to other colleges and universities.

Between the years 1916 and 1969 B. V. M. alumni contributed over $1,250,000.00 to the Congregation's projects. The closing of the various B. V. M. boarding schools and a number of their central high schools, as well as the many pressures resulting from the quickened pace of living, led to the final demise of the Federation on September 24, 1977 after sixty-five years of loyal and dedicated service. However, many of the local organizations continue to thrive and serve. [21]

In 1910 or 1911 Cardinal Mundelein established the Irish-Bohemian parish of Mary, Queen of Heaven in Cicero, Illinois, and appointed the Reverend A. J. Dedera, a Bohemian, as its pastor. Father Dedera immediately purchased the Morton Park club house to serve as church and school. Mrs. Kane, the mother of two future Jesuits, Terence and William, and a B. V. M. Sister M. Terence, induced the new pastor to apply for the B. V. M. Sisters to staff the school. Sisters M. Francis Fitzgerald, St. Basil McGinn and Irmina Doherty opened school on March 26, 1913 for 103 pupils. Until their convent was ready in August, they commuted from Blessed Sacrament. Sisters M. Sylvanna and Veturia Sullivan then joined the original group.

Mary, Queen of Heaven was one of the several parishes in the vicinity of the Western Electric plant at the time of the Eastland disaster in 1912. The young parish buried thirty-two of its victims.

The pastor was not too happy with his choice of Irish teachers for the Bohemian people of his parish. In 1917 he secured the services of a community of Bohemian Sisters and asked the B. V. M. 's to vacate school and convent. Mrs. Kane's daughter-in-law, an alumna of the Sacred Heart Academy near Holy Name Cathedral, canvassed the parish in favor of the B. V. M. 's. The matter soon reached the ears of the Cardinal. The Sisters had their trunks packed for departure when word came from him that they were to remain.

A new pastor, Father Griffin, replaced Father Dedera in 1923. He promptly built a new church and rectory, and enlarged the convent. A polyglot parish today, it is still served by the B. V. M. 's.

Emmetsburg, Iowa had boasted of its St. Mary Academy since its opening in 1908. Its first superior, Sister M. Benigna Ryan, and Sister M. Assisium Murphy taught music, while Sisters M. Euthalia Cash and Angelica Stackhouse shared the high school classes that first year with their thirty-one pupils. Sisters M. Leonella Roach, Carena Cass, Theodore O'Donnell and Eudora Crotty each taught two grades for a total enrollment of 224 pupils. Nine priests of the Sioux City diocese received their early education at St. Mary's. The B. V. M. Sisters continue to serve the school.

In 1914 St. Thomas Parish, Emmetsburg, opened its St. Ellen four-room grade school, with the Reverend M. McInerney, pastor and the Sisters of Charity, B. V. M. , in charge of the school. Both church and school had been built through the generosity of Thomas Tobin and his wife Ellen. Eighty-four pupils made up its original enrollment. Until the convent was built in 1926, the Sisters resided in the school, their living quarters on the second floor and their kitchen and chapel in the basement. Sister M. Virginia Lenihan, superior and her four companions, Sisters M. Bonaventure Sweeney, Aloysius Irwin, Thomas Martin and Cyrene Halloran made up the household.

Three girls of the McNulty family entered the Congregation from Emmetsburg, receiving the names of Sisters M. Eugene, Fabian and Eugenius. Their mother, an "old Mount girl, " and Mrs. Minnie McLaughlin Stewart, were benefactors of the school which grew and flourished. The public school officials were consistently cooperative and many of their pupils took music lessons from the Sisters. Graduates were at first required to take the county examinations until the high school staff had been satisfied as to the level of teaching the children were receiving. Like many small schools of Iowa, state demands for specified classes and equipment, and a shortage of Sisters, led to the closing of St. Ellen's in 1967.

When the Reverend J. A. Solon, pastor of St. Mary Parish, DeKalb, Illinois obtained the services of the B. V. M. Sisters for his school in 1913 his was the only parochial school for miles around. Until the first four Sisters came many of the children had never seen a Sister. Sister M. Evangelista Meehan, superior and music teacher, and Sisters M. Enda Snow, Teresita Julian and Alacoque McShane constituted the first little community. They found a well-built, well-equipped school and a comfortable home beside it. Attendance was much beyond expectations, and Sister M. Joan of Arc Shannon was sent promptly to relieve the load of the other Sisters.

The Normal Training College in DeKalb was not long in recognizing the excellent result of the Sisters' efforts, while the principal of the high school was so pleased with the first entrants from St. Mary's that he sent teachers to observe Sister M. Alacoque's English classes. The annual entertainment given by the children at the close of the school year drew priests and Sisters from surrounding towns, and the beautiful auditorium was filled with guests. However, as Sister M. Evangelista wrote: "To our sorrow we do not realize anything of monetary value from the proceeds. Were it not for the music class, we could not meet our expenses, and summer school would be out of the question. " Yet at the holidays the people of the parish were generous to the Sisters, and there was compensation in the ten young women who had entered the Congregation from DeKalb by 1929. For seven years the Sisters were without the Blessed Sacrament in their convent chapel, a deprivation which Bishop Muldoon saw supplied for when it was brought to his attention.

The B. V. M. Sisters continued in the school until 1970 when the School Sisters of Notre Dame assumed charge, serving it from their motherhouse then situated in DeKalb.

Archbishop Quigley established St. Gertrude Parish in Chicag in January 1912 to serve the north Edgewater area between St. Ignatius and St. Ita parishes. The Reverend P. F. Shewbrid was named its first pastor. A combination church and school wa being erected between Granville and Thome, adjoining the parish residence, when the B. V. M. Sisters arrived to open school in December. Their convent was situated at Broadway and Granville. That first staff included Sisters M. Verena Griffin, Ursina Dempsey, Ferdinanda Long, Tarcissius O'Shea, Benezetta Fosselman and St. Peter Tansey. By 1925 fourteen Sisters were occupied with 480 pupils. The present convent was completed in 1929 and the church two years later, handsome structures in matching stone. The school building followed shortly in the same good style. Many changes have come in the area, but not so complete a turnover of population as in many other parts of the city. While the enrollment is considerably reduced, the B. V. M. Sisters still staff the school.

St. Irenaeus Parish, Lyons, Iowa in 1913 provided a convent for the Sisters who had for many years resided at Our Lady of Angels Academy. The Reverend James Comerford was pastor at the time and the Sisters were Sisters M. Hortense Boland, Helen Donavan, Lourdes Brophy, Girolamo Dullard and Marguerite King. During the later pastorage of Father Jackson, the convent was closed and the Sisters returned to the academy. However, a residence across from the church has now served them for many years. Four Sisters staff the small school today.

Interesting innovations during the years 1912-1915, as noted in the Record of Events, include the installation of an electric dishwasher and a printing press at the motherhouse. The first issue of Our Herald, an intra-community periodical printed on it, was dated April 1, 1913. The first circular letter to be printed on the new press was that of November 14, 1913. Prior to that time such letters had been hectographed. Permission was given to the academy in Wichita for the purchase of an auto, the first in the possession of the Congregation. The full Holy Week services were initiated at the motherhouse in the spring of 1915, the Very Reverend Dr. A. Thier as principal celebrant. The first "sabbatical" for a B. V. M. was that taken by Sister M. Bertrand Foley when she went to St. Genevieve College, Asheville, North Carolina in 1913 for a year of rest. She used a portion of her leisure time there for the study of French.

The standard of musical excellence in the Congregation was established early, its principal protagonist Sister M. Gonzaga McCloskey. Sister was superior for many years at the Immaculate Conception Academy, Davenport. A graduate of the

academy conducted by the Sisters of Mercy in County Derry,
Ireland, Sister entered the B. V. M. Community at a time when
Sister M. Philomena Mullen was teaching music at the academy
on the Prairie. The daughter of a successful merchant in Philadelphia, Sister had had the advantage of excellent instructors
before her entrance into religion. Whatever the sources of her
own musical education, Sister M. Gonzaga was gifted and a
perfectionist.

Sister quickly recognized the possibilities of the youthful
novice, [22] Sister M. Editha Flanagan, when she was assigned
to the teaching of music at the academy. When Sister M. Editha
entered the Congregation from St. Agatha Academy in Iowa City
she was already an accomplished musician. Sister M. Gonzaga
gave her many advantages which prepared her not only as a pianist
and teacher but as a composer of merit as well. [23] Something of
a result of their combined talents is illustrated by a commencement program for the class of 1878 at the academy. The entrance
march, "Marche de la Garde Imperiale, " was played by twelve
students on six pianos. The opening hymn, "O Cor Amoris
Victima, " was accompanied by one student on the organ and six
piano students. The closing hymn, Mozart's "Magnificat, " was
similarly accompanied. Harp, piano and vocal solos were inter-
spersed throughout the program.

It is then quite understandable that the Davenport Academy
should have been chosen as the center for the training of the
Congregation's music teachers, its title, the Mt. Carmel Conservatory of Music. Sisters who had studied under the Vienna-
trained Mary Wood Chase and the celebrated Silvio Scionti of
the American Conservatory of Music became instructors in summer sessions there. Scionti himself gave six weeks of instruction
there to ten of the advanced teachers, each one of whom in her
turn passed on her instruction to five Sister-pupils.

A highly professional teacher of both harp and piano, with
close ties to the music department of the University of Nebraska
in Lincoln, was Sister M. Melitta Fleming. Sister had studied
under W. S. B. Matthews, author of a well-known graded music
series. Two future B. V. M. 's to whom she passed on the training she had received were Sisters M. Teresine O'Shea and
Demetria Lodge, both of whom entered the Congregation in 1914.
As her pupils they had been called upon from time to time to
serve as accompanists in vocal concerts at the University. Both
also had performed that service in the Lincoln studio of the much
sought after vocal teacher, Clemens Movius of the Wesleyan University staff. Free vocal lessons were their reward for such
services. Both Sisters made the results of their training available
to their fellow religious.

Declining health was a detriment to Sister M. Teresine. Sister M. Demetria, however, attended the Gregorian Institute of America at Toledo, affiliated with the Solesmes School conducted at the Laval University of Quebec. There she studied under Dr. Robert Carroll, graduate of Boston College and the Sorbonne and Solesmes Institute of Chant in Paris. An assignment given her there resulted in a four-way index of the modalities of Latin chant in the entire Liber Usualis, a monumental work which is now in the library of the Solesmes in Paris. As a result of her work with Dr. Carroll, Sister compiled and published a text which combined the Gregorian or Latin chant notation with the Sol-Fegge system of sight-singing. In recognition of her work, Sister received from the Solesmes Institute in Paris the only diploma it had then issued to an American woman. It entitled her to the privilege of issuing certificates of excellence from the Institute on examinations she was authorized to conduct. Sister was for a number of years thereafter in charge of the chant choir of novices at Mt. Carmel. Her work there was followed by five years as piano supervisor for the Congregation.

Among the more remarkable of the Congregation's music instructors were the inspiring Sister M. Lumina Farrell who for many years directed the musical training of the novices at Mt. Carmel; Sister M. Meneve McMullen, who herself a great musician, taught harmony in the summer sessions at Davenport and was for many years director of the music department of Clarke College; Sister M. St. Ruth Connolly, an able successor to Sister M. Meneve; Sister M. Verda St. Clair who initiated the teaching of class piano; and Sister M. Rafael Bird who in later years was head of the music department at Mundelein College. Each of these Sisters added highly creditable music composition to their teaching. Others of note included Sisters M. Electa Cavanaugh, Francis Xavier Baldwin, Isabella Kane, Ignatia Pyne, Raphaella Talmadge and Bernard Farrell, together with many worthy successors of a later date.

We have witnessed the forward steps taken by Mother Ascension in the matters of teacher training and governmental changes, and the sensitivity she manifested in preparing the Sisters for the division into provinces. The love and respect which the Sisters had for her are evident in their reminiscences in her regard - her gentleness, kindly response and motherly solicitude for each. We find in her circular letters evidences of her concern for the Sisters' well-being and her desire to relieve them of any undue pressure. Witness the directive: "The Sisters must not be per-

mitted, much less required, to scrub or to mop the school-
rooms. " "No Sister should be left alone in the house while the
Sisters are away at Mass in the church or are absent for any
other reason. " "In some places, the Sisters are expected to
hear four Masses on Sundays. . . . It may be permitted, but
must not be required. "

Her efforts and those of her consultors to be faithful to the
strict discipline of their own early days are shown in other
directives. Their concerns are especially manifest in their
interpretation of poverty and in the fear of the relaxation involved in social contacts, even among the Sisters themselves.
These forbade "too frequent" visits even to their own convents,
requested the Sisters to refrain from conversations on the street
in street cars and on trains. For the last, it was suggested that
they say the rosary instead. When necessity or convenience required it, they were permitted to ride in automobiles, though not
in open cars and never for pleasure. Boat rides, except for
travel, were strictly forbidden. The Sisters were not to use the
telephone for private conversations "nor for repeating gossip
or matters of ordinary interest/from house to house. If this
abuse cannot be remedied in any other way, the telephone must
be taken out. "

Another curb on communication is found in the regulation
that forbade "unnecessary" letters. A superior in doubt as to
what was necessary was instructed to "send the letters to me
and I shall decide. " All shopping was to be placed in the hands
of an assigned purchaser, and the Sisters were not to go to
stores. This included even the purchase of shoes.

In school matters the Sisters were forbidden to take any cours
at a "Carnegie Institute, " to teach "elocution, "[24] or to tolerate
"certain /unidentified/ exercises in physical culture which were
not regarded as modest. The depth of Mother Ascension's con-
scientious[25] concern in matters of poverty and religious discipli
is manifested in this second of two letters to superiors dated
September 4, 1914:

> Please read both these letters aloud for the Sisters as
> soon as possible, and let me know the date of such reading.
> I am grieved to learn that some of our Sisters have failed
> in Obedience by travelling in street-cars on Sunday. No per-
> mission has been given for this; on the contrary, I have re-
> peatedly said that when necessity required travel on Sunday,
> a private conveyance, not a street-car, should be used.
> I learn also that some Sisters have so far forgotten the
> obligations of Holy Poverty as to make use of silk stockings

and underwear, and similar extravagances in attire. I hereby direct each superior to collect from the Sisters and to send to me at once, union suits and all such clothing as does not conform both in make and material, to the requirements of our Congregation. As one preparation for Perpetual Vows I beg the Sisters to dispose of all superfluities.

But more serious and alarming is certain information brought to me regarding the violation of our Rule of companionship in the parlor and other places. I beg our Superiors for the love of God and for the love they bear to our Sisterhood, to see that this Rule is observed, and I ask all the Sisters to let me know of any violation in order that I may be enabled to prevent it in the future. I forbid Superiors to give any exemptions from this Rule; each case must be referred to me, and if I think exemption is necessary my permission must be publicly announced to all the Sisters.

Confiding the safety of our loved Congregation to the Sacred Heart of Jesus through our faithful and fervent members, I am

Yours affectionately,

Construction was begun in 1914 on a bungalow, "the Loyola," to be built on the grounds of Mt. St. Gertrude Academy, Boulder to serve the Sister-victims of tuberculosis. However, by the time it had been occupied by its first contingent of Sisters in 1915, a city ordinance forbade those in danger of death to remain there. It was then necessary to return a number to the infirmary at Mt. Carmel. The result there was an overcrowding with some patients removed to the brick building which had formerly served as chaplain's residence.

Many tragedies, major and minor, struck during those brief three years. Those of world concern - the sinking of the Titanic on April 18, 1912, and the outbreak of World War I in the summer of 1914; the death of Pius X also in 1914, and the imposition on the frail shoulders of Benedict XV of the burdens of the papacy in a war-torn world. It was more in sympathy than congratulations that Mother Ascension sent the new pope through Cardinal Falconio an offering of $500.00. In presenting it the Cardinal took the opportunity of acquainting the Holy Father with the work of the Sisters, and of obtaining from him a special blessing on them and their labors. Regarding the check for $200.00 which Mother Ascension had enclosed for him, Falconio wrote: "I regret that you have again troubled yourself about me. The good work you are doing is the best recompense I can get for any service that I can render to your Institution. My blessing to all the Sisters. "[26] As a mark of appreciation he sent with his letter relics of St. Francis and St. Clare, which were promptly deposited in the chapel reliquary.

A succession of local difficulties began on New Year's Eve 1914 when word came during the dinner hour that the convent of the Holy Ghost Sisters in St. Anthony's Parish, Dubuque, was burning. A call to the pastor, Father O'Malley, offered hospitality for the Sisters. Then on January 10 Father Clark was seriously injured by a fall on the ice. He was subsequently hospitalized for some weeks. On the day after his fall, Sister M. Cyrilla Burke suffered a painful and disabling accident, having caught her hand in the laundry mangle. The death of Sister M. Gonzaga occurred on January 20, and on March 9 Mother Cecilia suffered a bad fall on the stairs. Her forty postulants were being received that day, and she was hastening to the dining room to leave at each place an affectionate greeting. As she was scheduled to give the profession retreat for the novices who would make vows on March 19, hurried arrangements were made for a Jesuit retreat master.

Two interesting proposals appear in Mother Ascension's circular letters to the Sisters. The first of these proposed the adding of a wing onto the motherhouse to provide space for Sisters who she anticipated would be returning regularly for summer study. The location of the chapel also concerned her. The usual path followed in the procession of clergy and servers on special occasions, and by the Sisters showing guests through the house, was up the main stairs to the second floor. Thus the way to the chapel led past the novice dormitories, hence through the "cloister. " The large groups of young people entering the Congregation threatened an overcrowding of the novitiate where the novices assembled for instructions and recreation. Both these later problems she proposed to solve by the use of the chapel for a novitiate, and the building of a new chapel on a lower level. Neither proposal seemed to find resonance among the Sisters and nothing came of either.

Almost nothing remains of Mother Ascension's business or her personal correspondence with the Sisters or others. Three short letters to Mrs. John Mullen of Lincoln, Nebraska giving indication of a warm and affectionate nature were returned to Mount Carmel after Mother's death. One of these, sent to console Mrs. Mullen on the death of an infant son tells us something of her deep spirituality. It says in part: "By the marvelous waters of Baptism your babe has entered into heaven, magnificer wise, full grown in the life of grace, to praise and to bless God forever. "

While Mother Ascension refused to be considered for re-election to the office of superior-general, she was destined to carry much of its burden during the next four years as vicar to the aging Mother Cecilia.

Mrs. Jennie Kane McEniry, graduate of the Class of 1878 of the Immaculate Conception Academy, Davenport, initiated the National Federation of B.V.M. Alumni, and was its first president.

Notes

1 Sister M. Marcelliana McFadden succeeded her as administrator of the infirmary.

2 While the music teachers taught singing in the classroom and trained the children's choir, these services were regarded as fair compensation for teaching accommodations available to each teacher in the convent for her private pupils.

3 In the light of all this the remark of a bishop in attendance at the bishops' meeting in Chicago in May, 1978 is of particular significance. When the president-elect of the Leadership Council of Women Religious mentioned to him the problem congregations of women faced in providing for the increasing proportion of retired Sisters, he responded: "That's your fault. You should have made the proper provision for it."

4 When on July 13, 1913 the council voted to direct the superior of Holy Cross to tell Father Hischen that all music money would be retained by the Sisters, Mother Cecilia was the only dissenting member.

5 The following April 25 the Archbishop yielded on this point, permitting the Sisters to invite Jesuits for retreats provided they were over forty-five years of age.

6 Mother Cecilia's letter included the following personal request: "As a special favor I ask that after the installation of the new officers on March 25th, the Sisters will omit the title of Mother in addressing me or in speaking of me, and thus they will kindly assist me in observing Art. 2, Chap. 4 of our Constitutions. In this request I am joined by our dear Mother Gertru who asks the same favor in her regard." That reference has been previously quoted and seems to the writer, as it did to the Sisters, to be irrelevant.

7 When on March 25, 1913 Archbishop Keane returned to the Sisters the copy of the proposed Constitutions, he asked that they include the following conditions: that no foundation be made without first consulting him; that the Congregation's financial reports be submitted to him, and that Sisters should be free to write to him without inspection of their letters. The first two conditions were reminiscent of Archbishop Hennessy and the Sisters' efforts for approbation by the Sacred Congre-

gation of the Propaganda. The conditions did not appear in the 1914 Constitutions.

8 Careful examination of the photograph as it appeared in the Early Days, page 197, shows that the features of Catherine Byrne replaced those of the original subject of the print.

9 In order to save the Bishops the prescribed canonical examination intended to insure that each Sister was acting with complete freedom in so committing herself, each was required to give her signature to a form which gave that assurance. Her signature was attested by two witnesses.

10 Sister M. Stella Reid, a patient in the infirmary, was near death on November 17. Lest she would not linger until the day assigned, she was permitted to pronounce her vows on that day with Mother Ascension and many others gathered about her bed.

11 On December 4, 1914 Mother Ascension had requested that each Sister under vows send to her by January 15 a list of four names of those whom they regarded as suited to the office of provincial, signing or not as she wished.

12 In the course of its history the Church had experienced many situations in which the state closed all religious houses and confiscated their properties. In such an event the dowry would make at least immediate provision for those expelled from their convents.

13 Mother Ascension had been installed in office on March 26, 1912.

14 Grades for these were to have 60 - 95 as their outer limits. Sister M. Edwina Tansey recalls that during her brief assignment to Cathedral School in the year 1910-1911 in Lincoln, Nebraska, when Sister M. Ascension was in charge, the school made use of devices which did not appear until many years later elsewhere. Among these were the standardized report card, absence and tardy slips, and a card used for recording teacher-pupil relations, such as conferences on studies, etc. (Letter addressed to Sister M. Thomas More - Doris Walsh - September 16, 1968).

15 Tansey letter.

16   The college made frequent changes in its name. It was St. Joseph's College, 1873-1914; Dubuque College, 1914-1920; Columbia College, 1920-1939; and Loras College since 1939.

17   Dr. McCormick was later to become a bishop and rector of the University. Dr. Turner was also later raised to the episcopate.

18   The laboratory course in biology that summer resulted in three cases of malaria among the Sisters, attributed to the presence of larvae in the specimen material provided.

19   The writer is indebted to Sister Mary Eunice Mousel, OSF, PhD, for the above interesting quotation. It occurs in her history of the Sisters of the Third Order of St. Francis of the Holy Family, entitled They Have Taken Root. (New York: Bookman Associates, 1954), pp. 218-219.

20   The Catholic University extension courses were re-instituted in 1934 and continued until 1963. The College then continued a graduate program in the fields of English, history and education.

21   Details from "National Federation of B. V. M. Alumni," by Sister M. Kevin Gallagher, B. V. M. (Salt, Fall issue, 1977), pp. 6-7.

22   Sister M. Editha was scarcely older than fifteen years when she was assigned as a novice to teach music at the Davenport Academy.

23   A certain majesty and splendor marked her religious choruses which, unfortunately, have never been published.

24   Superiors faced with the problem of hiring seculars for the teaching of elocution substituted "expression" on their schedules and life went calmly on.

25   The first letter announced that permission had been received for perpetual vows.

26   We see the same "holy indifference" on the part of Cardinal Giovanni Bonzano, then Apostolic Delegate, expressed in his letter of December 13, 1913 to Mother Ascension: "I found enclosed in your letter a check for fifty dollars. Not knowing for what it can be, I am herewith returning it to you."

PICNIC AT RIVERVIEW PARK. CHICAGO, 1908. COAL–BURNING STEAM ENGINE.

Chapter Twelve

THE FORMING YEARS HAVE FLED

Mother Cecilia was seventy-seven, frail and with seriously failing eyesight, when the chapter of 1915 returned her to the office of superior-general. It was not the easiest of all times in which to direct the destinies of a rapidly growing religious congregation. A World War was in progress; an epidemic of major proportions was to sweep the country; shortages and rising costs were adding to administrative pressures. And within the Congregation the problems and possibilities of provincial government were just beginning to unfold. Then there were the growing costs of and arrangements involved in the preparation of the entire teaching body for the certification and degrees necessary to meet the new accrediting requirements.

The Congregation's first chapter had decreed the opening of a teacher's college at Mt. Carmel, affiliated with Mt. St. Joseph and offering classes for postulants and senior novices, an arrangement which only later came to be. It had further determined on the establishment of a board of education for the general direction of the Congregation's growing system of schools. The efforts required to meet such varied exigencies would tax the powers of the ablest.

Mother Ascension, vicar to the superior general, excellent woman that she was, lacked the necessary breadth of vision, concerned, as she had shown herself, with personal minutiae. Yet much of the burden was to rest on her shoulders. The able and resourceful Loyola and Octavia were no longer of the council, nor was Mother's faithful friend, Sister M. Basil Healy. Besides Mother Ascension, it included instead the untraditional Sister M. Bertrand Foley of Mt. St. Joseph College, Sister M. Editha Flanagan who had been Mother Cecilia's superior during her trying years at the Davenport Academy, and Sister M. Esther Warren, administrator of the infirmary, all new to the

problems of general administration. Sister M. Crescentia
Markey, the secretary general, was to spend many months as
a patient in the infirmary, leaving her secretarial duties to Sister M. Bertrand. The procurator was the newly chosen Sister
M. Urban Bermingham; Sister M. Angela Fitzgerald continued
in the office of novice mistress. Fortunately many of the details
of administration had been transferred to the four able women
who would set the tone and establish the pattern of provincial
government for the Congregation of 1,065 members, then operating seventy-six schools with a total enrollment of 28,498 pupils.
Mother Cecilia had protested her reelection, but apparently the
chapter members were firm in their choice.

The struggle to meet educational needs by building projects in
many areas, as well as the construction of the motherhouse, had
resulted in a total investment of $1,861,000, according to the
report the retiring treasurer general presented to the chapter.
Against this there was an interest-bearing indebtedness of
$172,700.00.

The chapter created the new office of assistant novice mistress
which, for the time, however, seems to have indicated the duties
of a postulant mistress. To it Sister M. Gervase Tuffy was assigned.

We see a growing pragmatism in requests made of the chapter
of 1915. One request presented to the committee on discipline
suggested that the subject matter of the spiritual reading, cus-
tomarily taken in common, be so chosen as to serve as preparation for the teaching of catechism. A similar request,
presented to the committee on teaching, asked that an aid to
the catechism teacher might be found in a study of MacEachen's
Moral and Dogmatic Series, to be substituted for the usual
spiritual reading. Fortunately the matter was settled by the
reminder that the practice of spiritual reading was intended to
serve the Sisters' own spiritual life and growth, a more fundamental, though less immediate, preparation for their apostolate
of teaching.

Previous to the chapter of 1915 information had been sought
from Dr. Edward A. Pace of the Catholic University of America
on the functions and organization of a board of education. As
authorized by the chapter, the board was composed of the superior general and her four councillors,[1] the four provincial
superiors and their directresses, "and as many other experienced teachers as the Mother General may appoint." The first
appointees were Sisters M. Columba Donnelly,[2] Gervase Tuffy,
Ida Harty and Urban Bermingham. To Sister M. Columba was
delegated the task of writing its constitution. Of the board's

three departments, judicial, legislative and executive, the Mother and her councillors were to be involved in the first department and the provincials and their directresses in the second, while the execution of the board's special functions rested with the directresses.

Among the directives from the board, one required that no high school teacher be permitted to follow more than one branch of study during the school year lest her health or classroom work suffer. A second urged the local superiors to arrange for drawing and sight singing lessons for their elementary teachers who were expected also to undergo examinations on Christian Doctrine

A weakness in the operation of the board resulted from the temptation to assign directresses as substitutes for local superiors who had become ill. The first instances of this came in 1919 when superiors at St. Francis Xavier in St. Louis and St. John's, DesMoines were thus substituted for.

We gain much insight into Mother Cecilia's personality from the little notebook she kept of visitations made during her final years. Was it the joy the Sisters felt in having her with them which is reflected in so large a proportion of her reports? Was life for them always so idyllic as her comments suggest? It is interesting that when the occasion warranted, Mother Cecilia proved herself nonetheless a realist. She suggested but did not make changes. These she left to the respective provincials. Excerpts from her 1915 visitation record include:

Holy Cross, Sister M. Sinella, superior: All well and good. Blessed be God.

Holy Rosary, Sister M. Ignata: Thank God again and again for the good spirit here. Superior governs wisely and well.

Holy Angels Academy, Sister M. Agnella: Blessed be God for the good spirit here, and for the good done by all. Thanks be to God!

A few shadows fell in 1916:

Lincoln, Nebraska, Sister M. Xavier: Can nothing be done about salary here? Can't Sister M. Oswald return to Chicago?

Council Bluffs, Sister M. Philip: ----- should be changed. ----- is a dead failure with boys. ----- should be changed from here and should never have the care of altar, sacrist or altar boys.

St. Vincent's, K. C., Sister M. Ludivine: Nourish the body if you expect it to work, but never at the expense of the soul. The spiritual life first.

St. Aloysius, K. C., Sister M. Pulcheria: Charity covers a multitude of sins. Silence, charity.

But again:

Pontiac, Sister M. Henrietta: A lovely, happy mission this. Thank God! Six Sisters, eight grades, a secular housekeeper.

St. Paul's, Frisco, Sister M. Conradine: A very happy mission. Thank God!

Mt. St. Gertrude, Sister M. Oswald: Very, very good - considering conditions. Blessed be God!

The picture was still bright in 1917:

St. Mary's, Sioux City, Sister M. Harold: A convent home most pleasing to God. Blessed be His Holy Name!

St. Mary's, Emmetsburg, Sister M. Felician: Sisters miserably accommodated but very edifying - no murmuring, no complaining, happy and good. Thanks be to God!

Marcus, Sister M. Bernardine: This is a lovely little mission. Thank God! All happy, comfortable, good. ----- should be with Italians in Chicago. ----- not strong enough for three grades but an excellent teacher. Will prepare for higher grade. A singing teacher badly needed.

Presentation, Sister M. Edmund: All is well here. Blessed be God! A bright, hard working, well-meaning crowd of Sisters. May God bless and protect them.

The year of 1918 was all sunshine at St. Gertrude's under Sister M. Verena; Rock Island with Sister M. William; the Davenport Academy, Sister M. Ignatia; Cedar Falls, etc. The situation seems a bit dubious in Rapid City where Sister M. Dominica was superior, for the comment reads: "Come Holy Ghost. Without Thee man is nothing." It was the feast of Pentecost and the unpredictable John J. Lawler was the Bishop.

A number of new missions were established during these
years! St. Bridget's, Omaha, has left no account of its beginnings save that it opened in 1914 with Sister M. Electa Cavanaugh
as superior and music teacher. The household included Sisters
M. Ramon O'Hara, Odelia Brady, Celeste Murphy, Honorata
Riley, St. Charles Behan, Claudius Emerson and Philippa
Sheridan, three of whom were quite elderly. Difficulties must
have risen in the household for all save Sisters M. Honorata
and Claudius were replaced the following year. Sister M. Melitta
Fleming, also a music teacher, succeeded as superior.

In September 1915 five B. V. M. Sisters opened the St. Mary
School in the small town of Waucoma, Iowa, the Reverend Martin
Hogan, pastor. They were Sisters M. Annunciata Durkin,
Rosamond Donlin, Salvina Hurley, Christopher Carey and Sylvius
Schanborn, one of these a music teacher and another a house-
keeper. Of the ninety-three pupils enrolled, thirty were in the
ninth and tenth grades.

On November 11 a tornado completely demolished the church,
tore off part of the roof and broke windows in the school. Strangely enough, although the altar was crushed with debris, the ciboria
were left standing upright in the tabernacle.

It was real missionary work which the Sisters had undertaken.
Operating in the school basement and with no equipment, they
were faced with the necessity of preparing the children for the
county examinations. This they were able to do with remarkable
success. When the Archbishop came to give Confirmation he
returned to Dubuque with glowing accounts of their work.

The Reverend James Sheehy soon built a beautiful brick church.
However, the account of the parish tells that he "used rather
strange language to our Sisters in the presence of the children
and denounced them from the altar of the public church. " If
this continued it was Mother Cecilia's intention to lay the case
before the Archbishop and withdraw the Sisters. Matters must
have been adjusted for they continued in Waucoma until the
diocesan school reorganization in 1968.

On March 4, 1916 the newly installed Archbishop George
Mundelein established the parish of St. Thomas of Canterbury
in Uptown Chicago for the five hundred families of the area.
He assigned the Reverend Francis M. O'Brien as its first pastor
and the Reverend J. Malloy, a former pupil of the B. V. M. 's,
as his assistant.

The first Mass was said in the Lakeside Theatre, while the Dorset Hotel at 5009 North Sheridan served thereafter until the permanent church-school structure was ready for use. Its dedication on June 24, 1917 was signalized by a dancing party at which Governor and Mrs. Dunne were honored guests. The new building was the first Catholic structure in the city to feature the colonial style of architecture, a style which Mundelein, by then Cardinal, chose for the St. Mary of the Lake Seminary established in Mundelein, Illinois in time for the Eucharistic Congress in 1926.

The Canterbury Primary School and Kindergarten, which included the first four grades, was opened in September 1917. The B. V. M. Sisters, with Sister M. Eulalia McSwiggin[3] as superior, taught the first forty pupils in the former Grosvenor residence at 4827 North Kenmore. The building later served as the Sister's convent.

The nature of the Uptown area with its many businesses, the popular Aragon Theatre, apartment buildings and residential hotels overshadowing its family residences, gave the school a character different from that found in other areas of the city. By 1937 the school enrollment had reached just 260 pupils. The transient nature of the parish was then accented by the influx of many Spanish-speaking people. The Sisters remained in the school until 1972 when local situations and the shortage of personnel led to their withdrawal.

Archbishop Mundelein was less than a year in Chicago when he established several new parishes on the South Side. On June 30, 1916 he appointed the Reverend John B. Scanlan pastor of the new St. Dorothy's. Father Scanlan said the first parish Mass in a hall at 81 East 71st Street. His appeal for Sisters led to the rejection of one received from Bishop Libert Boeynaems of Honolulu, to the great regret of many of the Sisters. Six B. V. M. 's with Sister M. Lamberta Fitzgerald as superior[4] arrived on November 15, 1917 to take charge of ninety-six pupils in makeshift quarters. By June the number had almost doubled. The Archbishop dedicated a combination church and school on May 12, 1918. Five years later ground was broken for a convent, the Sisters having occupied temporary quarters in the school building to that time. The new church was dedicated on April 16, 1928, and parish and school grew rapidly.

The parish is today made up of middle class Blacks. A shortage of Sisters has greatly reduced its faculty and the large convent has been left to serve as rectory and to provide other parish needs.

In 1917 the DePaul High School for Girls was separated from the St. Vincent Grade and High School, with Sister M. Lambertina Doran as principal and superior. With her were Sisters M. Roberta and Tertulla Reynolds, Antionette Murphy, Veneranda Mulcahey, St. Henry Collins, Callista Campion, Simon Foley, Feliciana Walsh, Urbanita Stapleton and Fidelia McGonigal. Though a successful venture, its life was cut short in 1922 by the opening of the Immaculata High School. Only first year students were accepted at the new site when classes opened in September 1921 in the Greenlee mansion. When the new building was ready in 1922, it was prepared to receive all four years of high school. Details pertinent to the establishment of a separate high school appear later.

The discovery of gold in a gulch near Deadwood, South Dakota in 1875 led to the rapid growth of the town of Lead, site of the Homestead mine, the largest gold mine in the world at that time. The first Mass in Lead, then the diocesan seat, was said in 1876 by the Bishop in residence at St. Patrick Parish. The first religious in the Lead school were the Sisters of the Holy Cross, who taught in the church basement. They were followed by the Sisters of St. Benedict. The church, destroyed by fire in 1900, was rebuilt in 1902. The Sisters were withdrawn the following year. In 1906 the Sisters of St. Francis from Niagara, New York came and served into 1911.

Difficulties with the Homestead Mining Company led the Most Reverend Joseph F. Busch, Bishop of Lead, to transfer his seat to Rapid City in 1913 and to close the school.

His successor, the Most Reverend John J. Lawler, reopened the school in 1916, and six B. V. M. Sisters were assigned to serve it, their first mission in the Black Hills. Sisters M. Ursuline Desmond, Rafael Bird, Idus Slattery, Anna Sweeney, Mamerta Walsh and Barnabas Dwyer formed the first staff for the grey stucco school Bishop Busch had erected. The Sisters' home was not ready when they arrived, and for six weeks they traveled by trolley to and from the Benedictine Hospital in Deadwood. Classes opened with eighty-nine pupils.

During the flu epidemic of 1918 the school was closed and the Sisters helped in the nursing of its victims. This led to close ties with the people of the parish. The Sisters withdrew from the mission in 1966, just fifty years after their first coming.

In September 1917 Bishop Lawler invited the B. V. M. Sisters to serve the Immaculate Conception School in the new see of Rapid City. The six Sisters who were assigned to the mission were M. Dominica Burke, Olive Regan, Emilita Brennan, Prudens Costello, Adorinus McGuire and St. Austin Revill. There seem to have been areas of conflict with the Bishop in those early years, though the school flourished. The Sisters continued to serve in Rapid City until 1976 when a loss of numbers and the isolated situation of the mission led to their withdrawal in that year.

St. Paul's, San Francisco, was the second California parish to seek the services of the B. V. M. Sisters for its school. The new building awaiting their arrival in 1916 was a massive structure of granite and masonry, a model school containing eighteen large classrooms. Special features were a roof garden with sun and lunchrooms, and a ground floor play room for inclement weather. Areas for the teaching of drawing and painting, music and commercial courses were provided. An auditorium with a seating capacity of 1, 200 had a well equipped stage.

Adjoining the school on the left was a four-story convent in matching style. These, together with a rectory, occupied an entire city block. The pastor, the Reverend M. D. Connolly, had known the B. V. M. Sisters from his years at St. Brigid's, and the first superior of the new school, Sister M. Conradine Davies, had served there for fourteen years.

The Sisters were received warmly by the congregation, were shown the city, taken for a visit to St. Brigid's, and given a public reception. The convent was not ready, and Sister M. Conradine and her fifteen companions[5] lived for a time in the school, taking their meals at the rectory. Classes began with an enrollment of 529 boys and girls, but before the week's end the number had grown to 600. At the end of September, Sister M. Benedicta, provincial, and Sister M. Florence Clowry, her directress, came for visitation and were highly pleased with all they found.

When the influenza struck in 1918, the school was closed for two months while the Sisters shared in the care of the sick, for the parish was one vast hospital. The convent kitchen served as dispensary of soups and other provisions for the poor. Just two of the Sisters contracted the flu.

War efforts undertaken by the children included the purchase of Liberty bonds and thrift stamps and the production of patriotic programs. The enrollment grew to 1, 300, the boys remaining in the school through eighth grade and the girls through ninth and, if they wished, for commercial courses.

A second school building was dedicated by Archbishop Edward J. Hanna on November 7, 1920. Two years later Sister M. Rose Rourke, a native of San Francisco who had succeeded as superior, opened a high school department for girls, introducing one year at a time. A high school building was ready for occupancy in 1925. The total enrollment at St. Paul's reach 1, 500 pupils with a staff of thirty-six Sisters in three school buildings.

In September 1928 the well-loved Sister M. Conradine returned to St. Paul's as superior of the grade school. But the joy of her former acquaintances was cut short when on December 7 Sister succumbed to pneumonia.

Many vocations have come to the Congregation from St. Paul's. But, as in so many other urban situations, the parish is no longer the flourishing establishment that it was. Both grade and high school continue in operation, but the convent intended for the high school faculty is now able to accommodate that and the grade school faculty as well.

Mother Gertrude was eighty-nine when she celebrated her diamond jubilee, the first to do so in the Congregation. As a child of fourteen she had entered the sisterhood after some time as a pupil at the Sacred Heart Academy in Philadelphia. All the others in that first novitiate had been laid to rest in the Prairie graveyard. She too was feeling her years. In October 1912 Mother Cecilia had written Sister M. Renata Colvin, a convert to the faith whose entrance to religion had completely estranged her family: "Won't you write dear Mother Gertrude? She is very poorly. She always loved you, and it will comfort her to hear from you. Tell her about your dear father. She will pray for him, and her prayers are worth having. "

Mother Gertrude lived quietly in her little room down the novice corridor, rarely visiting the novitiate, and working when she was able, on the community accounts. When she was caught up with these, her gnarled but busy fingers made scapulars or small relics for the Sisters from bits of garments of Mother Clarke and Father Donaghoe. Sister M. Eileen Curran told of the great rejoicing on a day that nineteen new postulants arrived. Mother Gertrude joined the merry group, holding a treasure gathered in her full serge apron. Opening it up to their

surprised eyes, she invited each to claim a fresh, warm dough-
nut. Sister M. Cordelia, mistress of the sewing room and
faithful caretaker of Mother's wardrobe, would find herself with
a task, reclaiming the apron.

Jubilee days are times of recollections, as Sister M. Louise
Clark thought when she wrote of her memories of Mother Gertrude:

> I had my first chat with Mother when she was on her way
> home from San Francisco about Easter, 1891. I was a pupil
> at St. Francis, Council Bluffs. I think some Sister must
> have mentioned me to her, because she asked to see me.
> I do not recall what we spoke about. I was impressed by
> her simplicity and holiness, and I have never seen anything
> to change it. . . .
>
> I remember being her companion from Dubuque. As soon as
> we got started, we began the rosary, and we prayed about
> all the way. . . .
>
> In 1907 she was very ill and had her room near the novitiate.
> I was home for the summer. Monday morning I went to the
> laundry and asked Sister Mary Esther if there was anything
> there I could do. She replied that I could help her more by
> going up and staying with Mother. For the next several weeks,
> I was either her day or night nurse. She never complained.
> One day we thought she was dying. You could see she was in
> great pain. She did not die until 1919. . . . She must have
> had great vitality.

It was Mother's earnest wish that her diamond jubilee celebration to be held on September 24, 1916 be a quiet one, observed religiously and wholly within the Congregation, and the
Sisters conformed to her wishes. The only slight exception was
a simple program at the Mount, given in her honor and climaxed
with the presentation of a basket of seventy-five red roses.

In those later years Mother Gertrude had the happiness of
contact with a grand-nephew, John Regan, S. J., preparing for
the priesthood in Hillyard, Washington. A letter of May 17, 1918
to "My very dear Aunt, " observed that due to their apathy a
missionary's work among the Italians in the west "was even
harder than among the Chinese. " He expected then to be ordained
in about three years, and promised that if he were assigned to
Woodstock for his theology he would stop off at Mt. Carmel for
a visit, adding: "Thanks for the scapulars. The priests took
some for the other scholastics. "

John's Christmas letter written from Santa Clara told that "'flu took one priest and two scholastics, one, Mr. Peacock, brother of a B. V. M. "[6] The Jesuits had lost one boy at the university. John had called on the Sisters at St. Brigid's and had "never had the pleasure of meeting a more edifying and humble community. . . . We have a good number of boys from St. Brigid's. In the opinion of all the teachers, they are the best boys that come to our college. "

At the table under the crucifix in the large motherhouse refectory, the two Mothers sat adjacent to each other. To their novice server each seemed eager to outdo the other in thoughtfulness. Ill health often kept Mother Gertrude in her room, however, and age was taking its toll.

On April 4, 1917 a certain Mlle. Marie Hannagan presented herself at Mt. Carmel asking admission. Hers was an interesting story, and to confirm it she presented documents from the Archbishop of Paris, Cardinal Mercier of Belgium and the Holy See. She told how as a member of the Religieuses Zelatrices de la Sainte Euchariste, she had left France when in 1905 the French government dispersed the religious orders. Five of the Sisters, she said, opened two houses in Brussels. When the Germans overran Belgium in World War I, the Sisters fled the country, and she took passage for America.

Her case was presented to Archbishop Keane and he sanctione her reception into the Congregation. As might be expected, the newly received Sister M. Reparatrice with so dramatic a background was the center of interest for young and old. She played her part well. Doubtless, too well, for an investigation was shortly under way. This resulted in three letters from as many superiors of Dominican congregations, each of which had dismissed her. Her brother, on learning of her whereabouts, recognized her as his erratic sister Bridget, who had not been out of the country in the previous twenty years. October 25, 1920 saw her on her way to other high adventures. Where she obtained such apparently valid credentials remains a mystery.

On June 13, 1917 Mother Cecilia wrote a confidential letter to superiors asking that they

> Please send me in the enclosed envelope the names of five Sisters more or less, not now in office whom you consider to be spiritual women, exact observers of Rule, but of

sound judgment knowing when to exempt; motherly, kind and thoughtful, impartial, treating all alike, considerate of the Sisters' health, their needs and their feelings, not given to particular friendship, jealousy or suspicion, possessing good common sense together with the ability required to take charge of a Convent and School. If you know none who combine these qualifications, please name the Sisters who according to your judgment approach nearest to doing so. You are not limited to your own House or Province - select from the whole Community.

In August 1917 Mother Cecilia prepared a long and understanding vade mecum for the superiors going into office. We get something of the tone of it from the following:

The spirit of the religious life is the spirit of love; manifest it toward your Sisters. Bear in mind that their subjection is to God, whom you represent. It is voluntary, not forced. Do not cultivate a rigid mannerism. Receive your subjects kindly, and treat them with courtesy at all times. The office of Superior should be associated with refinement of manner, word and act. Never refuse to accept an apology or listen to an explanation. . . .

You hold a Mother's place. You are the only one in your Mission to whom the subjects can turn for help. If their relations with you are shadowed, or you are prejudiced against them, all manner of evil or unhappiness will be the result.

On the following April 26 a letter directed to all the superiors contains a paragraph which gives us pause in view of present day attitudes.

The temporary Professed are not your equals. You will more easily keep them in their place if you prove you are their superior in every sense of the word. If they see in you what they are one day to be, you will be a strong influence in their spiritual life, and the bond of charity, which is "love for one another, " will unite young and old to the Heart of God.

Mother Cecilia appealed to Archbishop Keane on September 23, 1917 for permission to shorten the novitiate of five senior novices by seven weeks and seventeen for five months to meet the demands for teachers which the provincials were facing in the missions under their charge. A year later, with the country in the throes of war, she presented a similar petition and forty senior novices were professed on August 22, shortening the novitiate of ten of them by one month, two by three months and twenty-eight by seven months.

On May 27, 1918 the Congregation appealed to Archbishop Keane to permit no other college for Catholic women to be opened under his jurisdiction until Mt. St. Joseph had become firmly established. That year also Mother Cecilia announced that with proper approbation, the college would be removed from the jurisdiction of a provincial and placed directly under the control of the Mother General, the four provincials to constitute with her a board of trustees.

A letter came to Mother Cecilia from Elizabeth King, president of the National Federation of B. V. M. Alumni, dated March 14, 1917. It announced the decision of the organization to undertake the support of two orphans for a year. Notification having been sent to Cardinal Mundelein, he forwarded the offer to St. Mary Training School in Des Plaines, Illinois.

That year Sister M. Antonia Durkin, prefect of studies, and Clara Russell, chairman of the English department of Mt. St. Joseph College, were commissioned to represent the Congregation at the annual convention of the National Catholic Education Association in Buffalo, New York. At a later council meeting they reported on significant trends as they had noted them in secondary and collegiate departments.

On July 11, 1919 Father Jennings, pastor of Presentation Parish, Chicago, wrote Mother Cecilia offering to help provide a vacation site for the Sisters. The response sent in Mother Cecilia's name said that she would send Sisters to inspect the property which he suggested at Crystal Lake, Illinois. Unfortunately the matter seems to have progressed no further.

The fall of 1917 witnessed the opening of St. Joseph School in New Hampton, Iowa, situated not far from the small town of Waucoma in which the Sisters were already established. The Sisters of St. Francis from Clinton, Iowa had just been withdrawn from the parish of which Father Carey, [7] brother of Sister M. Salvator, B. V. M., was pastor. Seven Sisters went to occupy the former rectory, [8] the pastor having moved into his new residence shortly before. Coming as teachers were Sisters M. Bernardino Gorman, superior, Malachy Geraghty, Edwarda Maher, Thoma and Naola Brennan and Amandus Flynn, with Sister M. Germanus Heiberger as housekeeper.

Many items in the convent were rejects when the new rectory

was furnished. The cracked and crazed dishes were especially disreputable. Matters of the kind came to the attention of officials at Mt. Carmel through newsy letters to Sister-friends, and two Sisters were promptly dispatched to New Hampton for a first hand survey of the situation. They wasted no time in replacing the most unsuitable items of convent furnishings.

When Mother Cecilia made her visitation of the mission, she was sufficiently impressed by the remoteness of the situations of Waucoma, Cresco and New Hampton that she gave permission for the Sisters to exchange visits from time to time. However, she seems not to have been her own master, for on her return to the motherhouse she was obliged to write the Sisters withdrawing the permission. [9]

The city of Butte, Montana was experiencing rapid growth, and the Flats were filling up with residences. The increased population called for more parishes and new schools. These were opened in 1918 at St. Ann's with Sisters M. Liberata Chambers, Robertus Sutton and Viatora O'Malley as staff and the Reverend F. X. Leshner, pastor. That at St. John's brought Sisters M. Joannes Kelly, Roderick Burke and Zoella Murphy. The pastor there was the Reverend P. J. Crawley. The several Butte schools have now merged, though the Sisters now teaching in Butte live in St. Ann's Convent.

Archbishop Mundelein had seen in the success of St. Mary High School a possible pattern of such schools strategically located throughout the city. The existence of thriving elementary schools under the direction of the B. V. M. Sisters at Our Lady of Lourdes, St. Vincent's, Annunciation, and Holy Name, and the prospects for further growth at St. Thomas of Canterbury suggested to him the wisdom of assigning the North Side to them for the location of a second central high school for girls. The burden of debt resting on the Congregation led Mother Cecilia to tentatively refuse the assignment, while she requested that the prospect be left open for a time. In a letter dated May 23, 1917 the Archbishop indicated that "the Community deserves special consideration in the diocese," and that he would be glad to give the time for her to think the proposition over. The North Side, he suggested, had special claims on the B. V. M.'s because of their several elementary schools in that area. He would make no offer to other Congregations, preferring to give the Sisters the time they needed to weigh the matter. [10]

Not until the election of Mother M. Isabella Kane in late 1919, after the death of Mother Cecilia, did the plan go forward with the purchase of the Greenlee mansion at Irving Park and the Lake. The story of the school's inauguration and building under Sister M. Justitia Coffey in 1921 and 1922, and its many years of successful operation await a future chronicler, its entire history lying beyond the scope of this book.

Few details remain to us of the cooperation the Sisters gave the war effort aside from a booklet indicating the participation of the students in patriotic programs, the sale of bonds and thrift stamps, Junior Red Cross activities, knitting, the rolling of bandages, etc. However, a letter of Mother Gertrude's in response to one from Sister M. Salvator Carey, who was then superior of St. Ambrose, DesMoines, has survived. It was doubtless the boys at Fort DesMoines that Sister was befriending. Mother had shared Sister's letter with Sister M. Annunciata Durkin, superior of the motherhouse, hoping that the Sisters there could "do something for the poor soldiers, since the Sisters at DesMoines were working every spare moment for them and any reading matter they can get goes out to them. " The letter reads:

It seems too bad the altar linens should be so black for the holy sacrifice. It was a charity for you to have sent some clean ones. I'm sure they had a welcome for the organ you begged for them. I am very sorry for your nephew to be obliged to leave the younger members for the war. God will take care of them since he obeys orders to help. We are all praying for peace. May it be God's will that it may soon be restored to the entire world.

A letter went to the Sisters urging them to refrain from any least complaint of wartime regulations, and to pray earnestly for peace.

The influenza scourge which struck the county in 1918, resulting in thousands of deaths in army camps and elsewhere, and especially among young mothers and the elderly, providentially left Mt. Carmel untouched. There were but remarkably few deaths among the Sisters in the various missions, though many took advantage of the closed schools to care for the sick and the dying. We catch echoes of the situation in Mother Cecilia's correspondence. On October 16, 1918 she wrote that she was "influenza bound, " not daring to continue her visitations lest she bring the flu to her large household at Mt. Carmel. However, she added: "Dr. Lenihan died last night, his cousin last week and his sister has been taken to the hospital - influenza. " Her letter begged for prayers and adoration for the preservation of all. On the 18th her letter to a Sister, probably in California, read:

We have an awful time through Iowa fighting the "Flu" - Spanish influenza. Have you got it there? May God protect us from it! The churches and schools are all closed and people dying by wholesale, especially priests and doctors - grand men. I dare not travel now.

Mother Cecilia's days were drawing to a close. Her letters tell the story, as they indicate also the warmth of her relations with her Sisters. Recovering from a serious illness resulting from digestive disorders, she wrote on September 2, 1916 to Sister M. Basil Healy, then in California.

. . . I am myself again, only my poor legs are quite wobbly yet. But I hope to go to the coast in August, God willing. I'm beginning to eat again. What do you think of that! Mother Gertrude is much better too.

As early as November 14, 1910 she had written the Sisters asking prayers to St. Lucy for the improvement of the failing vision in her clear blue eyes, her most distinctive feature. She wore then the thick glasses prescribed for her by Dr. Schneider of Milwaukee whom she visited regularly. At that early date she had found it necessary to have others read her mail and answer it for her.

On April 17, 1917 Mother remarked in a letter to Sister M. Realmo,[11] still a patient at the Loyola in Boulder,[12] that her "eyes are almost sightless. " She mentioned having sent Mother Ascension and Sister M. Esther in her place to the bedside of Sister M. Octavia Burke, then dyi ng of pneumonia. On January 14, 1918 she responded to Sister M. Realmo's complaint of having received no recent word of her. The letter read:

If you understood conditions here - and my years - 80 - and my half-blind eyes and my visitations and the work that accumulates in my absence and must be done by myself, I don't think you would blame me. . . . My letter-writing days have passed. I don't know when I wrote a letter to anyone. My writing consists in business scratches, generally on cards with indelible pencil.

The Reverend Arthur M. Clark, the Sisters' chaplain, was named domestic prelate by His Holiness, Benedict XV, on April 19, 1917. He had been in failing health for some time, and the doctor had warned him that death might come suddenly. It came on Sunday evening, December 8, 1918, as Monsignor Clark entered the sacristy to vest for Benediction. Fortunately three of the college priests were with him - Dr. Thier, Father Craney and Father Schulte - when he was stricken.

Mother Cecilia, in a letter to "My loved Lumie" /‾Sister M. Lumina Farrell7, wrote:

> You know our saintly old cranky Rev. Father has left
> us for his Heavenly Home. His death was beautiful - in the
> sacristy where three priests /were7 vesting him and them-
> selves for Solemn Benediction - we all waiting after supper -
> when down he dropped on the floor of the sacristy. They
> laid him down, his head nearly in the sanctuary - and there
> he died - all in about 7 minutes. We had him two nights -
> one in his own house and one in our own chapel - and one
> in the Cathedral. Solemn High Mass by the College Boys -
> 700 soldiers. 13

His obituary in the next issue of Our Herald reads in part:

> Monsignor Clark was born in Framingham, Massachusetts
> on August 3, 1853. He belonged to a non-Catholic family,
> and in May, 1882, he was ordained an Episcopal minister
> and assigned to the Church of the Advent in Boston. On
> December 5, 1882 he received the grace of the Catholic
> faith and made his submission to the Church. In 1885 he
> was ordained to the priesthood by the Most Rev. M. A.
> Corrigan, Archbishop of New York. The next fourteen
> years were spent in the mission field as a member of
> the Congregation of St. Paul. Finally, his health could
> no longer withstand the continual strain and he sought
> work that would be less strenuous. He obtained from his
> friend, Most Rev. John J. Keane, Archbishop of Dubuque,
> the appointment of chaplain at Mount Carmel where he
> remained for eighteen years.

In accordance with his last wishes after a funeral Mass at the Cathedral, Monsignor Clark was buried in Mount Olivet Cemetery, Dubuque.

By 1918 the malignancy from which Mother Gertrude was suffering was slowly taking over. Early in the spring of 1919 this led to emergency surgery. Sister M. Frances Rose Urbanowski, a trained nurse newly received, was assigned to Mother's care. After the operation she was wholly confined to her room, this time in the infirmary, where death claimed her on July 10, 1919. With her passing the Congregation's last tie with its origins in Philadelphia was broken. Archbishop Keane preached at her funeral Mass to a large assemblage of priests and Sisters. In it he reviewed the history of the Congregation in which Mother Gertrude had played so conspicuous a part. The body of the Congregation's second Mother General was laid to rest close by the mausoleum which held the remains of Father Donaghoe and the first five, whom she had known so well.

Mother Cecilia was in poor health from the first of the year 1919. Writing on January 13 to Sister M. Realmo, then superior at St. Mary's, Sioux City, she thanked her for her "lovely letter which raised my heart." She spoke of herself as "low down these days. So much trouble for want to help - teachers and housekeepers. Do you have any trouble in Sioux City about teachers' certificates? We are worried to death over them. We have started out in the novitiate to get at least county certificates next summer. . . . "

Mother Ascension was filling many gaps at the time, presiding at council meetings and keeping in touch with the Sisters as necessary. She wrote them on February 10 that Mother Cecilia had been ill for sometime, "suffering from intestinal trouble such as caused so much anxiety two years ago. While Mother seems to be improving slowly and there is no immediate danger, still her condition is somewhat serious." She urged the Sisters for prayers.

By April Mother Cecilia was able to be moved to the College for convalescence. As the spring came on she spent long hours in her wheel chair "on the beautiful lawn at Mt. St. Joseph in the scorching sun." On her return to the motherhouse in mid-July she was established in the large, airy "St. Mary's," close to the chapel where the Sisters could visit her frequently. A series of strokes accompanying a vascular condition heralded the nearness of death. Her doctor, a sufferer from alcoholism who had long felt the support of her confidence, knelt beside her dying bed to receive her blessing, then, leaning his head on the fireplace mantel, he wept like a child.[14]

It was the evening of Sunday, September 7, 1919 and, as had become their custom, the novices were gathered under Mother's window singing the hymns she loved best, among them her favorite, "O Mary, my Mother." The Sisters were gathered around her bed to recite with the chaplain[15] the prayers for the dying. Death came quietly as the sun went down. It was the eve of the feast kept in honor of the nativity of the Blessed Virgin.

Mother's remains in a simple black casket lay in the motherhouse library where the murmur of the rosary sounded night and day until her funeral Mass on Thursday morning. Into the chapel, hung with the papal colors, the procession moved, led by more than sixty vested priests. Following were Monsignors Hoban and Fitzsimmons of Chicago, Flavin of DesMoines, McLaughlin of Clinton and Heer of Dubuque. The Very Reverend presidents of Loyola and DePaul Universities, John B. Fury, S.J., and D. J. McHugh, C.M., with Father William B. Rogers, S.J., of Gesu, Milwaukee, later president of Saint Louis University. Bishops Lenihan of Great Falls, Montana and Edmund Heelan of Sioux City, in full vestments, preceded the principal celebrant, Archbishop Keane. Six priests served as pallbearers. The pews were filled to overflowing with representatives from many congregations of religious women, and four hundred professed Sisters. The priests' choir from Dubuque College sang the Mass at which the Archbishop spoke - of those qualities which had won the respectful love of so many. Interment was beside the mausoleum in which reposed the Congregation's founding members.

As vicar for the mother-general, Mother Ascension called an extraordinary chapter for the election of a new superior for the Congregation. It met November 15, 1919, choosing Sister Mary Isabella Kane, then provincial of the Sacred Heart Province.[16] The councillors chosen were Mother Mary Ascension Lilly and Sisters M. Bertrand Foley, Basil Healy and Editha Flanagan. Sisters M. Crescentia Markey, Urban Bermingham and Angela Fitzgerald retained their respective positions. A firm hand was now at the helm, an organizer and a builder.

The council minutes of February 2, 1913 speak of a plan proposed by Sister M. Isabella Kane, then superior of the Immaculate Conception Academy in Davenport, for the sale of that property and the purchase of a more suitable site for the school'

location. No action was taken at that time. When Sister was
named a provincial in 1915 she was succeeded at the academy
by Sister M. Ignatia Pyne, who was of somewhat the same mind.
The plan rested until the death of Mother Cecilia in 1919; Sister M. Isabella was chosen as superior-general. With the consent of her council she then offered the property to the Palmer
School of Chiropractic, situated just to the rear of the grounds,
for $225, 000. 00, and the sale was contracted for.17 However
when Palmer could not arrange for the necessary loan, he had to
withdraw from the purchase. (After the opening of the co-insti-
tutional Assumption High School, the property remained idle for
a couple of year, the Congregation finally accepting an offer of
$38, 000. 00 from the Palmer School of Chiropractic.)

Meanwhile Bishop James Davis of Davenport and the pastors
of the city anxious lest the Catholic girls of the city be denied
the services of the Sisters met with Mother Isabella and other
official members, pledging financial assistance for their building at a new site. No steps could be taken, however, for the
purchase of the site or contracting for the proposed building
until sale of the original property was assured. Negotiations
with the Lend-a-Hand Club, a philanthropic organization of
women, were next under way. The club joined with the Y. W. C. A. ,
and the purchase was arranged for. Again the sales contract
failed to materialize, for the banks held back on a loan, and
the Sisters were left with the property. The effort to sell had
cost the Sisters the 2 1/2% commission, amounting to $5, 625. 00,
paid to the real estate agent, Thomas Dougherty, for his services.

It i s probable that Mother Isabella never knew the source of
the opposition that blocked each sale. Certainly there was opposition enough in the ranks of the Congregation, for many of
the Sisters had strong ties of affection for a school which was
so closely associated with the Congregation's early history.
However, the effective force came from the outside - from
friends and patrons of the academy under the leadership of Dr.
Glynn, brother of Sister M. Xavierita Glynn of Davenport. It
was they who put the necessary pressure on the banks to withhold the loans and thus obstruct both attempts of a sale.

Mother Mary Isabella (Mary) Kane was the youngest of six
children and the family's only girl. Born in County Clare, Ireland on November 15, 1855, at the age of ten she came with
her widowed mother and brothers to this country, settling in
Chicago. There her first teachers were the Religious of the
Sacred Heart who, in addition to their boarding academy on

Taylor Street, conducted a school for the children of the Holy
Family Parish. When the B. V. M. Sisters came to Chicago in
1867 she enrolled in the small St. Stanislaus School opened
that September. Eventually St. Stanislaus became the nucleus
of the Sacred Heart Parish. From there Mary entered the Congregation on May 25, 1870 at the age of fourteen. Primarily a
music teacher, Sister taught voice, piano, violin, organ and
harp, and conducted classes in art as well. Sister studied music
for a time at the New York conservatory of Madame Marchesi.
She taught for some years at Wichita Academy, and for eighteen
years served as instructor of both art and music and as superior
at the parish girls' school, Lourdes Academy, in Burlington,
Iowa. Sister was superior at the Immaculate Conception Academy,
Davenport when she was named the first provincial of the Sacred
Heart Province, with headquarters at St. Mary's, Chicago.

Elected superior general in November 1919, Mother Isabella's
work stretched much beyond the confines of this volume. However
a brief survey of her subsequent career seems warranted. Her
first major enterprise was the building and staffing of the Immaculata, a central high school for girls on Chicago's north side.
In her selection of Barry Byrne[18] of the Frank Lloyd Wright
school of architecture for the planning of the Immaculata, she
was pointing the way for his work in the construction of Mary
Frances Clarke residence hall at Clarke College and for Holy
Angels High School, Milwaukee, both completed during her
twelve years in office. To these she added the remodeling of St.
Mary High School and additions to Mt. Carmel Academy, Wichita,
and Mt. St. Gertrude Academy, Boulder. She was responsible
also for the artistic renovation of the motherhouse chapel.

Mother Isabella's major accomplishment, however, was the
erection of Mundelein College for Women, opened in 1930. At
the time Cardinal Mundelein approached Mother with the request that she undertake that project, she had been for some
time in negotiation with Marquette University regarding the
planned opening of a women's college in affiliation with the university. The college he proposed was intended to be a unit in
a great midwestern university, its crowning institution a school
of theology, the "queen of the sciences."[19] Cardinal Mundelein's
proposal to Mother Isabella was for a day college for young
women of modest circumstances and as such easily available
from other parts of the city.

Mother Isabella's first move was the purchase of the beautiful Wheeler[20] residence at Sheridan Road and the Lake. Plans
for the present fourteen story structure were quickly under way,
Mother's own artistic ability directing both the major features

of the structure itself and of its interior ornamentation. Construction began in 1929 under the direction of Sister M. Justitia Coffey.

Financing the undertaking and providing faculty called for heroic measures, for financially it could not have been less timely. The crash of the stock market in the course of its construction, and the great depression which shadowed its formative years taxed Mother Isabella's faith and the Congregation's resources to the utmost. Though its close neighbor, Loyola University, cooperated generously with the struggling venture, there was no plan for affiliation.

In addition to these major projects, the Congregation added twenty-one new missions in the course of Mother Isabella's twelve-year superiorship. To meet the immediate educational needs of the large groups of young women entering the Congregation, Mother established a junior college at Mt. Carmel in affiliation with Clarke College.

In recognition of Mother Isabella's success as an organizer and administrator, Loyola University awarded her the honorary degree of Doctor of Laws, a signal honor for a woman at the time. [21]

It was indeed a strenuous life for a woman of her years. Mother enjoyed but a brief retirement, dying on October 29, 1935 at Mt. Carmel after a four-day struggle with pneumonia. She was eighty years of age at the time of her death. Monsignor Thomas Conry, president of Loras College, wrote of her:

Few women of this generation have done so much to advance the cause of religion as did this great daughter of charity. For your Congregation and for all of us her memory will remain a hallowed inspiration.

Samuel Knox Wilson, S. J., professor of history at Loyola University, delivered her funeral sermon. After suggesting the range of her labors and her virtues, he singled out for special stress the spirit of generosity by which she gave her all for the Congregation she had been chosen to serve.

Notes

1 The term "councillor" was first used by this chapter, replacing the earlier "consultor. "

2 Sister M. Columba had shown promise as an educational leader when in 1911 she had asked and been granted an opportunity to try out her pedagogical theories with primary classes. She had received an A. B. degree from the Catholic University in 1912, and through summer study in 1914, 1915, 1917 and 1918 received a Master's degree in 1920 also from Catholic University.

3 Other members of the household were: Sisters M. of the Rosary Kirby, Francis Borgia McLaughlin, Leola Oliver, Eugene McNulty and Annunciation Leyden.

4 Other members of the staff were Sisters M. Laurentia Donahoe, Francis Clare Golinvaux, Agnes Clare Carroll, Callistus Schulte and Noelite Corrigan.

5 The Sisters who first staffed St. Paul's were: Rosina Harrigan, Amanda Graney, Wilhelmine Derry, Enda Snow, Regiola Maher, Camilla McLaughlin, Nazaretta Madden, Rembert Salz, Gasper Maguire, Rose of Lima Kelly, Cunegunda Gayman, Sarita O'Sullivan, Catherine Braniff, Placidia Sweeney and Basil Healy.

6 Sister M. St. Philip Peacock, B. V. M.

7 Father Carey's sister Kate kept house for her brother. When Kate needed surgery, Sister M. Salvator, superior at Tigard, Oregon was exchanged with Sister M. Clarissa Sullivan, then at New Hampton.

8 The pattern by which a pastor built a new rectory and assigned the old to the several Sisters who staffed his school was far from unique. There was the Chicago pastor who, having found his rectory inadequate for himself and his assistant, built a new one and turned the old over to the thirteen Sisters who staffed his school.

9 Details provided by Sister M. Edwarda Maher.

10 It had been the hope of the council that such a school would serve the Sisters for retreats and summer study, a service which

it was to perform in a manner somewhat less than ideal, for those who made those first retreats have long memories of a gym equipped with army cots and orange crates, with only the shadows of the night providing privacy. At a later stage an army cot in the front of a classroom afforded refuge from the crowds that assembled for the eight days of spiritual renewal.

11 One of the problems faced in the matter of personal correspondence in this work has been its imbalance. Only that remains which was carefully preserved by the recipient, and then only if it was returned to the archives. There is almost a complete dearth of such correspondence for Mother Ascension, and that which has been preserved for both Mother Gertrude and Mother Cecilia is relatively meager.

12 Sister M. Realmo had recovered her health when by September 1917 her provincial, Sister M. Adora Caverly, took her to Kansas City where she returned to classroom duty. She seems never to have suffered a relapse, and was destined to spend a number of years as the Congregation's treasurer general.

13 Members of the Reserve Officers Training Corps being trained at the College.

14 Account by Mother's nurse, Sister M. Frances Rose Urbanowski.

15 Dr. Thier of Dubuque College.

16 Sister M. Hilary Regan was chosen by the new council to take Mother Isabella's place as provincial of the Sacred Heart Province.

17 The council minutes of December 12, 1919 indicate that the Sisters were borrowing $250,000 for the erection of a new building at Mt. St. Joseph, $50,000 for Our Lady of Angels Academy, Clinton, $75,000 for Holy Angels Academy, Milwaukee, and $75,000 for Mt. St. Gertrude. The possibility of an entirely new plant in Davenport was certainly a gamble considering the other financial needs.

18 Brother of Sister M. Ursulita Byrne, B.V.M.

19 While the colleges and subsidiary universities arose according to his plan, as did the magnificently conceived St. Mary

of the Lake Seminary in Area - now Mundelein, Illinois - the fusion under one great master plan was never realized.

20 The residence of Italian marble was constructed by Albert G. Wheeler who died shortly after its completion. Its second owner was Albert M. Johnson, from whom the Congregation purchased it.

21 For the above details, see the study by the former Sister M. Aquin Lally, B. V. M. , published in the BVM Vista of September 1959, entitled "Woman of Decision. "

Mt. Carmel Chapel, on a Reception and Profession day after the Redecoration by Mother Isabella. August 15, probably 1925

RESPICE - PROSPICE

"There is no point to newness for the sake of newness, but there is point to newness for the sake of
recapturing old things that have gotten lost. "
                                        Robert McAfee Brown

It has been our effort to capture again that which was significant in the old - the spirit and the vision of Mary Frances
Clarke, and of those who shared her love, her labors and her
dedicated service. That those who followed were women of
lesser stature, with preoccupations in building and expansion,
more deeply engrossed in the practicalities, is not to be wondered at. They faced great and pressing problems. Though
they shared in Mother Clarke's vocation and her charism, the
radiance of the vision had dimmed through the complexities of
a changing world, and dimly they passed it on.

Relics of a narrow asceticism early imposed on our Sisters
still clung. These were reinforced by the codification in 1918
of anachronistic laws governing the religious life of women,
resulting in a sterile legalism which militated against the
human spirit. The necessity for meeting ever-growing demands
in a changing milieu, while encased in the mold of days long
gone, had brought our Sisters to the point at which the Church
too found herself - the point of renewal or decline.

The liberating enactments of the Council have brought us
into harmony with the needs and realities of the apostolic life.
They have rekindled the religious spirit, placing love above
law, with the center of that love the living Christ.

In freedom of spirit, armed with the experience of past years,
with a broadened vision and deepened insights, we seek a return to the original inspiration which brought our Congregation
into being, the revitalizing of all that was good in the old, the
enrichment of it with the insights of the new.

It is ours now to move into the future with that same intrepid
spirit that brought Mother Clarke across the stormy sea in an
unseaworthy vessel, and out to an untamed wilderness; with the
spirit that reclaimed the community of women she had founded,
after thirty-six years of alienation from her guidance, and, with
them, penetrated the future, and planned a Congregation prepared in mind and heart for all that future held.

We are heirs of a pioneering spirit, the spirit of courage to
meet new needs strengthened through prayer and simple living.
In that spirit let us move into the future with firm step and

assured trust. Not newness for newness' sake, but newness for God's sake, and for the sake of the service to which He is calling us.

THE B. V. M. S' RESPONSE TO OPPORTUNITIES FOR
HIGHER EDUCATION

(For the sake of unity, the following study is disengaged from the chronological account of the Congregation's history.)

In reviewing the possibilities that had been opened up to the Sisters for higher education in Catholic universities and the response made by the B. V. M. Congregation, we turn first to Marquette University as leader in that movement. While the direction initially taken by the Congregation was to assign just the secondary and college teachers to university study, the availability of Marquette to the Sisters at Holy Rosary and Gesu, elementary schools in Milwaukee, as well as to those at Holy Angels Academy, may have led to their enrollment also. As with other schools in a time of rapid change, the keeping of records was an art yet to be developed. Apparently the only remaining source of data regarding the early enrollments of the Sisters at Marquette is the "Register of Alumni" in the Marquette Bulletin, covering the years 1890-1918, among the materials provided by the University archivist, the Reverend Robert Callen, S. J. Even that has its limitations, for it lists the Sisters without either their family names or the Congregations to which they belonged. Matching religious with family names of B. V. M. secondary teachers, we venture to list the following as having received the A. B. degree at Marquette University during the years 1914-1918.

S. M.	Angelita Stackhouse	1915
	Benedicta Prendergast	1918
	Bertranda Wenninger	1915
	Clotilde Williams	1916
	Constantia O'Leary	1916
	Consuela Martin	1918
	Eutropia Flannery	1916
	Florence Clowry	1918
	Helene Hargett	1915
	Immaculata McCann	1918
	Julius Shanley	1916
	Madeline Shanley	1915
	Miriam Russell	1918
	Pulcheria McGuire	1914
	Realmo Sullivan	1916
	Ricarda Ryan	1915
	Remi Harrington	1914

S. M.	Seraphica Nagle	1918
	St. Helen Donahue	1916
	Tarasius Kehoe	1918
	Veronica O'Neil	1915
	Vincentius Collins	1915

Sister M. Remi Harrington received a B. S. degree in 1913.

While DePaul University, Chicago, in inaugurating its summer sessions and extension courses for women in 1911 aimed primarily at teachers in the public school system, the enrollment of religious women was large from their beginnings. Records are limited here also. However, the College of Liberal Arts, in its catalog of 1918, included a listing of those enrolled during the years 1911-1917. Though this list does not include religious affiliation, it does indicate the schools from which the Sisters came. It is thus possible to identify sixty-one B. V. M. Sisters among them - fourteen from St. Mary's, four from DePaul High School for Girls and three from Holy Name High School. Fifteen of the Sisters teaching at St. Vincent's and twelve from other elementary schools in Chicago, as well as twelve from missions outside Chicago, were in attendance. A. B. degrees were conferred on the following B. V. M. Sisters during those years: Sisters M. Clemenza Leahey, 1912, Lambertina Doran, 1913, and Sisters M. Adolina Walsh, Edna Lynch and Roberta and Tertulla Reynolds in 1917. In addition the Master's and Doctoral degrees were conferred on Sister M. Lambertina[1] doubtless giving consideration to her two published works. Sister was to loom large in Father McCabe's continued efforts to establish a college for women in affiliation with DePaul University. [2]

The story of DePaul University's efforts to provide for the educational needs of women is a long one, involving the B. V. M. Congregation through the years 1911-1917. We have presented Mother Cecilia's letters regarding the plan for instituting a women's college in 1911. The New World published on October 7, 1911[3] under the heading "A Great and Good Undertaking, " a letter of Archbishop J. E. Quigley addressed to 'Rev. Mother Superioress, Sisters of Charity, Chicago. " The editor commented on the need of such an institution as follows:

The Catholic young women today must receive their academic and qualified training in Chicago in either the University of Chicago or the Northwestern University in Evanston, and this at great danger to their Catholic faith. . . .

The Archbishop's letter, dated September 26, 1911, reads:

> Rev. dear Mother:
> I have heard with satisfaction that the Sisters of
> Charity are preparing to establish a college for women
> in the city of Chicago. An institution of this kind is
> greatly needed in Chicago, as there are many Catholic
> women following university courses with a view of ob-
> taining degrees in non-Catholic colleges and universities.
> The work therefore has my entire sympathy and full-
> est approbation. This work needs only to be mentioned
> to our Catholic people to be appreciated and supported.
> I feel confident that many Catholics of our great city,
> and particularly the Catholic societies of women, will
> give it encouragement and financial support.
> Wishing God's blessing on this undertaking. . . .

We have seen that another Archbishop, that of Dubuque,
viewed the matter in a different light and the Sisters were
obliged to withdraw from the project. However, the Very
Reverend F. X. McCabe, president of the University, was
willing to bide his time.

The death of Archbishop Quigley in Buffalo, New York on
July 10, 1915 brought a change of climate toward any such
undertaking in Chicago. Archbishop George Mundelein was
named as Quigley's successor on December 9 of that same year.
His correspondence with Mother Cecilia in 1916 in regard to
the establishment of a women's college in Chicago was mild
enough, expressing regret that Mother found such a venture
beyond her resources. It was his hope that a benefactor might
be found to make the project a possibility.

The purchase by the University of the Doyle apartment building at 2242-44 Osgood in early 1917 as a site for a women's college seems to have changed Mother Cecilia's stand, and the
April 17, 1917 issue of the DePaul Minerval announced the September opening of the "Jeanne d'Arc College for Women" under
the direction of the Sisters of Charity, B. V. M. The Archbishop,
making his visitation of the parish shortly after the announcement "had some choice words for Father McCabe when McCabe
persisted in his endeavors"[4] to open the college.

With those "choice words" hopes for the "Jeanne d'Arc
College" met their death. The apartment building was given
over to high school classes. The St. Vincent High School[5],
previously under the same principal as the elementary grades,
was now renamed the DePaul High School for Girls and placed

under the charge of Sister M. Lambertina whom Father McCabe had intended to head the proposed college. It was to the school's alumnae that Father McCabe appealed when his hopes for Jeanne d'Arc College were high. In an undated letter he made a plea for a personal contribution of $25.00 toward the college fund to be pledged as a means of paying a debt of gratitude to their former teachers whose Congregation would conduct the college. [6]

Even in the face of the Archbishop's apparent displeasure, Father McCabe made one more effort on behalf of the higher education of women. On September 14, 1917, on the wish of his provincial, Father Finney, C. M. , that he take no step "without consulting Your Grace, " he addressed a plea that the many young women applicants for entrance to the College of Liberal Arts and Sciences be permitted to enroll. He reminded the Archbishop that Catholic high schools in the city had become coeducational without apparent harm, and that the classes of women would be largely conducted in the separate Lyceum building. The response of the Archbishop, dated September 25, however, left no doubt of his position in the matter. It follows:

> My dear Father McCabe:
> I have gone rather carefully into the contents of your letter of the 14th inst, and asked advice of those who are competent to give it and likewise of those who may have some claim in this matter, and, as a result I wish to re-affirm again the decision that I gave you before, which is in accordance with the instructions given you by the Very Rev. Father Finney, your Provincial, to the effect that I do not desire DePaul University to accept any young women as students in your College of Liberal Arts and Sciences.
> You will readily understand that I have given this matter quite some thought and that this comes to you not in the form of a snap judgment and that the decision is therefore final. Wishing you and your Fathers every success in your work, I beg to remain, dear Father McCabe. . . . [7]

As for the high school, classes did not long remain in the apartment building for it failed to meet the city's code for schools. A move of classes into the Lyceum was made by Sister M. Leandre Swift who succeeded Sister M. Lambertina after just a year. The school was closed in 1922 with the opening of the newly constructed Immaculata High School at Irving Park and the Lake. The Lyceum was then turned over to the boys' academy.

The Jesuit Fathers from St. Ignatius College on Chicago's
west side began a series of lectures for the Sisters and public
school teachers at St. Mary High School in 1911. The first
course appearing in their catalog, however, consisted of forty
lessons entitled "The Scientific Study of Religion." It was conducted by the Reverend Charles Coppens, S. J., and the Reverend John M. Lyons, S. J., [8] in the school year 1913-1914. The
enrollment included twenty-nine B. V. M.'s, two Sisters of St.
Dominic and two Sisters of Mercy, together with twenty-nine
others, doubtless public school teachers. Among those enrolled
there appear familiar personalities, Sisters M. Josita Baschnagle, Justitia Coffey, Hilary O'Regan and Pulcheria McGuire.

From that time until the early thirties extension courses had
an acknowledged place in the Jesuit's teaching schedule, with
later centers at Xavier High School on the South Side, Immacula
on the North, and Maria Immaculata in Wilmette, as well as
courses at the various Catholic hospitals. [9] A charge of $6.00
was made for each course.

The roll of lecturers for the extension courses through the
years 1917-1920 included nine Jesuits, four laymen and seven
lay women. Jesuit lecturers were: Fathers Claude J. Pernin,
English literature; Charles Coppens, history of philosophy;
Joseph C. Flynn, American literature; William H. Agnew,
ethics; George W. Mahowald, psychology; Samuel Knox Wilson,
American history; Aloysius S. McCormick, logic; Frederick
Siedenburg, sociology; and Francis Gerst, mathematics. Of
these none was more popular than Father Claude Pernin, a
superb teacher, with Father Wilson high among favorites.

Loyola University was still very young at the time. The Reverend Henry Dumbach, president of St. Ignatius College, moved
in the direction of its establishment in 1906 with the purchase
of a large tract of land in Rogers Park on the lake, eight miles
north of the Loop. An academy and Jesuit residence were soon
in the process, with the construction of Dumbach Hall in 1908
and Cudahy Hall in 1910. [10] By 1909 the acquisition of a pro-
prietary medical school and the opening of departments of law
and pharmacy, together with the long established St. Ignatius
College of Arts and Sciences constituted it a university.

The Reverend Frederick Siedenburg, S. J., returned from
study in Europe with the innovative idea of opening a school
of sociology to be eventually incorporated into the University.
St. Ignatius had already been accredited by both the State of
Illinois and the North Central Association of Schools and Colleges. Affiliating his school with the College, he was readily
able to secure accreditation. The training of social workers

could not be limited to men, but introducing women onto the campus of either the College or the University was out of the question as coeducation had no place in the educational philosophy of the Society. Father Siedenburg solved that problem in 1913 by the rental of space in an antiquated building in the Ashland Block at the corner of Randolph and Clark Streets, [11] and this became Loyola's first downtown school. (The Very Reverend John L. Mathery, S. J., president of the University, 1909-1915, was succeeded by the Reverend John B. Fury, S. J., who served 1915-1921.)

But the most pressing need of the day was the higher education of women for the teaching profession. Realizing this, the resourceful priest, under the umbrella of sociology, opened in 1913-1914, by way of summer school and evening and Saturday classes, a full panoply of college and normal courses. The enrollment listed for 1917 included 317 Sisters out of a total of 579 students, with a few men among them. The entire list included sixty B. V. M. 's, among them the familiar names of Sisters M. Lambertina Doran, Raphaella Talmadge, Clemenza Leahey, Josita Baschnagle, Edmundine Mahoney, Eileen Curran, Hilary Regan, and St. Victor Lesner.

Among those receiving bachelor's degrees in 1916 were Sisters M. Emerentia McHugh, St. Genevieve Nash and Azaria Flynn. Many others were to follow. The opening of the Correspondence Study Division of Loyola University in 1921 extended the services available to the Sisters. [12]

When Creighton University of Omaha faced the problem of education of women, it was ready for the challenge. Established as a boys' school in 1878 and endowed by the wealthy financiers, Edward and John Creighton, it attained to the status of a college in 1888. By 1913 it was solidly established as a university. As soon as assurance had come from the Jesuit Father General, Francis X. Wernz, in Rome, permitting the teaching of women, "even nuns," Father William H. Grace, S. J., president, set about arranging for the University's first summer session, to be conducted in 1913 chiefly for the benefit of teachers. Since there were no living quarters at the University for women before 1918, efforts were made to provide for the Sisters in local convents and academies. [13] Tuition for the six weeks was at the remarkably low rate of $15.00, with "special rates to religious communities sending five or more students to the session." In 1918 the University provided housing for a limited number of religious, while the 1919-1920 Summer Bulletin stated that:

Through the kindness of Archbishop Harty, O'Connor Hall will be available for the use of out of town Sisters who come for the Summer Session. The hall is located a block from the Arts College, and is equipped with every modern convenience. The charge for room and board will be $6.00 per week.

Lectures were given from eight until noon, Monday through Saturday. A wide range of courses was offered - in methods, pedagogy, Christian doctrine, philosophy, mathematics, science, history and languages. Afternoon lectures on professional subjects and a series of sixteen educational moving pictures enriched the summer's program.

By the opening of its second summer session, Creighton was authorized to grant teacher's certificates on the same basis as the University of Nebraska. In this respect Creighton stood alone among Catholic universities. Two years of college work with twenty hours of professional courses gave title to a state certificate.

However, the B. V. M. Sisters did not enroll at Creighton until the summer of 1915 when five were assigned there for summer work. By this time the Very Reverend Eugene A. Magerney, S. J., had been named president, and the long-remembered Reverend William P. Whelan, S. J., supervisor of professional colleges. [14] Those who came were Sisters M. Edwardine Tierney and Osmund Whalen from Lincoln, Nebraska and Sisters M. Emerita Fahey, Noella Flynn and Rosaline Cash from Council Bluffs. Sisters M. Noella, Osmund and Rosaline returned the following year, together with Sister M. Ethelreda Bracken from Marcus, to whom the A. B. degree was awarded in 1917. None were present at the summer session of 1917. The six who came in 1918 included Sisters M. Alberic Duane from Boulder, Cecilian Gannon, Lincoln, Clotilde Williams, Dubuque and Ermine McCarthy, Council Bluffs.

The summer of 1919 witnessed a great influx of B. V. M. 's, seventy-five in all. Forty of these merited certificates of various levels by the summer's end. Listed as post graduate students that summer were Sisters M. Benedicta Prendergast, Consuela Martin, St. Helen Donahue, Julius Shanley, Lambertina Doran and Richard Bordeaux.

The B. V. M. enrollment dropped to fifty the next year and forty-eight in 1921. Degrees granted in 1920 included the Master's to Sister M. Clotilde Williams, B. V. M. The 1921 graduating class included Sisters M. Bertille English, Richard Bordeaux and Xavier McNeill who received Master's degrees and Sister M. Emerita Fahey, the Bachelor's. By the summer of 1929 Creighton had granted thirteen Master's and twenty-nine Bachelor's degrees, together with a large number of teacher's certificates to B. V. M. Sisters. [15]

Meantime, in 1917, Mt. St. Joseph College arranged for summer sessions for the Sisters. Its program included the completion of high school courses for those with that need and preparation for teacher's certificates, as well as the usual collegiate subjects. The College[16] was accredited to the North Central Association the following year. A listing of the courses covered together with teaching staff is given on page Completion of the collegiate course, involving certain required studies, entitled a graduate to state certification, qualifying her to teach in any public school in Iowa or any state of the Northwest Territory.

Coeducation at Saint Louis University followed a different pattern according to its historian, the Reverend William B. Faherty, S. J. [17] In a letter of April 26, 1978, addressed to the writer, Father Faherty discusses the inhibiting effect of the program for scholastics at the University, not only in the matter of coeducation but of openness to fresh thought in the field of philosophy. He wrote:

> The basic negative power /delaying the move to coeducation at Saint Louis University7 was the scholastic establishment. They allowed nothing that would interfere with the scholastics' philosophy and theology courses - as they saw it. Thus they questioned at the first NCEA meeting in 1904 the recommendation of the president of the University, William Banks Rogers, one of the two best presidents SLU ever had, that the philosophy department recognize the existence of modern schools of philosophy. Father Thomas Sherman, the General's son, a renowned public orator, recommended coeducation at the same time. The scholastic establishment publicly questioned both. . . .

In 1915 the provincial of the Missouri Province, the Very Reverend Alexander Burrowes, opened a discussion on the subject of coeducation[18] with the presidents of colleges and universities in that province. The effective response for SLU was negative. A compromise plan, however, instituted to meet the pressing needs of the religious woman for higher education

REGULATIONS

for the

Summer School, Ninteen=Ninteen.

—◆>•◆<◆>—

1. Centers of Study.

1. The Sisters preparing for degrees will take up their work at the following Centers:

Marquette University	Dubuque College
De Paul University	Mount St. Joseph College
Creighton University	St. Mary's High School (Loyo

2. Third and Fourth Year High School classes will be open at Mount St. Joseph College; classes at St. Mary's High School and at the Academy in Lyons; First Year classes at St. Aloy and De Paul High School, Chicago. The Normal Centers will be as follows:

a — For the Iowa teachers, at Mount St. Joseph College, St. Joseph's Academy, Des M Immaculate Conception Academy, Davenport.

b — For the Nebraska teachers at Creighton University.

c — For the South Dakota teachers at Lead, and

d — For the Butte teachers at the Immaculate Conception School, Butte, Montana.

Classes will also be held at Wichita, Kansas City, St. Louis, and Milwaukee; In Chicago, Methods in Eighth Grade will be open at Presentation School; a Center for Methods in Se Holy Cross School, and a Center for Methods in Fifth and Sixth Grades at Help of Christian

3. The Music Teachers will study the *Mary Wood Chase* Method with our own Sisters i St. Mary's, Lourdes, and Annunciation; in Des Moines at St. Joseph's Academy; in Davenpo maculate Conception Academy; and in Fort Dodge at Corpus Christi.

II. Expenses.

1.		Tuition	Laboratory
	Marquette	$ 20.00	$ 5.00
	De Paul	25.00	5.00
	Creighton	10.00	3.00
	Dubuque	25.00	5.00
	Mount St. Joseph	00 00	5.00

The Loyola Extension will give two College subjects at $6.00 each.

Board — $5.00 per week.   Retreat — $5.00

2. Every Sister, whether she be teacher or student, should be supplied with money for boar turn fare, and the necessary books and stationery. The Sisters should deposit their money wit

Mount St. Joseph College Summer School 1919

HORARIUM

A. M.

8:00   History of Education.........College Hall (114) .... S. M. Antonia

Cicero ....Aquinas (115)........ S. M. Justitia

English B — High School......English Hall (112).....S. M. St. Clement

8:45   Agriculture (Normal)...... .Academy Hall.........S. M. Rachel

French 1 ....Aquinas (113) ....S. M. Vincentius

Spanish 1 ....English Hall...........S. M. Carmencita

9:35   Psychology II ....English Hall........... S. M. Ritter

Home Economics (Normal)...Home Ec. Kitchen......S. M. St. Clara

Caesar....................Aquinas (113) .... S. M. Josephina

College Algebra..... ... ...Mathematics Hall........S. M. Resignata

10:25 General Methods............English Hall (112)......S. M. Columba

Home Economics (Normal)..Home Ec. Kitchen.......S. M. St. Clara

Algebra 1 H. S..............Mathematics Hall (4) ...S. M. Helene

Geometry 1............. .. College Math. Hall (81)..S. M. Resignata

11:15 College English............English Hall (112)......S. M. Clara

English A. (H. S.)..........120 .... S. M. St. Clement

French II.................Aquinas (113).........S M. Vincentius

Algebra 1 [2nd Semester]....Mathematics Hall (4)....S. M. Helene

P. M.

1:30   Normal Reviews   To continue throughout afternoon

Vergil.............. ......Aquinas [113]...........S. M. Justitia

Physics.................. Physics Laboratory (120) ..S. M. Remi

* Biology................ Biological Laboratory [52] ...S. M. Evangela

Chemistry................ Chemistry Laboratory.......S. M. Regina

2:15   Physics..................Physics Laboratory [120].... S. M. Remi

Biology........ ....Biological Laboratory [52] ...S. M. Evangela

3:00   Physics.................. Physics Laboratory [120].....S. M. Remi

Biology ....Biological Laboratory [52] ....S. M. Evangela

4:00   Church History............College Hall.... ....S. M. Josephina

4:00   Scripture..Sat. and Sun.......College Hall.............. S. M. Crescentia

4:45   VISITS

included the opening of extension courses. In the summer of
1916 Father Shannon, S. J. , conducted a science class at the
Visitation Convent. Two years later Saturday afternoon classes
were initiated on a regular basis at the Sacred Heart Academy
some blocks west of the University. The faculty of Jesuits offered a fairly broad choice of subject matter for the time -
psychology, ethics, English, physics, Latin, geometry, trigo-
nometry and education. With the opening of the fall term in
1919, similar courses were instituted at Maryville College,
Visitation Convent and St. Elizabeth Academy. For the B. V. M.
Sisters teaching at St. Francis Xavier, the Sacred Heart
Academy was conveniently close and they attended classes
there regularly.

Sister M. Augustina Ray, B. V. M. , superior at the time,
was among those in attendance. Others included Sisters M. St.
Lucian Deckelmayer, Juliana Bowen, Antoine Leslie and
Margaret Mary Doran, all presently residing at Mt. Carmel.
These Sisters received credit from the University for a course
in Shakespeare taken during the early twenties which Sister M.
Augustina taught them at their own convent. It is their belief
that Sister was thus the first woman accredited to teach at the
University. [19]

Saint Louis University has contributed much to the higher
education of B. V. M. 's since its hesitant beginnings as a coeducational institution.

With the concentration of B. V. M. Sisters in the San Francisc
area, the question arose as to the response the Jesuit University
of San Francisco made to the need for the higher education of
women. There were in the area three colleges - the San Francisco College for Women conducted by the Religious of the
Sacred Heart and familiarly known as Lone Mountain, Holy
Name College in Oakland and Dominican College in San Rafael,
all for women and all in close proximity. A kind of infused
predilection for the Jesuits, and the need on the part of some
for Master's degrees would have directed the B. V. M. Sisters
to San Francisco University had classes there been available.
However, coeducation there lay in the future. The delay may
well have been in deference to the three women's colleges.

There seems no exact data as to when women were admitted
to the University beyond the recollections provided by the Reverend Lloyd R. Burns, S. J. , alumni chaplain, to whom the
question was referred by the office of the University registrar.
His simple memorandum forwarded by that office reads:

I was here as a student 1911-16. No women. I was here
as a scholastic from 1923 to 1926 and there were no women
in the day college or in the evening department. I think the
first women were admitted after the college moved to the
present Campion Hall. The graduating picture of 1930 shows
two women and I think that they were Masters of Law - one
for sure. Women were in the evening /classes7 mostly for
dramatics. I don't know when the first day Summer Session
was /held7, but Sisters then came in great numbers. B. V. M. 's
were here in great numbers at that time. The reaction to the
first girls (as nurses, RNs to get a college degree) was not
very favorable, but it died down.

In a subsequent letter, June 27, 1978, Father Burns wrote:

When we first opened USF to women the B. V. M. 's came
in droves to Summer Sessions and we have over one hundred
who received their degrees from here. Later on fees became
too high for Sisters, and we lost a great deal of them to
other universities. This year we gave a reduced rate again
and there are many Sisters on campus for the Summer Session.

Father Burns' letter adds that

. . . . The B. V. M. 's had great records at our St. Ignatius
High School in San Francisco in the 1920's. Most of the
scholarships were won by boys from Most Holy Redeemer,
St. Paul's and St. Brigid's schools, so much so that the
principal invented another way that would give others a
chance. I think that the other convent schools who did not
have the Sisters to coach before school in the morning complained a great deal about the B. V. M. 's.

It is to be questioned whether all the zeal shown by the Sisters in those years was directed toward the glory of God, as
Mother Clarke had hoped for her Sisters.

A letter sent out by the four provincial superiors to the Sisters under their jurisdiction under date of May 1, 1919 reads:

The War, as you are well aware, has left in its train many
very grave problems for Church and State, and it is not
surprising that we, Religious teachers, should be called

upon now to meet conditions that test our courage and our
loyalty to the great cause of Catholic Education. The legis-
latures of nearly all the States are framing laws providing
for inspection of our schools and certification of our teachers. These laws will be effective in a few States next September, and the time is near at hand when they may be
read in the Statute books of every State in the Union. Now,
Sisters, we must all face these new conditions with such
generous courage as will assure both our friends and our
enemies that we are not unprepared for them. Far from
showing faintheartedness, we will submit patiently to
the new requirements, regarding them as opportunities
for proving to the public that our Sisters are capable,
devoted, self-sacrificing teachers. We are now, more
than ever before, in the fore-front of the battle for the
faith of our little ones. We must therefore be more than
ever generous and unsparing in our efforts to meet the new
conditions successfully and the good God in Whose service
we are spending our best energies will be our Strength
and our Shield in the day of battle, as well as our Reward
exceeding great when the victory is won.
. . . Certification of teachers is the immediate and imperative need. We have, therefore, opened Normal Centers
in Iowa, Nebraska and other States, where the Sisters may
take a thorough review of the common branches and study
Agriculture and Domestic Science under competent teachers. . . .

Novices were then required to take county examinations for
certification, and summer classes were held at the motherhouse
with teachers from the state universities in the less traditional
subjects of agriculture and domestic science. Certainly every
effort was made to acquire the necessary credentials. Diocesan
regulations were under revision, and none too soon, if we are
to judge from the contract presented by the Archdiocese of
Chicago to religious congregations in 1920. It specifies that

All teachers of the fifth and of a higher grade shall hold
a high school certificate. Time will be given until September,
1925 to carry out this provision, after which time no exception will be admitted. Schools of eight or more rooms
shall have a directress.

That the condition was not without application to the B. V. M.
Sisters we realize from the fact that Mt. St. Joseph College

was still devising examinations for Sisters in the seventh and eighth grade subjects. Many high school graduates would be daunted by them today, however.

The sudden rush for certificates and degrees was to have a profound effect on the life of the religious teacher and on her community. The double burden of teaching and learning crowded her hours and divided her interests. A second-grade teacher who rushed off at the end of a school day or year to classes in political economy and the French Revolution could scarcely do justice to either. The lack of proper guidance or opportunity for course sequence easily led to superficiality. Pressures for time meant something had to give - community exercises, quiet reading, class preparation, prayer life - all must yield in one degree or another. An ambition for hours, high grades and degrees, rather than a growth in scholarship, led many to a distorted sense of values and mistaken goals.

The six weeks' summer sessions were necessarily preceded by the preparation of classrooms and convents to be closed for the summer, by sewing and laundering all the details of head-dress and habit, the packing of trunks lest the end of the summer retreat bring a change of assignment, and finally, the stowing into boxes and travel bags a sufficient supply of starched linens to last until late August when each Sister expected to be back in her mission. Study, retreat, possibly a brief two days' home visit or off as companion to another, then the necessary reorganization and preparation for school, all this was scarcely conducive to composure of spirit and the self-possession necessary to the successful teacher. Yet it was the real world at a time that called for change, and life must be lived. For many it meant chiefly strain and frustration. Others grew as scholars and as teachers with horizons broadened and interests awakened as their educational levels rose.

The new Chicago Archdiocesan contract of 1920, long in the making, was manifestly intended to correct abuses and assure an equitable arrangement for both religious communities and Chicago parishes. Financial arrangements included the following:

The directress and each grade teacher shall receive a salary of $35.00 per month for each of ten months. Where there is no parish convent for the use of the Sisters, the directress and each teacher is to receive $45.00 per month.

The Sisters may conduct a music school in their residence and retain for themselves the income therefrom. However, no music classes are to be given to the pupils of the school during school hours.

The sale of school books and stationery is to be left to the Sisters, and the profits of the sale belongs to them. The cost and selling prices of these books and articles should be submitted to the pastor.

On the other hand, "There will be no entertainments, collections or sales for the benefit of the Sisters, " a practice which the meager returns from the schools had in a great many cases rendered imperative.

Provisions to be made by pastors in the convent and its furnishings were explicit, while reasonable limits were put upon communities regarding the transfer of Sisters and forbidding their abandonment of a parochial school without the written consent of the Archbishop. The Sisters were expected "to take charge of Sunday school classes and children's sodalities, " and "to prepare and conduct commencement and graduating exercises and one other entertainment during the year if the pastor so desires, " duties which might well fall to their lot. It was the basis on which Mother Cecilia's successor would be expected to direct her Chicago schools.

While the time lies somewhat outside the scope of our study, it is of interest that the first woman candidate accepted for a doctoral degree at the Catholic University of America was a B.V.M., Sister M. Joseph Therese Geiger. [20]

The story provides unusual insights. In the summer of 1926, Mother Isabella assigned Sister to the Catholic University for a doctorate in science, not realizing that science courses were taught only on the campus during the academic year when women were not allowed. Sister M. Realmo Sullivan was then at Sisters' College, working on a Master's in Latin. Her graduate research, directed by Dr. Deferrari, could be conducted in his seminar library on campus only on weekends because of the University's restrictions on women students.

Enrolled in the summer session which was open to women, Sister M. Joseph Therese was able to take prerequisite courses on the University campus. When fall came it seemed unlikely that she would be able to continue her work. Her situation was spelled out when Monsignor McCormick, director of Sisters' College where Sister was in residence, informed her that no woman had ever studied on the University campus during the academic session, and "none ever will." Discouraged, Sister wrote to Mother Isabella. Meanwhile, during the interim weeks before the fall session, Dr. J. B. Parker, head of the biology department, permitted Sister to make use of the laboratory.

In a chance encounter Dr. Edward A. Pace, acting rector, inquired of Sister the occasion of her presence in the university building. Repeating Monsignor McCormick's remark, Sister outlined her predicament, saying that the only recourse open to her was to pursue her work at the University of Illinois. [21] He responded bluntly: "McCormick isn't running the University. I'll see what I can do." Meantime Sister received word to return to Dubuque. Dr. Pace wrote her there of her acceptance in the biology department.

When in the course of registering Sister M. Joseph Therese took her checkbook from her purse, Dr. Pace, who had accompanied her to see that all went well, waved it away. "You will have earned your tuition by the end of the year," he assured her. A part of the price was the trip back and forth to the campus - through a woods, across railroad tracks, and through the grounds of the Notre Dame House of Studies, its alternate a walk along a mud road and a roundabout streetcar ride.

Tests in both French and German faced Sister at the end of her first year, along with the intense courses she was following. Dr. Parker, chairman of the biology department, could scarcely believe her when at the end of three years Sister presented to him the evidence of courses completed and of her readiness for comprehensives. She received her doctoral degree in science in June 1929. Her companion, Sister M. Joseph Aloysius Buck, was granted her PhD in the classical languages at the same time, having taken her class work at the Sisters' College.

In 1928 the new rector of the University, Bishop James H. Ryan, opened registration to all properly qualified women. Many years later Dr. Parker wrote his former student: ". . . of all the nuns I met during my tenure of office, I doubt whether there was another one that would have had the courage to put up the fight you made. . . . but we have the satisfaction of knowing that many a nun today is doing better work in our schools because of the opportunity" opened up to them by Sister's perseverance and his support of her efforts. [22]

Notes

1 Sister is listed for study at Loyola University' School of
Sociology in the summer of 1917, at Creighton University,
1919 and 1920, and as having been granted a Master's degree
by the University of Wisconsin, Madison in 1921.

2 All materials concerning DePaul have been provided by
the Reverend Patrick Mullins, C. M. , the University's archivist
and historian.

3 Page 4, Col. 4.

4 Letter, the Reverend Patrick Mullins, archivist, DePaul
University, June 7, 1978, to the writer.

5 It is of interest that the St. Vincent High School for Girls
had attained sufficient maturity by 1909 to have an alumnae association. That year it held a banquet on June 26 in the Grille
Room at Fields, at which Mary Coffield-Callahan of the class
of '98 read a review of the years. (Leaflet in the DePaul Archives.

6 See DePaul Archives.

7 DePaul Archives.

8 See Loyola University Catalogue, "44th Annual Commencement, " office of University Registrar.

9 Their lecture courses included out of town engagements.
Father Claude Pernin, S. J. , gave a two-weeks' course in
literature and Father Frederick Siedenberg, S. J. , a succession
of lectures in sociology at Mt. St. Joseph College, Dubuque in
the early twenties. (Sister M. Benedict Phelan, B. V. M.)

10 The academy opened in 1909 in Dumbach Hall with an
enrollment of approximately sixty students. Both students and
clergy moved to Cudahy Hall on its completion in 1911. The
Jesuit residence was ready for occupation in 1922. By 1925
the University enrollment had grown to 5, 000 students.

11 Later transferred to Franklin Street.

12 The above materials were supplied by Mary L. McPartlin,
director of the Correspondence Study Division, the Reverend

Robert C. Hartnett, S. J., archivist, and the early catalogs of the University.

13 St. Bridget Convent, opened in 1914, was able to accommodate a small number of B. V. M. 's. None attended, however, until 1915 when the first five came.

14 Having two nieces, Sisters M. St. Edna Whalen and Edwarda Maher, among the B. V. M. Sisters, Father Whalen was adopted by all as "Uncle Willie, " and responded by extending to all B. V. M. 's a proper avuncular regard.

15 All data concerning Creighton University were provided by Ms. Sandi Nichols, secretary to the registrar, for whose extensive research in our behalf we are deeply grateful.

16 The name was changed to Clarke College in 1928 at the time the new Mary Frances Clarke Residence Hall was dedicated.

17 Father Faherty is the author of Better the Dream, Saint Louis University and Community, 1818-1968. Except as indicated, the writer is indebted to Father Faherty's work for all the above data.

18 Father Faherty's history calls attention to the fact that the St. John College, Toledo, had conducted since 1914 a Sisters' College similar to that affiliated with the Catholic University of America. (p. 278)

19 In a note to Sister M. Juliana, Father Faherty wrote on May 30, 1978, "I shall pursue a plan to find out if indeed Sister Mary Augustina was the first nun to teach an accredited course at Saint Louis University. "

20 Sister M. Antonia Durkin had been granted a PhD by the University in 1926, but for work done at and through its affiliated Sisters' College.

21 As we see from the following directive from the Archbishop of Dubuque addressed to Mother Cecilia on April 14, 1919, this would have involved his written permission. It read:
I beg to advise that no religious over whom we have jurisdiction may attend a secular or non-Catholic educational

institution without our written permission.

I advise, moreover, that such permission cannot be given unless the Rt. Rev. Ordinary of the territory in which such educational institution is found is advised and permits such attendance, or at least allows such attendance in the case of Sisters of his jurisdiction.

Sincerely,

James J. Keane

Archbishop of Dubuque

22 Early in her studies Monsignor Pace chose to present Sister to a session of the University senate, presided over by Dr. William Kerby, head of the School of Sociology. As former faculty member of the men's college in Dubuque, Dr. Kerby was well acquainted with the B. V. M. Sisters. Rising from his place he came forward and greeted Sister warmly. To make sure that things continued to go well, Dr. Pace occasionally dropped in on Sister at the laboratory. Because she was investigating the corm or "bulb" of the gladiolus plant, the subject of her dissertation, he fell into the habit of substituting for her many syllabled religious name the less conventional "Cormie. "

BIOGRAPHICAL BRIEFS

Only scant biographical details remain of most of the early Sisters. For some, even of those who made conspicuous contributions to the life and works of the Congregation, there is often little more than a death notice. The following brief sketches give at least some indication of the backgrounds of those for whom some record remains and the extent of their services.

Sister M. Seraphina (Margaret) Short entered the Congregation on October 7, 1855 at the age of fifteen, having been a pupil at the St. Mary Academy, Dubuque. Sister was assigned to St. Agatha Academy, Iowa City, and later as superior at the Gesu School, Milwaukee; Holy Family, Chicago; and St. Francis Xavier, St. Louis. A highly gifted woman, both intellectually and spiritually, she endeared herself to students and parents alike. Her death at Mt. Carmel, September 4, 1925, ended seventy years as a religious.

Sister M. Maurice (Catherine) Duffy entered the Congregation on August 15, 1865 at the age of eighteen, and was professed December 23, 1866. Mother Clarke named Sister the first superior of St. Brigid School in San Francisco, opened in December 1887. In 1900 she was recalled from California to serve as assistant novice mistress under Mother Gertrude who was much taken up with the duties of first consultor and assistant to Mother Cecilia. Sister was herself consultor for four terms, while she continued as novice mistress save for her last term. As a result of ill health she resigned that position to Sister M. Esther Warren. Sister had undergone surgery for cancer on April 1, 1907 in St. Joseph Hospital, Chicago and continued poorly until her death at Mt. Carmel on June 17, 1908. Sister had three Sisters in the religious life, Sister M. Genevieve, B. V. M., and Sisters M. Alberta and Alexius, OP. Of Sister it was said that "few were more universally loved in life and more tenderly mourned in death, the inspiration of many a young heart. " The charges made for Sister's twelve weeks' stay in the hospital and her care there seem unreal today: for her private room, $10. 00 a week, for a private nurse on twenty-hour duty, $20. 00 a week, and for anesthesia and surgical dressings, $5. 00.

Sister M. Loyola (Alice) Rutherford, her mother and brother became converts to the faith. Born in Vermont she came with her family to Iowa where she spent some years as a high school teacher in the Muscatine public schools. Her father, a devout Puritan, was so disturbed by the conversion of members of his family that he finally left the home to live with a Protestant daughter. In the end, however, both he and the daughter came into the Church. Sister entered the Congregation on October 22, 1867 on the death of her mother. She was then thirty-one years of age. Her early training and her aptitude for management made her a valuable superior at Annunciation and St. Pius, Chicago, and St. Joseph Academy in Dubuque. As assistant to Mother Cecilia, and in the positions of councillor and procurator for the Congregation, she supervised the laying out of the grounds at the new motherhouse and the building of the infirmary, St. Mary High School, and the rest home for tubercular patients on the academy grounds in Boulder. Sister died December 18, 1915 from influenza and an ear infection.

Sister M. Crescentia (Mary) Markey entered the Congregation on July 16, 1870 at the age of fifteen. She served as the foundress and superior of Holy Rosary Mission, Milwaukee in 1885, and taught for some years at St. Mary High School, Chicago. The Sisters under her leadership visited the reform schools and jails of the various cities in which she served, including Chicago, Muscatine and Iowa City. She was among the first six Sisters to go to Washington, D. C. for study, receiving her master's degree from the Catholic University of America in 1914. She served as secretary general to the Congregation 1915-1926, during which time she was also on the faculty of the young Mt. St. Joseph College. Never rugged, Sister gave up active work in 1926. She died at Mt. Carmel August 1, 1930.

Sister M. Casia (Bridget) O'Connor, born in Wisconsin in 1860, was the first postulant from Council Bluffs. She entered on March 26, 1876 at the age of fifteen. She was professed on July 16, 1878 and was assigned to St. Bridget's, Chicago where she served for twenty-one years. It was here that Sister grew to love and be loved by the poor and the lowly, characteristics which marked her to the end. Sister was superior at St. Joseph', Kansas City for a three-year term, then asked to be transferred to St. Brigid's, San Francisco to be near her aging parents. In 1904 she was assigned as superior to St. Dominic's, Chicago, where she served six years. This was followed by a year in Cresco, Iowa, five years in Petaluma and fifteen years in the care of the sick at Loyola in Boulder, her most cherished duty, the loving care of the sick. Ill health then forced her to return to Dubuque. On her way she stopped in Chicago. All her "old boys" gathered about her there to review deeply cherished memories. Sister spent her last years a patient in the infirmary where she died on September 13, 1943.

The Casia Club, established at St. Dominic's by Sister's former pupils, continued to give loyal support to the Sisters, monetary and otherwise, until the close of the school in 1959.

Sister M. Hilary (Margaret) O'Regan was born in Davenport, Iowa on July 27, 1856. She was the daughter of James O'Regan and his wife Delia Cornwall, pioneer Irish who then settled near Waterloo, Iowa. It was from there that Margaret entered on May 24, 1878, at the age of twenty-two. Seven years later Mother Clarke named her superior of St. Mary Academy, Elgin, the first of a number of such assignments. Sister replaced Sister M. Agatha at Holy Family Convent after the closing of St. Aloysius School in 1896, when the Sisters assumed the education of the boys as well as the girls of the parish. Regret for the necessity of giving up the higher classes for the girls at that time was a factor in the opening of the St. Mary High School in 1899, with Sister M. Hilary in charge. She was to serve a second six-year term there following a superiorship at St. Jerome's, Chicago. When Sister M. Isabella Kane was named Mother General in late 1919, Sister M. Hilary replaced her in the office of provincial for Sacred Heart Province.

The alumnae of St. Mary High School to which she had contributed so much of her energies and her spirit had meantime formed a Hilary Club in her honor, having for its purpose the advancement of the interests of their alma mater. In her years of retirement, Sister supervised the library at Our Lady of Angels Academy, Clinton, Iowa. Her last years were spent at Mt. Carmel's infirmary where she died of leukemia on Thanksgiving day, November 26, 1942, at the age of eighty-six.

A resemblance to Mother Cecilia in manner as well as in physical likeness had caused Sister to be taken many times for Mother.

Sister M. Esther (Mary) Warren entered from Burlington, Iowa on September 1, 1881 at the age of twenty-one. Having served as superior at Presentation Convent, Chicago, she spent the last twenty-six years of her life at Mt. Carmel, as superior of the motherhouse, general councillor and novice mistress, and was for many years in charge of the infirmary. She loved to think of herself as "servant of the sick and the suffering, " a work to which she gave herself with heroic generosity. Sister died at Mt. Carmel on May 14, 1932 at the age of sixty-three, the result of pneumonia and peritonitis.

Sister M. Angela (Catherine) Fitzgerald was one of eight children of James and Honor (Grace) Fitzgerald. Sister entered the Congregation from Holy Family Parish, Chicago on August 15, 1885, following into religion her three sisters, Sister M. Wendolin and the twins, Sisters M. Lamberta and Thomasina. A brother, Thomas A., entered the Jesuits and served a term as provincial. Sister taught music at the St. Mary Academy, Elgin; Holy Cross, Chicago; St. Francis, Council Bluffs; St. Joseph's, DesMoines; and Mt. St. Joseph Academy, Dubuque. After a term as superior at Holy Rosary, Milwaukee, she was named novice mistress, an office in which she contined from February 2, 1909 to January 7, 1928. After a period of rest in Wichita, Sister M. Angela was named provincial of the St. Joseph Province. Completing her term there she then retired to Mundelein College where she died April 2, 1944. She had to her credit the training of 929 novices in the course of her nineteen years in that capacity.

Sister M. Adora (Nellie) Caverly was in her seventeenth year when she entered the Congregation at the motherhouse on the Prairie on August 15, 1886. Born in London, England, she came as a small child to Chicago where she attended school at Annunciation. She was missioned as music teacher to the Immaculate Conception Academy in Davenport where she formed close bonds of friendship with Sisters M. Regina Lynch, Carlino Guyton and Antonia Durkin. She served as superior at the Cathedral Convent, Sioux City, at the Immaculate Conception Academy in Davenport and Holy Angels, Milwaukee. Named provincial in 1915, Sister made her residence at the Wichita Academy. At the time of her death on July 29, 1936, she was superior at Our Lady of Angels Academy, Clinton, Iowa. Becoming ill on a visit to the motherhouse where she had been invited in anticipation of her golden jubilee, she died following an emergency operation in Waterloo. Sister was a kindly and much loved person.

Sister M. Benedicta (Bridget) Prendergast was born in Tipperary, Ireland, one of the nine children of James and Margaret (Burke) Prendergast. Seven of the nine were given religious vocations, three becoming priests, a fourth dying in the seminary, and two sisters joining the order of St. Ursula.

Sister entered under Mother Clarke on August 15, 1887, and served as superior at Emmetsburg and Sioux City, Iowa; Mt. Carmel, Wichita; and St. Vincent's, Kansas City. At the division of the Congregation into provinces in 1915, Sister was named provincial for the St. Joseph Province with headquarters at the St. Joseph Academy, DesMoines. She served briefly as postulant mistress in 1926. Sister died June 21, 1940 of an embolism resulting from a fall in which she suffered a broken hip and wrist. A woman of refinement, Sister had a keen sense of humor and a manner of great graciousness.

Sister M. Redempta (Mary) Coleman was born in Louisville, Kentucky on February 22, 1871, the daughter of James and Catherine (Power) Coleman, both of whom were Irish born. She was a boarding student at St. Francis Academy, Council Bluffs from early childhood, entering the Congregation on August 15, 1888, at the age of seventeen. Sister taught at the Cathedral School in Dubuque; St. Aloysius, Chicago; St. Mary's, Emmetsburg; Petaluma, California; Our Lady of Victory, Waterloo; St. Mary's, Chicago and Holy Angels, Milwaukee. She was the second superior at St. Brigid's, San Francisco, and served in that capacity in Petaluma, at the Mt. Carmel Academy, Wichita, and Presentation School, Chicago. Sister was the first directress for Holy Family Province, provincial for the Immaculate Conception Province, and councillor at Mt. Carmel from 1931 to 1949. Sister died in the Sisters' new infirmary, Marian Hall, on February 15, 1961, of a duodenal ulcer. Sister M. Georgina, B. V. M., was her well loved sister.

Sister M. Urban (Nell) Bermingham was born in Lincoln, Illinois, March 29, 1876. She entered at the motherhouse on the Prairie on September 8, 1893, shortly before the move into Dubuque. Professed on January 6, 1896, Sister taught in high schools at St. Ambrose, DesMoines; St. Mary's, Clinton; and St. Vincent's, Chicago. Having received a B. A. degree at the Catholic University of America in June 1913, she continued her studies at the Sisters' College there through the following year. She served as procurator general at Mt. Carmel 1914-1926. For the following six years she served as superior and principal at St. Francis Academy, taught college subjects to the novices at Mt. Carmel, 1932-1937, and was then named third councillor, serving until 1943 when she returned to her classes with the novices. An injury to her knee in her early career had an increasingly crippling effect which seriously handicapped her in her later years. Death occurred in Mercy

Hospital in Dubuque on January 6, 1957 after a confinement of four years in the infirmary. Sister was survived by twin brothers, Walter and James, and two sisters, Mrs. Bernard Clifford and Ann Bermingham, and a niece, Mrs. Evelyn Coogan.

Sister M. Justitia (Alice) Coffey was born in 1875 in North Hadley, Massachusetts. She was graduated from the Northhampton High School in 1893 and taught school in Worcester, Massachusetts for some years before she, her parents and her brother John moved to Granville, Iowa. From there Alice entered the Congregation on July 13, 1900, at the age of twenty-five. As a novice Sister served for two years as directress the St. Cecilia Academy, Holden, Missouri. She was then assigned to St. Mary High School, Chicago where she taught, save for the year of study, 1911-1912, at the Catholic University of America, until her appointment as superior of the new Immaculata High School in 1921. She had completed her studies for the Master's degree at Loyola University that summer. The Greenlee mansion served a first year class during the construction of the new high school building. The full enrollment was received on its opening in September 1922.

Upon the expiration of her term of office in 1927, Sister M. Justitia was named provincial of the Holy Family Province with residence at the Wichita Academy. After little more than a year, she was called upon to superintend the building of Mundelein College, then assigned as its president for the term 1930-1936. A year at Wichita and two at Clarke College then intervened before Sister was returned to the office of president of Mundelein College. At the end of her second six years in 1945, Sister spent several months of rest and health care at the Sacred Heart Sanatarium in Milwaukee. Suffering from arthritis and with failing eyesight, Sister M. Justitia spent her little remaining time in retirement at the College under the care of Sister M. Vincentine Lewis. Death came on November 5, 1947 at the age of seventy-two.

An honor guard of students in cap and gown formed an avenue for the simple black casket as it was carried to the hearse after a two days' wake in the large reception room of the College. The funeral cortège, accompanied by a motorcycle escort, a feature which had characterized many occasions Sister had directed, moved to St. Ignatius Church. There the Very Reverend Joseph Egan, S. J., provincial, the Reverend J. Sullivan, pastor, and the Reverend William R. Murphy, chairman of the College religion department, celebrated a solemn Mass of requiem. The Reverend Robert Kelley, S. J., long associated with Sister's educational labors, spoke of the extraordinary contribution Sister had made to Catholic education in the two major institutions which she had nurtured through their formative years. The Most Reverend Bishop Bernard J. Sheil gave the final blessing. Burial was in Mount Carmel Cemetery.

Sister M. Antonia Durkin was the younger sister of Sister M. Balbina Durkin who spent her years as a simple grade school teacher. The former is presented to us, on the other hand, as scholar, teacher and author as well as a religious. Sister entered the Congregation on May 24, 1887 at the age of twenty-three. She was missioned at the St. Francis Academy, Council Bluffs, the Immaculate Conception Academy, Davenport, and St. Joseph Academy, DesMoines where she served as superior for a three-year term. Having taught religious education and the classics at the motherhouse, Sister was then occupied for ten years as dean of studies at Clarke College. Sister was a faculty member at Mundelein College when she was appointed president of Clarke in 1935. It was at the close of her six years there that death claimed her on July 7, 1941, the result of a cerebral hemorrhage.

Sister M. Antonia is reported as having exerted influence which hastened the opening of classes for women accredited by the Catholic University of America, though such classes were not for many years permitted a place on the campus. She was one of the six B. V. M. 's who attended those first courses, earning the A. B. degree there in 1912, and the Master's degree the following year. After a further period of study at Sisters' College affiliated with the University, Sister merited the PhD degree in 1926. Her dissertation, The Preparation of the Religious Teacher, was published as a college text, as was also her work, Introduction to the Studies of Newman.

The Reverend E. A. Fitzgerald, registrar at Loras College and later Bishop of Winona, celebrated the Mass of Requiem, assisted by other members of the Loras faculty, the Reverends S. D. Luby, Emmett Kelly, J. T. Gannon and Monsignor J. M. Wolfe. Burial was in Mount Carmel Cemetery.

Sister M. Clemenza (Honora) Leahey, born September 2, 1869, was the daughter of Irish born John Leahey and his wife Julia Nolan of Lanesboro, Minnesota. Having attended a year of commercial in Lanesboro and completed the normal course at Winona, Minnesota, Sister entered the Congregation on September 20, 1894 at the age of twenty-five. Assigned to Mt. St. Joseph as a novice, she taught eighth grade and high school classes. When a college department was added in 1901 she was engaged with education courses there. In 1909 Sister was transferred to St. Mary's, Chicago, and three years later to Holy Name High School. In 1914 she was named superior of St. Mary's. At the close of her term of office in 1920, Sister was assigned to the Wichita Academy. Having been awarded the A. B. degree by DePaul University in 1912, she was granted the Master's degree by Loyola in 1921. Her assignment in 1923 as superior of the Academy was cut short by her appointment to the office of provincial for the Holy Family Province. For a number of years thereafter, Sister served as librarian at the St. Francis Xavier School in St. Louis. Elected general councillor in 1940, she took up residence at Mt. Carmel where she taught a course in American government to the novices. Her last active years were spent as secretary general. Sister died on March 24, 1946 at the age of seventy-seven.

Sister M. Rose (Catherine) Rourke was the daughter of John Rourke and his wife Hanna Healey, both of Ireland. She entered on August 15, 1890. After four years in the high school classrooms at Cresco, Iowa, Sister was assigned to St. Brigid's, San Francisco. This was followed by a single year at St. Vincent Chicago, when she was named superior of Presentation Convent. Four years as teacher of high school classes at St. Vincent Academy, Kansas City were followed by six years as superior and teacher at St. Vincent's, Petaluma. In 1922 Sister was assigned to the superiorship of St. Paul's, San Francisco, following three classroom years at St. Francis, Council Bluffs. Briefly serving as travel companion to Sister M. Angela in 1928, she was then assigned to replace the recently deceased Sister M. Conradine at St. Paul's, San Francisco. A year there was followed by one year's stay at St. Joseph's, DesMoines and one year of rest at Boulder. Sister then returned to Petaluma for a five-year stay when she retired to St. Brigid's to supervise the bookroom. A much-loved woman, Sister M. Rose died of a heart attack at the age of eighty-six after sixty-one years in religion.

Sisters M. Octavia (Mary) and Edmunda (Annie) Burke were the daughters of Edward and Catherine Burke of Council Bluffs, Iowa. Their mother was an unusual woman, for on her death at the age of eighty-eight, the local newspaper acclaimed her "one of the most genial and saintly women we have ever known. . . . In her every day life she seemed to practice the presence of the divine. " Her daughters inherited many of their mother's admirable traits of kindliness and generosity, combined with an uncommon degree of common sense, which fitted them for lives of faithful and able service.

Mary Burke entered the Congregation on September 1875, at the age of twenty-one. Early among Sister M. Octavia's assignments was the superiorship of St. Pius, Chicago, 1891-1897. For fifteen years she served as visitor of the various houses of the Congregation under the direction of the superior general. This brought her into contact with nearly everyone of its members. Sister M. Octavia was one of the principal factors in the drawing up of the "Course of Studies for the Parochial Schools of Chicago. " Copies of this were in the mail for the pastors of the city on April 10, 1919, the day she died of pneumonia at Presentation Convent, Chicago, where she was serving as superior. The Reverend J. J. Jennings, pastor, spoke at her funeral Mass with unusual warmth and deep regret of her passing, her charity to all, her high level of intelligence, and of the loss her death was to the parish as well as to the Sisters. Hers was an unbroken example of devotion to the Congregation, and of loyal support to those who served it in the office of superior general.

The life of Sister M. Edmunda Burke had much in common with that of her older Sister whom she outlived by many years. As Annie Burke she entered from Missouri Valley, Iowa on September 8, 1879, at the age of twenty. Her years alternated between teacher and local superior, save for the six years in which she served as one of the four first provincials, an office in which she was beloved for her charity and her loyalty to her institute. Sister died on August 18, 1936 at the Mt. Carmel infirmary, at the age of seventy-seven.

Sister M. Regina (Mary Louise) Lynch was the granddaughter of Patrick Quigley, a significant figure in early Dubuque. Patrick, a native of Londonderry, Ireland had settled in St. Louis as a merchant, where he met and married Catherine Rooney in 1824. The fact that they were the parents of five children when the lands of Iowa were opened for sale in 1833 did not deter them from an immediate move north. The daughter Catherine, who would become Sister M. Regina's mother, was born in Dubuque on December 15, 1833, and was nearly six months old when a traveling missionary, probably Father Fitzmaurice briefly stationed in Galena, Illinois, baptized her, the first white child to receive that sacrament in all of future Iowa.

The two-story home of logs - later weather-boarded - constructed by Patrick Quigley at First and Bluff Streets was but a

short distance from the site of Dubuque's first cathedral for
which he contributed the land. It was Father Fitzmaurice who
celebrated Dubuque's first Mass in a south room of the Quigley
home. The room was thereafter reserved for visiting mis-
sionaries and served for nearly two years as residence of the
Dominican, Samuel Mazzuchelli. When Bishop Loras landed in
Dubuque in the spring of 1839, the entire Quigley family were
lined up on the river bank to greet him - quite a sizable group
even then for the family in time numbered thirteen children
and one adopted daughter.

Catherine Quigley was in attendance at the Sisters' St. Joseph
Academy on the Prairie when the boarding school was moved to
the Fourteenth Street Hill, Dubuque, in 1859. It is not clear
what took her east thereafter, to Syracuse, New York, but either
there or earlier she met and married Denis Lynch. Until his
naturalization, Denis was a man without a country, for he had
been born in mid-ocean of emigrant parents. Their daughter,
Mary Louise, was born in Syracuse, July 18, 1870. The family
were in Dubuque, however, living in a small frame house at
Fourth and Bluff by the time their daughter was ready for seventh
grade. From this she entered the new Mt. St. Joseph Academy
where she remained for five and a half years, until her graduation
in 1888. She entered the novitiate on the Prairie a year later,
on July 2, at the age of nineteen. An aunt, Sister M. Angela
Quigley, had preceded her into religion by many years.

Sister spent just a year at each of her first three missions,
Council Bluffs, Rock Island and St. Pius, Chicago. Assigned
to the Davenport Academy in 1894, she remained there until
1911 when she became one of the group of six B. V. M. Sisters
to go to Washington, D. C. for a year of study. Having received
the A. B. degree in 1912, Sister was able by home and summer
study to complete requirements for the Master's degree in 1914.
Meantime she had taught at Holy Angels Academy, Milwaukee.
Now assigned to Mt. St. Joseph College, she was on the staff
there until 1922 when she spent an additional year of study at
Columbia University, New York. Named superior of Cathedral
High School, Lincoln, Nebraska, Sister M. Regina had remained there but a year when she was transferred to the superiorship of the Davenport Academy. In 1932 Sister returned to
the Mount, now Clarke College. While she had by then specialized in biology and confined her teaching to that subject, she
had earlier awakened great love of the poet Browning and had
shared with her students her interest in the life and labors of
St. Paul. In 1932 Sister was named provincial of Holy Family
Province. At the close of her term of office, Sister M. Regina

took up residence at Mt. Carmel where she worked on the scholastic records of the Sisters until she became a bed patient in the infirmary. Death came on June 4, 1958 following a cerebral hemorrhage.

Sister M. Lambertina (Charlotte Ellen) Doran was born April 16, 1857 in Milwaukee, the daughter of James Lalor Doran and his wife Ellen O'Meara, both of Ireland. She entered from Holy Family Parish, Chicago on May 24, 1877 at the age of twenty. Sister taught as a novice at St. Mary's, Clinton, then at the academy in Davenport, and at Mt. St. Joseph Academy, Dubuque. She then was named superior of All Hallows Academy, Wichita, and after three years continued in that office at Mt. St. Joseph Academy. Returning to the classroom, she taught at Holy Angels Academy, Milwaukee; St. Mary High School, Chicago; and St. Joseph Academy, Dubuque. She served briefly as superior of the Cathedral School, Sioux City, being then elected secretary general at Mt. Carmel in February 1906. After nine years there she was named superior at St. Pius School, Chicago where she remained just two years. Meantime plans were underway for the opening of the Jeanne d'Arc College for Women which was to be affiliated with DePaul and to open in September 1917 under the B. V. M. Sisters. Father McCabe, C. M., president of the University, had negotiated for Sister's services to head the new college. However, on the demise of this second effort for a women's college, Sister was given the principalship of the parish high school, and named superior of its community of teachers. The St. Vincent High School for Girls became that fall the DePaul High School, situated in the former Doyle apartment building which the Vincentian Fathers had purchased at 2244 Osgood - now Kenmore - as the site of the proposed college.

Sister's own schedule of assignments indicates that she served just one year in her new situation, years 1918 and 1919 being assigned to "writing" at the motherhouse. The summers of 1919 and 1920 found her in summer school at Creighton University. Records of the University of Wisconsin at Madison indicate that Sister was granted the Master's degree from that school in October 1921, though her schedule does not indicate attendance there. Having taught Spanish and literature at the Mount for several years while residing at the motherhouse, she was elected secretary general and second councillor to Mother Isabella in 1925, offices to which she was reelected in 1931. Sister died at Mt. Carmel on October 10, 1946.

S.M.Edmunda Burke   S.M.Loyola Rutherford   S.M.Octavia Burke

S.M. Carlino Guyton   S.M.Regina Lynch
S.M.Adora Caverly, Antonia Durkin, Evangela Henthorne

S.M.Benedicta Prendergast   S.M.Justitia Coffey

APPENDIX I

A CRITICAL ERA IN AMERICAN CHURCH HISTORY

Rome had long held that error has no right to exist, and that it is the responsibility of the state to give all necessary support to the Church as the depository of truth. The idea of the separation of church and state, as held in America, official Rome regarded as not less than revolutionary, especially since the Roman Pontiff had for centuries performed the double function of political ruler of the Papal States and spiritual head of the universal Church. This double function lent weight in the minds of American Protestants to the conclusion that the Catholic's loyalty to the Holy Father was allegiance to a foreign prince whose political philosophy was a threat to American institutions.

This is not without significance in the final decades of the nineteenth century, a critical era for the American Church. The story, told in the lives of its leading prelates, is of a struggle on many fronts. The first of these involved the American hierarchy's efforts to maintain its lawful autonomy in the administration of a Church faced with unprecedented problems. It was their responsibility to adapt to a new and strongly Protestant land the hordes of Catholic and largely impoverished immigrants pouring into its ports from the countries of Europe. Besides, they had to make clear to official Rome the unique character of the American governmental pattern as it related to the Church, and the advantage as well as the necessity of church-state separation in a pluralistic society. Furthermore, the bishops faced the necessity of explaining to a solidly entrenched Protestant majority the nature and purposes of the Catholic Church. As a recent writer succinctly states it:

> Rome could not understand how a truly loyal Catholic
> Church could pledge allegiance to a state which did not
> accord it special privilege. Protestant America could not
> recognize that the Church which was loyal to the Roman
> Pontiff was not a menace to democratic institutions. [1]

The situation would seem to have been critical enough if the American hierarchy were of one mind. But, unfortunately, they were not. The most aggressive, and in some respects, the most far-seeing prelate of the liberal wing was John Ireland, Archbishop of St. Paul; a staunch and voluble patriot. In general agreement with his liberal stand was the urbane James Cardinal Gibbons, Archbishop of Baltimore and primate in all but name[2] of the American Church. Like Ireland, Gibbons was in every respect a "first citizen," participating in and lending support to civic enterprises at every level. [3]

A third distinguished member of the liberal wing was John Lancaster Spalding, first Bishop of Peoria, orator and writer. A man of great intellectual gifts, he was subject to moods, and temperamentally unable to work closely with others. These characteristics greatly reduced his effectiveness as a leader. A third prominent liberal, John Joseph Keane, Bishop of Richmond was a loyal supporter of Ireland and Gibbons. He was to become the first rector of the Catholic University of America, and later, Dubuque's second Archbishop.

In opposition to the progressive stance of the liberals, though not always openly, was the conservative Archbishop Michael A. Corrigan of New York. His inclination was to confine his loyalties to the Church and to take the Roman view on critical issues. Furthermore, he bitterly resented the influence and the over-riding methods of John Ireland. The more outspoken Bernard McQuaid, Bishop of Rochester and, as such, suffragan of Corrigan, was his faithful confederate. A third thoughtless conspicuous conservative was the Archbishop of Philadelphia, Patrick Ryan, lifelong friend of Archbishop Hennessy of Dubuque. Their ranks were swelled by a number of strongly nationalistic German bishops, the most significant of whom was Bishop Frederick Katzer, Bishop of Green Bay, and later Archbishop of Milwaukee It was Ireland's battle against the nationalistic tendencies of the Germans that drove them into the camp of the conservatives.

Archbishops of Baltimore until that time had kept open the lines of communication with Rome, and had served as papal representatives in the three Plenary Councils. But problems had grown with the rapid growth of the country. Means of safe-guarding the faith among the great numbers of Catholic immigrant and of composing national differences, were matters of concern to official Rome. The phenomenal growth of secret societies and the divisions within the American hierarchy in this regard as in other matters were subjects of confusion and concern. Then there was need of a papal arbiter to settle issues arising between the people and the clergy in their relations with their bishops. A liaison person with adequate status was indeed necessary if Leo XIII was to deal wisely and fairly with the American Church.

However, the American hierarchy were at one in their opposition to the appointment of a papal representative. His coming they were convinced, would revive old prejudices and bring an outcry against Roman influence. [4] But there was the even more relevant threat to the autonomy of the bishops. To forestall the establishment of a papal delegation, they promptly inaugurated a counter move: the commissioning of an agent to represent the American Church in Rome.

Their choice fell on Msgr. Denis O'Connell, to whom they gave the official position of rector of the North American College in Rome. O'Connell was a man of superior intelligence, of broad experience, and, as he was to prove, of considerable diplomatic skill. He soon aligned himself with the liberal group of "Americanizers. "

As O'Connell's allegiance to the liberals became manifest, the forces of opposition under Archbishop Corrigan of New York established their own agent, Ella B. Edes. [5] Her reports of proceedings in Rome bore the slant which conformed to their purpose. Both forces converged on the person of Leo XIII, and the difficulties of his position were further complicated by conflicting counsels of members of the Propaganda, under whose jurisdiction its missionary status placed the American Church.

Among the many issues which arose between liberals and conservatives in the course of the era was the "German Question. " The preponderance of Irish in the American hierarchy - though their number was not greatly out of line with the size of the Irish Catholic population - was a point at issue. Equipped from the beginning with the language of the country, and deeply appreciative of the advantages to be found in the land of their adoption, the Irish were generally inclined to an aggressive support of all the country stood for. On the other hand, loyalty of the Germans to their native language and customs, and their desire to preserve these intact extended so far as to demand that their clergy be trained in German seminaries. This demand, together with efforts of the German bishops to increase their own number and influence, met the resistance of the liberals. The filling of the largely German Milwaukee see left vacant by the death of Archbishop Michael Heiss was made an issue when Ireland spearheaded opposition to the German Katzer, Bishop of Green Bay, and urged instead the appointment of Spalding of Peoria to that archdiocese.

To further complicate the situation, Peter Paul Cahensly, a devout Catholic from Nassau, Germany, came to the States to establish a branch of St. Raphael's Society for Protection of German Catholic Immigrants, who, he believed, were otherwise in danger of losing their faith. His efforts were regarded as foreign influence, and as such were resented by the American clergy, and led to international complications. From him the

German movement derived its name, Cahenslysm, and his activities became a point of focus to the opposition.

A triumph for the German cause came in 1890, when Frederic Katzer was named Archbishop of Milwaukee. His appointment was a signal to the liberals that their influence in Rome was far from secure.

Ireland had been involved in a conflict with conservative bishops, and, finally, with Rome on a school matter, details of which will be given later. In a state of euphoria after the satisfactory resolution of this problem, O'Connell, who had supported Ireland with the full force of his position, now supported Pope Leo's determination to appoint an apostolic delegate to the American Church. O'Connell's new position of cooperation would cement relations with Rome for the liberals, and would, they hoped, remove America from the status of missionary country, and thus from the control of the very conservative Congregation of the Propaganda. [6] A pretext could be found for bringing a representative of the Holy Father into the country by inviting a Vatican representative to be present for the opening of the Columbian Exposition in Chicago in October 1893. O'Connell could safely assume the role of interpreter.

Cardinal Francisco Satolli was the Pope's choice. To forestall the possibility of his falling into the hands of the conservatives, O'Connell alerted Cardinal Gibbons and a party of friends to meet Satolli and himself and escort them to the residence of Archbishop Corrigan. The latter had not been notified in time to be present himself at the ship's landing. They were there entertained at dinner, but Corrigan's absence from the welcoming party was taken by Satolli as a personal slight, one which, however, would in the end work to the undoing of the liberals. [7]

After a brief stay in New York, Satolli was taken by special train to Baltimore "to join the entourage of liberals as they made their triumphal progress through the country. "[8] In Washington, where Keane joined the others, the party paid a visit to the Secretary of State. Ireland then met the group on August 18 and traveled with them to Chicago again by special train. There he delivered an oration at the dedication of the buildings erected for the Columbian Exposition. The party then set out for St. Paul, where they remained until the opening of the meeting of archbishops in New York on November 16. So far Satolli's coming had been a complete triumph for the liberal faction.

At the meeting in New York, Satolli spoke of the Pope's desire to appoint an apostolic delegate with the concurrence of the American hierarchy. To this the assembled archbishops declined to agree, asking delay until they could confer with their suffragans. Unfortunately, neither O'Connell nor Ireland had informed Cardinal Gibbons that Satolli's permanent appointment had been previously decided upon. Gibbons' subsequent letter to the Holy Father declaring that the American hierarchy did not favor the establishment of an apostolic delegation placed him in an ambiguous position. This complication required more than the facile explanations offered by O'Connell, already in difficulties, his career in Rome soon to be cut short. He had, further, over- shot himself in his maneuver against Corrigan, who had later won the naturally conservative Satolli to his side. O'Connell's temporary victory led to his dismissal from the rectorship of the North American College, and in 1895 to his withdrawal as Roman agent. Keane too was to feel the revenge visited on the liberals. In the following year he was dismissed from the rector- ship of the Catholic University. His position there had been undermined by a German faction in the university faculty who had gained the ear of Satolli, then in residence there. At the urging of Gibbons and Ireland, Keane went to Rome hoping to clarify his position. There in the minor positions assigned to him, he was faced with various humiliating frustrations until his appointment to the Archdiocese of Dubuque on the death of Archbishop Hennessy in 1900. [9]

After Corrigan's death in 1902 and the replacement of Satolli, the animus against O'Connell lessened, and he was appointed to the rectorship of Catholic University, [10] following the assign- ment of the ineffectual Bishop Thomas Conaty to the Monterey- Los Angeles diocese in 1903. His appointment, however, was no sinecure. The University, then under the jurisdiction of Satolli, the fully accredited apostolic delegate, was small, of exclusively graduate level, and in serious financial straits. O'Connell's rectorship did not prove particularly successful, though he did secure the University's finances through an annual collection in the parishes of the country. His dealings with the faculty, however, failed to reflect the genial-mannered diplomat he had previously shown himself to be. His subsequent career as auxiliary to Archbishop Patrick Riordan of San Francisco and then as Bishop of Richmond, from 1912 to his death in 1926, was not outstanding.

Meanwhile, however, another major source of conflict had arisen over an unfortunate French translation of Elliott's life of Isaac Hecker, founder of the Paulists, which had been published in 1897. Hecker, a convert to the faith from Protestantism, had found his way into the Church after a long and earnest search. [11] It was his desire to mediate his new faith to the Protestant world, and, while his doctrine was sound, his terminology had a strange ring in the ears of Catholic theologians. The translation of his biography in an abbreviated form seemed adapted to the purpose of French liberals in their support of the new republic, then grappling with the problems of church-state separation. The book's preface seemed to align with modernism Hecker's efforts to harmonize Church's teachings with recent scientific developments. His stress on the guidance of the Holy Spirit was taken as an unwarranted independence of ecclesiastical authority. French monarchists gave the label "Americanism" to all that they regarded as erroneous in his teachings. In concert with other European arch-conservatives, they sought to have the biography placed on the Index of Forbidden Books.

Both O'Connell and Ireland realized the disastrous effects such an action would have on the young Paulist society, already remarkably successful in winning converts to the faith. Their further concern was for the misinterpretation being placed, not only on Hecker's teaching, but on their own efforts to reconcile traditional Church polity with the realities of Catholic life in a republic and in the presence of an intellectual awakening. Both men appealed directly to European audiences, especially pointing out the injuries the Church had sustained in the course of the centuries through church-state involvement. In contrast they set forth the advantages which had accrued to the American Church from the free exercise of religion.

However, the whole liberal cause had now come under a cloud, both at home and abroad. No longer able to ignore the imputations of heresy which had been pressed upon him, on January 22, 1899, Leo XIII issued the encyclical Testem Benevolentiae. While it did not condemn the principles actually advocated by the "Americanizers," but rather the errors attributed to them, it appeased the conservatives on both sides of the Atlantic. The liberals, on their part, regarded their cause as vindicated since they could not accuse themselves of ever having held the strange tenets condemned by the encyclical. However, little more was heard thereafter of the "phantom heresy," Americanism. But the battle for an intellectual awakening was not won. In fact, with the passing of the "Americanizers" the cause had few able champions, and the intellectual life of the American Church received a half-century setback from which only Vatican II could revive it.

Since the early American clergy were all foreign born, the seminaries they established followed the European pattern and so bore the scars of their prototypes, chiefly French. Controversies over Jansenism, Gallicanism and the rationalist teachings of the Enlightenment, the devastation wrought by the

French Revolution and the fall of the Napoleonic empire had divided and decimated the European clergy. Through it all, Rome had felt the repercussions. It was an embattled Church, then, that faced the future, a Church fearful of the philosophies and political movements that had threatened its very existence. With the world about it changing in its every aspect, and science preempting the thoughts of the intelligentia, the clergy could feel secure only in preserving its own tight little pattern of thought and of discipline, reflected especially in its seminaries.

Patterns of seminary training introduced into this country in 1791 by the French Sulpicians were marked by conservatism and a highly disciplined regularity. The desire of each bishop and each religious order for its own seminary resulted in a proliferation of small, weak institutions inadequately provided for either in staff or library resources, and with the students frequently called on for manual labor or for teaching in the parish schools. Rote learning from Latin theological manuals, and a heavy emphasis on apologetics reflecting the Church's siege mentality, were expected to prepare the young cleric for leadership, not only in religion but in life. Yet his indoctrination included the assurance that the teaching of the Church provided adequate answers for all life's problems, and led to indifference if not scorn for the rapidly developing sciences.

In Europe, and especially in France, there were coming to the fore men, lay and clerical, who were making earnest efforts to bridge the gap between the seminary and the intellectual life of the rising universities, and to reconcile the new learning with the Church's teaching.

The strongly conservative body of French clergy allied with at least as conservative members of the Congregation de Propaganda Fide in Rome, proved less than friendly to such efforts, with the result that in 1864 Pius IX issued a listing of eighty propositions lifted out of previous encyclicals as a Syllabus of Errors to be strictly avoided as threatening heresy. Stifling as it was to the intellectual life of the Church, it had slight significance for the American seminarian who had little exposure to the dangers it envisioned.

Anti-intellectualism continued to deface the image of American Catholicism, [12] though again there were those, the "Americanizers" included, who sought to bring the Church out of the ghetto and into her rightful teaching role in the world. With the coming of the twentieth century all the old fears of heresy were awakened, and the preponderance of ultra-conservatives to be found about the papal throne led in 1907 to the decree of Pius X on the threat of "Modernism," as outlined in the encyclical Pascendi Dominici gregis. This again left the American clergy practically untouched though there were evidences of a growing intellectualism in the Church which boded well for the future.

It was the aftermath of the promulgation, however, that wrought havoc, setting back by half a century the scholarly efforts of Catholic leaders. The conservatives, having won their cause, followed up their victory with a witch hunt for any to whom the label modernist could be attached. [13] Bishops were required to establish vigilante committees to search out among priests and laity any possible trace of the "heresy. " Every priest and seminarian was required to pledge his allegiance to the provisions of the encyclical. Suspicions and rumors of suspicions multiplied, and priests, bishops and seminarians were subjected to investigation even in the absence of evidence. With the undermining of confidence and growing uncertainty as to what might be impugned as error, scholarly work came to a halt, and able writers turned their talents to less vulnerable pursuits or went underground. Not until the scholarly Benedict XV came to the papal throne in 1914 was the sinister search called off. Beset as he was by the tragedy of World War I, he yet took the occasion to issue as his first encyclical Ad beatissimi which made it clear that no private person was

> either by the publication of books or journals, or by delivering discourses publicly, /to/ assume the position of a master in the Church. . . Concerning matters in which, since the Holy See has not pronounced judgment, saving faith and discipline, discussion may take place pro and contra; it is certainly lawful for everybody to say what he thinks and to uphold his opinion. [14]

And especially directed to the self-appointed guardians of orthodoxy he wrote:

> let him not imagine he is justified in casting suspicion on the faith or discipline of those who hold a contrary opinion because they differ from him. [15]

Though it came too late to redeem many losses, the encyclica came like a breath of spring to many in the Church. Though recovery was slow, it was certain, and by the 1960's there were those prepared to guide the deliberations of the Council that would carry us into a whole new era in the life of the Church.

Notes

1 Gerald P. Fogarty. The Vatican and the Americanist Crisis: Denis J. O'Connell, American Agent in Rome, 1885-1903. (Roma: Universita Gregoriana Editrice, 1974), p. vii.

2 From the establishment of the American hierarchy with Bishop Carroll as Bishop, then Archbishop of Baltimore, Roman pontiffs had conducted the affairs of the American Church through the head of the see of Baltimore. The Archbishop of Baltimore still takes precedence over the other bishops in all processions of the clergy.

3 Both men were on excellent terms, not only with local governmental officials, but also with successive presidents, whose problems often merged with those of the Church. Ireland was commissioned by the Holy Father to use all his influence with President McKinley to prevent war between the United States and Spain. Both his and Gibbons' cooperation with Theodore Roosevelt in the settlement of land claims by the Friars in the Philippines are cases in point. In all this they strove to remove the foreign label from Catholicism, showing, as they did, their firm allegiance to the nation. See John Tracy Ellis, The Life of James Cardinal Gibbons, Archbishop of Baltimore, 1834-1921, 2 Vol. (Milwaukee: Bruce, 1952), p. 133 ff., and James H. Moynihan, Life of Archbishop Ireland. (New York: Harper Bros., 1953).

4 The American Protective Society (A. P. A.) established in Clinton, Iowa in 1887 by Henry F. Bowers pledged its members to active opposition against Catholics as threats to American institutions. Tom Watson, a frustrated Southern radical, in 'Watson's Paper, " decried the "Foreign foe at our gates, " "spies within" who would 'unlock the country's portals. " The Menace, published in Aurora, Mo., did a rousing business in anti-Catholic books, arranging engagements for anti-Catholic lecturers, and, through its columns circulating much calumnious and inflammatory copy.

5 "The strangely influential 'Signorina' who . . . siding with New York prelate, would show a growing and implacable opposition to Gibbons. " John Tehan, Prince of Democracy, James Cardinal Gibbons. (Garden City, N. J.: Hanover House, 1962), p. 105.

6 The United States remained in the status of a missionary country, however, and so under the jurisdiction of the Sacred Congregation of the Propaganda until 1908.

7 Fogarty, p. 237.

8 Ibid., p. 234.

9 See Chapter VIII, Patrick H. Ahern, The Life of John J. Keane, Educator and Archbishop, 1839-1918. (Milwaukee: Bruce 1954).

10 Fogarty, p. 299ff.

11 Rev. Walter Elliott, The Life of Father Hecker. (New York: Columbus Press, 1898).

12 There was "hardly a trace of intellectual activity in the Church in America." Quoted from the professor of church history Albert Erhard by John Tracy Ellis in his study "The Formation of the American Priest: An Historical Perspective," contained in The Catholic Priest of the United States: Historical Investigation (Collegeville: St. John's University Press, 1971), p. 74.

13 For a careful study of moderism in the American Church see also Michael V. Gannon, "Before and After Modernism, The Intellectual Isolation of the American Priest," pp. 293-383 of the above volume.

14 Ellis, op. cit., p. 73.

15 Ibid.

APPENDIX II

EDUCATION - A CRITICAL ISSUE

It was at the insistence of the Holy Father, Leo XIII, that the Third Plenary Council of Baltimore occupied itself in 1884 with the establishment of a system of parochial schools. As early as the year 1875 the Sacred Congregation, in its "Instructions to the Bishops of the United States Concerning Public Schools, " insisted that

. . . there is nothing so needful to this end as the establishment of Catholic schools in every place - and schools no whit inferior to the public ones. Every effort, then, must be directed toward starting Catholic schools where they are not, and where they are, toward enlarging them and providing them with better accommodations and equipment until they have nothing to suffer as regards teachers nor furniture by comparison with the public schools. [1]

Aware that it was not always possible to meet acceptable standards, the directive conceded that parents could be permitted by their bishop to send their child to public schools where proper cause existed:

Generally speaking, such cause will exist where there is no Catholic school in the place, or the one that is there cannot be considered suitable to the condition and circumstances in the life of the pupils. [2]

However, parents were not to take lightly their responsibility toward the religious education of their children.

Parents who neglect to give this necessary Christian training and instruction to their children, or who permit them to go to schools in which the ruin of their souls is inevitable, or, finally, who send them to the public schools without sufficient cause and without taking the necessary precautions to render the danger of perversion remote, and do so while there is a good and well-equipped Catholic school in the place, or the parents have the means to send them elsewhere to be educated - that such parents, if obstinate, cannot be absolved, is evident from the moral teaching of the Church.[3]

Both the Sacred Congregation and the Council decreed that when a bishop granted permission for attendance at a public school, "no one, layman or cleric, should presume to denounce or condemn such an action, much less pastors make it a pretext to refuse the sacraments to the child or its parents."[4]

The Council decreed that within two years of its adjournment a school was to be established in every parish and that it was to be maintained "in perpetuum" "unless the bishop, on account of grave difficulties, judge the postponement to be allowed." A pastor, who through "grave negligence" did not carry out the provisions of the decree "deserves removal from that church.'[5]

That the parish school should "have nothing to suffer as regards teachers and furniture by comparison to the public schools, was not always to set high standards. Normal training schools for teachers were non-existent in large areas of the country, and many of those which existed did little more than review the subject matter to be taught. Public school teachers, especially in rural situations, were frequently but little ahead of their older pupils in age and attainment.[6] The one-room country school which provided the elements of education for a fairly large section of the population continued through the early 1900's in primitive simplicity and with a paucity of instructional materials.

In the late nineteenth and early twentieth century public school teaching was still regarded as an occupation for youth, and was recompensed with youth's pay.[7] As such it came to interest fewer and fewer young men. The girl who boarded around with the families whose children she taught was scarcely regarded as a professional. Not always a high school graduate, she may have attended a four-weeks' institute in teacher training organized by the county, or qualified for a single-term certificate based on an examination an elementary school graduate might be expected to pass. Even so, many exceptions were made, despite the efforts of legislators to raise standards. If the status of an occupation can be judged by the compensation offered, the average pay of a female teacher in 1900 of $30.24[8] a month for a seven or eight month year is significant. Fortunately for the young woman, teaching ordinarily served only as an interim occupation before marriage.

In contrast the religious teacher expected to give her life to the work of the classroom. Hers was a dedication not ordinarily to be expected of a hired teacher. For her community solidarity involved a pooling of resources in education and methods. However, as standards rose and the curriculum broadened, her need for higher education grew beyond the power of the community to supply.

While the Third Plenary Council had recognized the need for high schools and colleges, it left their establishment and support open to religious orders of men and women. However, it decreed the founding of a Catholic university to be organized along the lines of the University of Louvain and subject to the direction of the bishops. [9] Its purpose was the post-seminary training of the American clergy. Opened in 1889, the University experienced much turbulence during its early years. Its first setback was Spalding's refusal of the rectorship. The building problems, the assembling of a faculty, and begging tours for its support, all fell to the lot of John J. Keane, Bishop of Richmond. Then there was the all-pervasive problem of secret opposition on the part of the conservative bishops. Although Archbishop Corrigan of New York and his friends had signed their names to the petition seeking approbation from Rome for the venture, Corrigan had fed suspicion and opposition to it in his communications with the Holy See. [10] The same conservatives gave support to certain German professors whom Keane had hired but whom he soon recognized as elements of disruption. Their purpose was accomplished with Keane's dismissal in 1896. The appointment of the less effectual Bishop Thomas Conaty to the rectorship, and a financial disaster involving nearly a million of the University's limited funds through bankruptcy proceedings against the school's financial agent, [11] combined to threaten its very existence.

Although the University was established as a graduate school for clerics, [12] only the later admission of laymen and the inclusion of undergraduate courses enabled it to survive. Its relation to the parochial school system came much later.

It was the problem of financing the system of parochial schools that most seriously concerned the bishops of the country. They took the logical position that the service rendered by their schools in the education of a significant portion of the nation's future citizens entitled the schools to a proportionate share of the school taxes.

Prior to the establishment of the public school system, the populace had entertained no scruples about the provision of funds to those Catholic schools which provided the only education facilities in an area. [13] However, the bishops' appeal now met a hue and cry about the separation of church and state, as a similar appeal by Archbishop John Hughes of New York had done in earlier years.

Archbishop Ireland sought a solution to the problem by an ar-

rangement with the public school boards of Faribault and Still-
water, Minnesota, towns in his archdiocese. Here the boards
rented the Catholic school buildings during school hours and the
Sister-teachers were certified and paid by the school boards.
Religion classes were held outside the regular hours. Although
similar arrangements were in operation in a number of other
dioceses, Ireland's action in this, as in so many of his endeavors, drew fire. To the conservatives, public schools were "gat
of hell, " "hotbeds of vice, " and "sources of corruption. " The
general outcry over Ireland's arrangement from the conservativ
wing of the hierarchy led to embroilment on both sides of the
Atlantic, until Leo XIII issued his tolerari potest, [14] regarding
the Faribault plan. However, the expression of tolerance came
late, for the public school authorities had reacted to Protestant
pressure and had already withdrawn from the arrangement.

Catholic schools had already proven the most effective instru
ment in acclimating the vast numbers of immigrants and establishing loyalty to their adopted land. Yet, without public support
few parishes could provide better accommodations for the educa
tion of their children than church basements or other makeshift
quarters, crowded, poorly heated, lighted and ventilated, and,
as such, breeding places for epidemics of illness. The stipends
pastors could allot for teaching services were at subsistence
levels, and were not always collectable. Yet, many could do
no better. In the end it was the religious teacher who was to
bear the heaviest end of the load, not only in the classroom but
in personal poverty and consequent hardships and inconvenience

Decree 205 of the Council's Acta and Decreta imposed on the
religious congregations of women, not only the provision of an a
quate number of teachers, but under the threat of Rome, the est
lishment of normal schools for the training of those teachers:

> In order that there may be always ready a sufficient number
> of Catholic teachers, each thoroughly equipped for the holy
> and sublime work of the education of youth, we would have
> the bishops concerned to confer with the superiors of con-
> gregations dedicated to the work of teaching in the schools,
> either directly on their own authority, or, if need be, in-
> voking the authority of the Sacred Congregation, for the
> establishment of normal schools where they do not exist,
> and there is need for them. These are to be suitable estab-
> lishments, in which the young may be trained by skillful
> and capable teachers, during a sufficient period of time
> and with a truly religious diligence, in the various studies
> and sciences, in method and pedagogy and other branches

pertaining to a sound training for teaching. [15]

Not only were young religious to be prepared by normal courses, but each classroom teacher was expected to have earned a teacher's diploma from the educational authorities of the state, in addition to her certification by a proposed diocesan school board.

Was the deposit of learning within the pioneer communities sufficient to meet the educational needs of a rapidly progressing society, as well as the professional requirements the Council demanded? If not, how was it to be supplemented? The only Catholic colleges and universities in existence in the country were strictly masculine preserves, with priests either forbidden to or discouraged from the teaching of women. Religious women as late as 1912, were forbidden to take courses from laymen. [16] At the same time the attendance of religious at secular universities was severely restricted by many bishops[17] as a danger to the religious spirit and a source of scandal to Catholic people who were forbidden to send their children to these institutions.

While the many European congregations that had come to the States before the Civil War were by this time fairly Americanized, the congregations the bishops were now recruiting faced many of the same problems experienced earlier. Educated in a vastly different milieu, trained in their own convent schools, these Sisters belonged largely to the upper social classes. [18] Many of them were cloistered, living under solemn vows, and as such were quite unprepared for the open life required of them in the New World. Class conscious, and trained to the refinements of a conventional society, prepared for teaching in the exclusive finishing schools of the continent, [19] they were shocked by the frank and casual ways of young America. Their students, on the other hand, were unaccustomed to their gentle piety, and psychologically unattuned to a training in the elegancies of manner familiar to the European élite. Especially distasteful to the young was the position accorded by the Sisters to the lay members who were assigned to menial tasks and set apart from the choir Sisters by their humble attire. These reactions complicated by their expression in a strange tongue were sources of puzzlement and dismay to the Sisters.

Financial problems were entirely new to many of the recent arrivals. Accustomed to assured support in well-endowed convents to which they had themselves brought substantial dowries, they had long provided free schools for the poor as adjuncts to their fashionable academies. But there were no such endowments in the New World, and those who entered their ranks had little to offer by way of dowry. The number of girls prepared to pay full tuition in select schools was small indeed in comparison with those too poor to pay at all.

Bound as these Sisters were to their own traditions, and by directives from their European superiors, they were often seriously hampered in their efforts to serve those most in need of their help. Their regulations against admitting boys to their classrooms, a relic of the Janenistic influence, further limited their usefulness, as it did the service of American foundations influenced by their prestige.

Not least to be considered were the problems faced by those European sisterhoods that responded to the glowing promises of bishops, only to find themselves in remote situations, badly housed, illy provided for, and required to conduct their classes under the most unfavorable circumstances. While the Sisters had little recourse, the bishops who had sought their coming looked to their separation from their European foundations, exacting such changes in their rules as would make their services effective in the respective dioceses. All this could not be accomplished without pain for those with deep loyalty to their origins. Some grew discouraged and returned to their homelands, while others eventually freed themselves from the jurisdiction of their bishops by applying to Rome for the status of papal institutes.

For these and for the many later migrations - Polish, Lithuanian, etc. - assigned to national schools, the requirement that they teach their candidates in their own normal schools was to isolate them further from the American scene, though it appealed strongly to their nationalistic inclinations.

The Council's requirements for full novitiate training and teacher preparation were largely nullified by the pressure of bishops and pastors to obtain teachers for the ever-growing number of classrooms.

The stalemate in the effective training of Sisters continued until in the early 1900's state demands for compulsory education of all children under certified teachers threatened the entire parochial system. While religious women had long struggled in silence against their own inadequacies, they were well aware that even their best efforts were unequal to the challenge they faced. Their only alternatives were attendance at secular universities or laying the responsibility for the Catholic school system on the consciences of clerical educators. Their efforts were reinforced by the many Catholic women teaching in public schools who were determined to improve their own educational status without endangering their faith.

As women's colleges established under Protestant influence in the east antedated those Catholic by nearly half a century, so state universities in the midwest opened their doors to women before Catholic institutions of higher education by about the same margin.

Professing fear that the intellectual struggle would prove disastrous to the fragile female constitution, the universities had only with great reluctance admitted women to the sanctuaries of learning. Iowa, the first of the state universities to do so, experimented with a normal department, admitting girls of twelve and boys of fourteen who possessed as prerequisite a slate and pencil, a notebook and a dictionary and atlas. [20]

The University of Wisconsin first tolerated the presence of women in order to fill seats left vacant by Civil War enlistees. It later segregated them on another campus. Only in 1870 did the University of Michigan permit the "contamination" of the institution by coeds.

After 1870 the University of Missouri, having discovered slowly that "the Normal did no matter of harm," cautiously admitted women to some of the recitations and lectures in the University itself, "providing always they were to be marched in good order with at least two teachers, one in the front and one at the rear of the column as guards." Women were next cautiously admitted to chapel, [21] though seated discreetly apart and restrained from raising their voices in prayer. On continued good behavior they were gradually granted full privileges. [22]

The first breakthrough in Catholic institutions came in 1911 in the form of summer sessions. These were quickly followed by extension courses and more gradually by the admission of women to classes during the academic year. The advantage was mutual, for the religious congregations tended at first to send their older and more able members. The pace these set for study reacted on teachers and students alike. [23] Increasing pressure for degrees later involved all, however, with less happy results, both for scholarship and the religious spirit.

In the matter of teacher preparation the Sisters, and consequently parochial schools, owe their deepest debt to the Reverend Doctor Thomas E. Shields. Father Shields was a Minnesota priest whose doctoral studies at the Johns Hopkins University Archbishop Ireland had sponsored, later sacrificing his services to the Catholic University of America. Having himself suffered greviously at the hands of inept teachers, [24] Dr. Shields concentrated, with a strong sense of mission, on the building of a school for the training and education of religious teachers. [25] To this he added the compiling of a pedagogically sound series

of religious readers of high cultural value. With the encouragement and cooperation of Dr. E. A. Pace, the vice-rector of the
University, Dr. Shields set about the establishment of a Sisters
college[26] to be staffed by University professors - the University
campus was then, and would continue for many years to be, holy
ground, sacred to the male of the species.

Shields' first step was to establish correspondence courses
available to the Sisters. As a further prelude to his venture, he
spent several summers conducting teachers' institutes in centers throughout the country. His first summer school session
for Sisters was held in Washington, D. C., in 1911, the Sisters
living wherever accommodations could be found. A large port-
able building, set up on the grounds of the Benedictine Sisters'
convent for the holding of classes, was later removed to the
grounds he had purchased for the proposed Sisters' college,
despite the studied opposition of many to that project. [27] In this
setting classes were held until the opening of Brady Hall, the
gift of Mrs. Nicholas Brady, in the summer of 1916. The new
institution was henceforth known officially as the Catholic
Teachers' College.

Dr. Shields had succeeded in bringing women to the edge of
the Catholic University, but the campus remained secure from
them except for six-weeks' summer sessions. Even his most
heroic efforts could not provide the Sisters' College with satisfactory library and laboratory facilities for the bachelor's
degree - certainly not for the master's for which there was
growing need. Strenuous begging tours in which his greatest
appeal was to the country's Catholic women received a serious
setback when in 1914 the University rector, Bishop Shahan,
proudly announced on his return from Rome that he had received
from the Holy Father permission for the erection of a national
shrine in honor of the Immaculate Conception on the University
grounds. His appeal too was directed to the nation's Catholic
women. [28]

The summer of 1911 witnessed a summer session for women
at DePaul University in Chicago. While the Jesuits were not
authorized to teach women, they began a series of lectures at
St. Mary High School, Chicago, that fall. Marquette University
in Wisconsin attempted, though unsuccessfully, to provide for
the education of Sisters by sponsoring the foundation of a Sisters' college affiliated with the University and under the directio
of the B. V. M. Sisters. In 1910 it had affiliated with a coeducational school of journalism. This complicated matters for the
school, unauthorized to teach women, and it could only comprom
by permitting Sisters to audit university classes that summer an

the summers following until the teaching of women could be regularized. The older and endowed Creighton University of Omaha responded promptly to the educational needs of the Sisters. The Holy Cross Fathers at Notre Dame delayed until 1918[29] when their first summer session was opened to women.

Few men's colleges and universities remained closed to them after that, save only the Bishops' Catholic University. It was not until 1924 that the first woman, under the patronage of the Most Reverend Joseph Busch, Bishop of St. Cloud, was admitted to graduate work at the Catholic University. Sister M. Inez Hilger, OSB, was in that year enrolled for a master's degree in the downtown school of social studies. [30]

Under the sponsorship of Dr. Pace, Sister M. Joseph Therese Geiger, B. V. M. , who had done prerequisite work during the summer of 1926, was permitted to register for doctoral studies in biology. Two years later, Bishop James H. Ryan, newly installed as rector of the University, dropped the bars against women in most university classes. It was not until the 1960's, however, that the School of Theology was opened to women. [31] Then the Sister Formation movement brought pressure to bear on the University in view of the needs of women religious for master's and doctoral degrees in that field. This seems strange in view of the fact that the general level of religious instruction in the whole Catholic school system had been for many years largely dependent on their adequacy as its teachers.

Meantime many Catholic academies for girls had added postgraduate work to their secondary courses. For these the teachers had prepared themselves as best they could by private study, correspondence courses, and series of lectures brought to their campuses for their own benefit as well as that of their students. [32] In these endeavors, however, they trailed by nearly half a century leading non-Catholic schools in the east. There lay women, finding doors to higher education closed to them - save for the limited access granted by midwest state universities - and encouraged by generous benefactors, had established their own colleges, all, however, with a strongly Protestant orientation. These included the Lyons Female Seminary, Smith, Vassar, Radcliffe, Bryn Mawr, Barnard and Wellesley, though in their beginnings the general lack of preparation for collegiate work on the part of their students held the schools at the preparatory level through a number of years. [33]

With so strong a lead given by these eastern institutions, it was to be expected that the earliest Catholic colleges for women would have their start in the east.

The Academy of Notre Dame in Maryland petitioned for the

right to give degrees, granting their first for a four-year progra
in 1899. [34] Almost simultaneously the Sisters of Charity of Moth
Seton obtained a charter for St. Elizabeth Academy at Convent
Station, New Jersey, conferring their first degree in 1903. St.
Joseph College, founded by Mother Seton in Baltimore as an
academy, and later moved to Emmitsburg, graduated its first
four-year students in 1906, though it had conferred its first college degree in 1898. [35]

St. Mary Academy, Notre Dame, Indiana, closely associated
with the men's College of Notre Dame (later University) offered
post graduate work as early as 1872. In 1903 the name was
changed to St. Mary College, when it began to give the baccalau-
reate degree in four fields. (It was a pioneer again when, under
Sister Madeleva, its president, it opened a school of theology
for graduate study in 1944.)[36]

Trinity College, Washington, D. C. , was the first institution
initially established for the higher education of women. Like St.
Mary's, Notre Dame, it could draw on a university for many of
the professors of the Catholic University gave support and encou
agement to the venture. The new institution received its first
students - seventeen of them - in September 1900, graduating its
first class in 1904. [37]

In the midwest St. Clara College, conducted by the Sisters of
St. Dominic of Sinsinawa, Wisconsin, obtained its first charter
in 1901. Equating the last two years of academy training with
the first two years of college, its academy graduates of 1902
entered the college course as "juniors. " Its two graduates of
1904 were then in reality junior college graduates. The school's
first four-year graduate received her degree in 1910. [38]

St. Teresa College, Winona, Minnesota, grew out of the Our
Lady of Lourdes Academy[39] conducted by the Franciscan Sisters
of Rochester. Sister Leo Tracy, OSF, mistress of the academy,
desiring to raise the school to college level, acquired in 1907
the services of Mary Molloy, just graduated with a doctoral
degree from Cornell University. Mary initiated the college by
carrying four Franciscan Sisters through the full four years of
undergraduate work in preparation for teaching positions in the
Congregation's schools. By 1910 she issued a brochure which
brought its first secular students. [40] Finances were never a
serious problem, for the growing St. Mary Hospital at Rochester
shared its resources with the budding college.

The Sisters of St. Joseph of St. Paul, with the encouragement
of Archbishop Ireland and of Dr. Thomas Shields of Catholic University, inaugurated a college program at St. Catherine Academ
in 1905, though Ireland had anticipated such a move as early as

1887. [41] With royalties from his own writings and donations he encouraged, he paved the way for the construction of the first college building. In 1916 the institution became a four-year accredited college. The dominant figure in those years was Sister Antonia McHugh, CSJ. As a teacher in the academy she took her first collegiate courses in 1902 and 1903 by correspondence from the University of Chicago. Then followed four successive summer courses and a full year of study at the University. By 1909 she had received a master of philosophy degree. Other Sisters had also attended the University of Chicago, the University of Minnesota, or Harvard preparatory to college teaching. [42]

As early as 1896 graduates of Mt. St. Joseph Academy in Dubuque, under the direction of the Sisters of Charity of the Blessed Virgin Mary, had been returning for post graduate work. This, with the encouragement of the newly installed Archbishop Keane, led to the opening in 1901 of a three-year college department which granted its first bachelor of arts degree in 1904. A charter for a four-year course was granted in 1912, and by 1915 Mt. St. Joseph College was offering the full four years of college work and a teacher's certificate to those completing its educational courses. The school was fully accredited in 1918. It thus became the first all-woman's college in Iowa and the first Catholic woman's college on record west of the Mississippi. [43]

Thus by the opening of the twentieth century the various sisterhoods had begun to provide for their members training for the bachelor's degree. In each case, courses preparatory to teaching were offered, leading to the necessary certification. While supplanting normal schools, they provided preparation for entrance into the universities at the graduate level. By 1915 there were fifty-seven women's colleges in the United States conducted by Catholic sisterhoods. [44] The challenge met by Catholic women, [45] religious and lay, brought them into leadership roles in many fields, calling forth talents which had long lain fallow for want of the means of education.

Notes

1 Rev. J. A. Burns, PhD. The Growth and Development of the Catholic School System in the United States. (New York: Benziger Brothers, 1912), p. 190.

2 Ibid.

3 Ibid., p. 191.

4 Peter Guilday. A History of the Councils of Baltimore, 1791-1884. (New York: The Macmillan Company, 1932), p. 239. The following letter found in the Notre Dame Archives was addressed by Orestes A. Brownson, Jr., son of the famous convert, to his brother, tells of the difficulty he had experienced with Bishop Hennessy of Dubuque in 1869:

. . . I have felt very sad and hardly know what to do in regard to my school difficulties. Before commencing to teach here after Bishop Hennessy became Bishop of Dubuque, I went to him & consulted him about teaching the school to which I was appointed, viz., the First Ward Public School. He said, "Go and teach it. " I have done so. Now he prevents my children and all children that attend my school from the Sacraments, and from going to the Catechism classes in the Church or to the Sisters, & preaches against me, not by name but by insinuation, so that I cannot go to the High Mass for fear of abuse. I am glad you have told me what the Catholic doctrine is upon this subject. He has sent away all the Jesuit priests and monks that were here and only allows young or ignorant priests of his appointing. . . .

5 Burns, p. 199.

6 Sister Bertrand Meyers, in her doctoral dissertation on the education of Sisters, spoke of the many problems public school officials met in efforts to establish standards. Certificates were obtained through examination. However, she wrote, almost any grammar school graduate could qualify for at least a low-grade credential that would permit her to teach two years, taking another examination on the expiration of her certificate. The Education of Sisters. (New York: Sheed and Ward, 1941), p. 24.

7 Paper delivered by Professor Thomas Morain, Iowa State

University, Ames, at the conference of Women Historians in St. Paul in October 1977.

8 Report of the Superintendent of Public Instruction, Iowa, 1847-1901, contained in Morain's footnotes.

9 The University was, in fact, the brain child of Bishop Spalding of Peoria, whose own broad training had included graduation from Louvain. A pledge of $300,000 by a New York heiress, Mary Gweldoline Caldwell, had encouraged the Council to act.

10 Corrigan's opposition was based on the competition the new school would offer to the Fordham establishment in New York. He also proposed the Nation's capital as its site.

11 See John Tracy Ellis, The Formation Years of the Catholic University of America. (Washington: American Catholic Historical Society, 1946).

12 Seminary education at the time left much to be desired. See Appendix I, pp.

13 Mother Clarke's account books show a number of such payments.

14 "could be tolerated. "

15 Burns, p. 110.

16 In a circular letter to superiors sent by Mother Ascension Lilly in 1912, she wrote: "The Sisters are hereby forbidden to take lessons from laymen in any branch of study; laymen should not be brought in to teach either Sisters or pupils. This restriction is in accordance with directions from the Holy See. " Such a regulation seems less remarkable to us when we realize that until Vatican II, laymen were not acceptable for the teaching of seminarians.

17 Ever an independent in such matters, it was Archbishop Ireland who arranged for four of the St. Joseph Sisters of St. Catherine Academy in St. Paul to study at the University of Chicago through a succession of summers in the early 1900's, and to attend other universities in preparation for the expansion of the academy into a college, and thus to contribute substantially

to its success. (Karen Kennelly, CSJ, "Sister Antonia McHugh: Women's College Founder, " unpublished manuscript, 1977).

Prior to the opening of the College of St. Teresa in Winona, Minnesota by the Sisters of St. Francis of Rochester, "Sisters who were qualified had attended the University of Minnesota, Trinity College, Harvard University and the Minnesota School of Art. " (Sister Mary Caedmon Homan, OSF, Years of Vision, 1903-1928, A History of the Sisters of the Third Order Regular of St. Francis of the Congregation of Our Lady of Lourdes, Rochester, Minnesota. Unpublished Master's dissertation, Catholic University of America, Washington, D. C. , 1956), p. 43.

The Sisters of St. Dominic, Sinsinawa, Wisconsin ventured to send Sisters to the Universities of Wisconsin, Chicago, Howard and Washington (St. Louis) for summer sessions in the early 1900's. (Sister Mary Eva McCarty, OP, The Sinsinawa Dominicans: Outlines of Twentieth Century Development, 1901-1949. (Dubuque: Hoermann Press, 1952), p. 65.

It is possible that Ireland was cognizant of the fact that as early as 1897 an Italian order of Sisters had been granted permission for university attendance.

. . . They are not only allowed to attend lecture in the public universities in Rome, mingling there with laymen and listening to lectures by professors of every mental order, but they doff their religious dress to do so.

Also,

. . . The head of the French teaching Sisters of the Sacred Heart, a very progressive woman, went before the Vatican authorities . . . with an educational plan by which the novices of the order were to be allowed to take a normal course outside their convent restrictions and taught by up to date professors. (From an unidentified clipping found in Mother Cecilia's file.)

18 For this study of foreign congregation, the writer is indebted to the doctoral dissertation of Sister Mary Ewens, OP, The Role of the Nun in Nineteenth Century America: Variations on the International Theme.

19 There were notable exceptions, especially in the more practical German foundations with training colleges for teachers which enjoyed the advantage of able faculties under the direction of the bishops. An example may be found in the Congregation of the Sisters of Notre Dame. See Sister Mary Vincentia, SND, The Quiet Tread. (Milwaukee: Catholic Life Publications, Bruce Pres 1955), pp. 113-121.

20 Professor Robert E. Belding, Chairman/Professor of
American Educational History, University of Iowa, points out
still a room in the "Old Capitol, " University administration
building in which the female scholars were at first carefully
sequestered.

21 The feature of chapel services in state universities indicates the dominance of Protestant influence in these institutions.

22 The writer is indebted to Professor Belding for the above
data on midwestern universities. See his article, "Iowa's Brave
Model for Women's Education, " in Annals of Iowa, Summer Issue,
1976.

23 While Sister M. Ambrose Mulholland was a doctoral student in medieval history at Columbia University in the thirties,
the President, Nicholas Murray Butler, invited to dinner the
several Sisters studying in the Graduate School, together with
Cardinal Eugene Tisserant, then a visitor to the States. During
dinner the Cardinal turned to their host in jest and asked: "And
how are the girls behaving, Doctor Butler? " Butler's ready
response was: "I can't vouch for their virtue, Your Eminence,
but I can for their brains. According to their chairmen, they're
all the top students in their departments. " Sister M. Ambrose
remained in that category at Columbia, her dissertation receiving the distinction of publication by the University.
    Sister M. Augustina Ray was among the first women to merit a
degree from St. Louis University and later did distinguished research at Columbia University. Her PhD dissertation, American
Opinion of Roman Catholicism in the Eighteenth Century, earned
the University's award for the best dissertation in American
history submitted during the five-year period in which it was
presented.

24 Thomas E. Shields, The Making and Unmaking of a Dullard.
(Washington, D. C. : The Catholic Education Press, 1900).

25 See Justine Ward, Thomas Edward Shields, Biologist,
Psychologist, Educator. (New York: Charles Scribners Sons,
1947), p. 104 ff.

26 Bishop Spalding had long been an advocate of women's
education, holding that women had the same right in that regard
as men, and should have the opportunity for learning equal to that
provided for men. In his concern for the proper training of

teachers, he had proposed to his fellow bishops the establishment of a "central normal school, a sort of educational university" somewhat after the pattern of Teachers' College at
Columbia University. ("Normal Schools, " published in the
Catholic World, and quoted in Burns, p. 215.)

27 "So strong was the opposition still when the Rector of the
Catholic University went to Rome, he was amazed to be shown
letters (enough to fill a good-sized volume) from holy and conservative men and women requesting the Vicar of Christ to
withhold his approval! " Ward, op. cit. , pp. 138-139.

28 Ibid. , p. 212.

29 It is pleasant to contemplate the terms of that first summer session. Tuition fees of $30. 00, room rental, $1. 00 a week,
and a flat rate of $6. 50 for a week's board. As for religion
courses offered, there were two two-hour courses - apologetics
and methods of teaching religion. (See Bulletin of the University
of Notre Dame, Summer Session, University Press, January
1918.) Notre Dame at that time continued to maintain minims
and secondary departments.

30 Roy J. Deferrari, PhD, LLD, Memoirs of the Catholic
University of America, 1918-1960. (Boston: St. Paul Edictions,
1962), p. 231.

31 "Father Walter Schmitz, who was Dean of the School of
Theology for many years, informed me that he attended the
Vatican Council in Rome during the early to mid-sixties, and
with the permission of Bishop William McDonald, who was
Rector of the University at that time, was able to secure consent
for religious women and laymen to enter the Theology program.
These women were permitted, if qualified, to earn a Roman
Pontifical Theological degree. " Letter of April 20, 1977 from
Joseph C. Michalowicz, Registrar, the Catholic University of
America.

32 "There was no particular cause for discouragement in
the lack of degrees among the Sisters: when Bryn Mawr was
founded in 1885, women were teaching at Wellesley, Mount
Holyoke and Smith without even so much as a single college
course behind them! " Karen Kennelly, CSJ, "Mary Molloy, "
Women of Minnesota, Selected Biographical Essays. (St. Paul:
Minnesota Historical Society Press, 1977), p. 121.

33 See the delightful study of these colleges by Elaine Kendall, Peculiar Institutions, An Informal History of the Seven Sister Colleges. (New York: Putnam & Sons, 1976.)

34 Sister Marietta Bowler, M. A., A History of Catholic Colleges for Women in the United States. (Doctoral Dissertation, Catholic University of America, Washington, D. C., 1933), p. 21.

35 Edward J. Powers, A History of Catholic Higher Education in the United States. (Milwaukee: Bruce Publishing Company, 1958), p. 193.

36 Ibid.

37 Ibid., p. 192.

38 Sister Mary Eva McCarty, OP, The Sinsinawa Dominicans: Outlines of Twentieth Century Development, 1901-1949. (Dubuque: The Hoermann Press, 1952), pp. 51, 52.

39 The building occupied by the academy had been planned as a motherhouse and academy by the School Sisters of St. Francis, a German foundation, previously situated at New Castle, Wisconsin. Following its dedication, Bishop Ireland, who had officiated, informed Mother Alexia that the community was to receive no more recruits from Germany, and that the foundation was thenceforth to be diocesan, and so under his control. The response of the Sisters was to quietly vacate the premises, returning to their former location, and later constructing a new motherhouse in Milwaukee. See Sister Francis Borgia Rothluebber, OSF, He Sent Two: The Story of the Beginning of the School Sisters of St. Francis. (Milwaukee: Bruce Publishing Company, 1965), p. 94.

40 Kennelly, op. cit., p. 122.

41 Kathleen Kennelly, CSJ, "Sister Antonia McHugh, Women's College Founder," manuscript, 29 typewritten pages.

42 Ibid.

43 A more detailed study of this college can be found in chapter nine of this volume.

472

44 Bowler, op. cit., p. 69.

45 A study of the early colleges conducted by men and those by women, comparing their strengths and weaknesses, indicates that both "ignored the compelling prescription: one cannot give what he does not have or teach what he does not know. " Both, he says, "allowed their academies to become colleges before a faculty of college quality was assembled. " However, the author observes that women's colleges "probably came closer to approaching the primary aim of liberal education . . . for they were certainly not preparatory seminaries as most of the early colleges for men had been. " He points out a serious handicap under which women's colleges have consistently suffered:

Without the advantages for public notice enjoyed by most Catholic colleges for men /and especially the diocesan support which has been consistently confined to men's schools/ and Catholic coeducational colleges - advantages which often lead to benefactions - and almost totally devoid of endowments, Catholic colleges for women have used what resources they had to make an important contribution to American higher education. Powers, op. cit., pp. 195-197.

BIBLIOGRAPHY

SOURCE MATERIALS

The Congregation's source materials as listed in Volume I,
Appendix III,   and

Original handwritten copy of Rule as presented to Jesuit Fathers

Original handwritten copy of Rule by Father Donaghoe

Mother Clarke's Notes, Letters and Correspondence

Articles of Incorporation

Book of Minutes, Board of Managers and Council Meetings

Account Books, 1869-1920

Latin copy of the Rule as it went to Rome 1875

Bound copy of the same Rule in English

Manuscript list of changes to be made in the Rule before approbation, including descriptive titles of chapters

Bound copy of Rule as approved by Rome 1877

Notes of Consultor in Latin

72 letters, Father Trevis, regarding Rule

Decrees of Praise, and of temporary and final approbation

Notes by the Rev. Walter Hill, S. J. , regarding Rule as sent for
final approbation

Set of Books of Common Observances, Editions, 1882-1928

Set of Constitutions and Rules, Editions, 1875-1928

Set of Catholic Directories, 1835-1920 (Incomplete)

Photograph files

Minutes of Chapter Sessions

Mortuary list, giving causes of deaths (Statistics)

List of entrants and of departures (Statistics)

Record of Events, S. M. Pulcheria McGuire, 1900-1906
S. M. Lambertina Doran, 1906-1920

Diary, S. M. Crescentia Markey, 1894-1900

Letters and Correspondence, Mothers M. Gertrude, Cecilia
and Ascension

Book of the Missions, data on opening of missions and terms
of superiors

Architect's drawings for Motherhouse

Provincial Records, 1915-1920

Our Herald, Congregation's publication

Circular Letters, 1887-1920

Personal Folders

Folders of Individual Missions

Registers of Members

Partial Memoirs of Sisters

Personal Interviews

Taped Interviews with Retired Sisters, S. M. Angelita Kramer,
1953

Extensive Notes of Sister Doris Walsh, B. V. M. , on Mothers M.
Gertrude and Cecilia

Chapter Records of Visitation Convent, Dubuque, through 1910

Griffith Files, Davenport Diocesan archives

BOOKS AND UNPUBLISHED DISSERTATIONS

Ahern, Patrick Henry, MA, PhD. The Life of John J. Keane, Educator and Archbishop, 1839-1918. Milwaukee: Bruce, 1954.

Bauer, Gerald C. Protestantism in America. Philadelphia: The Westminster Press, ca. 1968.

Bowler, Sister Mary Mariella, MA. A History of Catholic Colleges for Women in the United States of America. Doctoral Dissertation, Catholic University of America. Washington, D. C., 1933.

Burns, Rev. J. A., PhD. The Growth and Development of the Catholic School System in the United States. New York: Benziger Bros., 1912.

Burton, Katherine. Leo the Thirteenth, the First Modern Pope. New York: David McKay Co., Inc., 1962.

Butts, R. Freeman and Lawrence A. Cremin. A History of Education in American Culture. New York: Henry Holt & Co., 1953.

Callan, Sister Mary Anna Rose, B. V. M. The Sisters of Charity of the Blessed Virgin Mary and Their Schools in Chicago, 1867-1940, unpublished Master's Thesis, Loyola University, 1941.

Callan, Sister Louise, RSCJ. The Society of the Sacred Heart in North America. New York: Longmans, Green & Co., 1937.

Carroll, Berenice A., editor. Liberating Women's History, Theoretical and Critical Essays. Urbana: University of Illinois Press, 1976.

Cogley, John. Catholic America. Garden City, N. Y.: Image Books, 1974.

476

Conroy, Rev. Joseph P., S. J. Arnold Damen, S. J. A Chapter in the Making of Chicago. Chicago: Benziger Brothers, 1930.

Coogan, Sister M. St. Joan of Arc. BVM, History of the Immaculate Conception Academy of Davenport, Iowa, and of the Foundations of Catholic Education in That City. Master's Thesis, Catholic University of America, 1941.

Cross, Barbara M., editor. The Educated Woman in America. New York: Teachers College Press, 1965

Dansetto, Adrien. Religions History of Modern France, Vol. II. New York: Herder & Herder, 1961.

Dedmon, Emmett. Fabulous Chicago. New York: Random House, 1953.

Deferrari, Roy J., PhD., LLD, editor. Essays on Catholic Education in the United States. Washington, D. C. Catholic University of America, 1942.

Deferrari, Roy J., PhD., LLD. Memoirs of the Catholic University of America, 1918-1960. Boston: St. Paul Editions, 1962.

Donaghey, Thomas J., FSC. Philadelphia's Finest: A History of Education in the Catholic Archdiocese, 1692-1970. Philadelphia: American Catholic Historical Society, 1972.

Driscoll, Rt. Rev. Msgr. Justin A. Driscoll, PhD. With Faith and Vision, Schools of the Archdiocese of Dubuque, 1836-1966. Dubuque, Bureau of Education, Archdiocese of Dubuque, 1966.

Durkin, Sister M. Antonia, B. V. M., MA. The Preparation of the Religious Teacher. Catholic Teachers' College of the Catholic University of America. Doctoral Dissertation. Washington, D. C., 1926.

Elliott, Rev. Walter. The Life of Father Hecker. New York: Columbus Press, 1898. (Fourth Edition)

Ellis, John Tracy, editor. The Catholic Priest in the United States: Historical Investigations. Collegeville: St. John's University Press, 1971.

Ellis, John Tracy, PhD. The Formative Years of the Catholic University of America. Washington, D. C. : American Catholic Historical Society, 1946.

-----. The Life of James Cardinal Gibbons, Archbishop of Baltimore, 1834-1921. 2 vols. Milwaukee: Bruce Publishing Co. , 1952.

-----. Perspectives in American Catholicism. Baltimore: Helicon, 1963.

Euper, Sister Jo Ann, OSF. Century of Service, The School Sisters of St. Francis. Milwaukee: n. p. , 1976.

Ewens, Sister Mary, OP. The Role of the Nun in Nineteenth-Century America: Variations in the International Theme. Unpublished doctoral dissertation submitted to the Graduate School of the University of Minnesota, 1971.

Fogarty, Gerald P. , S. J. The Vatican and the American Crisis: Denis J. O'Connell, American Agent in Rome, 1885-1903. Roma: Universita Gregoriana Editrice, 1974.

Garraghan, Gilbert J. , S. J. , PhD. The Jesuits of the Middle United States. Vol. III. New York: America Press, 1938.

Gilkey, Langdon. Catholicism Confronts Modernity: A Protestant View. New York: The Seabury Press, 1975.

Greeley, Andrew M. The Catholic Experience: An Interpretation of the History of American Catholicism. Garden City: Doubleday & Co. , Inc. , 1967.

Griffith, Rev. Charles F. History of the Diocese of Davenport, 1881-1906. Unpublished Master's Thesis, University of Iowa.

Guilday, Rev. Peter, PhD. A History of the Councils of Baltimore, 1791-1884. New York: The Macmillan Company, 1932.

-----. The National Pastorals of the American Hierarchy (1792-1919). Washington, D. C. : National Catholic Welfare Council, 1923.

Hayes, Sister Mary Francis Ann, OSF. Years of Beginning, A History of the Sisters of the Third Order of St. Francis of

Our Lady of Lourdes, Rochester, Minnesota, 1877-1902. Master's Dissertation, Catholic University of America, Washington, D. C. , 1958.

Higham, John. Strangers in the Land: Patterns of American Nativism, 1860-1925. New Brunswick, N. J. : Rutgers University Press, 1955.

Hoffmann, Rev. M. M. , editor. Centennial History of the Arch-diocese of Dubuque. Columbia College Press, 1938.

Hoffmann, Rev. Matthias M. Story of Loras College. Dubuque: Loras College Press, 1939.

Homan, Sister Mary Caedmun, OSF. Years of Vision (A History of the Sisters of the Third Order of St. Francis of the Congregation of Our Lady of Lourdes, Rochester, Minnesota) 1903-1928. Master's Dissertation, Catholic University, Washington, D. C. , 1956.

-----. Years of Expansion, 1928-1970. Unpublished manuscript 1975.

Huyghe, Very Rev. Msgr. Gerard. "What Do We Mean by Religious? " in Religious Orders in the Modern World, A Symposi Westminster, Md. : Newman Press, 1965.

Ireland, John, Archbishop of St. Paul. The Church and Modern Society, Lectures and Addresses. 2 vols. New York: D. H. McBride & Co. , 1903.

Kavanagh, Rev. D. J. , S. J. The Holy Family Sisters of San Francisco, A Sketch of Their First Fifty Years, 1872-1922. San Francisco: Gilmartin Co. , 1922.

Kendall, Elaine. "Peculiar Institutions, " An Informal History of the Seven Sister Colleges. New York: G. P. Putnam's Sons, 1976.

Kennelly, Sister Karen, CSJ. Sister Antonia McHugh, Women's College Founder. Unpublished Manuscript, 1977.

Kohler, Sister Mary Hortense, OP. Rooted in Hope, The Story of the Dominican Sisters of Racine, Wisconsin. Milwaukee: Bruce Publishing Co. , 1962.

McAvoy, Thomas T., CSC. The Great Crisis in American Catholic History, 1895-1900. Chicago: Henry Regnery Company, 1957.

McCarty, Sister Mary Eva, OP. The Sinsinawa Dominicans, Outlines of Twentieth Century Development 1901-1949. Dubuque: Huermann Press, 1952.

McGovern, Rev. J. J. Souvenir of the Silver Jubilee in the Episcopacy of His Grace, The Most Rev. Patrick Augustine Feehan, Archbishop of Chicago. Chicago: n. p. 1890.

Meyers, Sister Bertrande, PhD. The Education of Sisters. New York: Sheed & Ward, 1941.

Mousel, Sister Mary Eunice, OSF, PhD. They Have Taken Root, The Sisters of the Third Order of St. Francis of the Holy Family. New York: Bookman Associates, 1954.

Mulholland, Sister M. Ambrose. History of Clarke College, unpublished.

Montay, Sister Mary Innocenta, CSSF. The History of Catholic Secondary Education in the Archdiocese of Chicago. Washington, D. C.: Catholic University Press, 1953. Doctoral Dissertation.

Moynihan, Jas. H. Life of Archbishop John Ireland. New York: Harper & Bros., 1953.

Mulkerins, Brother Thomas M., S. J. Holy Family Parish, Chicago, Priests and People. Chicago: Universal Press, 1923.

Naber, Sister M. Vera, CSA. With All Devotedness, Chronicles of the Sisters of St. Agnes, Fond du Lac, Wisconsin. New York: P. J. Kenedy & Sons, 1959.

Nevins, Allen. A History of American Life, Volume VIII: The Emergence of Modern America, 1865-1878. New York: Macmillan Company, 1928.

O'Brien, Mother Gabriel, RSM. Reminiscences of Seventy Years 1846-1916. Chicago: Fred J. Rengley Co., 1916.

O'Connor, Sister Mary Paschala, OP. Five Decades - History of the Congregation of the Most Holy Rosary, Sinsinawa, Wisconsin, 1849-1899. Sinsinawa: The Sinsinawa Press, 195◄

O'Rourke, Alice, OP. The Good Work Begun, Centennial History of Peoria Diocese. Chicago: Lakeside Press - R. R. Donnell & Sons Co., 1977.

O'Neill, Sister Mary Rosinda. A Sketch of the Life of the Most Reverend James John Keane, Third Archbishop of Dubuque 1856-1926. Master's Dissertation, Catholic University of America, 1947.

Paul, Norma A., PhD. Study and Memos: Religious Orders and Their Schools in Illinois 1834-1939. Booklet, n.p. 1970.

Pierce, Bessie Louise. A History of Chicago, Volume III, The Rise of a Modern City, 1871-1893. Chicago: University of Chicago Press, 1957.

Power, Edward J. A History of Catholic Higher Education in the United States. Milwaukee: Bruce Publishing Co., 1958.

Ratte, John. Three Modernists, Alfred Loisy, George Tyrrell, William L. Sullivan. New York: Sheed and Ward, 1967.

Rothluebber, Sister M. Francis Borgia, OSF. He Sent Two. The Story of the Beginnings of the School Sisters of St. Francis. Milwaukee: Bruce Publishing Company, 1965.

Russell, Letty M. Human Liberation in a Feminist Perspective- A Theology. Philadelphia: Westminster Press, 1974.

Sanders, James W. The Education of An Urban Minority, Catholics in Chicago, 1833-1965. New York: Oxford University Press, 1977.

Sexton, Patricia Cayo. Women in Education. Bloomington, Ind.: Phi Delta Kappa. Educational Foundations, 1976. (Paperback)

Shannon, James P. Catholic Colonization on the Western Frontier. New Haven: Yale University Press, 1957.

Shields, Thomas E. The Making and Unmaking of a Dullard. Washington, D.C.: Catholic Education Press, 1900.

Sigwarth, Anthony William, BA. Some Facts About Catholic Elementary Education in Iowa as Interwove with the History of Public Schools. Dissertation for M. A. degree, St. Mary Seminary, Baltimore, Md. Unpublished.

Spiers, Edward F., M. A. PhD. The Central Catholic High School: A Survey of Their History and Status in the United States. Washington, D. C. : Catholic University Press, 1951.

Stuhler, Barbara and Gretchen Kreuter, editors. Women of Minnesota, Selected Biographical Essays. St. Paul: Minnesota Historical Society Press, 1977.

Sugrue, Francis. Popes in the Modern World. New York: Thomas Y. Crowell Co. , 1961.

Sweeney, David Francis, OFM. The Life of John Lancaster Spalding, First Bishop of Peoria, 1840-1916. New York: Herder & Herder, 1965.

A Symposium on the Life and Work of Pope Pius X, Commemorating the Fortieth Anniversary of His Encyclical, "Acerbo Nimis. " Washington, D. C. : Confraternity of Christian Doctrine, 1946.

Thèbaud, Rev. Augustus, S. J. Forty Years in the United States, 1839-1885. New York: U. S. Catholic Historical Society, 1904.

Vincentia, Sister Mary, SND. Their Quiet Tread, Growth and Spirit of the Congregation of the Sisters of Notre Dame Through Its First One Hundred Years, 1850-1950. Milwaukee: Catholic Life Publications, Bruce Press, 1955.

Ward, Justine. Thomas Edward Shields, Biologist, Psychologist, Educator. New York: Charles Scribner's Sons, 1947.

VARIED SOURCES

Azvedo, Rev. Marcello de, S. J. "Women Religious in the Church, " address given before major superiors of women religious in Rome, November 1975.

Belding, Robert E. "An Iowa School Girl - 1860's Style, " Palimpsest, Vol. 58, No. 1, January/February 1977.

-----. "Iowa's Brave Model for Women's Education, " Annals of Iowa, Summer Issue, 1976.

Buckley, Michael J. , S. J. "The Confirmation of a Promise, a Letter to George Ganss, S. J. , Studies in the Spirituality of Jesuits, Vol. III, No. 5, p. 187. American Assistancy Seminar on Jesuit Spirituality. St. Louis, Missouri.

Kempker, Rev. John F. The Catholic Church in Council Bluffs (Pamphlet) n. d. , n. p.

McCarthy, Caritas. "Constitutions for Apostolic Religious, " Supplement to the Way #14, Autumn, 1971.

Morain, Thomas. "The Entry of Women into the School Teach- in Profession in Nineteenth Century Iowa. " Paper read before Conference of Women Historians, St. Paul, Minn. , October 1977.

COMMEMORATIVE BOOKLETS

Silver Jubilee, Blessed Sacrament Church, 1890-1915

Souvenir of Dedication, Blessed Sacrament Church, May 1938

Golden Jubilee, Blessed Sacrament Church, 1890-1940

Diamond Jubilee, Blessed Sacrament Church, 1890-1965

Fifty Golden Years of Sisters of Charity, B. V. M. (Blessed Sacrament Parish) 1897-1947.

The Year of Jubilee, 1976, Our Lady Help of Christians, 1901- 1976

Fiftieth Anniversary, Mary, Queen of Heaven Church, Cicero, Illinois, 1911-1961

Holy Angels Academy, Milwaukee, Commemorating Seventy-Five Years - 1892-1967

Golden Jubilee, Our Lady of Lourdes Church, 1892-1942

The Story of Our Lady of Lourdes on Rededication, 1929

Dedication Ceremonies of the Church of Our Lady of Lourdes, 1916

Golden Jubilee, Our Lady Help of Christians, 1901-1951

Golden Jubilee, Our Lady of Angels Church, November 19, 1944

Jubilee Story of a Diocese, Lincoln, Nebraska, Seventy-Five Years

St. Mary High School, Fifty Golden Years, 1899-1949

Memories, St. Mary High School, Chicago, 1947-1951

Diamond Jubilee, Seventy-Five Years of Service by Sisters of Charity, B. V. M. , Chicago, 1943

Xavier High: A School and Its History since 1833. Jean Fahey Eberle. n. d. n. p.

SPECIAL JESUIT SOURCES

Ganss, Rev. George E. , S. J. The Constitutions of the Society of Jesus. St. Louis: Institute of Jesuit Sources, 1970.

------. "On How to Become Evangelically Poor. " Studies in the Spirituality of the Jesuits. Vol. 3, No. 2 and 3.

Buckley, Michael J. , S. J. "The Confirmation of a Promise, A Letter to George Ganss . . . " Ibid. , Vol. 8, No. 5.

Lozano, Juan Manuel, CFM. "Founder and Community: Inspiration and Charism. " Review for Religious, Vol. 37, No.

Summary and Common Rules (Society of Jesus)

Azvedo, Rev. Marcello de Carvalho, S. J. "Women Religious in the Church. " Talk given Major Superiors of Women Religious, Rome, November 1975.

McCarthy, C. "Constitutions for Apostolic Religious. " Supplement to the Way 14 (Autumn, 1971).

------. "Ignatian Charism in Women's Congregations. " Supplement 20.

Cain, James R. "Cloister and the Apostolate of Women. " Review for Religious, Vol. 27, 1968.

Futrell, John C. , S. J. "The Founder's Charism. " Supplement to the Way 14 (Autumn, 1971).

O'Connor, Friderico M. , S. J. The Community Life of Active Women Religious: An Analysis of the Special General Chapter of Four Congregations of Active Women Religious in the United States of America. Excerpted from a doctoral dissertation submitted to the Theology Faculty of the Pontifical Gregorian University. Rome 1971.

INDEX

494